THE RELEVANT MARKET IN INTERNATIONAL ECONOMIC LAW

This book provides what international trade law has hitherto lacked: a coherent analysis of product "likeness" under Article III of the GATT. Christian A. Melischek develops an economic approach to the interpretation of "like" products on the basis of a comparative analysis with antitrust theories on market definition. Not only does he propose a specific substantive economic test to render the notion of product likeness operational, he also examines the institutional and procedural frameworks for expert economic evidence necessary to implement an economic approach to the interpretation of product likeness. On a methodological level, the book adds a new interdisciplinary dimension to the legal debate by exploring the use of quantitative and econometric methods for the implementation of the proposed economic test.

CHRISTIAN A. MELISCHEK is a legal trainee at the Regional Court of Appeals in Hamburg. He was previously a visiting fellow at the World Trade Institute, University of Bern.

THE RELEVANT MARKET IN INTERNATIONAL ECONOMIC LAW

A Comparative Antitrust and GATT Analysis

CHRISTIAN A. MELISCHEK

CAMBRIDGE
UNIVERSITY PRESS

CAMBRIDGE
UNIVERSITY PRESS

Shaftesbury Road, Cambridge CB2 8EA, United Kingdom

One Liberty Plaza, 20th Floor, New York, NY 10006, USA

477 Williamstown Road, Port Melbourne, VIC 3207, Australia

314–321, 3rd Floor, Plot 3, Splendor Forum, Jasola District Centre, New Delhi – 110025, India

103 Penang Road, #05–06/07, Visioncrest Commercial, Singapore 238467

Cambridge University Press is part of Cambridge University Press & Assessment, a department of the University of Cambridge.

We share the University's mission to contribute to society through the pursuit of education, learning and research at the highest international levels of excellence.

www.cambridge.org
Information on this title: www.cambridge.org/9781107031524

First published 2013

A catalogue record for this publication is available from the British Library

Library of Congress Cataloging-in-Publication data
Melischek, Christian A.
Th e relevant market in international economic law : a comparative antitrust and GATT analysis / Christian A. Melischek.
p. cm. – (Cambridge international trade and economic law)
Includes bibliographical references and index.
ISBN 978-1-107-03152-4 (hardback) – ISBN 978-1-107-66635-1 (paperback)
1. International economic relations. 2. Foreign trade regulation.
3. Antitrust law. I. Title.
K3820.M45 2012
343.07′21–dc23 2012019853

ISBN 978-1-107-03152-4 Hardback

To my mother

CONTENTS

ACKNOWLEDGMENTS

This book is a revised and updated version of my doctoral thesis. It was accepted by the University of Hamburg, Faculty of Law, in 2011, and awarded the best doctoral dissertation prize for the academic year 2011–2012. I would not have been able to write it without the help of so many people.

I owe my deepest gratitude to my supervisor, Professor Peter Behrens. He guided me along my academic path which – owing to his encouragement – also became a geographic journey, leading me to Brussels, New York City and Bern. He allowed me the greatest intellectual freedom. At the same time, I was always certain to have his full support and to find invaluable advice. Moreover, I warmly thank Professor Thomas Eger for his very timely second evaluation report of the dissertation.

My inspiration for writing this book originates from a workshop organized by the *stagiaires* at the European Commission in 2008. In the following, I benefited greatly from my studies at New York University School of Law. In the stimulating environment at this most vibrant place, I had the possibility of working with a number of distinguished scholars. Professor Joseph H. H. Weiler was a brilliant teacher and I am thankful for the thought-provoking comments and insightful discussions on the topic of this thesis. I am also indebted to Professor Daniel L. Rubinfeld of the University of California at Berkeley, who introduced me to the world of antitrust economics and econometrics in his seminars. His thoughts on the technical aspects of the topic were very helpful to me. Moreover, I had the great privilege to work with Professor Robert L. Howse, under whose supervision I was able to develop aspects of the thesis topic in a research paper. I was also extremely fortunate that, thanks to Professor Howse, I was given the opportunity to pursue my thesis project as a visiting fellow at the World Trade Institute of the University of Bern. Professor Thomas Cottier, Professor Pierre Sauvé, the entire World Trade Institute team and the doctoral as well as the MILE students made my stay a most enjoyable experience and an extremely productive time. I would also like to express my appreciation to Professor Cottier as well as to Professor Petros C. Mavroidis of Columbia Law School for their comments on earlier versions of the manuscript. A very special thank you goes to Emma Dunlop, Carla Lewis, James Chapman, and Michael Kariya for countless hours spent on the linguistic polishing of the text. Finally, I wish to remark on the generous support provided by the Foundation of German Business (*Stiftung der Deutschen Wirtschaft*) through its postgraduate scholarship.

Mother, this book is dedicated to you – for your unlimited support and endless love.

ABBREVIATIONS

ABA	American Bar Association
BGH	Bundesgerichtshof
CFI	Court of First Instance
CPE	Cross-price elasticity
CTH	Consumers' tastes and habits
DCS	Directly competitive or substitutable
DoJ	Department of Justice
DSB	Dispute Settlement Body
DSU	Understanding on Rules and Procedures Governing the Settlement of Disputes (Dispute Settlement Understanding)
EC	European Communities
ECJ	European Court of Justice
ECMR	EC Merger Regulation
ECR	European Court Reports
EU	European Union
FRCP	Federal Rules of Civil Procedure
FRE	Federal Rules of Evidence
FTC	Federal Trade Commission
GATS	General Agreement on Trade in Services
GATT	General Agreement on Tariffs and Trade
HFCS	High-fructose corn syrup
HS	Harmonized system
ICJ	International Court of Justice
KG	Kammergericht
log	logarithm
Member	Member of the World Trade Organization
MFN	Most-favored-nation
NT	National Treatment
OECD	Organization for Economic Cooperation and Development
OJ	Official Journal of the European Union
OPE	Own-price elasticity
PPM	Process and production method

SATAP	So as to afford protection
SCM Agreement	Agreement on Subsidies and Countervailing Measures
SE	Standard error
SPS Agreement	Agreement on the Application of Sanitary and Phytosanitary Measures
SSNIP	Small but significant non-transitory increase in price
TBT Agreement	Agreement on Technical Barriers to Trade
TFEU	Treaty on the Functioning of the European Union
USC	United States Code
VCLT	Vienna Convention on the Law of Treaties
WTO	World Trade Organization

TABLE OF CASES

WTO Appellate Body Reports

WTO Panel Reports

Arbitrations: Article 22.6 of the DSU

GATT 1947 Reports and Rulings

European Court of Justice

General Court

European Commission

United States Supreme Court

United States Court of Appeals

United States District Courts

United States Federal Trade Commission

Judicial decisions of other jurisdictions

TABLE OF LEGAL TEXTS

Primary and secondary legislation of the European Union

United States legislation

Legislation of other jurisdictions

Introduction

> For the rational study of the law the black-letter man may be the man of the present, but the man of the future is the man of statistics and the master of economics.
>
> US Supreme Court Justice Oliver Wendell Holmes[1]

> A lawyer who has not studied economics ... is very apt to become a public enemy.
>
> US Supreme Court Justice Louis Brandeis[2]

I THE RESEARCH QUESTION AND SCOPE OF THE STUDY

"Identifying market boundaries is as much an art as it is a science."[3] Lawyers and judges, however, are uncomfortable being either artist or scientist. Nevertheless, the question of which products are sufficiently comparable to constitute a relevant market is central to the two legal disciplines of antitrust law and international trade law under the World Trade Organization's (hereinafter WTO) General Agreement on Tariffs and Trade (hereinafter GATT).[4]

The legal requirement to compare and distinguish products gives rise to a controversial interaction between law and economics in these two fields.[5] In US antitrust law, defining markets has been recognized as

[1] Holmes, "The Path of the Law," *Harvard Law Review*, 10 (1897), 457, 469.

[2] Brandeis, "The Living Law," *Illinois Law Review*, 10 (1916), 461.

[3] Geroski and Griffith, "Identifying Antitrust Markets," in Neumann and Weigand (eds.), *The International Handbook of Competition*, pp. 290, 294, (2004).

[4] With the inception of the WTO in 1994, GATT 1947 was incorporated into the WTO legal regime which refers to the articles of GATT 1947 as articles of GATT 1994.

[5] Glassman, "Market Definition as a Practical Matter," *Antitrust Law Journal*, 49 (1980), 1155: "The definition of relevant product and geographic markets in antitrust litigation requires the marriage of the economic and legal disciplines. The marriage is at best a troubled one, and divorce seems always imminent."

"in essence, an economic task put to the uses of the law," for which reason the "analysis perforce is directed to basic economic precepts."[6] United States antitrust law has hence developed into an arena for economists, with economic analysis successively penetrating all issues.[7] Posner even went as far as to suggest that antitrust law has become "a branch of applied economics."[8] While EU antitrust policy has ostensibly started to interact more heavily with economic theory, it does not match the long-standing history and tradition of economic analysis in the United States. Within EU antitrust law particularly, the "more economic approach" denotes the process of increasing influence of economics on all antitrust issues. It originated from market definition, and over the last decade has become a key talking point in European antitrust circles. It implies an evolution from a form-based tradition to an increasing focus on economic effects. It is also characterized by the expanding use of economic models and quantitative methods of analysis. Quantitative methods, also loosely described as econometrics, designate statistical techniques, such as regression analysis, applied to empirical data in order to obtain economically meaningful results.[9] Quantitative analysis is playing an increasingly important role also in court proceedings, most recently in the *Ryanair/Aer Lingus* case, where the General Court[10] did not hesitate to conduct an unusually exhaustive evaluation of the econometric analyses, more precisely the regression analyses, that were put forward by the Commission and the parties.[11]

[6] *United States* v. *Grinnell Corp.*, 384 US 563, 587 (1966) (Justice Fortas dissenting) and *SmithKline Corp.* v. *Eli Lilly & Co.*, 575 F.2d 1056, 1063 (3d Cir. 1978).

[7] The term "antitrust" is derived from US law. In Europe, the term "competition law" is usually used, with "antitrust" denoting more specifically non-merger analysis. For reason of simplicity, the term "antitrust" will be used here as a generic term that comprises all areas of legal rules on competition policy.

[8] Posner, *The Problematics of Moral and Legal Theory*, p. 229 (1999).

[9] This type of analysis is located at the intersection of statistics, mathematics, and economic theory. It looks "at relationships between explicit numbers such as prices, sales, or market shares," while qualitative analysis evaluates similar relationships from a non-numerical, descriptive perspective: Coate and Fischer, "A Practical Guide to the Hypothetical Monopolist Test for Market Definition," *Journal of Competition Law &* Economics, 4 (2008), 1031, 1054. See also European Commission, *XXIVth Report on Competition Policy 1994*, p. 280 (1995): "Qualitative methods could, for example, include the examination of product characteristics and the intended use of a product by consumers, whereas quantitative methods could involve the examination of price trends and the estimation of cross-elasticities using econometric methods."

[10] Formerly known as the Court of First Instance (CFI).

[11] Case T-342/07, *Ryanair* v. *Commission* [2010] C221 55, paras. 139–195.

Greater emphasis on economics in the exercise of defining markets has thus catapulted economics to the forefront in the two antitrust jurisdictions. Economic, and in particular econometric, analysis has even developed into what some now perceive as "a useful servant, but a terrible master."[12]

In GATT, the market definition problem surfaces in the context of the interpretation of "like" products or "directly competitive or substitutable" (hereinafter DCS) products; concepts that are central to the operation of the non-discrimination obligations. As a result, this "determination is one of the thorniest in WTO/GATT jurisprudence!"[13] For decades, trade scholars have asked the pertinent question: "If, therefore, trade lawyers must decide 'likeness' before applying GATT law, what test must they use?"[14] But neither jurisprudence nor doctrine has yet given a coherent answer. To say the least, this area is plagued by overwhelming confusion. With its infamous metaphor of the "like" definition stretching and squeezing like an accordion, WTO dispute settlement bodies appear to prefer the art of music over the science of economics.[15] Still, the absence of a coherent theory of interpretation has led to a hermeneutic cacophony. The interpretative pendulum in case law and scholarly literature has oscillated between three approaches. The dominant approach in case law and scholarship has been one of legal formalism based on qualitative criteria. A second approach has been a subjective and contextual aims-and-effects theory, allowing for regulatory purpose to enter the determination of whether products are "like." Although this approach was only a short episode in case law, it has received considerable support by important scholars. Also only of a temporary nature in case law, an economics-oriented approach sought to assess the competitive relationship of the products under scrutiny by additionally employing quantitative criteria. More recently, this last approach has seen a renaissance among several commentators.[16]

12 Kroes, European Commissioner for Competition, "Exclusionary Abuses of Dominance: The European Commission's Enforcement Priorities," Fordham University Symposium, New York (2008), available at: http://europa.eu/rapid/pressReleasesAction.do?reference=SPEECH/08/457&format=HTML&aged=0&language=EN&guiLanguage=en. All internet addresses in this book were last accessed on January 31, 2012.

13 Matsushita, Schoenbaum, and Mavroidis, *The World Trade Organization*, p. 158 (2003).

14 Bhala, *Modern GATT Law*, para. 1-003 (2005).

15 Appellate Body Report, *Japan – Taxes on Alcoholic Beverages* (hereinafter *Japan – Alcoholic Beverages II*), WT/DS8/AB/R, WT/DS10/AB/R, WT/DS11/AB/R, adopted November 1, 1996, at 21.

16 Most notably Choi, *"Like Products" in International Trade Law: Towards a Consistent GATT/WTO Jurisprudence* (2003); Emch, "Fiscal Discrimination in WTO Law and EU Law,"

The WTO is avowedly an economic institution.[17] That is why it is surprising that economics has only recently become increasingly involved in the analysis and litigation of WTO matters that call for economic interpretation and quantification. The use of sophisticated economic evidence and quantitative models by Panels has evolved from general reluctance to a growing willingness in recent times to embrace these types of evidence and methods.[18] For instance, economic analysis has played a more prominent role where, on occasion, a WTO discipline requires the analysis of the effects of a trade measure.[19] Quantitative methods have also figured more frequently in WTO arbitrations in order to calculate the maximum allowable level of retaliatory countermeasures.[20] These developments signal that there is a "systemic need for trade lawyers and economists to cooperate" in WTO legal practice.[21] But it is not clear what economics can, and cannot, do in WTO disputes that touch on the "like" and DCS definitions. Between 1996 and 2000, three landmark WTO Panel Reports introduced an economic approach to product comparison, also extending the assessment to quantitative methods, in particular, cross-price elasticities (hereinafter CPE)[22] of demand. Since then, economic analysis

Legal Issues of Economic Integration, 32 (2005), 369–415; Goco, "Non-Discrimination, 'Likeness,' and Market Definition in World Trade Organization Jurisprudence," *Journal of World Trade*, 40 (2006), 315–340; Diebold, *Non-Discrimination in International Trade in Services: A Contextual and Comparative Analysis of "Likeness" in WTO/GATS* (2010).

[17] The WTO is the "common institutional framework for the conduct of trade relations," Article II:1 of the 1994 Marrakesh Agreement Establishing the World Trade Organization (hereinafter WTO Agreement).

[18] For early reluctance on the use of statistical evidence see GATT Panel Report, *Treatment by Germany of Imports of Sardines*, BISD 1S/53, adopted October 31, 1952, para. 9 and GATT Working Party Report, *Netherlands Action under Article XXIII:2 to Suspend Obligations to the United States*, BISD 1S/62, adopted November 8, 1952, para. 4. For an overview of recent cases see WTO World Trade Report, *Quantitative Economics in WTO Dispute Settlement*, 2005, pp. 171–211, available at: www.wto.org/english/res_e/booksp_e/anrep_e/ world_trade_report05 _e.pdf.

[19] For instance, econometric simulation models were first used for the quantification of the effect of subsidies under Article 6.3 of the Agreement on Subsidies and Countervailing Measures (hereinafter SCM Agreement) in Panel Report, *United States – Subsidies on Upland Cotton*, WT/DS267/R, adopted March 21, 2005, paras. 7.1202–7.1209.

[20] See, e.g., *United States – Continued Dumping and Subsidy Offset Act of 2000 (EC) – Recourse to Arbitration by the United States under Article 22.6 of the DSU*, WT/DS217/ARB/EEC, adopted November 26, 2004, paras. 3.80–3.151.

[21] Keck, Malashevich, and Gray, "A 'Probabilistic' Approach to the Use of Econometric Models in Sunset Reviews," *World Trade Review*, 6 (2007), 371.

[22] For the moment it suffices to say that CPE is an economic measure of substitutability and that it is the ratio of the percentage change in demand for one product over the percentage change in price of another product.

has disappeared from the dispute settlement bodies' radar. Until very recently, the impression was that economics had been only a temporary episode for the "like" and DCS issue. But in mid 2011, two Panel Reports once again turned to quantitative methods for the assessment of product comparability, thus giving the discussion on an economic approach new and unexpected momentum.[23] Commentators have in fact been split on the issue of introducing economics into the determination of likeness and DCS. There are voices that strongly advocate an economic approach, but, beyond the argument for greater emphasis on economics, jurisprudence and scholarly work have revealed little regarding how to design the analytical framework for an economic approach that fits into the larger GATT framework. Moreover, those who advocate an economic approach have rarely looked at its limitations, and the question of how to implement an economic approach on a methodological level has been left open.

Against this background, the central theme of this thesis is to develop an economic approach to GATT market definition. This study explores how legal analysis can be guided by economic theories and insights on this topic. But the issue is not only merely one of *more* or *less* economics, but also of *how* economic analysis should be used, that is, how to integrate economics and law.[24] Thus, the aim of this book is a better integration of economic and legal analysis in the GATT market definition exercise, especially since economics has not been a familiar tool with which to analyze legal issues in international trade law.

Economics provides three things in this study: first, it provides the necessary underpinning for antitrust and international trade policy (Chapter 1); second, it gives a proper theoretical and conceptual framework on which to base the concept of market definition (Chapter 4), and, third, it provides a way of accessing appropriate evidence in order to implement the conceptual framework (Chapter 5). The second and third aspects are important because this study distinguishes between two levels for an economic approach to trade market definition: an overarching analytical framework based on economics and its implementation on a methodological level. On the first level, economics *frames* the analysis. It provides the design of a theoretical and conceptual framework within

[23] Panel Report, *Thailand – Customs and Fiscal Measures on Cigarettes from the Philippines* (hereinafter *Thailand – Cigarettes*), WT/DS371/R, adopted July 15, 2011; Panel Report, *Philippines – Taxes on Distilled Spirits* (hereinafter *Philippines – Distilled Spirits*), WT/DS396/R, WT/DS403/R, adopted January 20, 2012.

[24] Röller, "Economic Analysis and Competition Policy Enforcement in Europe," in van Bergeijk and Kloosterhuis (eds.), *Modelling European Mergers*, p. 13 (2005).

which the market definition analysis takes place. The framework designates what the necessary conditions are for a relevant market. It identifies the key factual issues that must be proven in order to support a legal finding of likeness, or DCS. On the second level, economics provide the (quantitative) tools that *drive* the analysis. Economics can be used to gather and evaluate evidence and thus to ascertain whether the conditions set by the framework are met.

The thesis of this book is twofold. On the first level, an overall conceptual framework based on economics is necessary for trade market definition. On the second level, economic methods, and in particular empirical methods, are useful, but they are not a panacea – and may sometimes even be a false friend.

With regard to the first level – the conceptual framework – the central insight has been adapted from antitrust law that market definition is not an aim in itself. Instead, the market definition inquiry must be guided by its underlying purpose. For the international trade law context, this means that the market definition paradigm must be based on the economic objective of preventing domestic protectionist measures. This paradigm draws inspiration from the modern antitrust approach. Yet this economic approach to international trade market definition is an approach specific to trade law, conceptually different from the antitrust model.

The call for an economic approach in the international trade law context has met widespread and intense opposition among scholars and adjudicators. One reason is the profound political dimension of the WTO, which seems to be irreconcilable with the strictures of economic analysis. Another is that economics is equated with the preeminence of quantitative methods, in particular CPE of demand. Quantitative methods are often labeled an obscure and cryptic discipline by the legal profession.[25] A lack of familiarity and understanding of such methods may be at the heart of the discomfort with an economic approach. On the second methodological level, this study therefore sheds light on the econometric estimation of CPE of demand. The most widespread statistical method used

[25] Note that the former president of the German antitrust agency, himself an economist, warned against the primacy of econometrics as "tantamount to a 'horror scenario' of competition law enforcement: some number-crunching economists feeding their computers with data of dubious quality, and finally presenting one single figure to serve as a lead": Heitzer, *Economic Assessment in Competition Enforcement: Developments in France and Germany – Statement for the Panel*, CRA International, Annual Conference "Economic Developments in European Competition Policy" (2008), p. 7, available at: www.bundeskartellamt.de/wDeutsch/download/pdf/Diskussionsbeitraege/081203_CRA.pdf.

for this purpose, multiple regression analysis, is presented as an approach that has already been applied in WTO case law on the definition of DCS on two occasions. A comparative analysis with regard to the antitrust experience allows for a much more nuanced picture of the virtues and vices of quantitative methods. The study underscores that quantitative analysis is an important, yet imperfect, tool that complements, but cannot replace, qualitative evidence. The conclusion is that a conceptual framework based on economic insights will not automatically lead to the sole reign of economic and econometric methods.

In addition to what role quantitative methods can play substantively, this study acknowledges that economic or quantitative evidence, usually introduced into litigation through expert economic testimony, also raises institutional and procedural issues. Thinking about an economic approach requires exploring whether the judicial system has the capabilities to handle sophisticated economic evidence. To put it bluntly, the issue is for adjudicators to remain undeceived by biased expert economic testimony. Again, the antitrust experience will be illuminating.

Ultimately, the analysis of both the substantive role of quantitative methods and the procedural handling of this evidence contributes to a better comprehension of the role economics can play in the definition of "like" and DCS.

The scope of analysis in this study is limited in two ways. First, it concentrates on one specific instance of product comparison in GATT. There is a multitude of provisions in GATT and WTO law more generally that prescribe an inquiry into the similarity of products (or services).[26] Yet this study is not an attempt to explore all these concepts. These concepts vary from provision to provision. They must be assessed on a case-by-case basis according to the text, structure, and purpose of each individual provision. Instead, the aim of this study is to examine the concept of product comparability in the non-discrimination provision of Article III of the GATT, which embodies the National Treatment (hereinafter NT) obligation. It is this provision that has been at the center of judicial and scholarly attention, and thus generates the most case law and scholarly debate.

The scope of analysis is limited in a second respect: the concepts of likeness and DCS are part of the legal elements of the non-discrimination obligations in Article III of the GATT. As such, they are closely intertwined and interdependent with the remaining elements of these

[26] For an overview of these provisions see *infra*, Ch. 2, fnn. 46 and 47.

obligations. Consequently, a particular interpretation of one element may require a specific interpretation of another element. An integral view would account for the interpretation of one legal element within the interpretation of another. This is a task of such complexity that numerous attempts by scholars have given rise to an equally large number of propositions.[27] For reasons of simplicity in an area that is known for its complexity due to the multitude of approaches, this thesis will break down the non-discrimination obligations of Article III of the GATT and focus exclusively on developing an *economic* interpretative approach to likeness and DCS.

As a consequence, this thesis leaves aside several interpretative issues that arise in the larger context of Article III of the GATT. First, it is not a further treatment of the linkage between trade liberalization and regulatory autonomy. This relates to the issue of whether or not to adopt an interpretative approach to the definition of likeness and DCS that accounts for the regulatory purpose of the disputed governmental measure.[28] Second, the thesis does not elaborate on the interaction between trade and other non-economic policy considerations, such as human rights, the environment, or labor standards.[29] Thus, it will not be discussed whether, for example, foreign products that do not comply with certain domestic human rights, labor, or environmental standards are "like" or DCS domestic products that adhere to these standards.

Article III market definition has in fact been discussed mainly with regard to the fundamental tension between trade liberalization and regulatory autonomy or other non-economic policy values. This is a highly controversial debate on the proper function of Article III of the GATT. Scholarship has already treated this topic comprehensively without bringing it nearer to a definite resolution.[30] This study acknowledges and briefly describes regulatory purpose and compliance with non-economic standards as alternative, non-economic approaches to market definition. But it does not take a position from a normative or hermeneutic perspective on which approach and therefore on which fundamental understanding of Article III of the GATT should prevail. The reason is that this has become

[27] The latest instance in scholarship is Diebold, *Non-Discrimination in International Trade in Services*. See also *infra*, Ch. 2, fn. 94.

[28] For an overview see Trebilcock and Howse, *The Regulation of International Trade*, pp. 108–111 (2005).

[29] On this conflict see, e.g., Cottier, Pauwelyn, and Bürgi, *Human Rights and International Trade* (2005); Vranes, *Trade and the Environment: Fundamental Issues in International Law, WTO Law, and Legal Theory* (2009).

[30] For references to the literature see *infra*, Ch. 3, fnn. 148 and 149.

a purely theoretical debate confined to the scholarly world. The Appellate Body has clearly and in a definite manner rejected the mentioned alternative regulatory purpose approaches to market definition. In today's world of WTO dispute settlement, trade law practitioners do not advise clients or argue before WTO dispute settlement bodies on the basis of those alternative approaches. Practitioners argue the issue of product similarity solely on the basis of the traditional approach. Acknowledging this reality of litigation, this study moves forward and sets aside the vexatious and complex questions associated with regulatory purpose and compliance with non-economic standards. Given the modern state of case law, the research question in this book focuses on whether an economic approach to product comparison can be developed as an alternative to the traditional approach.

II PRACTICAL RELEVANCE OF THE RESEARCH QUESTION

An economic approach does not necessarily lead to different results in defining markets than those provided by a non-economic approach. It does, however, certainly change the operational modes of professionals concerned with market definition. The immediate practical relevance of a well-designed economic approach lies in enhancing the predictability, transparency, and consistency – recognized objectives of the WTO legal system[31] – in the application of the relevant provisions. Ultimately, it thereby increases the acceptability and accountability of the WTO dispute settlement system. An economic approach based on quantitative methods will improve predictability, transparency, and consistency because it permits the formalization of a coherent methodology, generates reproducible and (even numerically) comparable results, and provides measures of precision and reliability. This makes it possible to discuss and evaluate the methods and models employed, and to follow a structured set of principles in the analysis.

On a more general level, the issue of market definition can be understood as exemplary for the interaction between law and economics. Taking the antitrust experience as a model, one may forecast that economic analysis and the use of econometric tools might also become central in

[31] Compare Article 3.2 of the Understanding on Rules and Procedures Governing the Settlement of Disputes, Annex 2 of the WTO Agreement (hereinafter DSU).

shaping lawyers' arguments and legal decision making in WTO disputes. Like antitrust lawyers, trade lawyers will therefore interact to an increasing degree with economists and statisticians.[32] Cynics may argue that the legal profession confronts this growing influence of economists with suspicion precisely in the manner of a monopolist fearing to lose its market. But the prime reason why economics often remains anathema to lawyers and judges is that while legal professionals traditionally demand "bright-line" tests – simple step-by-step rules – economic reasoning is perceived as inconclusive, incomprehensible, and inaccessible.[33] With the increasing use of economic concepts and the ensuing prevalence of economic and technical terminology, a language barrier arises that not only obstructs the dialogue between economists and lawyers, but also adds further complication to the lawyers' already existing daily problem of explaining legal "jargon" to their clients. Manifestly, without some understanding for the economics presented to them, lawyers and judges will likely ignore economic evidence, or refrain from giving it much weight. Thus, the priority for an efficient use of economic evidence is that economic presentation and arguments must be readily understandable and accessible to lawyers and adjudicators. Instead of remaining an independent subset of the legal inquiry from which the legal profession is excluded by language and lack of understanding, economics must become part of the legal proceedings through a dialogue with the economic expert. At the same time, where the discipline of *forensic* economics develops and gains increasing importance in legal decision making, the discussion also turns to the requisite standards for economic analysis in the legal context.[34] Against this background, this book has an interdisciplinary vocation. By virtue of a non-technical and accessible presentation of, in particular, econometrics, this book aims to contribute to the fruitful interaction of economic and legal analysis generally and, more specifically, to show that economic analysis is beneficial in order to put some science to the legal art of defining markets.

[32] See Desai, "The European Commission's Draft Notice on Market Definition: A Brief Guide to the Economics," *European Competition Law Review*, (1997), 473, 477.

[33] Fisher, "Economic Analysis and 'Bright-line' Tests," *Journal of Competition Law & Economics*, 4 (2007), 129–130.

[34] This can be observed in Germany, where the discussion on standards of forensic economics has now come to the fore following the recent publication of guidelines on expert economic testimony by the Federal Cartel Office, see Ewald, "Ökonomie im Kartellrecht: Vom more economic approach zu sachgerechten Standards forensischer Ökonomie," *Wirtschaft und Wettbewerb*, (2011), 15–47; Christiansen and Locher, "Die neuen Standards des Bundeskartellamts für ökonomische Gutachten in der Kartellrechtsanwendung," *Wirtschaft und Wettbewerb*, (2011), 444–453.

III METHODOLOGY AND STRUCTURE

The methodology applied in this book is that of a comparative analysis. It contrasts the differences and finds the commonalities between antitrust law and international trade law market definition. Drawing on the antitrust experience, this book aims to develop an independent market definition approach for Article III of the GATT. Indeed, it is only natural to turn to antitrust law for guidance on an economic approach because it is this field that has seen a proliferation of, and profound penetration by, law-and-economics analysis. Moreover, the comparison with antitrust law is logical because this discipline is familiar with the determination of competitive relationships between products. It thus offers rich practical experience and comprehensive scientific analysis of the delineation of markets.[35]

Consequently, a comparative view on Article III market definition is nothing new, rather it is something quite controversial. WTO case law has been inconsistent on this issue. On the one hand, as the analysis of WTO case law history will show below, almost the entirety of cases ignored an economics or antitrust-inspired market definition paradigm. One Panel even considered, and explicitly rejected, the antitrust law methodology as of practical guidance.[36] On the other hand, however, a small number of Panels have turned to economic tools well known in antitrust legal practice, such as CPE of demand, or even referenced to market definitions of national antitrust authorities.[37] Especially recently, commentators have repeatedly and to varying extents drawn parallels to antitrust law.[38] Yet those contributions have rarely attempted to conceptualize an overarching framework and did not go as far as exploring the methodological implementation of such an approach. Both shall be undertaken here.

The structure of this book is as follows. Chapter 1 sets out the basis for a comparative methodology. It establishes that antitrust and international trade law share fundamental commonalities that justify a comparative

[35] See the following prediction: "The competition's standards used to define markets will soon be used beyond the border of competition policy, in the pure regulatory field": Monti, European Commissioner for Competition, "Market Definition as a Cornerstone of EU Competition Policy," Workshop on Market Definition, Helsinki, 2001, available at: http://europa.eu/rapid/pressReleasesAction.do?reference=SPEECH/01/439&format=HTML&aged=0&language=EN&guiLanguage=en.

[36] Panel Report, *Korea – Taxes on Alcoholic Beverages* (hereinafter *Korea – Alcoholic Beverages*), WT/DS75/R, WT/DS84/R, adopted February 17, 1999, para. 10.81.

[37] See *infra*, Ch. 4, fn. 147. [38] See *supra*, Introduction, fn. 16.

analysis. These policy rationales determine the conceptualization of an economic approach to trade market definition at a later stage in this book. Chapter 2 explains the role of market definition in both legal regimes. Although market definition in each legal regime is about the comparability of products, it is shown that the ultimate aim of making this comparison differs between the identification of market power, on the one hand, and of protectionism, on the other. But the economic concept of market power will also become relevant when conceptualizing an economic approach to Article III market definition. Chapter 3 sketches the two legal regimes' similar historical evolution from a traditional non-economic and formalistic approach to an economic approach, and develops an explanation for this development. This case law survey indicates how lawyers have attempted to render operational the inherently economic endeavor of determining product similarity and how economics has – successfully or not – intruded into the realm of legal analysis. Chapter 3 also identifies reasons why the traditional approach has been problematic and why it needs to be replaced by an economic approach. Against this background, Chapter 4 formalizes the general analytical and conceptual framework for an economic approach to market definition under Article III of the GATT. It determines demand-side substitution as the relevant economic force and develops a price increase test to identify "like" and DCS products. Finally, Chapter 5 addresses how an economic approach could be implemented on a methodological level by the use of quantitative methods. In this context, the study turns, first, to the issue of whether evidence produced by quantitative methods can be reliably injected into WTO dispute settlement procedure. Fundamentally, this relates to institutional and procedural aspects of expert economic testimony. Subsequently, the focus is on CPE of demand as the economic measure for demand-side substitutability. The book outlines the precise role of CPE of demand in Article III market definition. Multiple regression analysis is then described as the most important quantitative technique to econometrically estimate CPE of demand. Its use in Article III market definition case law is critically assessed. On this basis, advantages of, and limitations to, quantitative methods in legal decision making generally can finally be addressed.

1

Comparison of antitrust and international trade law

Before embarking on a comparative analysis of antitrust and international trade market definition, a preliminary question is whether the two legal regimes can be usefully compared. As will become clear in the course of this book, market definition cannot be detached from the policy goals of the underlying regimes. This chapter outlines that the fundamental policy objectives in the two disciplines concur. It is the fact there are converging (economic) policy rationales that shape market definition in both legal areas that justifies a comparative analysis in this book.

The following description is developed at a simple introductory level. It is accessible both to experts in WTO law without a background in antitrust law and policy, and to antitrust experts without knowledge in WTO law and policy.

I EMPHASIZING DIFFERENCES OR COMMONALITIES?

At first glance, one may view antitrust and international trade law as diverging on their underlying policies.[1] As the Panel in *Korea – Alcoholic Beverages* put it:

> Trade law generally, and Article III in particular, focuses on the promo tion of economic opportunities for importers through the elimination of discriminatory governmental measures which impair fair international trade. Thus, trade law addresses the issue of the potentiality to compete. Antitrust law generally focuses on firms' practices or structural modifications which may prevent or restrain or eliminate competition.[2]

[1] See, e.g., Goco, "Non-Discrimination, 'Likeness,' and Market Definition in World Trade Organization Jurisprudence," p. 332.

[2] Panel Report, *Korea – Alcoholic Beverages*, *supra*, Introduction, fn. 36, para. 10.81.

From this extract, it appears that the different source of market distortion, that is, the distinction between state and private actors, constitutes the crucial difference between the two legal regimes. However this passage can also be interpreted differently to support the claim that they can be seen to be consistent with each other. Both are instruments to achieve the common objective of rendering markets more competitive: trade policy opens up markets to foreign producers, while antitrust policy provides an environment conductive to more open markets.[3] Fundamentally, the common denominator of both regimes is their simultaneous effort to ensure the effective equality of competitive conditions by eliminating market distortions.[4] More importantly, this is not an end in itself for the two disciplines. There is convergence toward the underlying (economic) rationale behind the objective to establish and maintain a level playing field for market participants. In each case, this rationale is the promotion of economic efficiency and (consumer) welfare. The two regimes share the ultimate objective of enabling an efficient, welfare-maximizing allocation of scarce resources through the competitive interaction of individual agents pursuing their private interests.[5] In fact, with their different focus on state and private actors, the two legal disciplines play complementary roles in promoting the common efficiency and welfare objectives through effective inter-firm rivalry in competitive markets.[6] The reason for their mutually reinforcing functionality is that market imperfections that impair efficiency and welfare goals may not be attributable to private firms only, but also to government intervention. Neither antitrust nor trade law could fully achieve its objectives without the other. Each would fail to address the type of impediment to efficiency and welfare gains that is addressed by the other. The extent to which there is accord

[3] WTO, Working Group on the Interaction between Trade and Competition Policy, Report on the Meeting of September 16/17, 1997, WT/WGTCP/M/2, para. 7, November 12, 1997.

[4] Bercero and Amarasinha, "Moving the Trade and Competition Debate Forward," *Journal of International Economic Law*, 4 (2001), 481, 502; Horn and Mavroidis, "Still Hazy after all These Years: The Interpretation of National Treatment in the GATT/WTO Case Law on Tax Discrimination," *European Journal of International Law*, 15 (2001), 39, 66.

[5] WTO, "Working Group on the Interaction between Trade and Competition Policy," Report on the Meeting of November 27/28, 1997, WT/WGTCP/M/3, para. 4, February 26, 1998. *Contra* Diebold, *Non-Discrimination in International Trade in Services*, pp. 280–282, who asserts that trade law is not about consumer welfare.

[6] WTO, Working Group on the Interaction between Trade and Competition Policy, Synthesis Paper on the Relationship of Trade and Competition Policy to Development and Economic Growth, WT/WGTCP/W/80, para. 29, September 18, 1998. In more detail on the complementary nature see Taylor, *International Competition Law: A New Dimension for the WTO?*, pp. 164–183 (2006).

in these economic goals will be outlined in greater detail in the following subsections. This will also prove to be important in the course of this study because insights on the underlying economic rationales are relevant when conceptualizing an economics-based market definition approach for Article III of the GATT.

II ANTITRUST LAW

In the early days of US antitrust policy, and to some degree still today in Europe, antitrust policy pursued various partially non-economic and, at times, conflicting goals. In the United States, antitrust statutes were inspired by the objective of busting trusts and keeping economic institutions small and locally oriented.[7] EU antitrust law was introduced originally as part of the broader context of the law of the European Communities, and thus embraced a multitude of economic, and also sociopolitical, goals, such as market integration. Therefore, aims besides economic efficiency and consumer welfare have long played a prominent role. However, modern antitrust policy is now considered to be primarily concerned with economic goals.

1 Introduction

Antitrust law may in fact be perceived as a policy instrument premised on neoclassical microeconomic price theory.[8] This economic theory contrasts the opposite extremes of perfect competition and monopoly.[9] The theory states that: (1) markets allocate society's scarce resources between competing end-uses; (2) economic efficiency refers to the optimal use and allocation of such resources by markets, thereby maximizing social welfare, that is, society's overall wealth; (3) competition enhances market efficiency and social welfare;[10] (4) monopoly or market power is anathema to competitive processes, and, in the presence of market power,

[7] See, e.g., *Brown Shoe Co.* v. *United States*, 370 US 294, 344 (1962) (hereinafter *Brown Shoe*): "We cannot fail to recognize Congress' desire to promote competition through the protection of viable, small, locally owned businesses."

[8] For a basic introduction see Wish, *Competition Law*, paras. 3–18 (2009).

[9] The archetypal state of perfect competition is premised on certain, yet in sum unrealistic, assumptions on market characteristics: a large number of buyers and sellers, homogeneous products, perfect information on the part of buyers and sellers, and the absence of entry or exit barriers.

[10] Regarding the notion of competition, it is commonly accepted that it connotes a dynamic process of rivalry, but beyond this there is no common understanding. For an overview

markets may not maximize economic efficiency and social welfare; and (5) antitrust laws regulate market power in order to promote competition, thereby enhancing economic efficiency and increasing social welfare.

The starting point under microeconomic price theory is that markets are decentralized mechanisms that allocate scarce resources through the collective transactions between profit-maximizing producers and consumers seeking to maximize their individual utility by purchasing the products they value most at the lowest available price.[11] An individual producer in a perfectly competitive market cannot unilaterally control market price. He has to take the price as given, that is, he is a price-taker. A profit-maximizing producer will therefore expand his production for as long as it is profitable to do so. Because the producer will always be able to add to profit where the cost of producing one extra unit of output ("marginal cost") is less than the price (or "marginal revenue"), the producer in a perfectly competitive market will keep increasing the units until the price obtained equals marginal cost. While production increases, the market price increases (supply function). Conversely, buyers will demand more as the market price falls (demand function). The market mechanism, that is, the interaction between buyers and sellers, pushes prices up and down, according to shortage in demand or surplus in production, until a stable equilibrium is obtained. Market equilibrium with equilibrium price and quantity is achieved where the level of supply meets the level of demand.[12] In this situation, market price and marginal cost coincide. The profit a producer makes by selling goods above the cost of production is known as the "producer surplus." Consumers realize a surplus utility in excess of the price paid to the producer, known as "consumer surplus."[13]

of the fundamental concepts of competition see Behrens, *Die ökonomischen Grundlagen des Rechts*, pp. 131–155 (1986).

[11] See Behrens, "Economic Law between Harmonization and Competition: The Law and Economics Approach," in Meessen (ed.), *Economic Law as an Economic Good: Its Rule Function and its Tool Function in the Competition of Systems*, pp. 45, 46 (2009): "Markets are large networks of interaction between market operators who all want to promote their individual welfare. Markets allow for the coordination of an indefinitely large number of individual 'welfare functions' by means of voluntary transactions between the market operators. They tend toward an allocation of scarce resources which mirrors the individual welfare objectives (preferences) of market participants, i.e., toward 'allocative efficiency.'"

[12] A graphical representation in form of a diagram can be found in every basic economics textbook, see, e.g., Pindyck and Rubinfeld, *Microeconomics*, p. 25 (2009).

[13] As a measure of the welfare that people gain from the consumption of goods, it is the amount that consumers benefit by being able to purchase a product for a price that is less than they would be willing to pay.

2 Promotion of economic efficiency

Based on these insights, the notion of economic efficiency will now be outlined. In economic theory, a policy change that produces a surplus of benefits over costs may be termed "efficient." The standard economic concept of economic efficiency is "Pareto" efficiency. A policy change is Pareto efficient when it produces net benefits for at least one individual affected by it, and does not leave anyone worse off than before. "Kaldor–Hicks" efficiency arises when the benefits of those who gain from a change in policy exceed the costs to those who lose from it. In contrast to *Pareto* efficiency, it thus recognizes the increase in the net wealth of society as a whole.

Economic efficiency embraces three fundamental categories: (1) "allocative efficiency" is achieved when society's scarce resources are allocated to produce the goods that are most desired by consumers. This equals the optimum utilization of a society's existing resources to meet consumer wants. (2) "Productive efficiency" is achieved when goods are produced at the minimum possible total cost with the available productive resources and thus in the most cost-effective way. This means that as little of society's wealth is expended in the production by using the most effective combination of resources. (3) "Dynamic efficiency" is achieved through an optimal rate of invention, development, and diffusion of new products and production processes.

The goal of promoting economic efficiency is recognized as a fundamental objective of antitrust policy in the United States as well as in Europe.[14] The advent of the efficiency paradigm came with the rise of the Chicago School thinking, which was highly influential on US antitrust policy in the 1970s and 1980s.[15] A fundamental principle that permeates current antitrust policy is that the ideal of perfect competition is economically optimal, while inefficiencies are the result of monopolies. Competition in markets is thought to achieve efficiencies for the following reasons: (1) sellers in such markets will produce the right amount of

[14] Kroes, European Commissioner for Competition, *Preliminary Thoughts on Policy Review of Article 82*, Fordham University Symposium, New York, 2005, available at: http://europa.eu/rapid/pressReleasesAction.do?reference=SPEECH/05/537: "In our view the objective … is the protection of competition on the market as a means of enhancing consumer welfare and ensuring an efficient allocation of resources."

[15] The first and most prominent proponent was Bork, *The Antitrust Paradox: A Policy at War with Itself* (1978). For an overview see Rubinfeld, "On the Foundations of Antitrust Law and Economics," in Pitofsky (ed.), *How the Chicago School Overshot the Market: The Effect of Conservative Economic Analysis on US Antitrust*, pp. 51–73 (2008).

goods (and sell them at marginal cost); (2) they produce them at the lowest cost; and (3) they have incentives to undertake research and development and to deliver innovation and technical progress. In other words, competition is perceived to serve the goal of enhanced efficiency in both its static (allocative and productive) and dynamic sense.

For economists, allocative efficiency is the central consideration in terms of antitrust's efficiency goal. The market equilibrium achieved under perfect competition has the effect that goods are produced in the quantities valued by society and allocated to those consumers who value the product most. This is the allocatively efficient outcome because it is the point at which the value consumers place on the last unit of the good (its price) is equal to the cost of producing it (its marginal cost). This situation is Pareto optimal because it is impossible to improve the welfare of any one individual, buyer, or seller without reducing the welfare of another.[16]

In contrast, a monopolist – as the single seller who provides all the buyers in the market – can control the market price. Since he is responsible for all the output, and since it is aggregate output that determines price through the relationship of supply and demand, he will be able to restrict output and thereby raise prices above the competitive level without losing so many sales that the price increase becomes unprofitable. Output decreases below the level under conditions of perfect competition. With fewer products produced, one portion of the consumers will still buy the products at higher prices and one portion of the consumers will stop buying. The former class of consumers now pays more than they would under perfectly competitive conditions. A transfer of wealth takes place from the consumers to the producer. In economic terms, a share of the consumer surplus is redistributed from the consumers to the monopolist, who increases his producer surplus by the corresponding amount, the "monopoly rent." This is the so-called price effect of monopoly. The latter group of consumers, who would have bought the product at the competitive price but cease to buy the product at the monopoly price, will now spend their money on other things. They are deprived of goods that they would have been prepared to pay for at the competitive market price. As the consumers stop purchasing the preferred product, their wishes are not fully satisfied. Their consumer surplus is not merely transferred to the monopolist, but lost altogether. This net loss is called the "deadweight loss." It is the so-called allocation effect of monopoly. Allocative inefficiency occurs because society's resources are not distributed in the most

[16] This is known as the First Fundamental Theorem of Welfare Economics.

efficient way: resources are diverted from more desired goods to less desired ones. The objection to monopoly in economic theory is not what laypeople would have in mind – that the monopolist is able to charge excessively for its products – but the loss to allocative efficiency.

The market equilibrium under perfect competition also has the effect that it allocates supply to those producers that use the least resources and thus enhances productive efficiency. Producers have the incentive to maximize producer surplus. Therefore, they continually strive to optimize production while minimizing production costs. The reason is that a producer is unable to produce and sell above cost (if he did, his customers would immediately desert him or more cost-efficient rivals would enter the market), and he will not, of course, sell below (because he would not make any profit). By contrast, a monopolist is productively inefficient; he is not constrained by competitive forces to reduce costs to the lowest possible level (known as "X-inefficiency"). Instead, the monopolist may spend resources inefficiently in acquiring or maintaining his monopoly position.

And, finally, competition delivers dynamic efficiency because producers who seek an advantage over competitors are motivated to optimize production and reduce costs, whereas a monopolist has no incentive to invent and innovate. Yet this assertion is highly contested; it is also claimed that monopolies can give a major innovation stimulus. This issue can, however, remain open for the purpose of this study.

3 Promotion of consumer welfare

A branch of microeconomic theory, welfare economics, identifies the welfare effects of perfect competition and monopoly. A perfectly competitive market, in most circumstances, maximizes society's welfare because it leads to efficiency. There are different concepts of welfare. The consumer surplus is the net welfare benefit accruing to consumers ("consumer welfare"), while the producer surplus is the net welfare benefit accruing to producers ("producer welfare"). The aggregate of the consumer and producer surplus is known as "total welfare" and is the traditional welfare economics measure of welfare gains. In terms of welfare maximization, the objection to monopoly is twofold: it transfers some consumer surplus to the producers. This may be neutral in terms of total welfare because the consumer surplus is not lost but absorbed by the monopolist (looking at the aggregate welfare effect reflecting Kaldor–Hicks efficiency). However, from an equity point of view, competition policy may, and usually does, make the normative argument that this leads to a situation with a less preferable welfare distribution (distributional or social justice goal). Moreover, the deadweight loss is a real and total loss of consumer surplus to the market. It lowers the total welfare of society.

Tension therefore exists between the welfare standards, with practical repercussions for antitrust policy. In the assessment of monopoly, economists – especially since the rise of the Chicago School – have traditionally focused on total welfare. Emphasis has thus been on the deadweight loss as the net loss to society and allocative efficiency assessed in terms of total welfare. At the same time, it is safe to say that today both US and EU antitrust policies value consumer welfare over producer welfare.[17] This means that antitrust policy's concern is the transfer of surplus from consumers to producers.[18] While antitrust policy neither matches the *Pareto* nor the Kaldor–Hicks criteria, the underlying welfare model is that of consumer welfare where – in contrast to a pure total welfare approach – consumers should be passed on efficiencies or, at least, not be made worse off.[19]

Against this background, it is more or less agreed that antitrust policy is an instrument to ensure that markets operate so as to achieve allocative efficiency and consumer welfare – even though the extent to which other goals should be pursued remains controversial.[20] In fact, allocative efficiency and consumer welfare are two objectives often stated alongside

[17] Kroes, European Commissioner for Competition, *European Competition Policy: Delivering Better Markets and Better Choices*, European Consumer and Competition Day, London, (2005), available at: http://europa.eu/rapid/pressReleasesAction.do?reference=SPEECH/05/512&format=HTML&aged=1&language=EN&guiLanguage=en: "Consumer welfare is now well established as the standard the Commission applies when assessing mergers and infringements of the Treaty rules on cartels and monopolies. Our aim is simple: to protect competition in the market as a means of enhancing consumer welfare and ensuring an efficient allocation of resources"; Pitofsky, FTC chairman, *The Effect of Global Trade on United States Competition Law and Enforcement Policies* (1999), available at: www.ftc.gov/speeches/pitofsky/fobebf1.shtm: "United States' primary commitment in enforcement of its antitrust laws is to serve the goal of the welfare of consumers."

[18] Bishop and Walker, *The Economics of EC Competition Law: Concepts, Application and Measurement*, 3rd edn., para. 2-017 (2010).

[19] van den Bergh and Camesasca, *European Competition Law and Economics: A Comparative Perspective*, paras. 41–45 (2006). Antitrust policy does not strive for *Pareto* efficiency (realized under conditions of perfect competition) because it is never the case that enforcement intervention takes place only if no individual (consumer or producer) would be worse off. The Kaldor–Hicks criterion (total welfare) is not the yardstick, since antitrust policy does not focus on the goal of maximizing the sum of consumer and producer surplus.

[20] van den Bergh and Camesasca, *European Competition Law and Economics*, paras. 35–40.

each other in antitrust enforcers' policy statements. Yet both are potentially conflicting concepts. Consumer welfare is concerned with the redistributive effect, while allocative efficiency is assessed in terms of total welfare for which it is irrelevant whether the consumer or the producer receives the wealth. The question of which of these two goals takes precedence in a trade-off remains open in the analysis. For present purposes, it is sufficient to note that allocative efficiency and consumer welfare are each achieved under perfect competition, whereas monopoly is detrimental to both. Thus it is the primary aim of any antitrust intervention by behavioral and structural regulation to prevent the aggregation of market power and, more specifically, to prevent the ability to increase price above competitive (equilibrium) level.

III WTO/GATT LAW

Traditionally, international trade has been explained from a purely economic perspective. The simple case for free trade can be made on the ground that it is efficiency and welfare enhancing in comparison with autarky. Since these economic objectives may be impaired by (governmental) trade barriers,[21] its aim is to reduce and ultimately eliminate trade restrictions.

Over recent decades, other explanations to international trade have gained increasing attention.[22] Still, economic objectives remain at the heart of any international trade agreement and also provide the common denominator for a comparative analysis with antitrust law. This book

[21] This is true with regard to efficiency and welfare effects on other nations, globally, and – in most instances – also the country imposing the trade barrier itself.

[22] One strand of the literature explains cooperation through international trade agreements as an escape to the prisoners' dilemma and a non-cooperative *Nash* equilibrium resulting from the fact that countries have the incentive to unilaterally set trade barriers higher than would be efficient. Economic externalities result in which one nation's self-interested policies may have negative spillover effects on global welfare and that of other nations. Another approach, the so-called commitment school, inspired by Public Choice Theory, alleges that binding trade agreements serve as a "hand-tying" mechanism that improves the bargaining position of each signatory government in relation to capture by various domestic interest groups, e.g., producer interests. Lastly, international trade agreements are explained in a political dimension with the motivation to achieve peace, security, and stability. See Irwin, Mavroidis, and Sykes, *The Genesis of the GATT*, pp. 177–197 (2008) and Schropp, *Trade Policy Flexibility and Enforcement in the WTO: A Law and Economics Analysis*, pp. 144–149 (2009).

therefore focuses on the core concept of "comparative advantage" as the primary basis and economic logic for international trade rules.

1 Introduction

The classical theory of international trade emphasizes the advantages of a liberal trade policy in which governmental intervention is reduced to a minimum. International trade is premised on the idea of specialization of production factors and labor division. The most prominent conception of international trade was expressed in the theory of comparative advantages formalized by Ricardo in his *Principles of Political Economy and Taxation* in 1817. According to this theory, welfare is enhanced when each country specializes in the production of those goods in which it has the greatest comparative advantage.[23]

A country is said to have a comparative advantage in the production of a good if it can produce it at lower opportunity cost (that is, at lower relative price) than another country. The opportunity cost of producing a certain product X is defined as the amount of another product Y that must be given up in order to produce one more unit of X at a given amount of factors of production and productivity. If a country must forgo less of product Y in order to produce an additional unit of product X than the amount of Y that another country would have to give up in order to produce an additional unit of X, it has a comparative advantage.[24]

For trade to be beneficial all that is required is for relative costs between countries to be different. Hence, even a country that only has an absolute disadvantage for all of its products (as it can produce them only at higher costs) can still benefit from international trade because there will be at least one good in which it has a comparative advantage. In each case, it is beneficial for the country to specialize in the production of the good in which it has the greatest comparative advantage and for its trading partner to do likewise, thus increasing total world output of both products.

[23] The economic foundations of free trade and the theory of comparative advantages are developed at length in many international economics textbooks, e.g., Kenen, *The International Economy*, pp. 19–62 (2000) and Krugman and Obstfeld, *International Economics: Theory and Practice*, pp. 27–87 (2009). Alternatively, see Bhala, *International Trade Law: Interdisciplinary Theory and Practice*, pp. 201–317 (2008).

[24] Note that a country only needs to be comparatively more productive than another with respect to a particular good. It does not need to have an absolute advantage, that is, be able to produce a product at absolute lower cost. In this way, the (absolute) production costs for the same product in two different countries are not compared, rather the relative production costs for two different products in two different countries.

Nations can exploit their comparative advantage by exporting the good that is relatively cheap locally (in terms of the other good) and importing the good that is relatively expensive locally (in terms of the other). The theory of comparative advantage therefore yields a simple prediction: nations will tend to specialize in the production of goods in which they have comparative advantages, exporting them to other nations in exchange for goods in which they lack comparative advantages.

The basic Ricardian two-country two-goods model is based on the sole precondition that the opportunity costs for the outputs are different across countries. It has been generalized to apply to any number of trading countries and any number of goods as long as this condition holds. Later refinements of the Ricardian theory explained in more detail the sources for comparative advantages.[25] Modern economics has further qualified this approach by noting that specialization according to comparative advantages cannot explain all facets of international trade.[26]

The theory of comparative advantage is therefore of only limited explicative value for international trade and is premised on simplified and, to a certain extent, unrealistic assumptions.[27] Despite subsequent refinements and qualifications, the model of specialization according to comparative advantages continues to be the theoretical basis for explaining international trade today.[28]

2 Promotion of economic efficiency

In the Ricardian model, the aggregate gains from the specialization of production factors and free trade can be described as "improvements in production and consumption efficiency," compared with autarky.[29] As it

[25] In particular, the Heckscher–Ohlim theory with regard to differences in "factor abundance."

[26] Especially the intra-industrial trade between industrialized countries with similar factor endowments cannot be explained by differences in comparative advantages, but by reference to, e.g., product differentiation, economies of scale, and imperfect markets.

[27] Among these assumptions are: zero transportation costs; costless and fully flexible reallocation of labor within each country; and zero factor mobility across borders, in particular zero labor migration between the countries.

[28] See, e.g., Lamy, Director-General of the WTO, "China hält sich an die Regeln," *Handelsblatt-Gespräch*, July 16/17, 2010, p. 6: "Für Arbeitsplätze und Wachstum entscheidend ist jedoch, welchen zusätzlichen Beitrag ein Land in der globalen Produktion der Unternehmen leistet. Es gibt immer die Möglichkeit, seinen Anteil dort zu steigern, wo man gegenüber der Konkurrenz einen komparativen Vorteil besitzt"; Utton, *International Competition Policy: Maintaining Open Markets in the Global Economy*, pp. 11, 17 (2006).

[29] Lester and Mercurio, *World Trade Law: Text, Materials and Commentary*, p. 49 (2008).

has been observed, free trade raises aggregate world production efficiency because global output of the two goods is increased, holding constant the resources devoted to productive activity in each country (only shifting them toward areas of comparative advantage).[30] This means that more of each product is produced with the same amount of input.[31] Free trade also improves aggregate consumption efficiency. Specialization and trade will increase the set of consumption possibilities of each nation, compared with autarky, and will enable an increase in consumption of both goods without increasing the resources that they devote to production. This implies that consumers have a more pleasing set of choices and prices available to them.

In terms of the above categories, international free trade generates allocative, productive, and dynamic efficiency. Specialization of production factors in accordance with comparative advantages leads to an optimal allocation and use of resources across and within industries. The producers that prevail are those that most efficiently produce the greatest amount of a good with a constant amount of input. And increased international competition leads to product and process innovation, which further reduces costs and expands consumer choices.

In the Ricardian model, the price of each country's comparative advantage good is lower than the price of the same good in the other country. The import of the comparative advantage good will thus lead to a decrease in the market price. At the same time, on the exporting country's side, once the domestic market opens to international trade, the market price of the now exported good will rise. Under these circumstances, the

[30] Sykes, "Comparative Advantage and the Normative Economics of International Trade Policy," *Journal of International Economic Law*, 1 (1998), 49, 61. Note that the Ricardian model assumes full employment and costless labor mobility, so that the domestic industry with the comparative disadvantage goes out of business, but the producer and the workers can immediately and gainfully switch to the comparative advantage industry.

[31] As an illustration, assume that the citizens in two countries value both products X and Y, and suppose that in autarky the labor force has been fully allocated in each country and that 100 units of X and Y are produced in each country. The labor requirement per unit of output in country A is 1 for X and 2 for Y and for country B, 2 for X and 3 for Y. Now imagine the following change in the allocation of labor: country A shifts 20 units of labor from the production of Y to that of X, sacrificing 10 units of the production of Y (it falls to 90) and increasing the production of X by 20 units (it increases to 120). Country B shifts 36 units of labor from the production of X to that of Y, sacrificing 18 units of the production of X (it falls to 82) and increasing production of Y by 12 units (it increases to 112). Country A then exports 19 units of X to country B in exchange for 11 units of Y. Each country now has 101 units of both X and Y to consume, more than they could possibly consume in autarky. Example taken from Sykes, "Comparative Advantage and the Normative Economics of International Trade Policy," pp. 60–61.

removal of impediments to trade is unlikely to be Pareto efficient.[32] On the side of the importing country, the reason for this is that the distributional impact of international trade and specialization will be harmful to certain individuals, such as domestic firms and workers operating in fields in which the country has a comparative disadvantage. On the side of the exporting country, consumers who cut back or stop their consumption are disadvantaged by the higher price. However, the efficiency argument from the national and global welfare perspectives for free trade rests on Kaldor–Hicks efficiency. It relates to the aggregate of consumer and producer welfare, and thus total welfare. On the importing market, the domestic consumers gain from a lower priced imported product.[33] As Sykes explained, this gain is greater than the attendant loss to domestic firms and workers producing import-competing products from an ensuing price decrease (loss in producer surplus).[34] On the exporting side, the loss to domestic consumers is smaller than the attendant gains to domestic firms and workers in the industry, which has the comparative advantage.

3 Promotion of total welfare

Recall that Kaldor–Hicks efficiency relates to the aggregate of consumer and producer welfare and thus total welfare. The movement of goods in free trade in accordance with the theory of comparative advantages generates Kaldor–Hicks improvements and maximizes total welfare nationally and globally. Governmental trade restrictions, by contrast, impair efficiency and thus reduce national and global welfare.[35] Restrictions on trade are harmful under a total welfare analysis. Focusing on the import side (as import restrictions are the usual form of trade barrier), imposing a trade restriction will increase the domestic price. The gains to domestic firms and workers in the industry from the higher price (in the form of domestic producer surplus) will be smaller

[32] However, see Srinivasan, "Nondiscrimination in GATT/WTO: Was there Anything to Begin With and is there Anything Left?," *World Trade Review*, 4 (2005), 69, 75–76.

[33] The increment in consumer surplus can be attributed to the gain for consumers who would have bought the products anyway but now pay less, and to the gain for consumers who enter the market at the lower price.

[34] Sykes, "Comparative Advantage and the Normative Economics of International Trade Policy," pp. 61–63.

[35] This is necessarily a generalization and requires certain qualifications because protectionist measures may, under certain circumstances, also increase national welfare, but usually at the expense of global welfare; see Sykes, "Comparative Advantage and the Normative Economics of International Trade Policy," pp. 68–77.

than the loss borne by domestic consumers (in the form of reduced consumer surplus).[36]

Modern conceptions of international trade policies that underpin the WTO/GATT regime are also based on this theoretical economic thinking. The theory of comparative advantages motivates the primary aim of the WTO to reduce and ultimately remove any form of trade barrier. This allows its Members to benefit from the economic advantages flowing from the liberalization of international trade. Thus, in economic terms, the principle of non-discrimination, of which Article III of the GATT is a part, is an instrument of the multilateral trading system that operates to prevent economic inefficiencies and losses in welfare that result from discriminatory protection of the domestic industry or of specific trading partners. It is designed to effectively determine the production, distribution, and consumption of goods according to the comparative advantages of countries.

More specifically, Article III of the GATT prevents discriminatory measures that enable inefficient and relatively high cost domestic producers to out-compete more efficient and lower cost foreign producers. This is known as "trade diversion," which creates the abovementioned welfare losses and allocative inefficiencies. When all producers are treated equally, the most efficient will prevail in competition. Welfare will then be enhanced because of savings in resources in the production and increased consumption possibilities in the form of lowered consumer prices or increased consumer choice.

IV CONGRUENCE IN EFFICIENCY AND WELFARE STANDARDS

Promotion of efficiency and welfare are identical core objectives of both legal regimes, even though each discipline follows a different, yet interrelated, underlying economic theory describing how efficiency and welfare are achieved (the model of perfect competition and the Ricardian theory of comparative advantages). Those theories concern different subject matters of regulation and thus rely on different causal mechanisms to

[36] Total welfare is reduced because of the deadweight loss associated with pricing some consumers out of the market and the deadweight loss associated with substituting higher cost domestic production for lower cost imports; see Sykes, "Comparative Advantage and the Normative Economics of International Trade Policy," pp. 65–66.

achieve the same efficiency and welfare goals.[37] Antitrust policy regulates private firms through behavioral and structural regulation in order to prevent excessive market power that may impair efficiency and welfare gains from competitive interaction. International trade policy regulates governmental intervention through trade liberalization in order to prevent (governmental) trade barriers that impair efficiency and welfare gains from specialization. But the theories do not only share these ultimate goals; they are also interrelated. The theory of perfect competition assumes that rational producers maximize their profits by minimizing their production costs. Such cost-minimizing behavior under (perfectly) competitive conditions should determine the type of specialization relevant to the theory of comparative advantages.[38] By contrast, a governmental barrier to trade is also an impediment to competition (in antitrust parlance, an "entry barrier") and thus not only prevents the achievement of comparative advantages, but also of conditions of perfect competition.

Still, some seek to make a distinction. The argument has been made that trade policy, and thus Article III of the GATT, primarily protects foreign products, and thus foreign competitors, which is inimical to the antitrust objective.[39] Antitrust policy is directed at the protection of the competitive conditions and of consumers, but not competitors.[40] For example, to substantiate an Article III complaint, the complainant must show an effect of the contested measure on the competitive opportunities of the foreign product; the effect on domestic consumers is irrelevant. In contrast, antitrust complaints are often required to show some detriment to the competitive process (in the EU) or to consumers (in the United States). Thus, with the alleged difference in producer versus consumer interests, international trade and antitrust policy are to be seen in conflict with each other.[41]

[37] See K. C. Kennedy, *Competition Law and the World Trade Organisation: The Limits of Multilateralism*, paras. 1.10–1.12 (2001).

[38] Taylor, *International Competition Law: A New Dimension for the WTO?*, p. 172.

[39] Diebold, *Non-Discrimination in International Trade in Services*, p. 282; Tarullo, "Norms and Institutions in Global Competition Policy," *American Journal of International Law*, 94 (2000), 478, 483, notes that "trade policy is usually concerned with promoting the interests of specific competitors, whereas competition policy is usually concerned with promoting competitive markets."

[40] See, e.g., *Brown Shoe*, *supra*, fn. 7, at 320 (noting that "the legislative history illuminates congressional concern with the protection of competition, not competitors").

[41] Chang, "Interaction between Trade and Competition: Why a Multilateral Approach for the United States?," 14 *Duke Journal of Comparative & International Law*, (2004), 1, 7.

Such a distinction is, however, overly simplistic and seeks to draw a dichotomy where there is in fact none. First, it will be shown below that the GATT regime in no way concerns individual rights of foreign producers or suppliers, and in particular is not about guaranteeing a share of the domestic market to foreign competitors.[42] Moreover, it is true that the above analysis has disclosed diverging welfare standards: consumer welfare in antitrust and total welfare in international trade policy. The latter, however, encompasses both consumer and producer interests. The protection of foreign products will therefore generate not only incidental benefits for domestic consumers. As it has been outlined, there is a crucial consumer welfare argument in favor of domestic consumers which makes international trade beneficial for the importing country under the Kaldor–Hicks efficiency criterion, and a total welfare standard. The key common denominator for both disciplines is (allocative, productive, and dynamic) efficiency and (consumer) welfare.

Where both legal regimes ultimately strive for the same economic goals, and the market definition inquiry in each context necessarily cannot be viewed as detached from these underlying objectives, a comparative analysis is useful and informative in order to develop an economic approach to market definition under Article III of the GATT.

[42] See *infra*, Ch. 2, fn. 83.

2

The role of market definition

This chapter provides the foundations for understanding the role of market definition. It sets the stage by introducing the legal framework and rationale behind market definition in antitrust law and Article III of the GATT. Section I presents market definition as a tool for antitrust law's analysis of market power. Section II, then turns to product comparison in the context of Article III of the GATT, and links the need for a determination of likeness and the identification of a DCS relationship to the concept of non-discrimination. It becomes clear that market definition in antitrust law is not a statutory requirement and has an auxiliary function that can be understood only when turning to the underlying market power rationale. By contrast, market definition under Article III of the GATT is a statutory requirement that is essential for the operation of the NT obligation.

I ANTITRUST LAW

1 Introduction

The basic purpose of antitrust market definition is to identify the competitive constraints faced by the firms involved. Put simply, it "is an effort to describe the array of firms that currently produce or potentially will produce products that are *sufficiently close substitutes*" for one another.[1] Market definition seeks to identify those products and geographic areas, commonly referred to as the "relevant market," which are *substitutable to a certain extent*. Thus, a relevant market has two components that reflect different dimensions in which competition occurs: (1) the "relevant product market," which identifies the products or services that compete with

[1] Pitofsky, "New Definitions of Relevant Market and the Assault on Antitrust," *Columbia Law Review*, 90 (1990), 1805, 1806 (emphasis added).

each other; and (2) the "relevant geographic market," which identifies the geographic area within which competition in the relevant product market takes place.[2] The notion of the two separate market dimensions was introduced by the US Supreme Court and has subsequently become part of market definition parlance.[3] Although the terms of relevant product and geographic markets are now conventionally used in antitrust law, they can be misleading. There is but one relevant market with a product and a geographic dimension. Separating the two dimensions is a practical necessity for courts and agencies, which usually start by looking at the product market and then turn to the geographic market.

2 Market definition as a statutory requirement

Although not expressly required by the statutes in US and EU antitrust law, market definition has become a prerequisite to antitrust analysis by judicial interpretation. It plays a pivotal role under all relevant provisions. This is true for prohibitions of anticompetitive vertical and horizontal agreements, which are agreements between a seller and a buyer either in the up- or downstream market, or between competitors at the same level of distribution, respectively. It is equally central in assessing the presence of monopolistic behavior. It also applies in assessing whether a proposed merger would generate anticompetitive effects. Broadly speaking, and as will be explained below, in each scenario market definition serves to identify whether the firm or firms under investigation have or will acquire a degree of influence that poses a significant risk to competition.

This section provides a brief overview of the most important statutes under US and EU antitrust law in which an analysis of the relevant market is employed.

In US federal antitrust law under section 1 of the Sherman Act,[4] which prohibits any form of agreement or conspiracy that restrains trade or commerce, courts have traditionally analyzed restraints using either the *per se* rule of illegality or the rule of reason. In the former case of agreements declared illegal as a matter of law, the delineation of a relevant market is

[2] Note that in rare cases a third temporal dimension may be relevant when competitive conditions vary significantly from one time period to another so that a firm may have market power at one point in time but not in another.

[3] *Standard Oil Co.* v. *United States*, 221 US 1, 61 (1911) (hereinafter *Standard Oil*). It appears that the term "relevant market" was first used in a US federal antitrust decision in *United States* v. *Columbia Steel Co.*, 334 US 495, 508 (1948).

[4] 15 USC § 1.

generally not required.[5] By way of contrast, the rule of reason requires that any anti- and procompetitive effects be balanced. This necessitates a definition of the market within which the effects may be evaluated.[6] As the *per se* rule has successively been replaced by extending the rule of reason to an ever growing number of types of restraints, under US Supreme Court precedent the vast majority of section 1 cases now fall under the latter rule and therefore require the delineation of a relevant market.

Section 2 of the Sherman Act[7] addresses unilateral, single firm conduct. The provision provides that it is unlawful to monopolize, attempt to monopolize, or conspire to monopolize "any part of the trade or commerce" among the states or with foreign nations. This quoted passage is understood to refer to the requirement of market definition.[8] "Without a definition of that market," the US Supreme Court observed, "there is no way to measure [a defendant's] ability to lessen or destroy competition."[9] Thus, proof of a relevant market is an essential element of all section 2 cases.

Section 7 of the Clayton Act,[10] as amended in 1950 by the Celler–Kefauver Act, prohibits mergers "where in any line of commerce in any section of the country, the effect of such acquisition may be substantially to lessen competition, or to tend to create a monopoly." The US Supreme Court held that the "determination of a relevant product market and geographic market is a necessary predicate to a finding of a violation of the Clayton Act," because of section 7's statutory directive that a substantial lessening of competition be shown "in any line of commerce or any section of the country."[11] Thus, the Supreme Court stated that market definition

[5] For references and exceptions see ABA Section of Antitrust Law, *Antitrust Law Developments*, 2007, p. 550, fn. 7

[6] *Continental TV, Inc.* v. *GTE Sylvania, Inc.*, 433 US 36, 45 (1977). For further references to lower courts see Kalinowski, Sullivan, and McGuirl, *Antitrust Laws and Trade Regulation*, vol. II, para. 24.01(3)(c), fn. 49 (2007). However, under a more recent doctrinal evolution, certain restraints may be condemned under a truncated rule of reason analysis, the so-called "quick look" doctrine, without defining the relevant market, if the requisite adverse effects on competition are clear and any procompetitive effects are unlikely or implausible, e.g., *FTC* v. *Indiana Federation of Dentists*, 476 US 447, 458–461 (1986).

[7] 15 USC § 2. [8] See *Standard Oil*, *supra*, fn. 3, at 61.

[9] *Walker Process Equip.* v. *Food Mach. & Chem. Corp.*, 382 US 172, 177 (1965).

[10] 15 USC § 18.

[11] *United States* v. *E. I. du Pont de Nemours & Co.*, 353 US 586, 593 (1957) (hereinafter *du Pont de Nemours–General Motors*). See also *United States* v. *Philadelphia Nat'l Bank*, 374 US 321, 356 (1963) equating "line of commerce" with "relevant product or service market" and "section of the country" with "relevant geographic market."

is required to determine whether a merger may have a substantial adverse effect on competition.[12]

In EU antitrust law, Article 101(1) of the Treaty on the Functioning of the European Union (hereinafter TFEU)[13] prohibits agreements, decisions by associations of undertakings, and concerted practices that are restrictive of competition. In contrast to early case law, the delineation of the relevant market is now ordinarily necessary before it can be determined whether an agreement, decision, or concerted practice has as its object or effect the prevention, restriction, or distortion of competition within the common market.[14] Market definition is also essential to the determination of whether or not an agreement *appreciably* restricts competition or trade, a further element of an Article 101(1) claim,[15] to the determination of whether or not an agreement substantially eliminates competition in the common market for the purposes of Article 101(3) of the TFEU, and, in most cases when relying on market share thresholds, whether a block exemption is applicable or not.[16]

Article 102 of the TFEU[17] – the European equivalent of the prohibition of monopolization – prohibits the abuse of a dominant position held individually or collectively. Very early, the European Court of Justice (ECJ)[18] determined the need to define a market when identifying a dominant position.[19] Ever since, it has been repeated that the Article's application requires the existence of a dominant position in a

[12] For other federal antitrust provisions that require market definition see ABA Section of Antitrust Law, *Antitrust Law Developments*, 2007, p. 549.

[13] Ex Article 81(1) of the EC Treaty.

[14] See, e.g., Case T-29/92, *SPO* v. *Commission* [1995] ECR II-289, para. 74; Cases T-25/95 etc., *Cimenteries CBR SA* v. *Commission* [2000] ECR II-491, para. 833. Note that there is only an obligation to define a relevant market under Article 101 of the TFEU when it is impossible, without such definition, to determine whether there is such an object or effect, Cases T-374/94 etc., *European Night Services* v. *Commission* [1998] ECR II-3134, paras. 93–95 and 103.

[15] *Commission Notice on agreements of minor importance which do not appreciably restrict competition under Article 81(1) of the Treaty establishing the European Community (de minimis)* [2001] OJ C368 12.

[16] For instance, Article 3(1) of Commission Regulation No. 330/2010 on the application of Article 101(3) of the Treaty on the Functioning of the European Union to categories of vertical agreements and concerted practices [2010] OJ L102 1.

[17] Ex Article 82 of the EC Treaty.

[18] Formerly known as the Court of Justice of the European Communities, it is called the Court of Justice of the European Union under the Treaty of Lisbon.

[19] Case 6–72, *Europemballage Corp. and Continental Can Company Inc.* v. *Commission* [1973] ECR 215 (hereinafter *Continental Can*), para. 32.

given market "which presupposes that such a market has already been defined."[20]

Finally, market definition is a condition *sine qua non* for merger control under the EC Merger Regulation (hereinafter ECMR).[21] A merger's compatibility with the common market is contingent upon whether or not the merger leads to a significant impediment to effective competition, in particular, as a result of the creation or strengthening of a dominant position. In this regard, it is established case law that "a proper definition of the relevant market is a necessary precondition for any assessment of any effect of a concentration on competition."[22]

While the foregoing highlights that market definition is a requisite for the central provisions of US and EU antitrust law, enforcement agencies and courts will often elect to precisely define the relevant markets only when market definition would be dispositive in the case. Otherwise, if the conclusion would be the same on either a wide or narrow candidate market, the precise definition of the market is left open.

Further, as a caveat, although the exercise of delineating a relevant market follows the same basic rules in the three contexts of prohibitions on cartels and monopolization as well as the control of mergers, the precise market definition for similar products need not be the same. The reason is that market definition adopts a prospective analysis under merger proceedings and a retrospective analysis under investigations of past agreements or anticompetitive conduct.[23] When carrying out a prospective market analysis, a dynamic – as opposed to the static approach characteristic of a retrospective inquiry – is required to take into account potential post-merger effects. Therefore, a prospective analysis of the future market

[20] Case T-62/98, *Volkswagen AG* v. *Commission* [2000] ECR II 2707, para. 231; Case T-61/99, *Adriatica di Navigazione* v. *Commission* [2003] ECR II-5349, para. 27.

[21] Council Regulation No. 139/2004 on the control of concentrations between undertakings [2004] OJ L24 1.

[22] Joined Cases C-68/94 & 30/95, *France* v. *Commission* [1998] ECR I-1375, para. 143. See also Case T-342/99, *Airtours* v. *Commission* [2002] ECR II-2585, para. 19 (hereinafter *Airtours*). Note that although this statement concerned the substantive test under the previous EC Merger Regulation No. 4064/89, it remains valid under the 2004 ECMR; see, e.g., Case T-177/04, *easyJet* v. *Commission* [2006] ECR II-1931, para. 55. Also the Commission Guidelines on the assessment of horizontal mergers under the Council Regulation on the control of concentrations between undertakings [2004] OJ C31 5 (hereinafter Guidelines on horizontal mergers), para. 10 specify market definition as the first analytical step.

[23] Behrens, "Der Marktbeherrschungsbegriff in Artikel 82 EG," in Ahrens *et al.* (eds.), *Marktmacht und Missbrauch*, pp. 37, 39–40 (2007).

structure and merged entity's position in the market may in some cases lead to a market definition different to that resulting from a market analysis based on past and present behavior. Finally, the market definition in different proceedings may differ for the same set of products, even under the same applicable antitrust statute if market conditions have changed in the meantime.

3 Market definition as an analytical tool in antitrust analysis

The preceding section showed that market definition has been interpreted by the judiciary as a prerequisite to all major antitrust statutes. This, however, does not explain the underlying logic for market definition. Its purpose as an analytical tool is outlined in the following.

A Overview

At the outset, it is important to realize that the fundamental question on the goals of antitrust policy has a direct bearing on the role of market definition. There are approaches to antitrust policy that reject market definition altogether as a decision-making tool.[24] As outlined above, and although the debate on the objectives of antitrust policy remains controversial, for present purposes it is an appropriate simplification to assume that the harmful efficiency and welfare effects of the economic power of firms, or "market power," are the primary concern of antitrust policy. The meaning of the term "market power" is ambiguous and will be analyzed more closely below. Further obfuscating matters, different terminology, such as "dominance" (under Article 102 of the TFEU), "monopoly power" (under section 2 of the Sherman Act), and "market power" (under section 1 of the Sherman Act), is used in different provisions and jurisdictions, with more or less no precise distinction. In this study, the term "market power" is used as encompassing any concept of economic power of firms. The prohibition of monopolization or abuse of dominance is most evidently aimed at outlawing behavior driven by market power. Merger control is also directed at preventing the concentration of excessive market

[24] The concept of freedom of competition ("*Konzept der Wettbewerbsfreiheit*"), introduced by Hoppmann, assumes that every product competes with every other in one unique and indivisible market: Hoppmann, *Fusionskontrolle*, pp. 10–12 (1972). Or, the Schumpeterian concept of competitive rivalry ("the process of creative destruction") discards the legal prerequisite to delineate the relevant market: Schumpeter, *Capitalism, Socialism, and Democracy*, pp. 81–86 (1942).

power in the position of the merged entity unilaterally or through coordination with remaining competitors. Finally, the prohibition of anticompetitive agreements is geared not toward prohibiting all possible types of coordination between firms, but, generally, only such coordination between firms with market power.[25]

Against this background, it is generally accepted today that market definition is not a goal in itself, but that its central purpose is the identification of market power. Early on, the US Supreme Court acknowledged this essential relationship between market definition and market power.[26] But it was not until the late 1970s that scholarship recognized the linkage.[27] As will be outlined later, it was the 1982 *Merger Guidelines*, a description of the agencies' enforcement policy, which for the first time offered a complete analytical framework for the use of market definition as a tool to identify mergers that may create or enhance market power.[28] Since then, the linkage between market definition and market power has become commonplace when courts or agencies describe the exercise of delineating markets.

B Legal definition of market power

In Europe, the link between market power and market definition has traditionally been made by the EU courts subscribing to a legal definition of market power. The key concept is that of "dominance," thought of as a position of substantial market power.[29] Resonating the German ordoliberalist view of protecting individual economic freedom, the ECJ has traditionally defined dominance under Article 102 of the TFEU as "a position of economic strength enjoyed by an undertaking which enables it to prevent effective competition being maintained on the relevant market by

[25] Exceptions are agreements known as hardcore cartels in Europe or *per se* infringements in the United States.

[26] *United States* v. *E. I. du Pont de Nemours & Co.*, 351 US 377, 391 (1956) (hereinafter *Cellophane*). The name derives from the fact that Du Pont was accused of having monopolized the market for cellophane wrappings.

[27] See, e.g., Sullivan, *Handbook of the Law of Antitrust*, p. 41 (1977): "Market definition is not a jurisdictional prerequisite, or an issue having its own significance under the statute; it is merely an aid for determining whether power exists"; Areeda and Turner, *Antitrust Law: An Analysis of Antitrust Principles and Their Application*, vol. II, p. 347 (1978): "In economic terms a 'market' embraces one firm or any group of firms which, if unified by agreement or merger, would have market power in dealing with any group of buyers."

[28] US Department of Justice, *Merger Guidelines* (1982), 4 Trade Reg. Rep. (CCH) § 13,102 (hereinafter *1982 Merger Guidelines*).

[29] Faull and Nikpay, *The EC Law of Competition*, para. 4.34A (2007).

giving it the power to behave to an appreciable extent independently of its competitors, customers, and ultimately consumers."[30] This judicial definition of dominance contains in itself the explicit requirement for the definition of a relevant market.

C Economic definition of market power

United States antitrust law has adopted the somewhat different, economically defined concepts of "market power" and "monopoly power." Economists often use these terms interchangeably to delineate power over price, while case law has often made a distinction.[31] The precise distinction does not require further discussion for the purpose of market definition, because courts and scholars use the term monopoly power in a manner that is compatible with the economic concept of market power, more precisely as a matter of degree where market power can rise in amount to monopoly power.[32]

Thus, in essence, courts, agencies, and scholars have variously used market power in its economic sense as the ability of a firm (or group of firms acting jointly) to restrict output and to raise prices above competitive levels without losing sales to the point that the price increase becomes unprofitable.[33] This clearly draws from the insights that have been outlined

[30] Case 27/76, *United Brands* v. *Commission* [1978] ECR 207, para. 65 (hereinafter *United Brands*); Case 85/76, *Hoffmann-La Roche* v. *Commission* [1979] ECR 461, para. 38 (hereinafter *Hoffmann-La Roche*). Note that the Commission has recently tried to reconcile the legal with the economic concept of market power in the Staff Discussion Paper on the Application of Article 82 of the Treaty to exclusionary abuses (December 2005) (hereinafter *Article 82 Commission Discussion Paper*), paras. 20 and 23, available at: http://ec.europa.eu/competition/antitrust/art82/discpaper2005.pdf) and the *Commission Guidance on the Commission's enforcement priorities in applying Article 82 of the EC Treaty to abusive exclusionary conduct by dominant undertakings* [2009] OJ C45 7 (hereinafter *Commission Guidance on exclusionary conduct*), paras. 10–11.

[31] Monopoly power has been defined as "the power to control prices or to exclude competition," see *Cellophane*, *supra*, fn. 26, paras. 391, 393.

[32] *Eastman Kodak Co.* v. *Image Technical Servs., Inc.*, 504 US 451, 481 (1992) (hereinafter *Eastman Kodak*). G. A. Hay, "Market Power in Antitrust," *Antitrust Law Journal*, 60 (1992), 807, 819–821; Hovenkamp, *Federal Antitrust Policy: The Law of Competition and its Practice*, para. 3.1 (2005).

[33] The economic definition has been adopted since *Fortner Enterprises, Inc.* v. *United States Steel Corp.*, 394 US 495, 503 (1969). See also US Department of Justice and Federal Trade Commission, *Horizontal Merger Guidelines* (1992), 4 Trade Reg. Rep. (CCH) ¶ 13,104 (hereinafter *1992 Merger Guidelines*), § 0.1. For scholarly literature see Landes and Posner, "Market Power in Antitrust Cases," *Harvard Law Review*, 94 (1981), 937, 937. Note that instead of a price rise above the competitive price level, one could also think of market power in non-price terms, such as the ability to profitably reduce the quality or service

above under the model of perfect competition and the theory of monopoly. Because the theory demonstrates that the harmful effects of market power stem from the monopolist reducing output and thus increasing price above a competitive level, focus is on the individual firm's discretion over price – the extent to which a firm could profitably price its products above marginal costs – as the proxy for market power.[34]

Importantly for this study, even under an economic approach to market power and regardless of the terminology, market definition is the conventional path taken in antitrust proceedings in determining the presence of economic power.

(i) Direct measurement of market power

Two different procedures for the assessment of economic market power exist: a "direct" and an "indirect" method. Under the economic definition, market power may be measured directly.[35] Market power can be depicted as the persistent setting of price in excess of the level that would prevail under perfect competition. The intuitive idea, therefore, is to measure market power directly by comparing the competitive price level with the actual price level. A separate definition of the relevant market would be unnecessary. The direct measurement of market power is becoming increasingly popular, in particular in merger analysis in the United States where evidence of direct effects is increasingly accepted by agencies and courts.[36] The (quantitative) analytical tools used for the direct measurement of market power obviate the need for a separate market definition exercise. They in fact integrate the evaluation of competitive alternatives into the market power analysis. However, as the direct approach poses great difficulties in practice and relies on the use of

below the competitive level, Fisher, *Market Definition: A User's Guide*, p. 11 (u.d.), available at: http://econ-www.mit.edu/files/2630.

[34] Motta, *Competition Policy: Theory and Practice*, p. 40 (2004); Hovenkamp, *Federal Antitrust Policy*, para. 3.1a.

[35] It appears that the first proposal for a direct measurement of market power was made by Landes and Posner, "Market Power in Antitrust Cases." See also Baker and Bresnahan, "Empirical Methods of Identifying and Measuring Market Power," *Antitrust Law Journal*, 61 (1992), 3–16.

[36] See US Department of Justice and Federal Trade Commission, *Horizontal Merger Guidelines* (2010), p. 7 (hereinafter *2010 Merger Guidelines*), available at: www.justice.gov/atr/public/guidelines/hmg 2010.html; most importantly in scholarship, Farrell and Shapiro, "Antitrust Evaluation of Horizontal Mergers: An Economic Alternative to Market Definition," *B.E. Journal of Theoretical Economics*, 10 (2010), available at: www.bepress.com/bejte/vol10/iss1/art9.

sophisticated econometric methods, it is not yet recognized as standard among regulators and courts.[37]

(ii) Indirect measurement of market power

With the direct measurement of market power often being unfeasible and not commonly accepted, the existence of economic market power is traditionally determined indirectly, by turning to circumstantial evidence of the firm's ability to control prices or to restrict output. This involves a structural approach, central to which is the determination of market shares as an indicator of market power. Market shares are also the most prominent indicator of dominance in EU antitrust law, and, as a result, high market shares have been held to be sufficient in themselves to establish dominance.[38] Thus, the need for market definition in EU antitrust law cannot be explained only with the express requirement in the legal definition of market power, but also with the judicial practice of relying on market shares to identify dominance.

For the indirect assessment of market power, three stages are common: first, the relevant market in its product and geographic dimensions is defined in order to identify the market participants that act as competitive constraints; second, market shares among competitors can be calculated, from which inferences about market power and anticompetitive effects can be made; and third, entry conditions are analyzed because market power can be maintained only in the case of entry barriers. This three-step process forms the typical progression of antitrust analysis universally followed by regulators and courts.

The use of market shares for the determination of market power is based on the view that high market shares indicate that competition is weak, while low market shares suggest the reverse. The doctrinal background for the so-called "structural analysis" of market shares is derived from the 1950s Harvard School way of thinking that it is the structure of a market that determines the conduct of the firms within the market, and, in turn, this determines the nature of

[37] Particularly, while the current price level can be easily observed, the competitive price level, i.e., marginal costs, are very difficult to calculate in practice, see Schwalbe and Zimmer, *Kartellrecht und Ökonomie Moderne ökonomische Ansätze in der europäischen und deutschen Zusammenschlusskontrolle*, pp. 62–64 (2006) and Carlton, "Market Definition: Use and Abuse," *Competition Policy International*, 3 (2007), 7, available at: http://ssrn.com/abstract=987061.

[38] *Hoffmann-La Roche*, *supra*, fn. 30, paras. 39, 41; Case C-62/86, *AKZO* v. *Commission* [1991] ECR I-3359, para. 60.

the market outcomes ("structure–conduct–performance" or the "SCP"-paradigm).[39] Accordingly, highly concentrated industries dictate the conduct of firms, which leads to poor market performance in the form of restricted output and increased prices. The structural presumption of high market shares as proxy for market power has been enshrined US and EU case law.[40] Modern economic theory has, however, cast substantial doubt on the SCP-paradigm and has revealed the intuition behind the use of market shares to be overly simplistic. Here, it suffices to say that courts and agencies now recognize that even very large market shares on their own may be insufficient for an inference of market power and require a more complete appraisal of the competitive conditions in the market, most importantly the analysis of entry barriers. However, for present purposes, perhaps the most glaring absence in the SCP-model is the complete lack of guidance for delineating appropriate markets.

Even though market shares are an incomplete proxy of market power from a modern perspective, their calculation and, therefore, the definition of the relevant market remains a well-established feature. Market definition is commonly thought of as a useful first step in the analysis for two reasons. First, it serves as a screening device, because high market shares or concentration indices calculated on their basis mean that an investigation will not be dismissed at an early stage. Second, and this is often believed to be the added value of the entire market definition exercise, the identification of a market permits a more detailed analysis of the competitive conditions in this market, which in the second step of the analysis is the basis for an overall competitive assessment. For this reason, market definition is the starting point in virtually all investigations in all areas of antitrust law. Merger control usually specifies a threshold level of market concentration based on market share level,

[39] Its most famous proponents were Mason, "Price and Production Policies of Large-Scale Enterprise," *American Economic Review*, Supplement Papers and Proceedings of the Fifty-first Annual Meeting of the American Economic Association, 29 (1939), 61–74 and Bain, "Relation of Profit Rate to Industry Concentration: American Manufacturing, 1936–1940," *Quarterly Journal of Economics*, 65 (1951), 293–324.

[40] See already *Standard Oil*, *supra*, fn. 3, at 33 (90 percent market share as proof of monopoly) and *United States* v. *Aluminum Co. of America*, 148 F.2d 416, 424 (2nd Cir. 1945) in which Judge Learned Hand famously opined that 90 percent of supply "is enough to constitute a monopoly; it is doubtful that whether sixty or sixty-four percent would be enough; and certainly thirty-three percent is not." For a similar market share classification in Europe see *Hoffmann-La Roche*, *supra*, fn. 30, paras. 51–63.

which triggers an investigation.[41] Investigations into various monopolistic abuses are usually centered on the leading firm in the market. And the analysis of anticompetitive effects in cartel proceedings may be based on market shares.[42]

II ARTICLE III OF THE GATT

1 Introduction

The WTO provisions for the liberalization of international trade are based to a wide extent on the concept of comparability of products or services.[43] Only if goods are comparable to a certain degree do many of the legal obligations of the multilateral trading system apply. The comparison of products is thus central to the operation of WTO law. In antitrust parlance, this requires the definition of the relevant product market. The geographical and temporal components have not received much attention, the relevant geographic market generally being the respondent's entire territory.[44]

Among the most prominent and important instances of product comparison are the concepts of "like" and DCS products.[45] These concepts are referenced some sixteen times in GATT alone,[46] and, along with related

[41] The Herfindahl–Hirschman Index (HHI) measures concentration and is calculated by summing up the squares of the market shares of individual market players. Other measures of concentration are concentration ratios, such as the combined market share of the top three (C3) or five firms (C5).

[42] See Kauper, "The Problem of Market Definition under EC Competition Law," in Hawk (ed.), *Annual Proceedings of the Fordham Corporate Law Institute, International Antitrust Law & Policy*, pp. 239, 240–242 (1997) and Friederiszick, "Marktabgrenzung und Marktmacht," in Schwarze (ed.), *Recht und Ökonomie im Europäischen Wettbewerbsrecht*, pp. 29, 34–35 (2006).

[43] As already indicated, this study focuses on product comparability. For a treatment of "likeness" under the General Agreement on Trade in Services (GATS) see Diebold, *Non-Discrimination in International Trade in Services*.

[44] Englisch, *Wettbewerbsgleichheit im grenzüberschreitenden Handel*, p. 296 (2008). Also note that the parties to WTO dispute settlement proceedings are the WTO Member countries, not private litigants. On the geographic reach of the inquiry, see most recently Appellate Body Report, *Philippines – Distilled Spirits*, WT/DS396/AB/R, WT/DS403/AB/R, adopted January 20, 2012, para. 168.

[45] For a survey of the likeness concept in various provisions see Choi, *"Like Products" in International Trade Law*.

[46] The requirement of product comparison appears in the following provisions of the GATT 1994: Article I:1 (on MFN treatment); Articles III:2 (1), *Ad* III:2, and III:4 (all on NT);

concepts of product comparability, also figure prominently under other WTO agreements.[47]

GATT's key concept of non-discrimination in the trade of goods, expressed in the most-favored-nation (hereinafter MFN) clause in Article I:1 of the GATT and the NT clause in Article III of the GATT, necessitates such a comparison of goods.[48] Focusing on Article III of the GATT, this provision prohibits less favorable fiscal and non-fiscal treatment of foreign imported products in comparison with domestic "like" or DCS products. If products are characterized as "like" or DCS, a WTO Member cannot apply differential treatment to imported and domestic products. For this reason, "it is only a bit of an overstatement to say that not only Article III, but also ... many other provisions of the GATT, depend first and foremost for their effective operation on the concept of 'like' products."[49]

The terms "like" or DCS products are a legal creation. In the absence of a general definition, the operation of these concepts depends on a case-by-case legal interpretation. However, whether two products are "like" or DCS cannot be said to be a purely factual question. As the Appellate Body stated, "the determination of whether imported and domestic products are 'like products' is a process by which legal rules have to be applied to facts."[50] The concepts of likeness and DCS thus constitute legal elements, which – under the interpretative approach developed in this study – require determination of the relevant facts by applying economic theories and insights.

Articles VI:1, VI:4, and VI:7 (on antidumping, "like commodities"); Article VII:2(a) and (b) (on customs, "like merchandise"); Article IX:1 (on marks of origin); Article XI:2(c)(i) and (ii) (on quantitative restrictions, "like" and "directly substituted" product); Article XIII:1 (on quantitative restrictions); Article XVI:4 (on subsidies); and Article XIX:1(a) and (b) (on safeguards, "like or directly competitive").

47 See, e.g., Article 5.5 of the Agreement on Trade-Related Investment Measures (TRIMs Agreement); Articles 2.1, 2.2, 2.6 and 4.1 of the Agreement on the Implementation of Article VI of the General Agreement on Tariffs and Trade 1994 (Antidumping Agreement); Articles 6.3, 11.2, 15.1, and Note 46 thereto of the SCM Agreement; Articles 2:1 and 4:1(c) of the Agreement on Safeguards; Articles 2.1, 5.1.1, 5.2.1, and Annex 3:D of the Agreement on Technical Barriers to Trade (hereinafter TBT Agreement); Annex C:1(a) of the Agreement on the Application of Sanitary and Phytosanitary Measures (hereinafter SPS Agreement).

48 For an analysis of the product comparison problem under the MFN clause see Davey and Pauwelyn, "MFN Unconditionality: A Legal Analysis of the Concept in View of its Evolution in the GATT/WTO Jurisprudence with Particular Reference to the Issue of 'Like Product,'" in Cottier and Mavroidis (eds.), *Regulatory Barriers and the Principle of Non-discrimination in World Trade Law*, pp. 13–50 (2000).

49 Bhala, *Modern GATT Law*, para. 1–004.

50 Appellate Body Report, *Canada – Certain Measures Concerning Periodicals* (hereinafter *Canada – Periodicals*), WT/DS31/AB/R, adopted July 30, 1997, at 22.

What may seem to be a dull exercise in legal construction has in fact far-reaching implications. In particular, the construction of likeness and DCS touches on fundamental policy questions. NT is the discipline of non-discrimination that has the deepest impact on the national autonomy of sovereign states. The Article III obligation affects all forms of internal state action, having an effect on international trade regardless of which branch of government is involved. Thus, Article III captures all types of internal policy measures in virtually all domestic policy areas, because almost all policies affect international trade directly or indirectly. This squarely poses the issue of intrusiveness. Depending on the interpretative approach chosen for likeness and DCS, tension arises between the multilateral trade discipline, on the one hand, and state sovereignty, on the other. An extensive or even over-inclusive interpretation of the terms would expand the scope of application of NT so as to include more imports under the protection of Article III of the GATT. By the same token, too broad an interpretation would restrict WTO Members in their sovereign fiscal and regulatory autonomy to choose internal taxation or regulation for legitimate policy goals, which are ultimately an expression of the values and identity of each particular state.[51] In contrast, a restrictive or even under-inclusive construction of the terms would unduly reduce the obligation's scope of application. Too narrow an interpretation would open the floodgates to a proliferation of protectionist measures and undermine the commitment to free trade.

The interpretation of the terms therefore poses the question of normative hierarchy. Is trade liberalization the default norm that prevails over other competing values such as state sovereignty? Otherwise, is it possible to strike a balance between the competing fundamental values of liberalizing trade in a non-discriminatory manner, on the one hand, and the respect of state sovereignty and, more fundamentally, of political and socioeconomic value choices, on the other? As will be discussed below, the substantive requirement of product comparability – as opposed to the other legal elements of the NT obligation or the exceptions from the NT discipline under Article XX of the GATT – has been the locus where these competing objectives have collided, shaping different interpretative approaches to product likeness.

[51] Senti, *WTO: System und Funktionsweise der Welthandelsordnung*, para. 697 (2000).

2 The non-discrimination obligation of national treatment

The underlying idea of the WTO/GATT system is the liberalization of international trade. Hence, the primary objective is the progressive reduction and the ultimate removal in a non-discriminatory manner of trade barriers between national markets. Trade barriers take many forms, including obvious restrictions, such as tariffs and quotas, as well as those that are less overt, such as domestic protectionist regulatory measures. To address such barriers, the WTO/GATT multilateral trading system adopted a negative integration scheme built on the central principle of non-discrimination.[52] The non-discrimination principle is widely seen as the cornerstone of the WTO/GATT trade regime. In abstract terms, it obliges WTO Members to avoid making distinctions between goods solely on the basis of their national origin, and requires that comparable domestic and imported goods be accorded similar treatment. In essence, it is about preventing WTO Members from putting goods of other WTO Members at a competitive disadvantage vis-à-vis their own goods or such goods imported from other WTO Members. The tenet of non-discrimination is enshrined in two fundamental principles that form part of the major WTO Agreements addressing trade in goods (GATT), trade in services (GATS), and intellectual property rights (TRIPS). The first fundamental principle is MFN treatment, which requires WTO Members to treat similar imported goods from all other Members in a non-discriminatory way with respect to customs duties and charges (that is, "border measures" that impede access to the market).[53] In contrast, the present study concentrates on the NT obligation, which constitutes the second pillar of the non-discrimination principle. With respect to trade in goods in the WTO, NT is embodied in Article III of the GATT. Since international trade is not only inhibited by measures imposed at the

[52] In other words, and with the notable exception of the Agreement on Trade-Related Aspects of Intellectual Property Rights (TRIPS), there is no compulsory adherence to international standards and no predefined set of policies to which all WTO Members must subscribe.

[53] By virtue of Article I:1 of the GATT, it extends to non-discriminatory treatment among imported products with respect to domestic measures, including both domestic taxes and regulations. Note that the term "border measures" also encompasses quantitative restrictions, or quotas. These are prohibited under Article XI:1 of the GATT. This provision is interpreted as a general prohibition of all types of non-tariff trade barriers at the border; see Bender, "GATT 1994," in Hilf and Oeter (eds.), *WTO-Recht*, § 9, para. 21 (2005).

border, this article provides that a Member must not discriminate against imports once they have crossed the border by treating them less favorably than comparable domestic products. At a minimum, it obliges Members to treat imported products *at least* equally as favorably as domestic counterparts. Thus, NT is a discipline on internal policies (that is, "internal measures" that apply once the product has cleared customs and has accessed the domestic market).[54] Typically, internal measures take the forms of taxes and regulations.

NT operates in two ways. First, it guards against the negation of the benefits of trade liberalization by preventing a Member from nullifying or impairing the effect of its tariff concessions by introducing a protectionist internal fiscal or regulatory scheme. Second, NT discourages Members from adopting disguised (that is, non-tariff, and more precisely, internal) restrictions on trade that favor domestic over imported products. These different modes will be addressed below in more detail.

3 The legal framework of GATT national treatment

Article III of the GATT has a rather complex – one could even say a poorly drafted – structure. Moreover, its words remain vague on its scope of application, which therefore has been a matter of jurisprudence. The following will shed some light on these issues.

A The structure of Article III of the GATT

The first paragraph of the provision (Article III:1) – the "Chapeau" – stipulates that taxes and other regulations affecting any stage or aspect of distribution and sale in the importing state "should not be applied to imported or domestic products so as to afford protection to domestic production."[55] Although the Chapeau is not an operative provision in itself, the Appellate Body has held that this "general principle informs the rest of Article III," and that it serves "as a guide to understanding the specific obligations contained in Article III:2 and in other paragraphs of

[54] Yet an internal measure that applies to imported as well as domestic products, such as a sales ban or a technical requirement, but is enforced at the border for administrative purposes remains subject to NT pursuant to *Ad* Article III of the GATT.

[55] Article III:1 of the GATT covers any "internal taxes and other internal charges, and laws, regulations and requirements affecting the internal sale, offering for sale, purchase, transportation, distribution or use of products, and internal quantitative regulations requiring the mixture, processing or use of products in specified amounts or proportions."

Article III."[56] This basic principle also constitutes an important guideline for the teleological interpretation of likeness and DCS.

The principal operative provisions of the NT obligation under Article III of the GATT are located in paragraphs 2 and 4. Thus, the obligation provides a bifurcated regime. It divides domestic policy interventions into fiscal (paragraph 2) and non-fiscal or regulatory measures (paragraph 4). The first sentence of paragraph 2 (Article III:2(1)) prohibits any fiscal discrimination of "like products"; its second sentence (Article III:2(2)) – read in conjunction with the interpretative note *Ad* Article III:2 in Annex I of the GATT – prohibits fiscal measures that do not similarly tax "directly competitive or substitutable products"; and paragraph 4 (Article III:4) forbids less favorable treatment by non-fiscal measures of "like products."

(i) Fiscal measures: Article III:2(1) and (2) of the GATT

For an internal fiscal measure to conform with Article III:2(1) of the GATT, it must satisfy a two-pronged legal test. It is necessary to determine: (1) whether the taxed imported product and the domestic product are "like"; and (2) whether the taxes or other internal charges applied to the imported product are "in excess of" those applied to the like domestic product.

The crucial legal element for the topic of market definition is the first prong, which requires the determination of likeness. The second prong has been interpreted strictly in its requirement of equal treatment, so that any excess in taxation – even if minimal – *ipso facto* amounts to a violation of the non-discrimination obligation.[57]

The second sentence provides that "no contracting party shall otherwise apply internal taxes or other internal charges to imported or domestic products in a manner contrary to the principles set forth in paragraph 1." The legal test can be discerned only when the provision is read in connection with *Ad* Article III:2, which is of binding legal status.[58] It indicates that a measure that is consistent with the first sentence would only be considered inconsistent with the second sentence "in cases where competition was involved between, on the one hand, the taxed product and, on the other hand, a directly competitive or substitutable product which was not similarly taxed." Thus, for a measure to meet the legal test under

[56] Appellate Body Report, *Japan – Alcoholic Beverages II*, *supra*, Introduction, fn. 15, at 18.

[57] Appellate Body Report, *Japan – Alcoholic Beverages II*, *supra*, Introduction, fn. 15, at 23 ("Even the smallest amount of 'excess' is too much.").

[58] Appellate Body Report, *Japan – Alcoholic Beverages II*, *supra*, Introduction, fn. 15, at 24.

Article III:2(2) of the GATT, as elaborated upon by the *Ad* Note, three elements must be examined: (1) whether the imported and domestic products are "directly competitive or substitutable"; (2) whether the DCS products are not "similarly taxed"; and (3) whether different taxes are levied on imported and domestic DCS products "so as to afford protection to domestic production."

Under Article III:2(2) of the GATT, the market definition issue arises in the context of the determination of a DCS relationship between products. Under the terminology of DCS, several questions immediately come to mind. First, the "or" separating "directly competitive" from "substitutable" appears to imply that there may be situations where products can be directly competitive but not substitutable, and vice versa. However, the drafting history shows that both terms were introduced by way of an additional interpretative note only in order to clarify the meaning of the provision.[59] The drafting history suggests that the terms should be read as being synonymous, without any intent to create separate conceptual ideas by their juxtaposition.[60] Such an interpretation is consistent with the way the Appellate Body views the relationship between the two terms.[61] The dispute settlement bodies do not distinguish between the concepts and treat the concepts together in their consideration of DCS. Another interpretative issue that arises is whether the qualifier "directly" was intended to modify only the word "competitive" or whether it is also meant to relate to "substitutable." Here, the authoritative French text of the Interpretative Note provides clarification that "directly" refers to both terms.[62] This, however, leaves open the meaning of "directly" – in contrast to what would be "indirectly" competitive or substitutable products. The drafting history suggests that nothing in particular was intended by this qualifier other than to clarify the meaning of the phrase.[63] Unfortunately,

[59] Fauchald, *Environmental Taxes and Trade Discrimination*, p. 149 (1998).

[60] Hudec, "'Like Product': The Differences in Meaning in GATT Articles I and III," in Cottier and Mavroidis (eds.), *Regulatory Barriers and the Principle of Non-discrimination in World Trade Law*, pp. 101, 105 fn. 5 (2000).

[61] Appellate Body Report, *United States – Transitional Safeguard Measure on Combed Cotton Yarn from Pakistan* (hereinafter *US – Cotton Yarn*), WT/DS192/AB/R, adopted November 5, 2001, para. 94: "A careful reading of our Report in that case [Appellate Body Report, *Korea – Alcoholic Beverages*, paras. 114–116] would show that we used the terms 'directly competitive' and 'directly substitutable' without implying any distinction between them in assessing the competitive relationship between products."

[62] It reads: "un produit directement concurrent ou un produit qui peut lui être directement substitué."

[63] Fauchald, *Environmental Taxes and Trade Discrimination*, pp. 148–149.

the text provides no guidance as to the content of the concept of a DCS relationship. Case law has differentiated between likeness and the concept of DCS, but their precise contours remain vague.

It stands to reason as to whether there is any point in differentiating between "like" and DCS products when the legal consequences under both sentences are identical in that any discriminatory fiscal measure would be outlawed. In fact, the Appellate Body admits that the distinction often does not change the legal conclusions in a case.[64] But beyond the mere textual difference, the practical reason why the dispute settlement bodies differentiate between "like" products, in the first sentence, and DCS products, in the second sentence, can be understood when considering the second element of the legal test (similar taxation). While the first sentence contains a strict prohibition on any kind of different treatment of "like" products, the protection mechanism for DCS products under the second sentence is more flexible. It forbids measures only once they fail to treat both products "similarly." For this to happen, the tax differential must exceed a *de minimis* level.[65] As a consequence, and depending on whether products are classified as DCS rather than "like," the second sentence permits a certain degree of differential treatment by the importing state.

According to the last prong of the legal test, the tax differential across two DCS products must operate "so as to afford protection to the domestic production" (hereinafter SATAP). This requirement derives from the language of the second sentence. Unlike the first sentence, the second sentence specifically invokes Article III:1 of the GATT by making reference to the principles set forth in paragraph 1. Thus, while the SATAP phrase serves only as an implicit "general principle" to the first sentence, it also acts as a stand-alone element that must be expressly addressed in the context of the second sentence.[66] For its interpretation, the distinction between a subjective inquiry into the protective intent of the regulating government (aims-based approach) and the objective assessment of protective effects of the measure (effects-based approach) is important. Although an impartial reading of the phrase SATAP may suggest the former was intended by the drafters, the Appellate Body has rejected

64 Appellate Body Report, *Japan – Alcoholic Beverages II*, *supra*, Introduction, fn. 15, at 21.

65 GATT Panel Report, *Japan – Customs Duties, Taxes and Labelling Practices on Imported Wines and Alcoholic Beverages* (hereinafter *Japan – Alcoholic Beverages I*), BISD 34S/83, adopted November 11, 1987, para. 5.11.

66 Appellate Body Report, *Japan – Alcoholic Beverages II*, *supra*, Introduction, fn. 15, at 25–26; Appellate Body Report, *Canada – Periodicals*, *supra*, fn. 50, at 24.

this understanding and has endorsed the latter: a definition of the term "protection" based on protective effects and not protective intent.[67] It has been held that large – more than *de minimis* – tax differentials can suffice for this requirement to be fulfilled. The Appellate Body, however, has refrained so far from giving any useful guidance on what constitutes a more than *de minimis* tax differential.[68] Moreover, the Appellate Body has directed the inquiry to other factors to discern the "protective application" of a measure, in particular the design, architecture, and the revealing structure of the measure.[69]

The application of the two different prohibitions of discriminatory taxation pursuant to Article III:2 of the GATT is contingent upon the degree of product comparability. With regard to the relationship between the two prohibitions, the Appellate Body "emphasized that the first and second sentences of Article III:2 are *closely related* and that those two sentences are part of a *logical continuum*."[70] In this logical continuum, it has been established by case law that: "'like' products are a subset of directly competitive or substitutable products: all like products are, by definition, directly competitive or substitutable products, whereas not all 'directly competitive or substitutable' products are 'like.'"[71]

Because "like" products are also automatically DCS, it follows that the case law on the definition of DCS products is *ipso facto* relevant for the interpretation of the term "like" product. However, the reverse inference cannot be drawn automatically, because not all DCS products are also "like" products.

[67] It can be understood as an objective assessment of protective intent as expressed, e.g., in Appellate Body Report, *Chile – Taxes on Alcoholic Beverages* (hereinafter *Chile – Alcoholic Beverages*), WT/DS87/AB/R, WT/DS110/AB/R, adopted January 12, 2000, para. 62: "The purposes or objectives of a Member's legislature and government as a whole" are pertinent "to the extent that they are given *objective expression* in the statute itself" (emphasis in original); Mavroidis, *The General Agreement on Tariffs and Trade: A Commentary*, p. 177 (2005) ("objective intent standard"). See also *infra*, Ch. 3, fn. 156.

[68] A differential in taxation of 27–47 percent was considered more than *de minimis*, Panel Report, *Chile – Alcoholic Beverages*, WT/DS87/R, WT/DS110/R, adopted January 12, 2000, para. 7.110.

[69] Appellate Body Report, *Japan – Alcoholic Beverages II*, *supra*, Introduction, fn. 15, at 29.

[70] Appellate Body Report, *European Communities – Measures Affecting Asbestos and Asbestos-Containing Products* (hereinafter *EC – Asbestos*), WT/DS125/AB/R, adopted April 5, 2001, para. 79 (emphasis in original and internal quotations omitted); see also the prior case Appellate Body Report, *Canada – Periodicals*, *supra*, fn. 50, at 24.

[71] Appellate Body Report, *Korea – Alcoholic Beverages*, WT/DS75/AB/R, WT/DS84/AB/R, adopted February 17, 1999, para. 118.

As a consequence of this relationship, and in order not to condemn measures under the strict terms of the first sentence that should be contemplated under the more lenient standard of the second sentence, the Appellate Body espouses a narrow interpretative concept of "likeness" in Article III:2(1) of the GATT.[72] In contrast to the smaller product scope under "likeness," DCS encompasses a broader category of products.[73] Yet the dispute settlement bodies left it open as to how much broader this category is. The Appellate Body held only that this would be a matter to be determined by the Panel based on all relevant facts in each individual case.[74] Essentially an admission to the lack of any bright-line standard, the Panels are conferred much leeway to determine the boundaries of likeness and DCS under a case-by-case fact-based interpretation. Furthermore, the Appellate Body's only other statement on this point does not contribute to any improved understanding: "While perfectly substitutable products fall within Article III:2, first sentence, imperfectly substitutable products can be assessed under Article III:2, second sentence."[75] Neither the law nor economics gives an unambiguous answer to the question of whether products are perfect or merely imperfect substitutes. As a clear distinction seems to be impossible to make in practice, Panels are usually content to analyze the product relationship under either one of the two prohibitions.

(ii) Regulatory measures: Article III:4 of the GATT

Article III:4 of the GATT applies the NT principle to "internal laws, regulations and requirements." These essentially cover all domestic public policies apart from taxation (covered by Article III:2 of the GATT), and subsidies and government procurement (exempted by Article III:8 of the GATT). Examples of non-fiscal domestic measures may be technical standards, or authorization and distribution requirements.

For a non-fiscal, regulatory measure to be in conformity with Article III:4 of the GATT, the following must be determined: (1) whether the domestic and imported products are "like"; (2) whether the laws, regulations, and requirements affect the imported product's internal sale,

[72] Appellate Body Report, *Japan – Alcoholic Beverages II*, *supra*, Introduction, fn. 15, at 19; Appellate Body Report, *Korea – Alcoholic Beverages*, *supra*, fn. 71, para. 118: "The notion of like products must be construed narrowly but the category of directly competitive or substitutable products is broader."

[73] Appellate Body Report, *Japan – Alcoholic Beverages II*, *supra*, Introduction, fn. 15, at 25.

[74] Appellate Body Report, *Japan – Alcoholic Beverages II*, *supra*, Introduction, fn. 15, at 25.

[75] Appellate Body Report, *Korea – Alcoholic Beverages*, *supra*, fn. 71, para. 118.

offering for sale, purchase, transportation, distribution, or use; and (3) as a result of the effect, whether "less favorable treatment" is given to the imported product.

Again, market definition revolves around the question of product likeness. One might assume that the identical terminology of "like" product in paragraphs 2 and 4 of the same Article suggests an identical interpretation of both terms. Notwithstanding the textual identity, the dispute settlement bodies have construed both terms differently on the basis of a purposive interpretation.[76] In contrast to the narrow interpretation of likeness under Article III:2(1) of the GATT, they have held that likeness under Article III:4 of the GATT necessitates a broader interpretative approach. In fact, the poor drafting of Article III of the GATT requires a construction of the paragraphs that runs counter to the literal meaning of the terms in Articles III:2(1) and III:4 of the GATT. Although the obligations of the two provisions each apply to "like" products, the structure of paragraph 2 differs in one important respect from that of paragraph 4. The former is divided into two distinct obligations regarding "like" and DCS products. In contrast, the latter contains only a single obligation with respect to "like" products, while the DCS discipline is noticeably absent. On the assumption that fiscal and regulatory measures can be used to achieve the same protectionist purpose, this poses a dilemma. Textually, paragraph 2 seems to be broader than paragraph 4. If, however, its product scope were to be interpreted more broadly than that of paragraph 4, a WTO Member could choose to impose a protectionist regulatory measure on a foreign DCS product which it could not impose in the form of a fiscal measure under paragraph 2. A different product scope of the two paragraphs would thus have the perverse effect of allowing protectionism contrary to the spirit of Article III of the GATT.

For this reason, the Appellate Body attempted to restore "harmony" between the two paragraphs by infamously stating "that, given the textual difference between Articles III:2 and III:4, the 'accordion' of 'likeness' stretches in a different way in Article III:4."[77] The Appellate Body is of the view that "likeness" in paragraph 4 is construed in a way that its product scope is broader than that of "likeness" in Article III:2(1), but "not broader than the combined scope" of Article III:2(1) and (2).[78]

[76] Appellate Body Report, *EC – Asbestos*, *supra*, fn. 70, paras. 94–95.
[77] Appellate Body Report, *EC – Asbestos*, *supra*, fn. 70, para. 96.
[78] Appellate Body Report, *EC – Asbestos*, *supra*, fn. 70, para. 99.

Note, however, that despite these apparent clarifications the precise scope of Article III:4 of the GATT is ultimately left open. The Appellate Body qualified its statement that it, in fact, did not "wish to decide if the scope of 'like products' in Article III:4 is co-extensive with the combined scope of 'like' and 'directly competitive or substitutable' products in Article III:2."[79] The reason for this reluctance might be that such an interpretative approach is evidently in tension with the clear wording of the provisions. In practice, however, the scope of Articles III:2 and III:4 of the GATT seem to be more or less co-extensive. For example, in *Mexico – Tax Measures on Soft Drinks and Other Beverages*, the only case where a breach of Articles III:2(2) and III:4 was claimed simultaneously with regard to the same products, the Panel confirmed the existence of the required product relationship under both provisions on the basis of an identical test applying the same criteria.[80] This approach is logical because only a co-extensive product scope prevents circumvention of the prohibition with respect to discriminatory fiscal treatment of DCS products by simply providing equal fiscal treatment but enacting discriminatory non-fiscal measures to the same effect.

Lastly, in light of the "less favorable treatment" requirement, Article III:4 of the GATT is clearly not an obligation prescribing equal or identical treatment. Instead, it prohibits discriminatory treatment. Under this precept, "like" domestic and imported products may be treated differently as long as this does not amount to a less favorable treatment accorded to the imported product. In the absence of an explicit reference to Article III:1 of the GATT, the legal test does not require a separate examination of the protectionist effect under the rubric of SATAP.[81] Rather, the "less favorable treatment" requirement already includes the notion of protection.[82]

[79] Appellate Body Report, *EC – Asbestos*, *supra*, fn. 70, para. 99.

[80] Panel Report, *Mexico – Tax Measures on Soft Drinks and Other Beverages* (hereinafter *Mexico – Soft Drinks*), WT/DS308/R, adopted March 24, 2006, para. 8.106: "As regards the likeness [under Article III:4], the factors to be taken into account – the products' properties, nature and quality; their end-uses in a given market; consumers' tastes and habits; and the tariff classification of the products – are the same as those examined by the panel when considering whether the two products [are] 'directly competitive or substitutable' under Article III:2, second sentence."

[81] Appellate Body Report, *European Communities – Regime for the Importation, Sale and Distribution of Bananas* (hereinafter *EC – Bananas III*), WT/DS27/AB/R, adopted September 25, 1997, para. 216.

[82] Appellate Body Report, *EC – Asbestos*, *supra*, fn. 70, para. 100.

B *The scope of the national treatment principle*

Two important aspects of the scope of application shall be addressed here: (1) the issue of who or what is the beneficiary of Article III of the GATT; and (2) the question of what type of discrimination is caught by the provision.

(i) Beneficiaries

The principle of non-discrimination in GATT applies exclusively to the *product* rather than to the foreign producer or importer.[83] Article III of the GATT has a specific object-related thrust, as it affords protection to products. This has been justified with the provision's explicit prescription of the treatment to be accorded to *products* and its description of activities related to the *product*, from its introduction into the market to its final consumption. There is, however, no similar prescription in relation to the foreign producer or importer.[84] Thus, the terminology of Article III of the GATT is expressly concerned with the products and not with the persons of other Members as the subject matter. In addition to the text itself, the negotiators during the Uruguay Round specifically noted that Article III of the GATT "had been set up for products, *not for producers*."[85] Though it may seem difficult to make this distinction in practice, it is therefore said that Article III of the GATT does not protect competitive opportunities of market actors, but rather those of specific products only. One may base this reasoning on the fact that governments exchange trade opportunities without allocating individual rights to exporters.[86] But one must at least concede that producers and importers are afforded some measure of indirect protection by way of protection of their products.

[83] GATT Panel Report, *Canada – Administration of the Foreign Investment Review Act*, BISD 30S/140, adopted February 7, 1984, para. 6.5. *Contra* Tietje, *Normative Grundstrukturen der Behandlung nichttarifärer Handelshemmnisse in der WTO-GATT-Rechtsordnung*, p. 240 (1998) and Choi, *"Like Products" in International Trade Law*, p. 35, who argue that GATT is aimed at protecting foreign producers.

[84] GATT Panel Report, *United States – Taxes on Automobiles*, DS31/R, circulated October 11, 1994, unadopted, para. 5.52.

[85] Group of Negotiations on Services, Note on the Meeting of September 15–17, 1987, MTN.GNS/10, October 15, 1987, para. 12, available at: www.wto.org/gatt_docs/English/SULPDF/92030029.pdf (emphasis added).

[86] DiMascio and Pauwelyn, "Nondiscrimination and Investment Treaties: Worlds Apart or Two Sides of the Same Coin?," *American Journal of International Trade*, 102 (2008), 48, 54.

(ii) Types of discriminatory treatment

As already stated, it is difficult to overestimate the potential reach of GATT NT. As Article III:1 of the GATT underscores, the NT obligation extends to any form of protectionist "laws, regulations and requirements affecting [the] internal sale, purchase, transportation, distribution or use" of foreign products. According to this non-exhaustive enumeration, the obligation covers virtually all governmental policies of its Members in all policy areas, which may affect any stage of the entire product cycle from the distribution, via the sale, to the use of imported products.[87] Article III of the GATT contains a comprehensive protection of foreign products against discrimination covering the entire spectrum of competitive situations. The application of the NT obligation is not contingent upon the form of the governmental measure, but the effect on the competitive conditions at any stage of the product cycle, aiming "not only [at] the laws and regulations which directly governed the conditions of sale or purchase but also [at] any laws or regulations which might adversely modify the conditions of competition between the domestic imported products on the internal market."[88]

In addition, although it is silent on the issue, the NT obligation has been interpreted broadly to cover all forms of less favorable treatment, whether explicit or implicit. On the one hand, Article III of the GATT prohibits *de jure* discrimination. This refers to origin-specific measures that differentiate on their face on the basis of the national origin of the product. On the other hand, the provision also prohibits *de facto* discrimination. This refers to an origin-neutral classification where the formally or facially neutral treatment is nonetheless applied so as to impose a disparate impact that is detrimental to foreign products in comparison with comparable domestic products.[89]

The *de jure–de facto* distinction is important to the issue of product comparison under Article III of the GATT. *De jure* discriminations are considered *prima facie* illegal under Article III of the GATT.[90] This means

[87] Puth, *WTO und Umwelt: Die Produkt-Prozess-Doktrin*, p. 234 (2003).

[88] GATT Panel Report, *Italian Discrimination against Imported Agricultural Machinery*, BISD 7S/60, adopted October 23, 1958, para. 12.

[89] The first report referring to a formally identical legal provision according *de facto* less favorable treatment was GATT Panel Report, *United States – Section 337 of the Tariff Act*, BISD 36S/345, adopted November 7, 1989, para. 5.11. See also Ehring, "De facto Discrimination in World Trade Law," *Journal of World Trade*, 36 (2002), 921–977.

[90] Hudec, "GATT/WTO Constraints on National Regulation: Requiem for an 'Aim and Effects' Test," *International Lawyer*, 32 (1998), 619, 623; Howse and Regan, "The Product/Process Distinction: An Illusory Basis for Disciplining 'Unilateralism' in Trade Policy,"

that if a complainant establishes that a WTO Member has imposed an origin-based distinction with respect to internal taxation or regulation, "imported and domestic products may be considered as like products, and a case-by-case determination of 'likeness' between the foreign and domestic would be unnecessary."[91] Although it has not been explicitly held as such in case law, this is tantamount to a presumption of likeness.[92] The rationale for such a presumption is that an origin-specific measure treats products, which are otherwise in all respects identical except for their origin, differently.[93] Therefore, an inquiry into likeness has been the focal point of the legal analysis for most dispute settlement proceedings under GATT 1947 and the WTO where the legality of an origin-neutral measure was contested.

For origin-neutral treatment, a further question arises as to whether only facially neutral discrimination (but with protective intent) comes under the ambit of Article III of the GATT, or whether facially neutral but benign discrimination (that is, such as with a legitimate purpose) might or should also be impugned under this provision. This question is of great significance because the latter would extend Article III of the GATT to non-protectionist internal policy measures that have only an incidental disparate impact on imported products. This issue has been debated fiercely under the topic of regulatory purpose and will be addressed below.

III CONCLUSION

It is obvious to economists that there is an implicit economic rationale to any exercise of market definition, and that this rationale is closely related to the economic theory underlying the particular context in which this

European Journal of International Law, 11 (2000), 249, 269; Zhou, *Non-discrimination and the Accordion of "Like Product,"* p. 21 (2007), available at: http://ssrn.com/abstract=1000173.

[91] Panel Report, *Colombia – Indicative Prices and Restrictions on Ports of Entry*, WT/DS366/R, adopted May 20, 2009, para. 7.182.

[92] See, e.g., Panel Report, *Indonesia – Certain Measures Affecting the Automobile Industry* (hereinafter *Indonesia – Autos*), WT/DS54/R, WT/DS55/R, WT/DS59/R, WT/DS64/R, adopted July 23, 1998, para. 14.113: "An origin-based distinction in respect of internal taxes suffices in itself to violate Article III:2, without the need to demonstrate the existence of actually traded like products"; for further references see Diebold, *Non-Discrimination in International Trade in Services*, p. 67 fn. 123.

[93] Regan, "Regulatory Purpose and 'Like Products' in Article III:4 of the GATT (With Additional Remarks on Article III:2)," *European Journal of International Law*, 11 (2002), 443, 455–456.

exercise is carried out (as described in Chapter 1). By contrast, when lawyers and judges have taken hold of the concept of market definition, they have not usually understood the market definition exercise as related to economic theory. Divorced from its economic roots, they think of it largely in a legally analytical way, as one of the elements that must be proven as part of a legal claim (as outlined in this chapter).

For antitrust market definition, however, this chapter has shown that it is neither a statutory requirement nor that it has its own significance in the relevant provisions; it is simply an analytical tool for determining whether concentration of economic power exists. In contrast, the criteria of "likeness" and DCS in international trade law, in fact, constitute distinct statutory elements with their own substantive significance in the analysis of non-discrimination.[94]

[94] Diebold, *Non-Discrimination and the Pillars of International Economic Law: Comparative Analysis and Building Coherency*, 2010, available at: http://ssrn.com/abstract=1632927, blurs the line between the separate legal elements of product comparability ("likeness") and differential treatment ("less favorable treatment"). He spells out his theory that the elements of non-discrimination obligations should not be applied as strictly separated legal conditions, but as soft-factors in an overall assessment of weighing and balancing. As a consequence, he proposes that the relevant market should be defined in view of "less favorable treatment" interpreted according to an asymmetric or disproportionate impact test. For this test, it is no longer sufficient that an imported product is treated less favorably in comparison with a particular "like" domestic product. It requires that the foreign product is more heavily affected in relation to the entire relevant market (which comprises all competing domestic products). This must be viewed cautiously. It may well be that "less favorable treatment" should not be found if a measure treats only one imported product unfavorably (failure to accord best treatment), but rather where imported products are disproportionately disadvantaged. Still, Diebold's approach renders redundant the separate inquiry into the likeness of a product pair and collapses the likeness issue into the definition of a wider relevant market under the "less favorable treatment" requirement. So far, this is not accepted practice in either case law or scholarship. In fact, with respect to "likeness" under Article III2(1) of the GATT, the Panel in Panel Report, *Thailand – Cigarettes*, *supra*, Introduction, fn. 23, paras. 7.422–7.428 has recently followed previous case law in that it held that the "like" product analysis does not require a comparison of "all" imported and "all" domestic products; therefore, at least under the "like" product inquiry, it does not require a comprehensive market delineation, but only evidence that the imported products at issue are like "at least some" domestic products. Likewise, the Panel Report, *Philippines – Distilled Spirits*, *supra*, Introduction, fn. 23, para. 7.120 most recently held that: "the competitive relationship does not need to occur throughout the *whole* market [but] actual direct competition [to exist] within at least a segment of that market [for the Panel] to find a direct 'competitive relationship' for the purpose of the second sentence of Article III:2 of the GATT 1994." However, Diebold's approach reflects the shift in analytical emphasis by some scholars from the analysis of the likeness requirement to the analysis of the element of differential treatment. See also *infra*, Conclusion, fn. 1.

Despite this difference in the operation of antitrust and international trade provisions, it is clear that much is at stake in both antitrust market definition and Article III product comparison. In antitrust analysis the outcome of a decision in many cases stands or falls on the precise market definition.[95] Whether an undertaking is perceived to have market power is largely a function of whether a narrow or broad delineation of the market is chosen. This, in turn, will almost invariably have a major effect on the outcome of the investigation or court case. An ill-defined market, therefore, has the dramatic consequence of implementing prohibitions that are either under- or over-inclusive.

Similarly, two competing values, the effectiveness of the NT obligation, on the one hand, and the preservation of the sovereign national domain, on the other, depend on the interpretation of the product comparability standards of likeness and DCS under Article III of the GATT. Often, emphasis is put on litigating over the issue of whether products are "like" or DCS. Thus, these interpretative issues usually form the focal points of battles between the parties. Depending on the interpretative approach, under- or over-inclusiveness of the NT obligation will have important repercussions on both of the competing values.

[95] *HDC Med., Inc.* v. *Minntech Corp.*, 474 F.3d 543, 547 (8th Cir. 2007); see also *Bathke* v. *Casey's Gen. Stores, Inc.*, 64 F.3d 340, 345 (8th Cir. 1995): "Antitrust claims often rise or fall on the definition of the relevant market."

3

Analytical evolution from the traditional to the economic approach

This chapter traces the approaches that case law in antitrust and international trade law have adopted toward market definition. Originally an exclusive domain of legal thinking, market definition has been shaped by legal adjudicators. But economic learning is increasingly gaining in influence. To a certain extent the chapter will reveal a parallel evolution from a legalistic and formalistic approach to a more economics-based approach. This experience will provide the foundation for conceptualizing an economic approach to Article III market definition in Chapter 4. Section I will outline the traditional formalistic approach. Section II will then describe the increasing economic orientation.

I THE TRADITIONAL FORMALISTIC APPROACH

This section outlines the traditional legal formalistic approach to market definition. The characterization of this approach as "formalistic" or "juridical" is not new.[1] But the label of formalism can be confusing and it requires clarification. Legal formalism may be understood to exist in opposition to substantive legal issues. In this study, however, a legal formalistic approach is contrasted to an economic approach. Both designate different doctrinal and interpretative – and thus substantive – modes of analysis for market definition. The traditional formalistic or legal approach to market definition is characterized by two main features: first, it lacks an overall economically sound framework that links the market definition exercise to the underlying goal of the regime's policy objectives; and, second, the importance attributed to a number of qualitative, and therefore subjective, criteria makes the traditional legal approach an

[1] Tsai, "'Like' is a Four-Letter Word: GATT Article III's 'Like Product' Conundrum," *Berkeley Journal of International Law*, 17 (1999), 26, 27; Trebilcock and Howse, *The Regulation of International Trade*, pp. 90, 95.

exercise of descriptive comparison of the goods according to their characteristics and uses, while disregarding the analysis of real world economic circumstances.[2] Overall, it is an empty – that is, uninformative – formalism based on legal – that is, descriptive – criteria.[3]

As will become clear in the course of the book, although this traditional, non-economic approach emphasizes the importance of qualitative criteria, it should be noted, however, that a qualitative approach cannot be equated with a non-economic approach. Rather, the distinction should be between the application of qualitative criteria in an economically unsound manner (that is, applied in a legal formalistic manner) and an economically sound manner (that is, giving an answer on the issue of demand-side substitutability).

1 Antitrust law

Antitrust statutes are short and imprecise and thus give judges enormous interpretative leeway. As a result, judges have, over the decades, developed judicial rules on market definition. But courts have not provided coherent guidance as to how the relevant market should be defined. In fact, as this section does, one can look back at decades of inconsistency in the application of the market definition concept. The requisite tests and criteria were often applied blindly, with little or no attempt being made to determine the dynamics of the marketplace.

A US antitrust law

In US antitrust jurisprudence, unreconciled conflicts in important judicial opinions led to a perception that "this whole area is a bloody mess."[4] Two parallel principles of the traditional approach to market definition can be traced back to two leading US Supreme Court decisions, providing for profound analytical inconsistency. In its seminal decisions in *United States* v. *E. I. du Pont de Nemours & Co.* (*Cellophane*)[5] and *Brown Shoe Co.* v. *United States*,[6] the US Supreme Court articulated standards which

[2] Lücking and Simon, "Definition of the Relevant Market," in Drauz and Jones (eds.), *EC Competition Law, vol. II: Mergers and Acquisitions*, para. 3.225 (2006).

[3] See Hudec, "GATT/WTO Constraints on National Regulation: Requiem for an 'Aim and Effects' Test," p. 633.

[4] Turner, "The Role of the 'Market Concept' in Antitrust Law," *Antitrust Law Journal*, 49 (1980), 1145, 1150.

[5] *Cellophane*, *supra*, Ch. 2, fn. 26.

[6] *Brown Shoe*, *supra*, Ch. 1, fn. 7.

control the definition of the relevant product market. To this day they remain virtually the Supreme Court's only significant words on the subject and still hold precedential value.[7]

Historically, the *Cellophane* case was the first landmark opinion on market definition. In this Section 2 monopolization case, the US Supreme Court expressed two alternative formulations of the proper test for the relevant market: the "reasonable interchangeability" test[8] and the CPE of demand test.[9] The "reasonable interchangeability" (or "functional interchangeability"[10]) standard has become a central concept in antitrust law both in the United States and in Europe. It focuses on the extent to which different products have similar qualities, that is, physical characteristics and uses. Therefore, it includes in the market "products that have reasonable interchangeability for the purposes for which they are produced – price, use and qualities considered."[11]

In a subsequent case, *United States* v. *E. I. du Pont de Nemours & Co. (General Motors)*,[12] the US Supreme Court endorsed what has been considered a "fundamentally different approach."[13] Instead of functional interchangeability, the Court adopted a "peculiar characteristics and uses" standard.[14] However, this and subsequent cases that followed suit,[15] rather appear as a reformulation of, and therefore as in continuity with, the approach in *Cellophane*.[16]

In summary of the case law of that time, it is possible to argue from the economist-lawyer perspective of Hale and Hale that "there is no disguising the fact that the legal tests applied in most of the reported decisions are basically irrational, arbitrary and hopelessly confused. It is also clear

7 For case law references since the *1982 Merger Guidelines* see Werden, "The History of Antitrust Market Delineation," *Marquette Law Review*, 76 (1992), 123, 139 fn. 89.

8 *Cellophane*, *supra*, Ch. 2, fn. 26, at 395 and 404.

9 *Cellophane*, *supra*, Ch. 2, fn. 26, at 394.

10 *Cellophane*, *supra*, Ch. 2, fn. 26, at 399.

11 *Cellophane*, *supra*, Ch. 2, fn. 26, at 404.

12 *Du Pont de Nemours–General Motors*, *supra*, Ch. 2, fn. 11. This case should not be confused with the *Cellophane* case, *supra*, Ch. 2, fn. 26, a year earlier, involving the same parties.

13 Keyte, "Market Definition and Differentiated Products: The Need for a Workable Standard," *Antitrust Law Journal*, 63 (1995), 697, 704.

14 *Du Pont de Nemours–General Motors*, *supra*, Ch. 2, fn. 11, paras. 593–594.

15 For instance, *United States* v. *Bethlehem Steel Corp.*, 168 F.Supp. 576, 592–593, fn. 34 (SDNY 1958).

16 *United States* v. *Columbia Pictures Corp.*, 189 F.Supp. 153, 184 (SDNY 1960) concluded that the "peculiar characteristics and uses" test was "but a different verbalization of the same criteria" under the reasonable interchangeability test.

that economic theory offers little in the way of a scientific method upon which the law could be reconstructed."[17]

In its 1962 *Brown Shoe* decision, the US Supreme Court introduced the notion of submarkets and recognized them as separate economic entities within a broader market. It held that submarkets can be identified on the basis of certain criteria:

> The outer boundaries of a product market are determined by the reasonable interchangeability of use or the cross-elasticity of demand between the product itself and substitutes for it. However, within this broad market, well-defined submarkets may exist which, in themselves, constitute product markets for antitrust purposes. The boundaries of such a submarket may be determined by examining such practical indicia as industry or public recognition of the submarket as a separate economic entity, the product's peculiar characteristics and uses, unique production facilities, distinct customers, distinct prices, sensitivity to price changes, and specialized vendors.[18]

In resorting to a reliance on "practical indicia," the Court simply listed a roster of factors to determine discrete submarkets. Therein it introduced a second strand of market definition interpretation. Although it seemed to have added another approach, the Court clearly did not regard the *Cellophane* approach (reasonable interchangeability and CPE) and the *Brown Shoe* approach as being two mutually exclusive tests. In the Court's view, the existence of a broad product market did not preclude the existence of submarkets.[19] However, this created considerable confusion. As it has been noted by Hovenkamp, it may be understood as suggesting that one should use economic criteria in defining a (broad) market, but use something other than economic criteria in defining a submarket.[20]

Following *Brown Shoe*, the submarket concept and its practical indicia as well as *Cellophane*'s reasonable interchangeability approach were the dominant themes in market definition thinking. Even after the introduction of a radically more economics-based approach in the *1982 Merger Guidelines* outlined below, courts are still today not necessarily guided by economic analysis. Although fewer cases have used the "submarket" terminology within the last two decades, occasionally courts still adhere to the *Brown Shoe* approach.[21] In a recent example of the conventional

[17] Hale and Hale, *Market Power: Size and Shape Under the Sherman Act*, p. 111 (1958).

[18] *Brown Shoe, supra*, Ch. 1, fn. 7, at 325 (internal citations omitted).

[19] *Brown Shoe, supra*, Ch. 1, fn. 7, at 325.

[20] Hovenkamp, *Federal Antitrust Policy*, para. 3.2c.

[21] For case law see Kalinowski, Sullivan, and McGuirl, *Antitrust Laws and Trade Regulation*, para. 24.02(2)(a). See, e.g., *Olin Corp.* v. *FTC*, 986 F.2d 1295, 1304 (9th Cir. 1993).

reasonable interchangeability thinking a District Court found that in determining the relevant market "it is the use or uses to which the commodity is put that control."[22] It found that the "defendants' viscoelastic foam mattresses may be very different from innerspring mattresses, but they are still a product on which people sleep."[23] Though manifestly the result of life experience, this was barely economic reasoning!

The *Brown Shoe* dictum did not provide any guidance on how to delineate the market. This weakness is particularly evident in the difficulty in distinguishing between broad and submarkets. The indicia were listed without any indication of priority or individual weight. Thus, lower courts (and commentators) have largely been left to fashion their own market definition methodologies, incorporating the factors in ways that suited on occasion. In practice, "peculiar characteristics and uses" became the factors that have been most often cited by courts in cases where submarkets were demonstrated.[24] This is unsurprising, since "peculiar characteristics and uses" are closely related to the concept of "reasonable interchangeability," in that both focus on the physical characteristics and end-uses of a product and as such were the prominent criteria under the *Cellophane* approach. This highlights the fact that, although *Brown Shoe* in part lays out different criteria to those in *Cellophane*, those that have been central for both broad and submarkets were essentially identical.[25]

For the following analysis of empirical methods, it is noteworthy that *Cellophane*'s alternative (economic) criterion, CPE, is also potentially reflected in the *Brown Shoe* list under the rubric of sensitivity to price changes. However, it did not play a significant role under either of the two approaches. There have been two ways of dealing with it. Either the CPE test was not mentioned at all, or, alternatively, courts mentioned it as a standard commonplace formula, but then turned to other criteria without in fact analyzing any elasticity. In this second case, courts adopted one of two approaches. The first approach turned to reasonable interchangeability, which was not only more widely used, but also a criterion that would trump elasticity estimates, in particular those of low value.[26]

22 *Jacobs* v. *Tempur-Pedic Intern, Inc.*, 2007 WL 4373980 at 4 (ND Ga. 2007).

23 *Jacobs* v. *Tempur-Pedic Intern, Inc.*

24 Kalinowski, Sullivan, and McGuirl, *Antitrust Laws and Trade Regulation*, para. 24.02(2)(c).

25 Note also that many of the *Brown Shoe* criteria have been used in determining *Cellophane*'s reasonable interchangeability test; see ABA Section of Antitrust Law, *Antitrust Law Developments*, 2007, pp. 559–561 fns. 40–46.

26 For instance, a finding of significant end-use competition may overcome a low CPE of demand, *United States* v. *Continental Can Co.*, 378 US 441, 453–454 (1964); *In re Warner-Lambert Co.*, 87 FTC 812 (1976).

As the second approach, courts mentioned the CPE test but addressed it in a non-technical way which did not give a mathematically calculated, discrete coefficient, but provided a somewhat anecdotal measure of CPE through a descriptive assessment of the traditional criteria.[27] For example, courts developed the "unfortunate tendency ... to rely on the *Brown Shoe* roster of factors," in particular peculiar characteristics and uses, rather than on precise numerical elasticities.[28]

Overall, the *Brown Shoe* approach has been sharply disapproved. A fitting summary on market delineation between 1962 and 1982 by one US District Court reads: "Reported cases have largely been limited to governmental concerns for protection of competition where courts have narrowed and broadened the product market without real criteria or consistency."[29] In particular, the idea of submarkets generated severe criticism as being an odd notion that served no purpose: "either there is or there is not a market in which competition may be affected."[30] Economists termed the submarket concept "an intellectual monstrosity" with "little economic justification."[31] As the US Court of Appeals for the Fourth Circuit stated:

> The use of the term "submarket" is to be avoided; it adds only confusion to an already imprecise and complex endeavor. For antitrust purposes a product group or geographic area either meets the listed criteria, in which case it is a relevant market; or it does not, in which case it is irrelevant for purposes of analysis. No fiddling with nomenclature will change the analysis or result.[32]

In an effort to formulate a coherent set of criteria, the US Department of Justice Antitrust Division (hereinafter DoJ) promulgated the first *Merger Guidelines* in 1968.[33] Although non-binding, courts have increasingly, but not invariably, endorsed them, or at least used the approach embodied in the *Guidelines* when defining markets. This is particularly true for the later revised versions of the *Merger Guidelines*, discussed below. Beyond their immediate merger context, they have been influential in all antitrust

[27] See *infra*, fn. 81.
[28] Pitofsky, "New Definitions of Relevant Market and the Assault on Antitrust," p. 1817.
[29] *Calnetics Corp.* v. *Volkswagen of Am., Inc.*, 348 F.Supp. 606, 617 (CD Cal. 1972).
[30] Hale and Hale, "A Line of Commerce: Market Definition in Anti-Merger Cases," *Iowa Law Review*, 52 (1966), 406, 426.
[31] Hall and Phillips, "Antimerger Criteria: Power, Concentration, Foreclosure and Size," *Villanova Law Review*, 9 (1964), 211, 219–220.
[32] *Satellite Television & Associated Resources, Inc.* v. *Continental Cablevision of Virginia, Inc.*, 714 F.2d 351, 355, fn. 5 (4th Cir. 1983).
[33] US Department of Justice, *Merger Guidelines* (1968), 4 Trade Reg. Rep. (CCH) ¶ 13,101.

areas. Although the *1968 Merger Guidelines* resisted the temptation to use the submarket concept, they remained committed to a non-economic, legalistic definition by referring to the opaque concept of "some significant advantage" that products in the relevant market distinguish from those outside.[34] In addition, they reiterated the "price, quality, and use" formula as the relevant criteria and thus espoused the prior *Cellophane* tripartite test.[35] In conclusion, they have done little more than subscribe to analytical continuity instead of conceptual revolution.[36]

B EU antitrust law

While confusion and error have been lamented in the United States, it has not been any better in Europe. For a much longer time "functional interchangeability" has remained the leading notion. Where goods can be regarded as interchangeable, they are within the same product market. In the past, both the European Commission and the EU courts have placed particular importance on the physical characteristics and intended use of the products when considering functional interchangeability. With more emphasis on products' attributes, the ECJ stated that:

> The definition of the relevant market is of essential significance, for the possibilities of competition can only be judged in relation to those characteristics of the products in question by virtue of which those products are particularly apt to satisfy an inelastic need and are only to a limited extent interchangeable with other products.[37]

Further, it held that:

> The possibilities of competition must be judged in the context of the market comprising the totality of products which, with respect to their characteristics, are particularly suitable for satisfying constant needs and are only to a limited extent interchangeable with other products.[38]

With regard to intended uses, the Court underlined:

[34] *Merger Guidelines* (1968), para. 3.

[35] *Merger Guidelines* (1968), para. 3(i).

[36] According to a government-sponsored task force headed by Stigler the guidance was "so loose and unprofessional as to be positively embarrassing," Report of the Task Force on Productivity and Competition, reprinted in *Journal for Reprints for Antitrust Law and Economics*, pp. 827, 846–847 (1969).

[37] *Continental Can*, *supra*, Ch. 2, fn. 19, para. 32.

[38] Case 322/81, *Michelin* v. *Commission* [1983] ECR 3461 (hereinafter *Michelin I*), para. 37; see also Case 31/80, *L'Oréal* v. *De Nieuwe AMCK* [1980] ECR 3775, para. 25.

> The concept of the relevant market in fact implies that there can be effective competition between the products which form part of it and this presupposes that there is a sufficient degree of interchangeability between all products forming part of the same market insofar as a specific use of such products is concerned.[39]

Accordingly, the ECJ's approach to assessing reasonable interchangeability has been consistently based on both physical characteristics and intended use.[40] This traditional approach also found its way into the definition of the relevant product market in the Commission Notice on the definition of the relevant market, a non-binding document published by the European Commission in 1997 which sets forth the principles of market definition for all areas of EU antitrust law.[41] It states that: "a relevant product market comprises all those products and/or services which are regarded as interchangeable or substitutable by the consumer, by reason of the products' characteristics, their prices and their intended use."[42] The "characteristics, price and intended use" formula, as Kauper observed, "appears regularly, in an almost ritualistic way" as the European Commission's standard definition for substitutable products.[43]

The *Commission Notice on market definition* stipulates that there is "no hierarchy of different sources of information or types of evidence," and even recognizes the limitations to the use of physical characteristics and intended use for the market delineation.[44] Yet it indicates that such an analysis may be useful as a preliminary step when considering possible substitutes.[45] Indeed, an analysis of the physical characteristics and intended end-use of the product, rather than the price, is the starting point of the analysis.[46]

[39] *Hoffmann-La Roche*, *supra*, Ch. 2, fn. 30, para. 28.

[40] For judicial decisions that rely on physical characteristics and intended use see the extensive case law references in Cárdenas, *Rolle, Kriterien und Methodik der kartellrechtlichen Marktabgrenzung*, p. 77 fn. 473 (2005).

[41] *Commission Notice on the definition of relevant market for the purpose of Community competition law* [1997] OJ C372 5 (hereinafter *Commission Notice on market definition*).

[42] *Commission Notice on market definition*, para. 7.

[43] Kauper, "The Problem of Market Definition under EC Competition Law," p. 245. See also, e.g., para. (7) of the Preamble of the Commission Regulation on vertical agreements [2010] OJ L102 1; Section 6 of merger notification Form CO, Annex I to the Commission Regulation No. 802/2004 implementing Council Regulation No. 139/2004 on the control of concentrations between undertakings [2004] OJ L133 1.

[44] *Commission Notice on market definition*, para. 25.

[45] *Commission Notice on market definition*, para. 36.

[46] Brinker, "Praktische Probleme der Marktabgrenzung aus rechtlicher Sicht," in Schwarze (ed.), *Recht und Ökonomie im Europäischen Wettbewerbsrecht*, pp. 41, 43 (2006). For

The complications arising from the use of characteristics and intended use are illustrated by several notorious and important cases in the field of market definition. Among the most controversial decisions is the seminal Article 102 case of *United Brands*. In this case, the ECJ decided on the basis of an evaluation of the product's physical characteristics that bananas constituted a distinct market from other fruit. Disregarding available economic evidence, in particular high CPE of demand with summer fruit, in favor of substitutability, the Court opted for a subjective test of what it regarded as the banana's "special features."[47] The market for bananas was determined by "certain characteristics": appearance, taste, softness, seedlessness, and easy handling nature.[48] The judgment did not make clear why these distinctive characteristics should impact on the determination of the product market. Yet it identified captive consumer groups, "the very young, the old and the sick," for whom those characteristics satisfied constant needs.[49] Since this was enough for a separate product market, the Court implicitly required virtually complete substitutability, which, as will be explained below, is another reason why this was a far from sound economic analysis.

Concurrence of end-uses has often been even more important than the identity of physical characteristics, because physically different products that serve the same purpose may still be considered functionally interchangeable. One prominent example is *Hoffmann-La Roche*, in which three separate markets were identified for vitamin C according to separate food, pharmaceutical, and technological uses.[50] Another important case was *Nestlé/Perrier*, in which still and sparkling mineral waters were held to constitute a market separate from soft drinks. The intended end-use was narrowly defined not as thirst quenching, but more specifically as thirst quenching from a healthy, natural source.[51] The qualifications of "healthy" narrowed down the market by excluding carbonated soft drinks, and "natural source" excluded bottled purified tap water. Since the publication of the *Commission Notice on market definition*, the European Commission has continued to rely heavily on the assessment of

case law references see Cárdenas, *Rolle, Kriterien und Methodik der kartellrechtlichen Marktabgrenzung*, p. 73 fnn. 451, 452.

47 Brinker, "Praktische Probleme der Marktabgrenzung aus rechtlicher Sicht," p. 22.

48 Brinker, "Praktische Probleme der Marktabgrenzung aus rechtlicher Sicht," p. 31.

49 Brinker, "Praktische Probleme der Marktabgrenzung aus rechtlicher Sicht," p. 31.

50 *Hoffmann-La Roche*, *supra*, Ch. 2, fn. 30, para. 28.

51 Case IV/M.190, *Nestlé/Perrier* [1992] OJ L356 1, paras. 10–12 (hereinafter *Nestlé/Perrier*).

intended uses.[52] Most recent EU case law is still replete with considerations of physical characteristics and intended end-use.[53]

Apart from the classic traditional criteria, market definition has, historically, also been a matter of a non-economic, market-detached, and speculative assessment of consumer perceptions on the basis of the subjective views of regulators and adjudicators. In Europe, this is a remnant of the heavy German influence during the first years after the inception of European antitrust rules in the 1957 Rome Treaties.[54] For this reason, a short glance at German antitrust law is informative. It still nowadays applies the notion of the "reasonable consumer" ("*verständiger Verbraucher*") as part of its demand market concept ("*Bedarfsmarktkonzept*") for market definition purposes.[55] Under the rubric of functional interchangeability, the assessment relies primarily on physical characteristics and intended uses as judged by a reasonably prudent consumer. The legal concept of the reasonable consumer implies that a subjective analysis is conducted by imagining the way in which a consumer of this type would view the market. Under this standard, no superficial or cursory perceptions of consumers are dispositive. Instead, those that result from a comprehensive process of weighing and balancing are decisive.[56] While the reasonable consumer standard has been influential, two major strands have developed in EU antitrust law. On the one hand, the European Commission often tends toward the assessment of actual consumer behavior, as evidenced by customer surveys or actual sales data. An analysis based on this type of data appears well in line with a market-based, and therefore

[52] For instance, Case T-65/98, *Van den Bergh Foods Ltd* v. *Commission* [1998] OJ L246 1, para. 132 (impulse ice cream, bought individually for immediate consumption, as a separate market from that of take-home ice cream, because "the consumers' intended purpose in purchasing the ice cream in turn determines the differences in characteristics and price between impulse and take-home products.").

[53] This is reflected in recent high profile Article 102 cases, e.g., Case COMP/37.7792, *Microsoft* [2007] OJ L32 23 (market for streaming media players distinct from market for media players not including streaming functionality). A survey of recent Commission merger control case law confirms that the Commission often embraces a traditional approach, e.g., Case COMP/M.3975, *Cargill/Degussa* [2007] OJ L316 53; Case COMP/M.4094, *Ineos/BP Dormagen* [2007] OJ L69 40; Case COMP/M.4215, *Glatfelder/Crompton* [2007] OJ L151 41.

[54] See Gerber, "The European Competition Law Story: Some German Roles," in Großfeld *et al.* (eds.), *Festschrift für Wolfgang Fikentscher*, pp. 654–670 (1998).

[55] Hildebrand, *The Role of Economic Analysis in the EC Competition Rules*, p. 282 (2002); see, e.g., KG, February 18, 1969, WuW/E OLG 995, 996 – *Handpreisauszeichner.*

[56] See, e.g., KG, December 1, 1976, WuW/E OLG 1748 – *GKN/Sachs*; BGH, December 16, 1976, WuW/E BGH 1447 – *Valium.*

economically-based, approach to assessing consumer perceptions. This is because attention is given to discerning what economists term "revealed preferences" – established through actual purchasing decisions.[57] On the other hand, EU law in general is based on the pervasive notion of a reasonably prudent consumer.[58] Thus, at least at times, EU antitrust law is also influenced by an idealized and typified consumer standard referring to the yardstick of "reasonable substitutability" or of the "typical" consumer.[59] In fact, even US antitrust law quite prominently has its proper reasonableness standard under which product characteristics and end-uses are assessed in order to ascertain whether products are "*reasonably* interchangeable by consumers."[60] As will be discussed below, such a standard is in tension with, and even potentially in opposition to, the realities of consumer perceptions in the market and therefore contrary to a market-based, and therefore economics-based, approach.

2 Article III of the GATT

WTO/GATT dispute settlement bodies and scholars have also expressed a variety of views regarding product comparability under Article III of the GATT. The rich case law that has emerged is, however, not a monument to consistency.[61] The methodical approaches can be summarized into three distinct schools of thought: the traditional approach; the aims-and-effects test; and the economics-based approach. The first two have been at the center of attention in the judicial and scholarly debate. After a brief appearance in the case law between 1996 and 2000, the latter has gained some attention with several commentators and has very recently resurfaced with respect to quantitative methods in two 2011 Panel Reports.[62]

[57] See, e.g., Pindyck and Rubinfeld, *Microeconomics*, p. 92.

[58] Immenga and Körber, "Artikel 2 Beurteilung von Zusammenschlüssen," in Immenga and Mestmäcker (eds.), *Wettbewerbsrecht Band 1 EG/Teil 2*, Art. 2 FKVO para. 42 (2007).

[59] Case IV/M.149, *Luca/Eaton* [1991] OJ C328, para. 28. Section 8.7(f) of the Form CO merger notification, Annex I to the Commission Regulation No. 802/2004, where the Commission requires a description of the "typical customer." See also Traugott, "Zur Abgrenzung von Märkten," *Wettbewerb und Wirtschaft*, 9 (1998) 929, 930; Rösler, "Der relevante Markt in der Europäischen Fusionskontrolle," *Neue Zeitschrift für Gesellschaftsrecht*, (2000), 761, 762.

[60] *Cellophane*, *supra*, Ch. 2, fn. 26, at 395 (emphasis added).

[61] For a recount see Trebilcock and Giri, "The National Treatment Principle in International Trade Law," in Choi and Hartigan (eds.), *Handbook of International Trade*, vol. II, pp. 185, 188–220 (2004).

[62] See references at *supra*, Introduction, fn. 16.

This section will first outline the traditional approach embraced by the dispute settlement bodies under all three non-discrimination obligations of Articles III:2(1), 2(2), and III:4 of the GATT. Further, this section will address non-economic alternatives to the traditional approach that have been debated, most importantly the famous aims-and-effects test, but also the role of product and process methods for product comparison. These alternatives, although advocated on numerous occasions by prominent proponents, have not succeeded before the adjudicating bodies. Importantly, this study does not continue the discussion on which of these non-economic approaches should prevail. Instead, it contrasts the non-economic approaches with a more economics-based approach, which will be described in the following subchapter.

A *The traditional approach: the* Border Tax Report

Given the different product scopes of the three non-discrimination obligations in Article III of the GATT, the unresolved question of interest is not about a one-size-fits-all definition, but the relevant criteria and their evidentiary weight. The adjudicating bodies have adopted a uniform catalog of criteria that was canonized by the GATT Working Party's *Report on Border Tax Adjustments* in 1970.[63]

(i) The *Border Tax* criteria

The *Report* concluded that the terms "like or similar" products in GATT law should be examined on a case-by-case basis. Further, it suggested the following criteria as pertinent for the interpretation of these terms: "the products' end-uses in a given market; consumers' tastes and habits, which change from country to country; the products' properties, nature and quality."[64]

These so-called "*Border Tax* criteria" were not revolutionary. Rather, the Report compiled what had already been used in prior case law. A criterion that was not originally part of the *Border Tax Report*, but which had already played an important role in earlier decisions, was that of tariff classifications of products. Since the *Border Tax* criteria list was not exhaustive,[65] tariff classifications were added to the list of what has

[63] *Working Party Report on Border Tax Adjustments*, BISD 18S/97, December 2, 1970 (hereinafter *Border Tax Report*).

[64] *Border Tax Report*, para. 18.

[65] See Appellate Body Report, *Japan – Alcoholic Beverages II*, *supra*, Introduction, fn. 15, at 20.

become known as the "basic" or "classic" approach, or the "traditional criteria" or "traditional analysis."[66] Reference to the *Border Tax* criteria often encompasses this extended list of factors, including tariff classifications, as outlined in this study.

The *Border Tax Report* did not provide any additional guidance beyond the mere listing of factors. No precise definition of the criteria was offered. Moreover, no guidance was given on their respective evidentiary weight or on how to apply those criteria to the facts. The Appellate Body in *EC – Asbestos* rendered them marginally more precise:

> These four criteria comprise four categories of "characteristics" that the products involved might share: (i) the physical properties of the products; (ii) the extent to which the products are capable of serving the same or similar end-uses; (iii) the extent to which consumers perceive and treat the products as alternative means of performing particular functions in order to satisfy a particular want or demand; and (iv) the international classification of the products for tariff purposes.[67]

Despite this attempt to clarify the terms, the prior criticism still persists that the dispute settlement bodies continue to invoke the criteria without any discussion of their relevance or the manner of their application.[68] Instead of developing a coherent methodology for applying these factors, the dispute settlement bodies have regularly insisted on the notion that an analysis must be conducted on a case-by-case basis. This amounts to saying that they are free to do anything and are not constrained by any general coherent framework that may reconcile the rulings with each other. In sum, inconsistency in the application of the criteria prevails to date.

Since their introduction, the *Border Tax* criteria have been applied to all instances of product comparison across Article III – and other provisions – of GATT.[69] They especially extend to the interpretation of DCS.[70] Although likeness and DCS encompass a different product scope,

66 Appellate Body Report, *Japan – Alcoholic Beverages II*, *supra*, Introduction, fn. 15, at 20; Panel Report, *China – Measures Affecting Trading Rights and Distribution Services for Certain Publications and Audiovisual Entertainment Products*, WT/DS363/R, adopted January 19, 2010, paras. 7.1146 *et seq.*, 7.1478 *et seq.*, 7.1558 *et seq.*; Raible, *Protektionismusverbote im Recht der Wirtschaftsintegration*, p. 216 (2005).

67 Appellate Body Report, *EC – Asbestos*, *supra*, Ch. 2, fn. 70, para. 101.

68 See Tsai, "'Like' is a Four-Letter Word: GATT Article III's 'Like Product' Conundrum," p. 30.

69 The *Border Tax Report* was concerned with the interpretation of Articles I, II, III, VI, VII, and XVI GATT; see *Border Tax Report*, para. 7.

70 See, e.g., Panel Report, *Mexico – Soft Drinks*, *supra*, Ch. 2, fn. 80, para. 8.106; Panel Report, *Philippines – Distilled Spirits*, *supra*, Introduction, fn. 23, para. 7.102.

their definition is thus based on the same set of criteria. However, it will become clear that in each context emphasis has been placed on different criteria from this list. This is why their respective significance and weight have varied considerably. Early case law stressed the role of physical characteristics and tariff classifications, which have generally been more important to the definition of likeness. In contrast, end-uses and consumers' tastes and habits (hereinafter CTH) have played an important role in the determination of DCS relationships. The evidence considered under the four factors has varied as well. Whereas inquiries into likeness have relied on qualitative and descriptive evidence, exceptionally in three cases between 1996 and 2000 the determination of DCS relationships – and as a novelty in two Panel Reports in 2011 also the likeness analysis – has extended to an appraisal of quantitative evidence.

(ii) Legal and *de facto* status

Neither the Working Party Report itself nor the Panel Reports that have endorsed the *Border Tax* criteria have legally binding *inter omnes* effect. Because Panel Reports only have *inter partes* effect, there is no doctrine of binding precedent in WTO law.[71] Moreover, adopted Panel Reports are not considered binding "subsequent practice" under Article 31(3)(b) of the Vienna Convention on the Law of Treaties (hereinafter VCLT) through which the *Border Tax* criteria could attain binding effect.[72] The *Border Tax Report* must also be seen as persuasive only because it does not have the status of primary international treaty law. The Appellate Body in *EC – Asbestos* said that: "these criteria are, it is well to bear in mind, simply tools to assist in the task of sorting and examining the relevant evidence. They are neither treaty-mandated nor a closed list of criteria that will determine the legal characterization of products."[73]

Instead of being bound by precedent and by a certain mode of analysis, the Appellate Body emphasized that Panels have to make a discretionary decision. Since product comparison is fact- and context-specific,

[71] See Articles 3.2 and 19.2 of the Dispute Settlement Understanding (hereinafter DSU).

[72] Appellate Body Report, *Japan – Alcoholic Beverages II*, *supra*, Introduction, fn. 15, at 12–15.

[73] Appellate Body Report, *EC – Asbestos*, *supra*, Ch. 2, fn. 70, para. 102. Panel Report, *Japan – Alcoholic Beverages II*, WT/DS8/AB/R, WT/DS10/AB/R, WT/DS11/AB/R, adopted November 1, 1996, para. 6.10 also rejected to consider the *Border Tax Report* as a "subsequent agreement regarding the interpretation of the treaty or the application of its provisions" pursuant to Article 31(3)(a) of the VCLT. This is evident since Article IX:2 of the WTO Agreement provides that only the Ministerial Conference and the General Council have the exclusive authority to adopt interpretations of WTO law.

it requires flexibility that "will always involve an unavoidable element of individual, discretionary judgment."[74] Against this background, the *Border Tax* criteria are in no way legally binding.

In stark contradiction to their theoretically recognized *de jure* non-binding nature, the *Border Tax* criteria have become *de facto* binding in practice. One reason is that the dispute settlement bodies have invoked the *Border Tax* approach almost invariably when terms "like" or DCS appeared. As the Appellate Body itself conceded, this overall approach has been followed in almost all adopted Panel Reports prior and subsequent to the *Border Tax Report* – although this does not mean that each and every criterion has always been invoked.[75] It has and continues to precede virtually every attempt to interpret and apply the terms to a given case. Even though there is no *stare decisis* doctrine, this factually binding effect may be explained with what has been recognized as "legitimate expectations" among WTO Members.[76] Somewhat self-perpetuating, once the *Border Tax* approach has been adopted in case law, Members can count on its continuing relevance. Therefore, it is reasonable to suggest that this list of criteria has actually gained a veritable canonical status and has become something of a mantra for subsequent dispute settlement bodies.

Moreover, despite the ruling that the *Border Tax* criteria are not a mandatory, closed checklist, the criteria have been elevated by the Appellate Body into a "doctrinal straightjacket" for Panels.[77] On the one hand, the list of factors is not exhaustive. On the other hand, the Appellate Body held in *EC – Asbestos* that all four *Border Tax* criteria must be assessed separately and individually in each and every case.[78] Leaving out a criterion would constitute a reversible error in law. On the whole, this means that the *Border Tax* criteria constitute a minimum requirement in the assessment of product comparability. This is confirmed by the recent jurisprudential evolution subsequent to *EC – Asbestos*. While at the beginning of dispute settlement practice only one or two selected criteria were exclusively dispositive in each case, it is standard today to look at the entire catalog examining the evidence relating to *each* of the four criteria. Then, in a second step, the Panel is to weigh all that evidence in making an

[74] Appellate Body Report, *Japan – Alcoholic Beverages II*, *supra*, Introduction, fn. 15, at 21.

[75] Appellate Body Report, *Japan – Alcoholic Beverages II*, *supra*, Introduction, fn. 15, at 20.

[76] See Appellate Body Report, *Japan – Alcoholic Beverages II*, *supra*, Introduction, fn. 15, at 14.

[77] Hudec, "GATT/WTO Constraints on National Regulation: Requiem for an 'Aim and Effects' Test," p. 635.

[78] Appellate Body Report, *EC – Asbestos*, *supra*, Ch. 2, fn. 70, para. 109.

overall assessment, or "overall determination," of whether products can be characterized to be "like" each other.[79] In fact, since *EC – Asbestos* the adjudicating bodies have invariably and mechanically applied the entire list of *Border Tax* criteria in the context of Articles III:2(1), (2) and III:4 of the GATT except for one instance, *Dominican Republic – Cigarettes*, which ignored CTH.[80]

(iii) The evolution of the traditional approach

The *Border Tax* approach is a qualitative and non-economic approach. Manifestly, physical characteristics and the uniform tariff classification of products are descriptive, qualitative criteria. It is less clear for end-uses and CTH. But, in practice, the unifying theme under all criteria has been that their analysis was made more or less "in the abstract," that is, separated from the marketplace. The criteria are understood and applied detached from the marketplace, or economic realities, and, in particular, isolated from the actual consumer perspective. This is true for the judicial treatment of physical characteristics. It also applies to end-uses, which were in most cases examined without paying heed to the perspective of market participants, either on the demand- or supply-side. The criterion of CTH may appear *a priori* as an expressly market-oriented measure. But instead of prompting the Panels to investigate actual demand-side perceptions and empirically inquiring into what the habits and tastes of consumers really were, they have often deemed it sufficient to substitute empirical facts with their subjective and unfounded speculations on consumers' perceptions. Overall, starting from the abstract in GATT 1947, the analysis of likeness and DCS seems to have returned to the abstract after a short flirtation with a more marketplace-based test. However, two 2011 Panel Reports may indicate the Panels' renewed interest in economics and quantitative methods in particular.

[79] Appellate Body Report, *EC – Asbestos, supra*, Ch. 2, fn. 70, para. 109.

[80] Panel Report, *Mexico – Soft Drinks, supra*, Ch. 2, fn. 80, paras. 8.30–8.35, 8.69–8.75, 8.106, 8.131–8.135; Panel Report, *Brazil – Measures Affecting Imports of Retreaded Tyres* (hereinafter *Brazil – Retreaded Tyres*), WT/DS332/R, adopted December 7, 2007, para. 7.415; Panel Report, *Thailand – Cigarettes, supra*, Introduction, fn. 23, paras. 7.433, 7.440 *et seq.*; Panel Report, *Philippines – Distilled Spirits, supra*, Introduction, fn. 23, paras. 7.30 *et seq.* But see Panel Report, *Dominican Republic – Measures Affecting the Importation and Internal Sale of Cigarettes* (hereinafter *Dominican Republic – Cigarettes*), WT/DS302/R, adopted May 19, 2005, paras. 7.165, 7.330.

(a) Prominence of physical characteristics and tariff classifications

(1) *Physical characteristics* Physical appearance might be the first property that comes to mind when comparing two products. That is why this criterion has played a significant role in GATT 1947 and WTO jurisprudence on product comparison. It is also a criterion under the *Border Tax Report*, in which it was referred to as the "properties, nature, and quality of the product." But the adjudicating bodies generally use the term "physical characteristics."

They have also stated and in practice attributed more relevance to the criterion under Article III:2(1) than under Article III:2(2) of the GATT.[81] In fact, as will be outlined, likeness is construed as a rather high degree of identity in physical characteristics, although case law has differed on whether to require near identity or to apply a more permissive standard. Because of the great importance of physical attributes for likeness, product comparison under Article III:2(1) of the GATT has also been labeled as the "physical characteristics test."[82] The prominence of the analysis of physical characteristics has been confirmed – under Article III:4 of the GATT – in a categorical statement: "Panels must examine fully the physical properties of products."[83]

While less prominent, physical characteristics have also played a role under Article III:2(2) of the GATT. Since likeness is a subset of the DCS relationship, the examination of physical characteristics has also been held to be useful in the latter context.[84] The criterion of physical characteristics has thus been applied in all cases involving the issues of "like" and DCS products. The following analysis of the case law will show that its examination has ranged from the close analysis of the physical-chemical composition to a more generalized examination of external

[81] See, e.g., Panel Report, *Chile – Alcoholic Beverages*, *supra*, Ch. 2, fn. 68, para. 7.51: "An examination of the physical characteristics of products is more critical in determining whether two products are 'like' than in the determination of whether two products are directly competitive or substitutable."

[82] Matsushita, Schoenbaum, and Mavroidis, *The World Trade Organization*, p. 159.

[83] Appellate Body Report, *EC – Asbestos*, *supra*, Ch. 2, fn. 70, para. 114.

[84] Panel Report, *Korea – Alcoholic Beverages*, *supra*, Introduction, fn. 36, para. 10.66: "The determination of whether two products are 'like' has traditionally turned to a greater extent (although not exclusively) on the physical characteristics of products. It would be an incorrect reading of the law to argue that products' physical similarities were somehow less relevant for the category of directly competitive or substitutable products than for the subcategory of like products. To put it another way, if two products are physically identical or nearly so, it is highly probable that they are 'like.' They should not then be found to be not directly competitive or substitutable."

characteristics, such as organoleptic properties. But more importantly, it will highlight that its application has usually been in a purely "objective" or "abstract" manner. This means that the examination of physical attributes has been conducted in what seems to be an aim in itself, without an inquiry into the significance of these properties for the purpose of product comparison.

(2) *Tariff classifications* Tariff classification is not an immediately obvious feature for comparing products. The idea behind using this criterion is that products that are uniformly classified in tariff nomenclatures are "like" each other. Some background on tariff classifications is necessary to understand the criterion. A key principle of GATT is that, as a general rule, all border measures that give a competitive advantage to domestic products should take the form of customs tariffs imposed at the border and that the level of such tariffs should be a matter for negotiation. Thus, with the exception of tariffs, GATT rules out all types of border measures, in particular, quantitative restrictions, such as quotas.[85] Multilateral rounds of trade negotiations aim at the successive reduction of tariffs. The resulting commitments of the WTO Members regarding tariff concessions and tariff bindings are listed in country-specific "schedules of concessions," which become an integral part of the GATT by virtue of Article II:7 of the GATT. They consist of the description of products and provide the respective maximum tariff level for each product category. Since tariff levels vary across different kinds of products, tariff classification systems that accord to product categories an identification number for customs purposes are necessary in order to apply the correct tariff rate to traded products. In principle, under the WTO/GATT regime each Member is free to maintain its own tariff classification system. Still, the tariff classification systems have been internationally harmonized for two reasons. First, the harmonization facilitates international trade, for example, by standardizing trade documentations and reducing transaction costs incurred by re-describing, re-classifying, and re-coding goods as they move from one classification system to another. Second, it facilitates negotiations on tariff concessions and tariff bindings, which would be very difficult if each Member used its own classification system. The harmonization took place under the auspices of the International Convention on the Harmonized Commodity Description and Coding System in 1983 (Harmonized System, or commonly "HS"), an international treaty developed by the

[85] See Article XI of the GATT.

Cooperation Council (today World Customs Organization).[86] The HS provides a framework for common scheduling of fiscal border measures (essentially tariffs, but also other measures).

WTO Members thus undertook to bind their tariffs of specific goods at a certain level by making commitments in their individual schedules and in accordance with Article II of the GATT. Both the schedules of concessions negotiated by the Members and the HS system provide tariff classifications, where the former can, but do not necessarily, comply with the product groupings under the HS system. Against this background, tariff classifications in either the tariff bindings or the HS were particularly important under GATT 1947 jurisprudence, especially in the context of Article I "like" product determination. It continues to be used frequently in the context of all three Article III obligations.

However, already at this point one has to be clear about the very limited usefulness of tariff classifications as a criterion in the comparison of products. It was not the intention that they be used for the purpose of defining the degree of product comparability under Article III of the GATT. Instead, they result from political negotiations and compromises among the signatories to an agreement and, in particular, for tariff bindings, reflect the parties' concessions rather than the likeness of or competitive relationship between products. In fact, the use of this criterion powerfully demonstrates the traditional approach based on formalistic legal line-drawing unfettered by real world economic considerations. It does not reflect the actual marketplace conditions of products, but the political realities of international trade negotiations and the practical realities of facilitating the functioning of the customs regime.

(3) *GATT 1947 jurisprudence* Early GATT 1947 jurisprudence on Article III of the GATT relied either on physical characteristics or tariff classifications.[87] With the same effect, cases subsequent to the *Border Tax Report* turned on either both criteria (with the additional consideration of end-uses under Article III:2(2) of the GATT) or solely on physical characteristics.[88]

[86] Cottier and Oesch, *International Trade Regulation*, p. 596 (2005); Trebilcock and Howse, *The Regulation of International Trade*, p. 188.

[87] Working Party Report, *Brazil – Internal Taxes*, BISD II/181, adopted June 30, 1949, para. 7; Working Party Report, *Australia – Ammonium Sulphate*, BISD II/188, adopted April 3, 1950, para. 9.

[88] GATT Panel Report, *EEC – Measures on Animal Feed Proteins* (hereinafter *EEC – Animal Feed*), BISD 25S/49, adopted March 14, 1978, para. 4.2; GATT Panel Report,

In particular, the Panels seemed to accord utmost importance to physical characteristics. They followed a very narrow interpretation under which, for Article III:2(1) of the GATT, products had to be "more or less the same."[89] At the same time, the Panels disregarded other (also more market-based) criteria submitted by the parties, some of which would actually later resurface under WTO jurisprudence.[90] One example of this very narrow interpretation of likeness and the abstract application of physical characteristics can be found in the earliest relevant GATT 1947 case, *Brazil – Internal Taxes*, where Brazilian conhaque and French cognac were considered different products due to additives and aromatic differences.[91] Another instance is *EEC – Animal Feeds*. Here, "varying protein contents and the different vegetable, animal and synthetic origins of the protein products" were sufficient for the Panel to conclude that various protein products were not "like" products, but in a DCS relationship.[92]

In contrast to the subsequent alcoholic beverages cases under the WTO regime, which espoused an economic approach, the first important alcoholic beverages dispute, still under GATT 1947, *Japan – Alcoholic Beverages I*, was exemplary in giving precedence to physical characteristics. On the one side, and contrary to the Brazilian case, the Panel seemed to admit some more flexibility by stating that likeness is not confined to identical products, but also to products that share similar qualities, regardless of minor differences in taste, color, and other characteristics.[93] On the other side, the Panel followed suit in applying the physical characteristics criterion abstractly. It considered that the "common characteristics" between Japanese shochu and vodka and other Western spirits, in particular, both being white clear spirits made from similar raw materials, weighed in favor of likeness and a DCS relationship under Article III:2.

Spain – Soyabean Oil, BISD L/5142, circulated June 17, 1981, unadopted, para. 4.7; GATT Panel Report, *Canada – Measures Affecting the Sale of Gold Coins* (hereinafter *Canada – Gold Coins*), BISD L/5863, circulated September 17, 1985, unadopted, para. 51.

89 GATT Panel Report, *Spain – Soyabean Oil*, *supra*, fn. 88, para. 4.6.

90 GATT Panel Report, *Spain – Soyabean Oil*, *supra*, fn. 88, para. 3.7: "[The complainant] argued that there was a strong case for considering sunflower oil and soyabean oil 'like' products under this paragraph in view of their interchangeability, similarity in processing, marketing and general price movement and comparable acid content." See also GATT Panel Report, *Canada – Gold Coins*, *supra*, fn. 88, para. 14, where the Panel ignored the submission to consider identical world market prices.

91 GATT Panel Report, *Brazil – Internal Taxes*, *supra*, fn. 87, para. 7.

92 GATT Panel Report, *EEC – Animal Feed*, *supra*, fn. 88, paras. 4.2–4.3.

93 GATT Panel Report, *Japan – Alcoholic Beverages I*, *supra*, Ch. 2, fn. 65, para. 5.7.

Only one out of nine GATT 1947 cases examined all four criteria,[94] and only two others examined the three criteria physical characteristics, tariff classifications, and end-uses. With the exceptions of one case, which exclusively relied on the analysis of end-uses,[95] and two cases, which adopted the aims-and-effects test,[96] the remaining cases all revolved around either tariff classifications and/or, more frequently, physical characteristics.

(4) *GATT 1994/WTO jurisprudence* The 1994 WTO Agreement established the WTO, and GATT 1947 was incorporated as GATT 1994. In this continuity of the legal framework, physical characteristics and tariff classifications remain important criteria.

The first cases under the WTO confirmed this.[97] Under the new legal regime, the first major case for the interpretation of likeness and DCS under Article III:2 of the GATT was *Japan – Alcoholic Beverages II*.[98] The United States, the EC and Canada complained about discriminatory taxation by Japan of Western alcoholic beverages, such as brandy, cognac, gin, liquors, rum, vodka, and whisky, in comparison with the domestic spirit shochu. The Panel emphasized the greater importance of physical characteristics for the determination of likeness under Article III:2(1) of the GATT than for that of DCS. In what seems to contradict the more relaxed reading of similarity of physical characteristics under *Japan – Alcoholic Beverages I*, the Panel postulated a strict standard for the determination of likeness based on near identity of physical characteristics. Products are "like" if they share "essentially the same physical

[94] GATT Panel Report, *Japan – Alcoholic Beverages I*, *supra*, Ch. 2, fn. 65, paras. 5.6, 5.7.

[95] GATT Panel Report, *United States – Taxes on Petroleum and Certain Imported Substances* (hereinafter *US – Superfund*), BISD 34S/136, adopted June 17, 1987, para. 5.1.1.

[96] *Infra*, Ch. 2, fn. 4.

[97] Panel Report, *United States – Standards for Reformulated and Conventional Gasoline* (hereinafter *US – Gasoline*), WT/DS2/9, adopted May 20, 1996, para. 6.9 (imported and domestic gasoline considered "like" under Article III:4 because of identical physical characteristics and tariff classifications); Panel Report, *European Communities – Regime for the Importation, Sale and Distribution of Bananas (Complaint by Ecuador)*, WT/DS27/R/ECU, adopted May 25, 1997, para. 7.62 (bananas from ACP and third countries as "like" because of identical physical characteristics and same tariff classification); Panel Report, *Canada – Periodicals*, WT/DS31/R, adopted July 30, 1997, para. 5.25 (similar characteristics between split-run and non split-run periodicals), reversed for a lack of factual basis on likeness by Appellate Body Report, *Canada – Periodicals*, *supra*, Ch. 2, fn. 50, at 20 *et seq.*; Panel Report, *Indonesia – Autos*, *supra*, Ch. 2, fn. 92, para. 14.110 (different car types, here Toyota Corolla and the Timor S515, as "like" because of identical physical characteristics).

[98] Panel Report, *Japan – Alcoholic Beverages II*, *supra*, fn. 73, at 23.

characteristics."[99] In this line of reasoning, it ruled that only vodka and shochu, which "shared most physical characteristics" and displayed "virtual identity," were "like" each other.[100] Differences in the use of additives and ingredients as well as in appearance were sufficient to disqualify the rest of Western spirits from being "like" shochu which, instead, were considered to be in a DCS relationship. Importantly, no other criteria, such as end-uses, were contemplated, which could have weighed in for likeness. This suggests that differences in physical characteristics preclude products from being "like," even in case of similarities under other criteria, but they do not necessarily seem to rule out a DCS relationship.

Korea – Alcoholic Beverages and *Chile – Alcoholic Beverages* are two further important alcoholic beverages cases, the most recent episode in this saga being *Philippines – Distilled Spirits*. All revolve around the issue of product comparability of imported and domestic distilled spirits under Article III:2(1) and/or (2) of the GATT. The two earlier cases concerned allegations of fiscal discrimination between Western spirits imported into Korea and Chile and domestically produced spirits, Korean soju and Chilean pisco. In both instances, the focus was on Article III:2(2) of the GATT, the pivotal issue being whether the Western spirits were in a DCS relationship with the respective domestic spirit.

Finally, both were seminal cases for the economic interpretation of the DCS phrase. Still, they also highlight the role of physical characteristics under the rubric of DCS – even under an economic approach. In *Korea – Alcoholic Beverages*, Western alcoholic beverages, such as brandy, cognac, gin, rum, vodka, and whisky, were held to be DCS with soju. Existing differences in color and flavor were deemed to be minor in comparison with the "fundamental physical similarities."[101] All products had the essential feature of being distilled alcoholic beverages, all had ethyl alcohol as the base ingredient, and all were bottled and labeled in a similar manner. The Panel in *Chile – Alcoholic Beverages* also concluded that Western spirits and pisco were DCS. In terms of physical characteristics, they had the "significant common feature" of being potable distilled spirits with high alcohol content.[102] As in *Korea – Alcoholic Beverages*, post-distillation differences due to the filtration, coloring, or aging processes of the beverages were not so important as to render the products non-substitutable.[103]

[99] Panel Report, *Japan – Alcoholic Beverages II*, *supra*, fn. 73, para. 6.22.
[100] Panel Report, *Japan – Alcoholic Beverages II*, *supra*, fn. 73, para. 6.23.
[101] Panel Report, *Korea – Alcoholic Beverages*, *supra*, Introduction, fn. 36, para. 10.67.
[102] Panel Report, *Chile – Alcoholic Beverages*, *supra*, Ch. 2, fn. 68, para. 7.53.
[103] Panel Report, *Chile – Alcoholic Beverages*, *supra*, Ch. 2, fn. 68, para. 7.54.

The Panel in *Philippines – Distilled Spirits* also concerned fiscal discrimination, and found foreign and domestic Philippine distilled spirits (gin, brandy, rum, vodka, whisky, tequila, and tequila-flavored spirits) to be "like" as well as in a DCS relationship.[104] The analysis under Article III:2(1) of the GATT was remarkably elaborate on the physical characteristics, considering alcohol content, color, physiological effects on humans, the process of production, organoleptic properties, and even going into the details of the chemical composition.[105]

Notably, in the course of the alcoholic beverages cases, physical characteristics remained an important criterion, but also seemed to evolve conceptually into a narrower reading under Article III:2(1) and a broader reading under Article III:2(2) of the GATT. What has, however, remained constant is the abstract analysis of physical characteristics, highlighted in both cases, for example, in the conclusions that all products in question have the common feature of being distilled alcoholic beverages.

Another landmark case in the context of Article III market definition has been *EC – Asbestos*. Upon the complaint of Canada, the dispute settlement bodies inquired into the legality under Article III:4 of the GATT of the distribution and sales ban of asbestos fibers and asbestos-containing cement in France. For the first time, the Appellate Body clarified the meaning of likeness under this provision. At the same time, both Panel and Appellate Body Reports, although coming to contradictory results, demonstrate how the criterion of physical characteristics has remained to play an important role despite concurrent efforts to move toward an economic approach to the market definition paradigm.

The Panel had concluded that chrysotile asbestos fibers and chrysotile asbestos-containing cement were "like" domestic asbestos-free fibers and non-asbestos cement, but justified the measure under Article XX(b) of the GATT on public health grounds.[106] It explicitly refused to consider the health risk (carcinogenicity) in the context of the application of the *Border Tax* criteria, relegating this consideration to the analytical stage of justification. In contrast, the Appellate Body appraised the physical and

[104] The Appellate Body upheld the Panel's finding with respect to its findings that each type of imported spirit was "like" the same domestic type and that all distilled spirits at issue were DCS, but it reversed the Panel's ruling with regard to the "likeness" of all spirits at issue, Appellate Body Report, *Philippines – Distilled Spirits*, *supra*, Ch. 2, fn. 44, paras. 172, 183, 243.

[105] Panel Report, *Philippines – Distilled Spirits*, *supra*, Introduction, fn. 23, paras. 7.34–7.47.

[106] Panel Report, *EC – Asbestos*, WT/DS125/AB/R, adopted April 5, 2001, paras. 8.121–8.126.

chemical composition in detail, and their relevance for human health.[107] From this, it negated the likeness of both product pairs on the basis that physical characteristics differed in view of the carcinogenicity of asbestos. It thus reversed the Panel's ruling.

Moreover, the Appellate Body Report in this ruling appears to privilege the investigation of physical characteristics. It ruled that physical differences impose a higher burden to establish likeness under the remaining *Border Tax* criteria.[108] Where the analysis of physical characteristics comes to the conclusion of unlikeness, the evidence under the remaining criteria must be virtually overwhelming to justify an overall, definitive judgment that the products are "like."[109] In fact, the Appellate Body seems to construct a rebuttable *prima facie* presumption of unlikeness where differences in physical properties exist.[110] This ruling has been made under Article III:4 of the GATT. Yet, logically, it is of significance for Article III:2 as well, since its product scope is practically co-extensive with that of Article III:4. Under this precedent, physical characteristics is now of preeminent importance for the assessment of likeness in Article III of the GATT. This is reflected in the subsequent case law, which has mechanically adhered to the *Border Tax* framework and continued to apply the physical characteristics criterion in the same abstract manner.[111]

[107] Appellate Body Report, *EC – Asbestos*, *supra*, Ch. 2, fn. 70, para. 114: "In the case of chrysotile asbestos fibres, their molecular structure, chemical composition, and fibrillation capacity are important because the microscopic particles and filaments of chrysotile asbestos fibres are carcinogenic in humans, following inhalation … This carcinogenicity, or toxicity, constitutes, as we see it, a defining aspect of the physical properties of chrysotile asbestos fibres"; and para. 134: "None of the substitute fibres … has the same structure, either in terms of its form, its diameter, its length or its potential to release particles that possess certain characteristics. Moreover, they do not have the same chemical composition, which means that, in purely physical terms, none of them has the same nature or quality."

[108] Appellate Body Report, *EC – Asbestos*, *supra*, Ch. 2, fn. 70, para. 118: "A 'higher burden' results where 'the products at issue are physically quite different' and a 'very heavy burden' follows where products have 'very different properties.'"

[109] Note that the Appellate Body does not affirm the converse that commonalities in physical characteristics increase the burden of establishing unlikeness on the basis of the other criteria. For the limited role of common physical characteristics see Appellate Body Report, *EC – Asbestos*, *supra*, Ch. 2, fn. 70, para. 111: "Although not decisive, the extent to which products share common physical properties may be a useful indicator of 'likeness.'"

[110] Appellate Body Report, *EC – Asbestos*, *supra*, Ch. 2, fn. 70, para. 121: "If there is *no* inquiry into [CTH], there is no basis for **overcoming the inference**, drawn from the different physical properties of the products, that the products are not 'like'" (emphasis in bold added).

[111] Panel Report, *Dominican Republic – Cigarettes*, *supra*, fn. 80, paras. 7.165, 7.330 (likeness of domestic and imported cigarettes under Articles III:2(1) and III:4, because of

Tariff classifications are a further criterion that most often has been examined as an annex to the consideration of physical characteristics. While it was a prominent criterion in the beginning of GATT 1947, it has henceforth been accredited lesser importance. Yet the outright rejection of this criterion in *Chile – Alcoholic Beverages* must be seen as an aberration in dispute settlement jurisprudence.[112] The Appellate Body in *EC – Asbestos* clarified that it is an element that is not, on its own, decisive, but which can provide some limited indication.[113] Hence, tariff classifications continue to be used to date – but only as a peripheral consideration – under all alternatives of Article III of the GATT.[114] The classifications have been drawn either from tariff bindings in the schedules of concessions of specific countries or, after its inception, from the HS system. In *Japan – Alcoholic Beverages II*, the Appellate Body acknowledged the relevance of tariff classifications based on the HS "as a helpful sign" if sufficiently detailed.[115] In contrast, it doubted the reliability of tariff classifications taken from tariff bindings in the schedules of concessions. Those "include broad ranges of products that cut across several different HS tariff headings."[116] Tariff bindings are therefore considered to sweep too broadly in order to provide the basis for the specific determination of likeness or DCS.

identical raw material); Panel Report, *Mexico – Soft Drinks*, *supra*, Ch. 2, fn. 80, paras. 8.32–8.35 (likeness of cane and beet sugar under Article III:2(1), because both are a form of saccharose with identical molecular structure and both are nutritive sweeteners or sweeteners with a caloric content. The same reasoning was applied to high fructose corn syrup (HFCS) and cane sugar under Article III:2(2) (*ibid.*, paras. 8.69–8.70); with the same reasoning, all products were also held to be "like" each other under Article III:4 (*ibid.*, paras. 8.105–8.106); imported soft drinks and syrup made with HFCS and beet sugar as well as domestic soft drinks and syrup made with cane sugar were deemed "like" products under Article III:2(1), because of their physical appearance, calorie content, manner of digestion and absorption, chemical composition, and labeling (*ibid.*, para. 8.131).

112 Panel Report, *Chile – Alcoholic Beverages*, *supra*, Ch. 2, fn. 68, para. 7.87 fn. 410: "Relying on tariff classifications [is] merely duplicative of examinations made in greater detail for the specific market in question in regard to such factors as physical characteristics and similar end-uses."

113 Appellate Body Report, *EC – Asbestos*, *supra*, Ch. 2, fn. 70, paras. 140, 146.

114 See, e.g., Panel Report, *Dominican Republic – Cigarettes*, *supra*, fn. 80, paras. 7.330, 7.165; Panel Report, *Mexico – Soft Drinks*, *supra*, Ch. 2, fn. 80, paras. 8.35, 8.75, 8.106, 8.135; Panel Report, *Brazil – Retreaded Tyres*, *supra*, fn. 80, para. 7.415; Panel Report, *Philippines – Distilled Spirits*, *supra*, Introduction, fn. 23, paras. 7.63–7.71, 7.132–7.134.

115 Appellate Body Report, *Japan – Alcoholic Beverages II*, *supra*, Introduction, fn. 15, at 21.

116 Appellate Body Report, *Japan – Alcoholic Beverages II*, *supra*, Introduction, fn. 15, at 22.

(b) End-uses The criterion of commonalities or differences in end-uses has been of only marginal importance in the context of Article III under GATT 1947.[117] This has changed under GATT 1994. Since then, it has been applied in every WTO dispute settlement case in which the comparison of products was called for under Article III of the GATT.

Despite its increasing use, the notion of end-use has remained elusive. Because the *Border Tax Report* phraseology refers to "the product's end-uses in a given market," it seems to suggest that a market-oriented inquiry is called upon.[118] By contrast, the Appellate Body later circumscribed the notion of end-uses more precisely as "the extent to which products are capable of performing the same, or similar, functions."[119] This circumscription corresponds to a definition of end-uses "in the abstract," or in "general" terms, and not to a notion of the term, which focuses on what is perceived as the relevant end-use in the marketplace.[120]

The concept of "general end-uses" defines end-uses according to the universal utility of a product. This means that adjudicators inquire about the product's end-use according to the general (universal) use of the product, that is, whether two products in general can fulfill the same functions. Under the traditional approach to market definition, it has been inferred from objectively or abstractly defined common end-uses that the products were "like" or DCS. At the same time, whether customers in a given market perceive the products as substitutable with respect to their end-use has been disregarded. General end-use is thus different from a "market-based end-use" in that the former is a more objective concept without reference to the marketplace or to the consumers of the products in the market. In contrast, the latter more subjective notion is determined according to the particular market conditions. Importantly, results under the two standards can diverge. Abstractly assessed, two products may have common end-uses. But they may not be substitutable in end-uses under the unique customer preferences and habits.

[117] GATT Panel Report, *EEC – Animal Feed, supra*, fn. 88, para. 4.3; GATT Panel Report, *US – Superfund*, supra, fn. 95, para. 5.1.1; GATT Panel Report, *Japan – Alcoholic Beverages I, supra*, Ch. 2, fn. 65, para. 5.7.

[118] *Border Tax Report*, para. 18.

[119] Appellate Body Report, *EC – Asbestos, supra*, Ch. 2, fn. 70, para. 117.

[120] Diebold, *Non-Discrimination in International Trade in Services*, p. 259 (2010) speaks of an objective determination of end-uses. Emch, "Fiscal Discrimination in WTO Law and EU Law," p. 409, and Choi, *"Like Products" in International Trade Law*, pp. 21–29, use the term "general end-uses." Melloni, *The Principle of National Treatment in the GATT*, p. 215 (2005) refers to "abstract end-uses."

As an example of the abstract assessment of end-uses, a Panel noted in one case that "vegetable proteins and skimmed milk powder were technically substitutable in terms of their final use," and thus were in a DCS relationship.[121] By the same token, in another case imported liquid hydrocarbon products and domestic crude oil, crude oil condensates and natural gasoline were found to be DCS because they "served substantially identical end-uses."[122] In *Japan – Alcoholic Beverages I*, the Panel prescribed that shochu and vodka had a common end-use in that they were a "well defined and single product intended for drinking."[123] In the crudest form, the first two examples display an abstract application of end-uses because they even refrain from defining what the relevant end-use is. Although the last case defines the end-use, it remains abstract for its broad and overly general interpretation of the end-use, which could encompass a multitude of beverages regardless of them actually being substitutes in end-use for customers.

As outlined above, in the alcoholic beverages cases one can observe an evolution from the abstract to a consumer-oriented determination of end-uses.[124] Whether this evolution is permanent or temporary remains open. The interpretative pendulum may have swung back on the occasion of the *EC – Asbestos* ruling. In this case, the Appellate Body clearly postulated an abstract understanding of end-uses by formulating the above-mentioned definition and by requiring an objective analysis of end-uses that is clearly separated from the other criteria, including the subjective analysis of CTH.[125] Several recent cases have applied the criterion of end-uses in this manner.[126] However, they provide rather limited insights, because likeness was not a disputed fact and the analysis was therefore brief. The Panel Report in *Mexico – Soft Drinks* is more instructive. As becomes evident from contrasting the Panel's analyses under the criteria of products' end-uses and CTH, the Panel appeared to make an effort to determine the end-uses with regard to a group of different sweeteners as well as to soft drinks and syrup in a more objective or abstract manner than the

[121] GATT Panel Report, *EEC – Animal Feed*, *supra*, fn. 88, para. 4.3.

[122] GATT Panel Report, *US – Superfund*, *supra*, fn. 95, para. 5.1.1.

[123] GATT Panel Report, *Japan – Alcoholic Beverages I*, *supra*, Ch. 2, fn. 65, para. 5.6.

[124] *Infra*, fn. 219.

[125] See Appellate Body Report, *EC – Asbestos*, *supra*, Ch. 2, fn. 70, paras. 109, 117.

[126] Panel Report, *Dominican Republic – Cigarettes*, *supra*, fn. 80, paras. 7.165, 7.330 (imported and domestic cigarettes "have the same end-use (i.e., they are smoked by consumers)"); Panel Report, *Brazil – Retreaded Tyres*, *supra*, fn. 80, para. 7.415 (imported retreaded tires and domestic retreaded tires have the "same end uses (to be used for respective vehicle types, such as passenger cars, buses and trucks, and air planes)").

subjective determination of CTH. For example, the Panel pointed to the objective interchangeability of the different sweeteners for the production of soft drinks and syrup.[127] When addressing the likeness of soft drinks and syrup, the Panel also reverted to a generalized assessment of end-uses, observing that "both types of products may be drunk for quenching thirst, providing energy or nourishment, or for socialization."[128]

(c) **Consumers' tastes and habits** Intuitively, CTH are the underpinning of any competitive relationship. As such, the criterion is inherently a market-based one. However, in the application of this criterion much has remained obscure and its application has oftentimes been conducted in a non-market-based manner which abstracted from marketplace realities.

Neither the *Border Tax Report* nor, for a long time, the case law specified what exactly is meant by the criterion of CTH. In fact, GATT and WTO jurisprudence considered the criterion at times only implicitly as part of end-uses, and at times it was not taken into account at all. After the *Border Tax Report*, it took the adjudicating bodies seventeen years to pick up CTH as a criterion. Once it had reached that point, the Panel "was of the view that the 'likeness' of products must be examined taking into account not only objective criteria (such as composition and manufacturing processes of products), but also the more subjective consumers' viewpoint."[129] At the same time, the Panel qualified that the probative value of this criterion may be compromised due to the discriminatory measure in question distorting consumer habits.[130] Another ten years later, the Panel in *Canada – Periodicals* embraced the criterion again. However, the Panel Report touched on CTH only briefly by asserting that "it was most likely that" the domestic and a foreign edition of a certain periodical "would have been designed for the same readership with the same tastes and habits."[131]

It was only in *EC – Asbestos* that the Appellate Body more specifically defined CTH as "the extent to which consumers are willing to use the products to perform [the same or similar] functions."[132] Put differently, the criterion concerns the question of whether the abstractly defined end-uses

[127] Panel Report, *Mexico – Soft Drinks*, *supra*, Ch. 2, fn. 80, paras. 8.32, 8.71.

[128] Panel Report, *Mexico – Soft Drinks*, *supra*, Ch. 2, fn. 80, para. 8.132.

[129] GATT Panel Report, *Japan – Alcoholic Beverages I*, *supra*, Ch. 2, fn. 65, para. 5.7.

[130] In more detail on this issue, see *infra*, Ch. 5, fn. 209.

[131] Panel Report, *Canada – Periodicals*, *supra*, fn. 97, para. 5.25.

[132] Appellate Body Report, *EC – Asbestos*, *supra*, Ch. 2, fn. 70, para. 117.

are perceived by the consumers in a market in a way that the products are considered as substitutable.[133] This approach has been implemented in an exemplary manner in the *Mexico – Soft Drinks* case. As already outlined, the criterion of end-uses had been defined abstractly, while subsequently the Panel examined consumers' perceptions and behavior with respect to these end-uses.[134] The Panel in *Philippines – Distilled Spirits* confirmed the reading of CTH as synonymous with demand-side substitutability by referring to "the ability or willingness of consumers to switch" and a "significant degree of competitiveness or substitutability."[135]

The Appellate Body Report in *EC – Asbestos* is highly important for another reason. During the preceding economically-oriented *Japan – Alcoholic Beverages II*, *Korea – Alcoholic Beverages*, and *Chile – Alcoholic Beverages*, CTH had not been addressed as a separate factor. But to the same effect, the adjudicators integrated consumer perceptions in their economic market analysis. Then, in *EC – Asbestos*, the Panel actually discarded the consideration of CTH altogether as useless. In response, the Appellate Body emphasized the significance of an independent and separate analysis of CTH, the examination of which being "indispensable – although not, on its own, sufficient."[136] More importantly, the Appellate Body put emphasis on the economic orientation of the test for likeness. Yet the concrete application of the CTH criterion did not fit squarely into what one would expect to be an economically sound marketplace orientation. The Appellate Body considered whether to distinguish from the perspective of CTH between asbestos-containing fibers and cement, and corresponding asbestos-free alternatives. From its reasoning followed significant confusion. On the one side, it underlined that "we do *not wish to speculate* on what the evidence regarding these consumers would have indicated"; on the other side, in the absence of any evidence at all, it concluded: "we *are also persuaded* that evidence relating to consumers' tastes and habits *would establish* that [health risks] influence consumers' behaviour."[137] Without any evidence on actual CTH at hand, the

[133] Appellate Body Report, *EC – Asbestos*, *supra*, Ch. 2, fn. 70, para. 117: "Evidence about the extent to which products can serve the same end-uses, and the extent to which consumers are – or would be – willing to choose one product instead of another to perform those end-uses, is highly relevant evidence in assessing the 'likeness' of those products under Article III:4 of the GATT 1994."

[134] Panel Report, *Mexico – Soft Drinks*, *supra*, Ch. 2, fn. 80, paras. 8.34, 8.72–8.74.

[135] Panel Report, *Philippines – Distilled Spirits*, *supra*, Introduction, fn. 23, paras. 7.50, 7.62.

[136] Appellate Body Report, *EC – Asbestos*, *supra*, Ch. 2, fn. 70, para. 139.

[137] Appellate Body Report, *EC – Asbestos*, *supra*, Ch. 2, fn. 70, para. 122 (emphasis added).

Appellate Body in fact based its conclusion solely on its own subjective convictions and speculations on how immediate and final consumers would, or ideally should, behave:

> A manufacturer cannot, for instance, ignore the preferences of the ultimate consumer of its products. If the risks posed by a particular product are sufficiently great, the ultimate consumer *may* simply cease to buy that product. This *would*, undoubtedly, affect a manufacturer's decisions in the marketplace. Moreover, in the case of products posing risks to human health, *we think it likely* that manufacturers' decisions will be influenced by other factors, such as the potential civil liability that might flow from marketing products posing a health risk to the ultimate consumer, or the additional costs associated with safety procedures required to use such products in the manufacturing process.[138]

The standard that the adjudicators applied for the analysis of CTH was whether the products would be substitutable in an "idealized" or "stylized" marketplace.[139] The analysis discloses "a sort of Alice-in-Wonderland view of the case" which is "based on a simplistic belief in the working of the market."[140] It presupposes that factors such as health risk, potential civil liability, or additional costs associated with safety procedures would deter customers from buying asbestos-containing products for which reason they are not substitutable with asbestos-free products. It also assumes fully informed, rational, and reasonable intermediate and final customers. But whether such hypothesized consumer behavior corresponds to the economic realities of the market is highly doubtful. In contrast to the Appellate Body's argument that there is no demand for asbestos for reasons of health risk, it is difficult to understand the ban unless intermediate and final consumers in fact treat asbestos-containing and non-asbestos products as substitutes. Moreover, in the real world marketplace with all its information asymmetries and imperfections, consumers may be willing to buy asbestos-containing products because of a lack of information as to its health risk, a conscious disregard of the danger, or for the reason

[138] Appellate Body Report, *EC – Asbestos*, *supra*, Ch. 2, fn. 70, para. 122 (emphasis added).

[139] Howse and Tuerk, "The WTO Impact on Internal Regulations: A Case Study of the *Canada – EC Asbestos* Dispute," in de Búrca and Scott (eds.), *The EU and the WTO: Legal and Constitutional Issues*, pp. 283, 301 (2001); Quick and Lau, "Environmentally Motivated Tax Distinctions and WTO Law," *Journal of International Economic Law*, 6 (2003), 419, 432.

[140] Respectively, Regan, "Regulatory Purpose and 'Like Products' in Article III:4 of the GATT (With Additional Remarks on Article III:2)," p. 466; Horn and Weiler, "EC – Asbestos European Communities: Measures Affecting Asbestos and Asbestos-Containing Products," *World Trade Review*, 3 (2004), 129, 149.

of collective action problems and the resulting prisoner's dilemma situation – in particular, where, as in the case of asbestos, negative externalities associated with the hazardous material have not to some extent been internalized.[141] For these reasons, stylized actions of economic actors do not necessarily comport with the actual behavior of market participants. In applying their intuition regarding the behavior of intermediate and final customers, the adjudicators are effectively doing nothing more than applying – more or less educated – guesswork about market participants' reactions. This is why, in practice, the application of the CTH criterion has been to abstract from what the adjudicators may perceive as real world minutiae. It follows that the test for likeness under the rubric of CTH remained in the marketplace, in name only, since there was no real world – in particular empirical, or otherwise economically founded – evidence of consumers' actually existing preferences. The Appellate Body *de facto* adopted a reasonable consumer test, speculating on their reactions in case of symmetry of information.

The recent case law provides an incoherent picture of how CTH are applied. The case subsequent to *EC – Asbestos*, *Dominican Republic – Cigarettes*, did not mention CTH at all. Also the assessment under *Brazil – Retreaded Tyres* was limited to the statement that there was "no evidence of any difference in consumers' perceptions and behaviour in respect of imported and domestic retreaded tyres."[142] The Panel in *Mexico – Soft Drinks* was more elaborate in its examination of CTH, but equally ambiguous. On the one hand, the Panel proceeded under the CTH criterion to proxy consumer perceptions by indistinguishable physical and other attributes, such as taste, smell, color, labeling, and marketing.[143] On the other hand, it assessed CTH by inquiring into actual market data from market studies based on actual sales data and by referring to market surveys and actual customer taste tests.[144] In the most recent Article III:2 cases, *Thailand – Cigarettes* and *Philippines – Distilled Spirits*, the

[141] As Trebilcock and Giri, "The National Treatment Principle in International Trade Law," p. 222, explained, the collective action problem arises from "the perceived futility of foregoing purchase of an otherwise better [i.e., non-hazardous] product if other consumers will seek to free ride on the self-sacrificing decisions of others."

[142] Panel Report, *Brazil – Retreaded Tyres*, *supra*, fn. 80, para. 7.415.

[143] Panel Report, *Mexico – Soft Drinks*, *supra*, Ch. 2, fn. 80, paras. 8.34, 8.134 (regarding the likeness of different types of sweeteners and the likeness of soft drinks and syrup), para. 8.74 (regarding the DCS relationship between different types of sweeteners assessed under CTH from the final consumer perspective).

[144] Panel Report, *Mexico – Soft Drinks*, *supra*, Ch. 2, fn. 80, paras. 8.72–8.73 (regarding the DCS relationship between different types of sweeteners assessed under CTH from the

Panels have, quite surprisingly in fact, engaged again in an economic and quantitative analysis under the criterion of CTH.[145] For the moment at least it appears that the Panels have moved away from assessing CTH in a non-economic manner, that is, in an idealized setting or abstractly from actual marketplace evidence, and have embraced an assessment of CTH in accordance with the proper economic realities.

B Other non-economic approaches

This section will give a brief account of other non-economic approaches to market definition developed in WTO/GATT law, but which have not prevailed in dispute settlement jurisprudence. Especially the choice between the *Border Tax* approach and the "aims-and-effects" theory as one of the competing non-economic approaches has been at the core of the "like" product controversy in jurisprudence and scholarship. The battles around these approaches have been fought in great detail. However, they are set aside here. As the objective of this study is to develop an economic approach, it does not take a position from a policy or hermeneutic perspective on which among the non-economic approaches is more convincing. Instead, the aim of presenting these alternatives to the *Border Tax* criteria is simply to show how the dispute settlement bodies have struggled with different non-economic approaches.

(i) The aims-and-effects test

To understand the first alternative approach, it is important to recall that market definition under Article III of the GATT rises to become a problem only when an origin-neutral measure is contested and, thus, where a claim of *de facto* discrimination is made. It has also been pointed to the issue of whether any type of *de facto* discrimination with an (objectively assessed) disparate impact on the foreign product would then come under the purview of Article III of the GATT. Alternatively, only cases of malign discrimination could be caught by the provision, discarding benign discrimination which only incidentally impacts on foreign products. Which path is taken has important policy repercussions. Either it ensures greatest effectiveness of the NT obligation by capturing all measures with

immediate consumer, i.e., industrial producer, perspective), para. 8.134 (regarding the likeness of soft drinks and syrup).

[145] Panel Report, *Thailand – Cigarettes, supra*, Introduction, fn. 23, paras. 7.442–7.451; Panel Report, *Philippines – Distilled Spirits, supra*, Introduction, fn. 23, paras. 7.52–7.57, 7.104–7.112.

an objectively ascertainable discriminatory effect, or it affords greater regulatory autonomy by excluding from the scope of application *bona fide* measures with an unintended protectionist effect. Against this background, the "like" product issue is not only a matter of differences in legal interpretation, but it enters the more fundamental realm of democratic regulatory autonomy, and political and socioeconomic value choices and identity.[146] It is hence at the core of normative tension between the multilateral framework for disciplining protectionism and the sovereignty to determine domestic policy choices.

Most commentators agree that "regulatory purpose" *should* be accounted for in Article III analysis.[147] But the question arises as to *how* it should flow into the analysis. This is where the controversy is sparked. Many competing approaches at different analytical steps have been proposed. There are at least four occasions where a Panel could incorporate the consideration of the regulatory purpose of a measure in the different principal operative provisions of Article III of the GATT: (1) it can be considered in comparing the products themselves, that is, within the likeness or DCS test; (2) or in the assessment of the SATAP criterion, at least under Article III:2(2) of the GATT, where it is indisputably a separate self-standing substantive element; (3) or in comparing the treatment of the products, as in the "less favorable treatment" element of Article III:4 of the GATT; (4) or, lastly, in applying the justification under Article XX of the GATT. For compounding further complication, regulatory purpose can operate in two ways: it can be considered in subjective terms, when looking at the protective intent of a measure; or in objective terms, when inquiring into the protective application of a measure.

The most widely discussed approach is a subjective approach to the definition of likeness and DCS. Here, exclusive focus will be on the role of regulatory purpose in this particular context. The issue of whether regulatory purpose could, or should, be taken into account at a different stage of the analysis is set aside and goes unresolved for the purpose of this study. In the context of "like" or DCS products, the debate has mainly crystallized two schools of thought. On the one hand, there are those who posit that likeness and DCS should be determined solely on the basis of the traditional criteria – while not necessarily ruling out regulatory purpose

[146] See, e.g., Horn and Weiler, "EC – Asbestos European Communities: Measures Affecting Asbestos and Asbestos-Containing Products," pp. 141–145.

[147] For the terminology of a "regulatory purpose" approach see, e.g., Trebilcock and Howse, *The Regulation of International Trade*, p. 109.

coming into the analysis at a later stage, in particular, in the context of determining the measure's protective nature.[148] On the other hand, are those who take the view that a determination of likeness or DCS should take into account – exclusively or in addition to the traditional criteria – regulatory objectives of the measure at hand.[149]

The latter school has become known as the "aims-and-effects" theory. It temporarily gained momentum under GATT 1947 during the early 1990s, when two GATT Panel Reports endorsed this approach.[150] Under this interpretative tenet, products would be considered "like" each other only if the purpose and effect of the challenged governmental measure was to afford protection to the domestic product. If the distinction between the products was made in pursuit of legitimate, non-protectionist domestic policy goals, the "aims" prong of the test would not be satisfied and the products would not be "like" each other. For its proponents, the attraction of this test lies in allowing for more legitimate domestic policies and, therefore, in enhancing the regulatory autonomy of WTO Members by rendering products "unlike" or not DCS. In contrast, Article XX of the GATT is considered to allow for too limited a number of legitimate policy goals by imposing an overly harsh burden on the regulating party (because certain exceptions require meeting a necessity test).

[148] For example, Horn and Mavroidis, "Still Hazy after all These Years," pp. 39–69, argue for an economics-based market definition and want to account for regulatory purpose under the SATAP element. Similarly, Choi, "Overcoming the 'Aim and Effect' Theory: Interpretation of the 'Like Product' in GATT Article III," *UC Davis Journal of International Law & Policy*, 8 (2002), 107–131; Ortino, *Basic Legal Instruments for the Liberalisation of Trade: A Comparative Analysis of EC and WTO Law*, p. 313 (2004). See also against regulatory purpose Davey and Pauwelyn, "MFN Unconditionality," p. 38 as well as Trebilcock and Giri, "The National Treatment Principle in International Trade Law," pp. 223–224.

[149] For example, Fauchald, *Environmental Taxes and Trade Discrimination*, p. 143; Hudec, "GATT/WTO Constraints on National Regulation: Requiem for an 'Aim and Effects' Test," pp. 619–648; Wille, "Recapturing a Lost Opportunity: Article III:2 GATT 1994 Japan – Alcoholic Beverages 1996," *European Journal of International Law*, 9 (1998), 4, available at: http://207.57.19.226/journal/Vol9/No1/sr1b.html; Tsai, "'Like' is a Four-Letter Word: GATT Article III's 'Like Product' Conundrum," pp. 28, 45; Regan, "Regulatory Purpose and 'Like Products' in Article III:4 of the GATT (With Additional Remarks on Article III:2)," pp. 443–478; Roessler, "Beyond the Ostensible: A Tribute to Professor Robert Hudec's Insights on the Determination of the Likeness of Products Under the National Treatment Provisions of the General Agreement on Tariffs and Trade," *Journal of World Trade*, 37 (2003), 771–781.

[150] GATT Panel Report, *United States – Measures Affecting Alcoholic and Malt Beverages*, BISD 39S/206, adopted June 19, 1992, paras. 5.25 *et seq.*, 5.71 *et seq.* and GATT Panel Report, *United States – Taxes on Automobiles*, *supra*, Ch. 2, fn. 84, paras. 5.17 *et seq.*

Due to its heavy reliance on the subjective factor of "aim," this test has been dubbed as the "subjective approach" to the interpretation of likeness. Notably, it has the feature that it does not attempt to define likeness *a priori*; rather, it allows any distinction to be made between products on non-protectionist domestic policy grounds – even if the products are in an intensive competitive relationship with each other.[151] Importantly for this study, where only policy and not market-based factors tip the scales, the approach can arguably be termed an "anti-economic approach" to market definition.[152]

The doctrinal difference in approaches has its roots in a fundamentally different understanding of Article III:1 of the GATT. The proponents of the aims-and-effects test argue that the ordinary meaning of the phrase SATAP in Article III:1 of the GATT is directed at purposeful protection, for which reason a measure is applied "so as to afford protection to domestic production" if, and only if, it is designed with protectionist intention.[153] Since Article III:1 of the GATT informs the rest of the paragraphs, a measure falling under any of its alternatives must meet this regulatory purpose test.

The Appellate Body's understanding of SATAP is diametrically opposed to the subjective interpretation. As it will be discussed below, it took the Chapeau's phrase as the basis for an objective approach based on the "competitive relationship in the marketplace" paradigm.[154] For the moment, however, it suffices to say that, after the aims-and-effects test figured in two Panel Reports, subsequent Panels and the Appellate Body made various objections.[155] First, the test was based on the words SATAP contained in Article III:1 of the GATT. Yet Articles III:2(1) and III:4 of the GATT make no reference to those words, thus lacking a textual basis for the test. Second, the burden of proof, normally on the defendant invoking Article XX policy exceptions, would be shifted to the complainant, who would now not only have to establish the discriminatory effect, but also a discriminatory aim. Third, in the regular case of multiple aims of a policy measure, it would be a difficult endeavor to determine which aim

[151] This is why for Regan, "Further Thoughts on the Role of Regulatory Purpose Under Article III of the GATT: A Tribute to Bob Hudec," *Journal of World Trade*, 37 (2003), 737, 750, the competitive relationship between the products is a necessary, but not by itself sufficient, condition for likeness.

[152] Choi, *"Like Products" in International Trade Law*, p. 82.

[153] See, e.g., Regan, "Regulatory Purpose and 'Like Products' in Article III:4 of the GATT (With Additional Remarks on Article III:2)," pp. 443–478.

[154] See *infra*, fn. 189.

[155] See Panel Report, *Japan – Alcoholic Beverages II*, *supra*, fn. 73, paras. 4.16, 6.17.

or aims should be determinative for the application of the test. Fourth, access to the legislative history necessary to establish a discriminatory aim could be difficult or impossible for the complainant. And, finally, the exhaustive list of general exceptions contained in Article XX of the GATT would become redundant and the strict requirements of the Chapeau of that Article circumvented by introducing additional, not multilaterally agreed upon exceptions not envisaged by Article XX. The dispute settlement bodies therefore quickly rejected the aims-and-effects test – at least under the likeness and DCS inquiry.[156] Some commentators consider that this has not been an outright rejection of the aims-and-effects test. They argue that the subjective approach has been transferred in recent case law from the likeness issue to the interpretation of SATAP, or that of "less favorable treatment."[157] For the present purpose of the definition of likeness and DCS, however, this can be left open.

(ii) Process- and production-based methods

Besides aims-and-effects, in the case of *de facto* discrimination the question has also been raised as to whether differences in process and production methods of products (commonly referred to under the acronym "PPMs") could be sufficient to consider otherwise "like" or DCS products as unlike or not in a DCS relationship.[158] This is particularly relevant

[156] Rejecting the aims-and-effects test in the context of Article III:2 Panel Report, *Japan – Alcoholic Beverages II, supra*, fn. 73, paras. 6.15 *et seq.*, confirmed by Appellate Body Report, *Japan – Alcoholic Beverages II, supra*, Introduction, fn. 15, at 19, 27–29. See also for a general rejection Appellate Body Report, *EC – Bananas III, supra*, Ch. 2, fn. 81, para. 241.

[157] See, e.g., Hudec, "GATT/WTO Constraints on National Regulation: Requiem for an 'Aim and Effects' Test," pp. 629–633; Howse and Regan, "The Product/Process Distinction: An Illusory Basis for Disciplining 'Unilateralism' in Trade Policy," pp. 264–266; Slotboom, "Do Different Treaty Purposes Matter? The Elimination of Discriminatory Internal Taxes in EC and WTO Law," *Journal of International Economic Law*, 4 (2001), 557, 575; Howse, "The Appellate Body Rulings in the Shrimp/Turtle Case: A New Legal Baseline for the Trade and Environment Debate," *Columbia Journal of Environmental Law*, 27 (2002), 491, 515; Verhoosel, *National Treatment and WTO Dispute Settlement: Adjudicating the Boundaries of Regulatory Autonomy*, pp. 52–64 (2002); Porges and Trachtman, "Robert Hudec and Domestic Regulation: The Resurrection of Aim and Effects," *Journal of World Trade*, 37 (2003), 783, 796; DiMascio and Pauwelyn, "Nondiscrimination and Investment Treaties: Worlds Apart or Two Sides of the Same Coin?," p. 65. In any case, the Appellate Body seems to have adopted an objective regulatory purpose test under the rubric of SATAP, which inquires into whether the application of the measure, that is, its design, architecture, and revealing structure, exhibits protectionist intent.

[158] The issues around PPMs go far beyond the problem of product comparison; see, e.g., Stepkowska, "Process and Production Methods (PPMs) in the GATT Agreement,"

for the question of whether physically identical but differently produced products can be treated differently under Article III of the GATT; for example, in cases where a domestic product is produced in an environmentally friendly way, whereas the imported product is not. The PPM test for likeness, therefore, does not refer to the comparison of the products themselves, but to the comparison of their production methods. Products with differences in the production process are not considered "like" or DCS, regardless of the intensity of the competitive relationship. This also amounts to a non-economic approach.

The dispute settlement bodies have held that PPMs are simply not covered by Article III of the GATT, and are thus not an issue of product comparison.[159] The reason is that one has to distinguish between the product "as such" and the production method. Article III of the GATT, mentioning "products" only, is confined to "measures affecting products as such."[160] In contrast, the provision does not speak of production methods and PPMs are not considered to affect products as such. Beyond the reasoning of the dispute settlement bodies, and on a more fundamental level, a PPM test for product comparison would be incompatible with the theory of comparative advantage. In many cases, comparative advantages will in fact stem from differences in PPMs. Making these differences the legitimate object of distinctions in treatment would undermine the driving economic rationale for international trade.

Against this backdrop, only characteristics that directly affect the product can be a basis for product comparison. This, however, does not exclude PPMs from entering the analysis of product likeness.[161] Actually, PPMs

Zeitschrift für europarechtliche Studien, (2007), 273–329. For PPMs to be considered in the likeness test, e.g., Howse and Regan, "The Product/Process Distinction: An Illusory Basis for Disciplining 'Unilateralism' in Trade Policy," pp. 249–289; Jackson, "Comments on Shrimp/Turtle and the Product/Process Distinction," *European Journal of International Law*, 11 (2000), 291–307; Bogdandy, "Verfassungsrechtliche Dimensionen der Welthandelsorganisation – 2. Teil: Neue Wege globaler Demokratie?," *Kritische Justiz*, (2001), 425, 434. *Contra*, e.g., Berrisch, "Das Allgemeine Zoll- und Handelsabkommen (GATT 1994)," in Prieß *et al.* (eds.), *WTO-Handbuch*, para. 44 (2003).

159 GATT Panel Report, *United States – Restrictions on Imports of Tuna (Tuna I)*, BISD 39S/155, circulated September 3, 1991, unadopted, paras. 5.11–5.14. The issue of measures based on PPMs was remitted to the prohibition of quantitative restrictions pursuant to Article XI of the GATT.

160 GATT Panel Report, *United States – Restrictions on Imports of Tuna (Tuna I)*, para. 5.11.

161 Panel Report, *Japan – Alcoholic Beverages I*, *supra*, Ch. 2, fn. 65, para. 5.7 ("'likeness' of products must be examined taking into account not only objective criteria (such as

have already played a role in the application of the traditional criteria. In particular, they can be seen as forming part of the wider category of physical characteristics. In this context, PPMs have been taken into account to the extent to which they are reflected in varying physical characteristics of the products. In both *Korea – Alcoholic Beverages* and *Chile – Alcoholic Beverages*, for example, the Panels examined the impact that differences in production methods had on the degree of physical similarity of products.[162] The Panel in *Philippines – Distilled Spirits* made clear, however, that production processes that do not result in the final products being different cannot be relevant to the inquiry into product "likeness."[163]

II THE ECONOMIC APPROACH

For both antitrust and international trade law, the economic market definition paradigm has the great virtue of focusing market definition on the underlying issue of interest, the identification of market power and of protectionism, respectively.

This section will outline the emergence of the general economic framework to antitrust market definition that has to be accredited to the enforcement agencies in the United States incorporating economic thinking into the legal exercise of market definition. In the application of this economic approach, recent case law has in practice moved significantly toward a more economics-based approach. Examples of the specific case law will be addressed at a later stage when addressing quantitative methods in more detail.

This section also shows that several Panels from 1996 to 2000 pushed the economic approach in GATT. This was nothing short of revolutionary. Yet dispute settlement bodies never conceptualized the approach into a coherent methodology – something to be undertaken later in this study. In 2000, the interpretative approach in WTO dispute settlement jurisprudence changed again. There was a backlash from a market-based approach to yet again a rather abstract and market-detached analysis of

composition and *manufacturing processes of products*) but also the more subjective consumers' viewpoint." (emphasis added)).

162 Panel Report, *Korea – Alcoholic Beverages, supra*, Introduction, fn. 36, para. 10.67 ("the differences due to filtration or aging processes of the beverages described are not so important as to render the products non-substitutable"); similarly, Panel Report, *Chile – Alcoholic Beverages, supra*, Ch. 2, fn. 68, para. 7.54.

163 Panel Report, *Philippines – Distilled Spirits, supra*, Introduction, fn. 23, para. 7.37.

the *Border Tax* criteria. In fact, while on the surface asserting the "competitive relationship in the marketplace" as the relevant standard, the Panels in actuality seemed content rigidly applying the *Border Tax* criteria in an approach that is neither embedded in an overall economic framework, nor has the goal of ascertaining the competitive relationship in the marketplace. Against the most recent developments in case law, however, the few cases adopting an economic approach now need not to be seen as aberrant market definition cases. *Thailand – Cigarettes* and *Philippines – Distilled Spirits* reflect a pragmatic approach of the Panels. Leaving the question of a sound conceptual framework based on economics aside, they employed the traditional criteria as well as quantitative methods.

1 Antitrust law

A US antitrust law

Though legal and economic analysis had already been closely intertwined in the United States, a watershed for market definition came in 1982, when the DoJ released drastically revised *Merger Guidelines*.[164] In those *Guidelines*, the two conventional formalistic strands of market definition developed by the judiciary were complemented by a more economic one proposed by the DoJ. Later, the *1992 Merger Guidelines* enshrined this approach – which, eventually, would to a large extent supersede the traditional one.

As the major theoretical contribution to market analysis, the *1982 Merger Guidelines* pioneered a new market definition paradigm by formally defining a product market as "a group of products such that a hypothetical firm that was the only present and future seller of those products could raise price profitably."[165] Elaborating on this test, the *1992 Merger Guidelines* define a relevant market as:

> a product or group of products and a geographic area in which it is produced or sold such that a hypothetical profit-maximizing firm, not subject to price regulation, that was the only present and future producer or seller of those products in that area likely would impose at least a "small but significant and non-transitory" increase in price, assuming the terms of sale of all other products are held constant. A relevant market is a group of products and geographic area that is no bigger than necessary to satisfy this test.[166]

[164] See *supra*, Ch. 2, fn. 28. [165] *1982 Merger Guidelines*, para. II. A.

[166] *1992 Merger Guidelines*, para. 1.0. See also the most recently revised version *2010 Merger Guidelines*, at 8–9.

According to the formulation in both extracts, this new approach has become known as the SSNIP test (acronym for "small but significant and non-transitory increase in price"), or "hypothetical monopolist test." In the United States, courts have usually insisted that they are not bound by the *Merger Guidelines*, but then regularly proceeded to endorse or apply the hypothetical monopolist paradigm.[167]

Under this "thought experiment"[168] the relevant market in its product and geographic scope is defined by the smallest set of products and geographic areas for which a SSNIP by 5–10 percent would be profitable for a hypothetical monopolist.[169] With regard to the product market dimension at issue here, the exercise proceeds in stages. The test begins with the smallest set of products (smallest market principle), usually the products of the type supplied by the firm(s) under investigation, for example, in the case of a merger the products of the merging entities. Then, the test asks whether a hypothetical monopolist with control over these products would be able to profitably raise the prices of those products significantly and permanently, that is, by 5–10 percent for the duration of approximately one year, assuming that the prices of all other products remain constant. If demand or supply substitution to the next best substitute makes a SSNIP unprofitable, the candidate market should not be considered the relevant market.[170] The basket of products is enlarged until a product is found with regard to which demand or supply substitution is so low as to make a SSNIP profitable. Importantly, this is equivalent to defining a relevant market as one in which market power can be exercised or enhanced. The SSNIP test identifies the smallest group of sellers who could exercise such power, or in other commonly used words, it defines a market as the smallest set of products worth monopolizing.[171]

[167] For references to the extensive US case law see Werden, "The 1992 Merger Guidelines and the Ascent of the Hypothetical Monopolist Paradigm," *Antitrust Law*, 71 (2003), 253, 263 fn. 37, 270–275.

[168] O'Donoghue and Padilla, *The Law and Economics of Article 82 EC*, p. 77 (2006); Hildebrand, *The Role of Economic Analysis in the EC Competition Rules*, p. 407 (2009) ("mental experiment").

[169] *Commission Notice on market definition*, paras. 15–19. For a more correct reformulation of the test see Werden, "Market Delineation and the Justice Department's Merger Guidelines," *Duke Law Journal*, (1983), 514, 542–545; ten Kate and Niels, "The Relevant Market: A Concept Still in Search of a Definition," *Journal of Competition Law & Economics*, 5 (2008), 297, 304.

[170] See *infra*, Ch. 5, fn. 152 on the importance of cost analysis in the assessment of profitability. For the (limited) role of supply-side substitution see *infra*, Ch. 4, fn. 67.

[171] Office of Fair Trading, *The Role of Market Definition in Monopoly and Dominance Inquiries*, para. 2.11 (2001), available at: www.oft.gov.uk/shared_oft/reports/

Setting the appropriate level for the requisite price increase is a difficult task. The range of 5–10 percent for around one year has become the usually adopted quantum, although it is inherently arbitrary. Yet these benchmarks are set on a normative judgment, according to which a price increase of this magnitude would be deemed unacceptable from a policy perspective.

B EU antitrust law

The infiltration of economic insights into EU antitrust law, and market definition in particular, took place with some delay in comparison with US antitrust law. In 1997, the European Commission published its Notice on market definition, which "tries to set out in coherent, readable fashion the economic principles on which the Commission bases its approach to the definition of relevant markets."[172] It provides guidelines for market definition in all areas of EU antitrust law, that is, Articles 101 and 102 TFEU and merger control. The *Commission Notice on market definition* borrowed heavily from the *1982* and *1992 Merger Guidelines* by introducing the SSNIP test as the common standard for defining relevant markets. In so doing, the Notice endorsed an economic approach toward the problem of how to delineate antitrust markets.[173] The hypothetical monopolist test has been fully acknowledged in Europe – if not yet fully embraced. The Notice does not reference the SSNIP test in articulating the conceptual definition of a market. Instead, as it has already been seen, it retains the functional interchangeability language and incorporates the traditional legal definition of the relevant market.[174] This "leaves the impression of new [economic] theories and techniques being injected into an orthodox legal straitjacket."[175]

comp_policy/oft342.pdf; Bishop and Baldauf, *Theoretische Grundlagen und praktische Anwendung wettbewerbsökonomischer Methoden in Bezug auf die Abgrenzung des relevanten Marktes und Fragen zur praktischen Anwendbarkeit des Herfindahl-Hirschman Indexes zur Ermittlung des Konzentrationsgrades*, (2006), p. 9, available at: www.bwb.gv.at/NR/rdonlyres/312D10EA-6476-4932-AFED-6280A0563C3C/28106/MarktabgrenzungrbbStudiefinal.pdf.

172 European Commission, *XXVIIth Report on Competition Policy*, (1997), para. 44, available at: http://ec.europa.eu/competition/publications/annual_report/1997/broch97_en.pdf.

173 Bishop, "Editorial: The Modernisation of DGIV," *European Competition Law Review*, 8 (1997), 481, 481.

174 *Commission Notice on market definition*, paras. 7, 8.

175 Camesasca and van den Bergh, "Achilles Uncovered: Revisiting the European Commission's 1997 Market Definition Notice," *Antitrust Bulletin*, 47 (2002), 143, 156–157.

The *Commission Notice on market definition* is mere "soft law." However, its considerable effect on case law comes from the weight of the decision-making practice of the European Commission and an increasing judicial awareness for economic reasoning since that time.[176] Even before the issuance of the Notice, there are instances in which EU case law experimented with the US approach. Several cases were clearly inspired by the *Merger Guidelines* when turning to an evaluation of how customers would react in response to a price increase.[177] The SSNIP test's European presence was therefore upstaged prior to its formalization in the Notice.

The SSNIP test is radically innovative in that it makes the critical connection between market delineation and market power – a link that the traditional approach had not made. By making the profitability of a price increase the yardstick, the SSNIP test ties the market definition exercise to the economic definition of market power, that is, the danger of persistent price increases above competitive levels. This examination is clearly different from the traditional legal approach, which seeks to define the relevant market on the basis of a comparison of characteristics of goods, but without ultimately being related to the identification of market power. The SSNIP methodology reflects the spreading view in the 1980s that market delineation must be based on the underlying concern with market power and thus with the ultimate goal of identifying market power – although the essential relationship between market delineation and market power had already been expressed by the US Supreme Court more than two decades before.[178]

[176] The ECJ in *Michelin I*, *supra*, fn. 38, para. 37, began extending the traditional market definition formula by stating that "an examination limited to the objective characteristics only of the relevant product cannot be sufficient: the competitive conditions and the structure of supply and demand on the market must also be taken into consideration." This was reiterated just before the publication of the *Commission Notice on market definition*, e.g., in Case T-83/91, *Tetra Pak* v. *Commission* [1994] ECR II-755, para. 63 (hereinafter *Tetra Pak* v. *Commission*) and Case T-504/93, *Tiercé Ladbroke* v. *Commission* [1997] ECR II-923, para. 81.

[177] Case IV/M.68, *Tetra Pak/Alfa-Laval* [1991] OJ L290 35, at IV.B.2.1(ii) (customer reaction "in the short to medium term in response to a small but significant price rise") and IV.B.2.2.2(ii) ("small but significant price increase"); *Nestlé/Perrier*, *supra*, fn. 51, para. 13 ("an appreciable, non-transitory increase in the price"); Case IV/M.214, *DuPont/ICI* [1993] OJ L13 7, para. 23 ("possibility to react to, for example, a significant increase in the price of one product by switching to the other products in a relatively short period of time"); Case IV/M.774, *Saint-Gobain/Wacker-Chemie/NOM* [1997] OJ L247 1, paras. 66, 220, 236 ("small but significant price increase").

[178] See *supra*, Ch. 2, fn. 28.

For the remainder of this book, it is important to underscore that the SSNIP test is neither a test in itself nor an operational technique. Preferably, it may be understood as a coherent conceptual framework for designing the analysis required for market definition.[179] It permits rigorous consideration of the relevant issues by formulating the right questions. It must be recognized that the test is formulated in a quantitative way, as it is phrased in terms of the magnitude of a profitable price increase that would be imposed by a hypothetical monopolist. But it should not be reduced to a mere arithmetic problem.[180] On the one hand, it should not be misunderstood as a purely quantitative method or formal econometric test. For instance, the SSNIP test does not require the calculation of the elasticity of demand based on an econometric analysis in each and every case. On the other hand, it should also not be confounded as a pure price test which does not take account of non-price elements of competition such as physical characteristics and intended use.[181] The SSNIP test does not predetermine what kind of evidence has to be adduced in order to satisfy the "thought experiment." Within the SSNIP test, quantitative as well as qualitative tests can be employed to address the market definition question. This is because customer reactions to a hypothetical price increase will depend not only on the "naked" price of a product, but also on its quality, service, and other factors.[182] If the price of a product rises, the customers will have to judge whether they accept this price given the quality of the product, service, the intended use, etc. Non-price elements are therefore implicitly included in the hypothetical monopolist test.

A merely "quantitative" or purely price-oriented interpretation of the SSNIP test would also not seem to have been the intention of the drafters of the *Merger Guidelines* or the *Commission Notice on market definition*. Many of the factors used to determine if switching occurs are conventional. With respect to product market definition, the *1982*

[179] van den Bergh and Camesasca, *European Competition Law and Economics*, p. 131; Faull and Nikpay, *The EC Law of Competition*, para. 1.147; Alese, *Federal Antitrust and EC Competition Law Analysis*, p. 184 (2008); Lücking and Simon, "Definition of the Relevant Market," para. 3.40. Jones and Sufrin, *EC Competition Law*, p. 361 (2008), seem to have a different understanding, contrasting the SSNIP test and qualitative assessments for market definition.

[180] Roth and Ackermann, "Grundfragen Art. 81 Abs. 1," in Jaeger *et al.* (eds.), *Frankfurter Kommentar zum Kartellrecht, Band II*, para. 375 (2009).

[181] For such erroneous criticism see, e.g., Baron, "Artikel 2 FKVO," in Bunte (ed.), *Langen & Bunte: Kommentar zum deutschen und europäischen Kartellrecht – Band 2 Europäisches Kartellrecht* at Art. 2 FKVO, para. 20 (2006).

[182] Lücking and Simon, "Definition of the Relevant Market," para. 3.40.

Merger Guidelines give weight to buyers' perceptions, similarities or differences between the products in customary usage, design, physical composition, and other technical characteristics, price movements, and evidence of sellers' perceptions.[183] Equally, in the *Commission Notice on market definition*, the SSNIP test is not presented in the context of the criteria and types of evidence for market delineation, but as a more general framework for the assessment of demand substitution. The Notice does not relinquish traditional considerations from the market definition exercise. Functional interchangeability considerations are intertwined in textual layout of the Notice, and the analysis of physical characteristics and intended use is retained as a "first step."[184] But the *Commission Notice on market definition* goes well beyond the simplistic analysis of product attributes, intended use, and customers' views, on which market definition was based up to that point. It cites a large array of evidence and more sophisticated analytical – yet from the point of view of contemporary economic practice rudimentary and incomplete[185] – measures valuable to market delineation, some of which will be looked at more closely below.

Overall, it is important for the following to emphasize that, conceptually, the economic calibration of the market definition exercise is twofold. First, the *1982 Merger Guidelines* and the *Commission Notice on market definition* introduced an economically sound general analytical framework by way of the SSNIP test, which by now has been adopted around the world.[186] Second, it introduced quantitative techniques to implement this economic approach. This second level of economic penetration of the market definition exercise will be addressed more closely below.

2 Article III of the GATT

A A market-based approach

The 1990s not only seemed to call for a more economics-based approach to market definition in EU antitrust law, but also to product comparison

183 *1982 Merger Guidelines*, at II.A. Note, however, that those criteria have not been kept under the *1992* and *2010 Merger Guidelines*.

184 *Commission Notice on market definition*, paras. 7, 8, 28, 36.

185 Coppi and Walker, "Substantial Convergence or Parallel Paths? Similarities and Differences in the Economic Analysis of Horizontal Mergers in US and EU Competition Law," *Antitrust Bulletin*, 49 (2004), 101, 108–109.

186 The latest instance is China, which adopted the hypothetical monopolist test in Articles 7 and 10 of the Ministry of Commerce of the People's Republic of China (MOFCOM) Guidelines for the Definition of the Relevant Market (2009) (unofficial translation available at: www.mwechinalaw.com/news/2009/guidelines_0709.html).

in Article III of the GATT under the newly founded WTO. While until then product comparison had been conducted as an issue of legal textual interpretation isolated from its teleological context (the aims-and-effects approach in the early 1990s was another example of an interpretative attempt to tie the market definition more closely to the *telos* of GATT), the case of *Japan – Alcoholic Beverages II* based the product comparison inquiry upon a new economic footing. The Panel in that case stated that "the appropriate test to define whether two products are 'like' or 'directly competitive or substitutable' is the market place"[187] – as "the forum where consumers choose between different products."[188] This approach was the result of an interpretation that now focused on the purpose of Article III of the GATT. It stressed that the antiprotectionist goal embodied in the "general principle" of the Chapeau in Article III:1 of the GATT. "Toward this end [of ruling out protectionism], Article III obliges Members of the WTO to provide equality of competitive conditions for imported products in relation to domestic products."[189] This was extended to encompass not only equal competitive conditions, but already the expectations of equal competitive relationships.[190] Given the objective of such comprehensive equality of competitive conditions, product comparison was now conceived as "fundamentally, a determination about the nature and extent of a competitive relationship between and among the products."[191] Since "the context of the competitive relationship is necessarily the market place,"[192] the interpretative principle connotes a relationship between the relevant products that can be essentially described as *in competition in the marketplace*. The Appellate Body recognized the *competitive relationship in the marketplace* as the uniformly "appropriate test" for all three non-discrimination obligations in Article III of the GATT. It was first

[187] Panel Report, *Japan -Alcoholic Beverages II*, *supra*, fn. 73, para. 6.22.

[188] Appellate Body Report, *Korea – Alcoholic Beverages*, *supra*, Ch. 2, fn. 71, para. 114.

[189] Appellate Body Report, *Japan – Alcoholic Beverages II*, *supra*, Introduction, fn. 15, at 16.

[190] Appellate Body Report, *Korea – Alcoholic Beverages*, *supra*, Ch. 2, fn. 71, para. 120 ("avoiding protectionism, requiring equality of competitive conditions and protecting expectations of equal competitive relationships"); see also the prior GATT Panel Report, *US – Superfund*, *supra*, fn. 95, para. 5.2.2 ("to protect expectations of the contracting parties as to the competitive relationship between their products and those of the other contracting parties … to protect current trade [and] also to create the predictability needed to plan future trade").

[191] Appellate Body Report, *EC – Asbestos*, *supra*, Ch. 2, fn. 70, para. 99 with regard to Article:4 of the GATT. While *EC – Asbestos* had still emphasized the distinction between Article III:4 and Article III:2 of the GATT, the Appellate Body has now extended this key passage to "likeness" under Article III:2 of the GATT, see Appellate Body Report, *Philippines – Distilled Spirits*, *supra*, Ch. 2, fn. 44, paras. 119 and 170.

[192] Appellate Body Report, *Korea – Alcoholic Beverages*, *supra*, Ch. 2, fn. 71, para. 114.

enunciated with regard to the definition of likeness and DCS in Article III:2 of the GATT in *Japan – Alcoholic Beverages II* remarking that the marketplace test "seems appropriate. The GATT 1994 is a commercial agreement, and the WTO is concerned, after all, with markets. It does not seem inappropriate to look at competition in the relevant markets."[193] It was then approved for Article III:4 in *EC – Asbestos* and, as it seems, even beyond that.[194] As it has been observed in the literature, the Appellate Body thus developed a "single notion" of a *competitive relationship in the marketplace* test, or in short "competition test," as the universal underpinning of any product comparability test.[195]

Yet the adjudicators have never given any concrete content to this test – a task that will be undertaken below. Taking this jurisprudence a little further doctrinally, the marketplace test can be construed as tying the Article III market definition more closely to the underlying aim of the provision, the identification of protectionism. It is submitted here that the economic approach to the product comparison of Article III of the GATT is best understood in an analogous way to the two-level significance of the economic approach to antitrust market definition. On the one hand, similar to the SSNIP test, it manifests itself as an overall conceptual framework in the form of the *competitive relationship in the marketplace* test. How to conceptualize this test will be addressed in detail below. On the other hand, within this general framework the economic approach addresses the way in which certain types of evidence (qualitative or quantitative) come into play. To generally trace the impact of the marketplace paradigm, its implementation on this second methodological level is addressed briefly, while a close scrutiny of how the dispute settlement bodies have dealt with quantitative methods will follow below.

[193] Appellate Body Report, *Japan – Alcoholic Beverages II, supra*, Introduction, fn. 15, at 25.

[194] Appellate Body Report, *EC – Asbestos, supra*, Ch. 2, fn. 70, para. 103. For what appears to be the same concept under the Agreement on Textiles and Clothing see Appellate Body Report, *US – Cotton Yarn, supra*, Ch. 2, fn. 61, paras. 95–98. But see the diverging rulings in Panel Report, *United States – Measures Affecting the Production and Sale of Clove Cigarettes* (hereinafter *US – Clove Cigarettes*), WT/DS406/R, circulated September 2, 2011, para. 7.99 and Panel Report, *United States – Measures Concerning the Importation, Marketing and Sale of Tuna and Tuna Products*, WT/DS381/R, circulated September 15, 2011, para. 7.225 on the "likeness" standard under Article 2.1 of the TBT Agreement.

[195] For the former citation Quick and Lau, "Environmentally Motivated Tax Distinctions and WTO Law," p. 429; for the latter, DiMascio and Pauwelyn, "Nondiscrimination and Investment Treaties: Worlds Apart or Two Sides of the Same Coin?," p. 79. See also Panel Report, *US – Clove Cigarettes, supra*, fn. 194, para. 7.99 ("competition-oriented approach").

At the outset, however, the Appellate Body appeared to be unaware of the above proposed conceptual distinction. Similarly, scholarship does not draw this distinction.[196] In *Japan – Alcoholic Beverages II* the Appellate Body still seemed to confuse both the conceptual and the implementing level, placing the marketplace test as an alternative alongside the other traditional *Border Tax* criteria.[197] In *EC – Asbestos*, the Appellate Body then implicitly adopted the above proposed understanding: distinguishing between the general requirement of an inquiry into the "competitive relationship in the marketplace," and the more concrete question of whether or not to apply the *Border Tax* criteria.[198] This was confirmed by the Panel in the case of *Mexico – Soft Drinks*.[199]

When outlining a marketplace test, one would expect a discussion of which criteria are relevant enough to shed light on the competitive relationship. Most surprisingly, this has not been discussed by dispute settlement bodies. All Panels continued to rely on the traditional criteria without questioning their relevance under the marketplace paradigm. The Appellate Body in *EC – Asbestos* even made their examination mandatory in each and every case irrespective of their probative value for the competitive relationship.[200] Only a very small number of Panels, which defined likeness and DCS more rigorously by reference to prevailing consumer perceptions in the marketplace, made additional use of economic

[196] Some consider the "marketplace" as an additional criterion to the traditional criteria, e.g., Hogg and Nawaz, "Japan – Alcoholic Beverages, Report of the Panel, 11 July 1996 and of the Appellate Body, 4 October 1996," in Cameron and Campbell (eds.), *Dispute Resolution in the World Trade Organisation*, pp. 343, 349 (1998).

[197] Appellate Body Report, *Japan – Alcoholic Beverages II*, *supra*, Introduction, fn. 15, at 25: "The Panel emphasized the need to look not only at such matters as physical characteristics, common end-uses, and tariff classifications, but also at the 'market place.'"

[198] Appellate Body Report, *EC – Asbestos*, *supra*, Ch. 2, fn. 70, para. 103: "We have noted that, under Article III:4 of the GATT 1994, the term 'like products' is concerned with competitive relationships between and among products. Accordingly, whether the Border Tax Adjustments framework is adopted or not, it is important under Article III:4 to take account of evidence which indicates whether, and to what extent, the products involved are – or could be – in a competitive relationship in the marketplace" (emphasis in original).

[199] Panel Report, *Mexico – Soft Drinks*, *supra*, Ch. 2, fn. 80, para. 8.68: "DCS connotes a relationship ... that can be essentially described as 'in competition' in the marketplace. In order to make this assessment, GATT and WTO bodies have examined the following factors: the competitive conditions between the products in the relevant market, in the light of the nature of both products, their physical characteristics, their common end-uses, consumers' perceptions and behaviour in respect of the products, and the products' tariff classifications."

[200] See *supra*, fn. 78.

and econometric evidence that parties had submitted to buttress their arguments for or against product comparability. The earliest – futile – attempt to select criteria of economic relevance was made in one of the first GATT 1947 cases, *EEC – Animal Feed Protein*.[201] But it was much later, in the 1990s, that dispute settlement bodies started to understand the concept of DCS as requiring "evidence that consumers consider or could consider the two products or groups of products as alternative ways of satisfying a particular need or taste."[202] From an antitrust point of view, it may seem logical to use established econometric methods to this end. Yet the only cases in WTO case law that touched on quantitative methods for product comparison were *Japan – Alcoholic Beverages II*, *Korea – Alcoholic Beverages*, *Chile – Alcoholic Beverages*, and, more than ten years later, *Thailand – Cigarettes* and *Philippines – Distilled Spirits*. While particularly *Korea – Alcoholic Beverages* embodied a simpler approach, more sophisticated and therefore more contested econometric analyses were introduced in *Japan – Alcoholic Beverages II* and *Chile – Alcoholic Beverages*. Those will be explored in greater detail below.

On these occasions, CPE of demand was a measure of substitutability introduced by the parties and which stirred much debate. It was endorsed by the dispute settlement bodies.[203] Yet quantitative methods were repeatedly seen only as one among a number of means for identifying "like" or DCS products and as such of only limited significance.[204] Moreover, the Appellate Body, in an awkward amalgam of economic (quantitative) concepts and legal (qualitative) analysis, underscored that focus should not be on the "quantity" of competition (as measured by a certain degree of substitutability or CPE), but on the "quality" or "nature" of competition.[205] Although it remains unclear how to determine the "nature" or

[201] The EEC's representative suggested that: "in his view, the concept of 'like product' was not based on purely legal criteria but should be determined case-by-case in a pragmatic manner, on the basis of criteria of an essentially economic character, such as the nature of the product, its intended use, commercial value and price, its character and substitutability. He maintained that price could be a fundamental criterion for the evaluation of what constituted a like product in the case of the EEC measures." GATT Panel Report, *EEC – Animal Feed*, *supra*, fn. 88, para. 3.4.

[202] Appellate Body Report, *Korea – Alcoholic Beverages*, *supra*, Ch. 2, fn. 71, para. 109.

[203] Appellate Body Report, *Japan – Alcoholic Beverages II*, *supra*, Introduction, fn. 15, at 25.

[204] See *infra*, Ch. 5, fn. 168.

[205] Appellate Body Report, *Korea – Alcoholic Beverages*, *supra*, Ch. 2, fn. 71, paras. 132–134; see also Howse and Tuerk, "The WTO Impact on Internal Regulations: A Case Study of the *Canada – EC Asbestos* Dispute," p. 297: "what is a [sic] stake is a contextual and qualitative judgment about competitive relationships, not merely the economic analysis of cross-elasticity of demand."

"quality" of a competitive relationship if not by quantification of substitutability, this points to the persisting rule of the qualitative over the quantitative approach. Yet in terms of quality and quantity, this thesis will argue that what is at stake is a qualitative judgment about competitive relationships, preferably, but not exclusively, on the basis of quantitative evidence.

Another example of a more economics-based approach in this period is the Appellate Body Report in *Canada – Periodicals*. While it ascertained the absence of likeness of "split run" and "non-split run" periodicals with reference to the *Border Tax* criteria, it did not refer to these criteria for the assessment under DCS. Under the latter rubric, it "found it appropriate to look at competition in the relevant markets."[206] To this end, it relied upon a report, based on a study by an economist, Leigh Anderson, which analyzed the competitive conditions with respect to price competition and to substitutability from the perspective of readers and advertising customers.[207]

Moreover, dispute settlement bodies in those instances also attempted to gear the traditional qualitative criteria toward elucidating current consumer perceptions in the marketplace. In this respect the Appellate Body emphasized the importance of both end-uses and CTH as highly relevant in the determination of a competitive relationship in the marketplace between products.[208] In particular, the focus under the end-uses criterion temporarily shifted from an abstract to a market-based one. This is already hinted at in the general observation that "'likeness' of products must be examined taking into account not only objective criteria … but also the more *subjective consumers' viewpoint* (such as consumption and *use by consumers*)."[209] Later, it was further refined in the statement that "the decisive criterion in order to determine whether two products are directly competitive or substitutable is whether they have common

[206] Appellate Body Report, *Canada – Periodicals*, *supra*, Ch. 2, fn. 50, at 25.

[207] Appellate Body Report, *Canada – Periodicals*, *supra*, Ch. 2, fn. 50, at 25–29.

[208] Appellate Body Report, *EC – Asbestos*, *supra*, Ch. 2, fn. 70, para. 117: "We note that these two criteria involve certain of the key elements relating to the competitive relationship between products: first, the extent to which products are capable of performing the same, or similar, functions (end-uses), and, second, the extent to which consumers are willing to use the products to perform these functions (consumers' tastes and habits). Evidence of this type is of particular importance under Article III of the GATT 1994, precisely because that provision is concerned with competitive relationships in the marketplace."

[209] GATT Panel Report, *Japan – Alcoholic Beverages I*, *supra*, Ch. 2, fn. 65, para. 5.7 (emphasis added).

end-uses, *inter alia*, as shown by elasticity of substitution."[210] However, the Panel did not find commonality in end-uses for vodka and shochu by actually inquiring into consumer perceptions. It proceeded to come to this conclusion by referring to the conclusions of *Japan – Alcoholic Beverages I* – which were the results of an abstract assessment. In the later *Chile – Alcoholic Beverages* case, the Panel reiterated the general principle that "the overall inquiry focuses on whether there are common end-uses by examining a number of factors which can include elasticity of substitution."[211] In that case, the subsequent examination of end-uses did then, in fact, revolve around the empirical analysis of substitutability.[212]

The dispute settlement bodies also directed the inquiry of physical characteristics from an abstract to a market-based assessment informative of consumer perceptions.[213] The Appellate Body stated in *EC – Asbestos* that "Panels must examine those physical properties of products that are likely to influence the competitive relationship between products in the marketplace."[214] Yet, as has already been outlined, the Appellate Body's assessment of physical characteristics confirms the persistence of the traditional approach in the concrete application of the criterion. It was a manifest contradiction that the Appellate Body directed, on the one hand, to strictly assess the competitive relationship and, on the other hand, to assess independently and separately each criterion.

This emphasizes the fact that the dispute settlement bodies never fully espoused an economic approach. Instead, they vacillated between two antagonistic positions, often within a single case. The economic approach has never received unanimous approval within the dispute settlement bodies; the primacy of the economic competitive relationships has been highly controversial in judgments. This is revealed in the concurring

[210] Appellate Body Report, *Japan – Alcoholic Beverages II, supra*, Introduction, fn. 15, para. 6.22.

[211] Panel Report, *Chile – Alcoholic Beverages, supra*, Ch. 2, fn. 68, para. 7.32.

[212] Panel Report, *Chile – Alcoholic Beverages, supra*, Ch. 2, fn. 68, paras. 7.31–7.47. But contrast Panel Report, *Korea – Alcoholic Beverages, supra*, Introduction, fn. 36, paras. 10.68–10.82, 10.87–10.94, where the analysis of end-uses was assessed objectively and empirical evidence was appraised under the separate rubric of "Prices."

[213] For the likeness definition under the SCM Agreement during the same period see Panel Report, *Indonesia – Autos, supra*, Ch. 2, fn. 92, para. 14.173: "Factors such as brand loyalty, brand image/reputation, status and resale value reflect, at least in part, an *assessment by purchasers* of the physical characteristics of the cars being purchased" and para. 14.176: "We must endeavour to find some reasonable way to assess the relative importance of the various differences *in the minds of consumers* and to devise some sensible means to categorize passenger cars" (emphases added).

[214] Appellate Body Report, *EC – Asbestos, supra*, Ch. 2, fn. 70, para. 114.

opinion in the Appellate Body Report in *EC – Asbestos*. The concurrence, a first in WTO/GATT case law, sharply criticized the other Appellate Body members' "conception of the 'fundamental,' perhaps decisive, role of economic competitive relationships in the determination of the 'likeness' of products under Article III:4."[215] *EC – Asbestos* in fact marked an end – at least until the *Thailand – Cigarettes* and *Philippines – Distilled Spirits* cases – to the short intermezzo with market-based evidence. The Panel in *EC – Asbestos* had applied the physical characteristics criterion abstractly by not accounting for the market relevance of carcinogenicity. The Appellate Body then reversed the Panel ruling and substituted a stylized market examination under the rubric of CTH. Overall, the analysis was qualitative, not quantitative.[216]

B Marketing strategies and distribution channels

As the *Border Tax* criteria list is not exhaustive, additional criteria have been introduced at times. Most recently, for example, Panels have "looked at internal [domestic] regulations [of the defendant] as a useful indicator of the degree to which a Member would tend to regard different products as being similar."[217] In the cases that emphasized the marketplace analysis, an examination of marketing and advertising strategies as well as distribution channels has been undertaken. These are considerations that reflect the attempt to incorporate the market vantage point to a greater extent, but that, as will be discussed below, are arguably of only limited relevance to the assessment of the competitive relationships under an adequately conceptualized framework.

The Panel in *Japan – Alcoholic Beverages II* pointed to the role of marketing strategies.[218] Marketing and advertisement strategies have been

[215] Appellate Body Report, *EC – Asbestos, supra*, Ch. 2, fn. 70, paras. 153 and 154: "the necessity or appropriateness of adopting a 'fundamentally' economic interpretation of the 'likeness' of products under Article III:4 of the GATT 1994 does not appear to me to be free from substantial doubt."

[216] Trebilcock and Howse, *The Regulation of International Trade*, p. 102.

[217] Panel Report, *Philippines – Distilled Spirits, supra*, Introduction, fn. 23, para. 7.31 (and paras. 7.72–7.74, 7.135) citing to Panel Report, *Thailand – Cigarettes, supra*, Introduction, fn. 23, paras. 7.441–7.442. Evidently, this criterion makes sense only in order to prove "likeness" where defendant's local regulation, contrary to the one in dispute, does not distinguish between the imported and domestic product.

[218] Panel Report, *Japan – Alcoholic Beverages II, supra*, fn. 73, para. 6.28: "Independently of similarities with respect to physical characteristics or classification in tariff nomenclatures, greater emphasis should be placed on elasticity of substitution. In this context, factors like marketing strategies could also prove to be relevant criteria, since what

considered a source of evidence because they shed light on how firms respond to or attempt to influence consumer perception. Thus, they were taken up in *Korea – Alcoholic Beverages* in the context of the assessment of physical characteristics.[219] The Panels' conclusions in *Korea – Alcoholic Beverages* and *Chile – Alcoholic Beverages* on overlapping end-uses were also supported by taking marketing and advertising strategies into consideration.[220] The domestic products, shochu and pisco, were changed in their physical characteristics and their marketing to match the imported Western-style alcoholic beverages. Further, they were expressly advertised as being in competition with those imports. Analogous considerations on marketing and labeling were made by the Panels in *Mexico – Soft Drinks* in the context of CTH and in *Philippines – Distilled Spirits* with regard to "likeness" in the context of CTH and with regard to DCS in the context of end-uses.[221]

An analysis of products' channels of distribution and points of sale was conducted for the first time in *Korea – Alcoholic Beverages* and then in *Chile – Alcoholic Beverages*, *Mexico – Soft Drinks*, and most recently in *Philippines – Distilled Spirits*.[222] They were understood to be reflective of consumer perceptions and thus significant for product comparison purposes.[223] They were also considered to reflect similarities and differences in intended end-uses.[224] The Panels in *Korea – Alcoholic Beverages* and *Philippines – Distilled Spirits* examined the distribution systems with regard to the consumption of the disputed alcoholic beverages "on-premise" (in restaurants, bars, etc.) and "off-premise" (at home).[225] In *Chile – Alcoholic Beverages*, the distribution in various outlets was

is at issue is the responsiveness of consumers to the various products offered in the market."

[219] Panel Report, *Korea – Alcoholic Beverages*, *supra*, Introduction, fn. 36, para. 10.65.

[220] Panel Report, *Korea – Alcoholic Beverages*, *supra*, Introduction, fn. 36, para. 10.79; Panel Report, *Chile – Alcoholic Beverages*, *supra*, Ch. 2, fn. 68, para. 7.46.

[221] Panel Report, *Mexico – Soft Drinks*, *supra*, Ch. 2, fn. 80, para. 8.134; Panel Report, *Philippines – Distilled Spirits*, *supra*, Introduction, fn. 23, paras. 7.51, 7.61, 7.82, 7.130, 7.131.

[222] Panel Report, *Korea – Alcoholic Beverages*, *supra*, Introduction, fn. 36, paras. 10.83, 10.84; Panel Report, *Chile – Alcoholic Beverages*, *supra*, Ch. 2, fn. 68, para. 7.55; Panel Report, *Mexico – Soft Drinks*, *supra*, Ch. 2, fn. 80, para. 8.133; Panel Report, *Philippines – Distilled Spirits*, *supra*, Introduction, fn. 23, paras. 7.122–7.123.

[223] Panel Report, *Chile – Alcoholic Beverages*, *supra*, Ch. 2, fn. 68, para. 7.59.

[224] Panel Report, *Korea – Alcoholic Beverages*, *supra*, Introduction, fn. 36, para. 10.83.

[225] Panel Report, *Korea – Alcoholic Beverages*, *supra*, Introduction, fn. 36, paras. 10.83–10.86; Panel Report, *Philippines – Distilled Spirits*, *supra*, Introduction, fn. 23, para. 7.123.

analyzed, going as far as the comparison of the presentation on shelf, while the Panel in *Mexico – Soft Drinks* found the high level observation of identical retail distribution sufficient to come to the conclusion of identical end-uses.[226]

III ASSESSMENT OF THE ANALYTICAL EVOLUTION

Having revealed striking parallels in the evolution of antitrust and Article III market definition case law, the following will put the developments into perspective in more detail and also provide some substantive assessment, in particular, of the complications encountered in the context of the traditional approach. The following will therefore first address the reasons for the initial (and in WTO law probably subsisting) reluctance toward an economic approach, second, turn to the reasons for the rise of economics and, finally, contemplate possible reasons why the economic approach in GATT law has not been adopted with lasting effect so far.

1 Reasons for the initial reluctance toward economics

Antitrust and Article III market definition both started from a purely legal understanding of delineating markets. At the outset, antitrust and trade lawyers, as they are prone to do, followed an approach of legal formalism. Rather than looking at the real world, the "marketplace" in WTO/GATT parlance, the market definition inquiry was reduced to a checklist of qualitative criteria. Among those, the most important in both legal regimes were physical characteristics and end-uses, which allowed for formalistic line-drawing along those categories. Thus, initially, there was an intuitive leaning toward legal formalism and a great discomfort with economics. This should come as no surprise. Several reasons can be identified.

First, both in the antitrust courtrooms and at the international trade negotiation table, lawyers and – probably legally trained – diplomats have reigned for a long time as sole and absolute rulers. For both groups, the initial discomfort with economic analysis may have much to do with their first-mover advantage. Antitrust and international trade lawyers came

[226] Panel Report, *Chile – Alcoholic Beverages*, *supra*, Ch. 2, fn. 68, para. 7.57; Panel Report, *Mexico – Soft Drinks*, *supra*, Ch. 2, fn. 80, para. 8.133.

well before economists, let alone antitrust or trade economists. Though the United States was the first legal system to adopt modern antitrust statutes with the enactment of the Sherman Act in 1890, while EU antitrust rules were established much later by the Treaties of Rome in 1957, the earliest antitrust legislation dates back as far as the Roman Empire around 50 BC.[227] The NT principle similarly has a long history in international trade law, reaching back to ancient Hebrew law and figuring in various commercial agreements in Europe of the Middle Ages.[228] Economics, in contrast, was acknowledged as an independent discipline much later. It was only in the eighteenth century that economists were first recognized as a profession.

Second, market definition has tended toward traditional evidence, because it was recognized itself as a central question in antitrust litigation and GATT case law long before the advent of empirical tools were developed and point-of-sale scanner data became available on a large scale.

Lastly, for a long time economists themselves did not define markets and only over recent decades have they addressed the problem more seriously. Still, in 1982 Stigler declared: "My lament is that this battle on market definition … has received virtually no attention from us economists. Except for a casual flirtation with cross-elasticities of demand and supply, the determination of markets has remained an undeveloped area of economic research at either the theoretical or empirical level."[229] Most economists not only scorned modern antitrust law at its outset when the Sherman Act was promulgated,[230] but among many there has actually been a tradition of hostility to reliance on market shares in assessing market power, and thus toward the whole idea of market delineation.[231] Without a

[227] Neven, *Economic Analysis in European Competition Policy: The First 2000 (or so) Years*, p. 2 (2008), available at: http://ec.europa.eu/dgs/competition/economist/oxera.pdf.

[228] DiMascio and Pauwelyn, "Nondiscrimination and Investment Treaties: Worlds Apart or Two Sides of the Same Coin?" p. 51.

[229] Stigler, "The Economist and the Problem of Monopoly," *American Economic Review*, 72 (1982), 1, 9. See also Horowitz, "Market Definition in Antitrust Analysis: A Regression-based Approach," *Southern Economics Journal*, 48 (1981), 1: "Because economists, from Adam Smith forward, have with confidence and enthusiasm, although not necessarily with shared views, written about markets, it is plausible to expect that they would have had quite a bit to contribute to the resolution of the market-definition issue. Plausible, but erroneous."

[230] Kovacic and Shapiro, "Antitrust Policy: Century of Economic and Legal Thinking," *Journal of Economic Perspectives*, 14 (2000), 43, 44.

[231] The first substantial discussion of monopoly power in the economic literature cautioned that market shares and concentration are not necessarily good indicators of market power; see Lerner, "The Concept of Monopoly and the Measurement of Monopoly Power," *Review of Economic Studies*, 1 (1934), 157, 166. See also *supra*, fn. 140.

long-standing economic grounding on which to draw, legal market definition developed its own legalistic and formalistic conception.

2 Reasons for the rise of economics

The preceding case law survey also underlines that both legal regimes underwent an evolution to an economics-based approach to market definition. Several determinants may have driven the process, which put antitrust and, temporarily, international trade analysis on a more economic footing and thereby opening the door to quantitative evidence. The following addresses some of them. For antitrust law, the paths along which the growing influence of economics occurred have already been explored in scholarship and will therefore be kept short here. For international trade law, the reasons have not been uncovered and for this reason shall be considered more extensively. Several observations may provide explanations, but they necessarily remain speculative in nature. In addition, there are several general reasons against the traditional approach and these can be put forward in favor of an alternative economic approach.

A *Paradigm shifts*

Within the confines of antitrust law, the increased demand for empirical methods is coincident with, and may be the result of, the evolution of economic theory in antitrust policy: the "economics revolution."[232] This explanatory approach is premised on the assumption that the outcome of the debate on the goals of antitrust policy cannot help but impact on the design of, and approach to, market definition. An emphasis on economic goals inevitably brings economics to bear in market definition. Thus, as the contours of antitrust doctrine and enforcement policy shifted to a focus on efficiency and welfare considerations following the advent of the Chicago School, market definition has also been driven more toward economics. As outlined above, both efficiency and welfare concepts translate into a concern for the rise of prices above the competitive price level. Where efficiency and welfare considerations come to the fore, it leads to the framing of market definition in terms of markets in which a price may increase as a result of the exercise of market power. In this regard, the SSNIP test is a logical consequence of the ascendancy of economic

232 Lipsky, "Antitrust Economics: Making Progress, Avoiding Regression," *George Mason Law Review*, 12 (2003), 163, 164.

concepts of efficiency and welfare standards in the discussion on the goals of antitrust law.

The corollary of the ascent of economic thinking is, on the "demand-side," the reception in case law of economic thinking. From around the same time, one can observe a growing judicial approval of, and explicit insistence upon, economic reasoning and analysis of economic effects in antitrust litigation.[233] In the United States in particular, courts are increasingly turning to economic principles to guide their interpretation of antitrust statutes. This is true, for example, with regard to the US Supreme Court's successive replacement of most form-based *per se* prohibitions of particular practices with a rule of reason analysis that explicitly accounts for efficiency and welfare considerations.[234] Moreover, measures were taken to improve the judiciary's ability to handle scientific information.[235]

Over the last few years, EU antitrust policy has also made attempts to gradually evolve away from structural presumptions and to introduce a more economically thorough analysis of likely competitive effects of mergers, agreements, or single firm conduct;[236] although much remains unclear in EU antitrust policy, and statements by the European Commission are often contradictory in this respect. As a result, the economic estimation of the direction and magnitude of these effects has become an integral part of antitrust analysis, in particular, with regard to theories of harm and efficiencies.

Similarly to the United States, the European judiciary has played an important role in increasing the awareness of economics. A series of important judgments in which the EU courts identified weaknesses in

[233] In *Leegin Creative Leather Products, Inc.* v. *PSKS, Inc.*, 551 US 877, 888 (2007) (hereinafter *Leegin*) the US Supreme Court cited ten works of economists. Although a lack of economic citations does not necessarily demonstrate a lack of economic reasoning, this is in stark contrast to the *Dr Miles Med. Co.* v. *John D. Park & Sons Co.*, 220 US 373, 404–405 (1911) decision which was overruled by *Leegin*. The 1911 decision relied solely on legal treatises, one published in 1628 on English common law and, as such, irrelevant to modern business practices or their economic effects.

[234] The line of decisions that successively cut back the *per se* rule extends from *Continental TV, Inc.* v. *GTE Sylvania Inc.*, *supra*, Ch. 2, fn. 6, at 57–58 to *Leegin*, *supra*, fn. 233.

[235] For instance, the first edition of the Federal Judicial Center's *Reference Manual on Scientific Evidence* was issued in 1994.

[236] Neven and Coninck, *Best Practices on the Submission of Economic Evidence and Data Collection*, (2010), p. 1, available at: http://ec.europa.eu/dgs/competition/economist/neven_deconinck_best_practices.pdf. Generally on the rise of economics in EU antitrust law, see Friederiszick, "Economic Analysis in EU Competition Cases," in Drexel *et al.* (eds.), *Economic Theory and Competition Law*, pp. 3–19 (2009).

the European Commission's consideration of economic arguments, and in which they demanded greater economic rigor, were the catalyst for increased economic analysis in enforcement policy.[237] However, these decisions came after the introduction of the *Commission Notice on market definition*, and therefore were not themselves the impetus for an economic approach to market definition. Instead, they provide the broader picture where not only the European Commission, but also the courts instigated a process of pervasive economic penetration of all areas of EU antitrust law.[238] The European Commission has been proactive in these developments in terms of decision making and in the reform of the legal framework.[239] For example, shortly before the Notice was promulgated, a series of three important European Commission decisions – starting with *Nestlé/Perrier* in 1992 – paved the way for the use of quantitative methods for market definition.[240] They may also have been significant in drawing attention to the potential of economic analysis beyond market definition. Since then, the European Commission has resorted more and more frequently to econometric studies in the areas of the estimation of merger effects and the delineation of markets. Further attempts to facilitate the penetration of economic methodologies into the legal practice are manifested in numerous expert reports.[241] And, finally, the legislative framework has been revised successively in all areas to account more for economic and effects-based considerations.[242]

In international trade law, there has not been a shift in economic learning. The dispute settlement bodies' move from strictly textual to more teleological interpretation is, however, characteristic of a different important shift in paradigm. It is the evolution of institutions which have gained

[237] See *Airtours*; Case T-310/01, *Schneider* v. *Commission* [2002] ECR II-4071; Case T-5/02, *Tetra Laval* v. *Commission* [2002] ECR II-4381.

[238] See Table 2 in Neven, "Competition Economics and Antitrust in Europe," *Economic Policy*, (2006), 743, 751 for the positive trend in the number of published decisions in which reference is made to economic advice since the implementation of the Merger Regulation.

[239] For an overview of subsequent notices, guidelines, and regulations in the areas of Articles 101 and 102 of the TFEU and merger control see Neven, "Competition Economics and Antitrust in Europe," pp. 753, 755–759.

[240] *Nestlé/Perrier, supra*, fn. 51, Case IV/M.430, *Proctor & Gamble/VP Schickedanz* [1994] OJ L354 32 (hereinafter *Proctor & Gamble/VP Schickedanz*); Case IV/M.623, *Kimberly-Clark/Scott* [1996] OJ L183 1.

[241] These expert reports are available at: http://ec.europa.eu/competition/mergers/studies_reports/studies_reports.html.

[242] 2004 ECMR; *Guidelines on horizontal mergers*; *Commission Guidance on exclusionary conduct*.

a basic level of legitimacy.[243] With the inception of the WTO legal order, three major developments have contributed to this evolution.

First, with the introduction of novel Agreements, such as the SPS and the TBT agreements,[244] dealing with scientific and technical issues, the international trade regime itself became increasingly scientific and technical, and overall more sophisticated and complex. Those agreements explicitly adopted scientific and technical criteria of legality, such as the requirement to base sanitary or phytosanitary measures on a risk assessment.[245] Quite naturally, for their application there has been a general tendency toward recourse to scientific and technical expertise.[246] Thus, use of economic expertise and evidence fits into this overall disposition to consult and utilize specialized knowledge.

As a second major shift in paradigm, the WTO dispute settlement bodies were embedded in a more robust adjudicatory framework. This was the consequence of the "judicialization" of the dispute settlement procedure with the establishment of the WTO.[247] Under the dispute resolution procedures of GATT 1947 the approach to resolving disputes was "negotiation-based." It was primarily "aimed at lowering tensions, defusing conflicts and promoting compromise," and was characterized by the flexibility of procedures, the control of the dispute by the parties, and the freedom to accept or reject opinions and proposed settlements.[248] These equitable and diplomatic solutions were favored by international trade negotiators and diplomats, who accorded priority to mutually satisfactory and politically acceptable solutions to disputes. Justice was not a priority to them. The requirement for a unanimous adoption of Panel Reports, even requiring assent by the losing party, exemplifies this characteristic of GATT 1947 dispute settlement procedure. That is why dispute settlement

[243] Howse, "Adjudicative Legitimacy and Treaty Interpretation in International Trade Law: The Early Years of WTO Jurisprudence," in Weiler (ed.), *The EU, the WTO, and the NAFTA: Towards a Common Law of International Trade?* pp. 33–69 (2000); Weiler, "The Rule of Lawyers and the Ethos of Diplomats," *Journal of World Trade*, 35 (2001), 191–207.

[244] *Supra*, Ch. 2, fn. 47.

[245] Article 5.1 of the SPS Agreement.

[246] See *infra*, Ch. 5, fn. 35.

[247] For the description of the dispute settlement system under the DSU as of "judicial" or "juridical" nature see, e.g., Jackson, *Sovereignty, the WTO and Changing Fundamentals of International Law*, p. 136 (2006).

[248] Lowenfeld, "Remedies Along with Rights: Institutional Reform in the new GATT," *American Journal of International Law*, 88 (1994), 477, 479; Gupta, "Appellate Body Interpretation of the WTO Agreement: A Critique in Light of *Japan – Taxes on Alcoholic Beverages*," *Pacific Rim Law & Policy Journal*, 6 (1997), 683, 684.

jurisprudence was viewed as the "manifestation of a distinctive jurisprudence [that is] primarily the work of diplomats rather than their lawyers."[249] As has been noted, a major "rationale for diplomats' rather than lawyer's jurisprudence in GATT was the perception that handling disputes over matters of international commerce was too important to be left to lawyers and judges," as such disputes were inherently political.[250]

In contrast, the new WTO procedure, framed under the Dispute Settlement Understanding (DSU), marked a profound change in which "lawyers triumph over diplomats."[251] In a decided shift from the diplomatic approach toward adjudication-based litigation, it emphasizes impartial and objective procedures and the prominence of the rule of law within the dispute settlement mechanism administered by the newly established Dispute Settlement Body (hereinafter DSB). The DSU created compulsory adjudication with binding outcomes in a two-step procedure of an initial *ad hoc* fact-finder (the Panel) and a standing Appellate Body. It is characteristic of a true legal process and a rule-oriented system of dispute resolution.[252]

The consequence of the ascendancy of pure legal jurisprudence is increased judicial activism by the adjudicators through interpretation. In fact, in a more legal-oriented system, the dispute settlement bodies are required to tailor their deliberations to precise fact-finding, strict legal interpretations, and doctrinal justifications. As the DSU strives for more transparency, consistency, and predictability,[253] adjudicating bodies have gained assertiveness in clarifying terminology, providing precise definitions, developing rigorous legal tests, and ensuring a predictable application of the law. This has led to a definition of the obligations of Article III of the GATT in greater detail and a more coherent structure of the analysis of the legal elements.

Concurrently to their strengthened judicial role, and manifestly for this reason, the dispute settlement bodies embarked upon a mission of more pronounced and forceful judicial decision making. Thus, the shift to a more purposive, economics-based interpretative approach can also be

249 Hudec, *Essays on the Nature of International Trade Law*, p. 17 (1999).

250 Srinivasan, "Nondiscrimination in GATT/WTO: Was there Anything to Begin With and is there Anything Left?," p. 70.

251 Young, "Dispute Resolution in the Uruguay Round: Lawyers Triumph over Diplomats," *The International Lawyer*, 29 (1995), 389, 389.

252 See Mora, "A GATT with Teeth: Law Wins Over Politics in the Resolution of International Trade Disputes," *Columbia Journal of Transnational Law*, 31 (1993), 103, 136–141.

253 Compare Article 3.2 of the DSU.

put within the general context of a stricter and more intrusive application of the NT obligation.

A primary aspect of the more pervasive application of the NT obligation is the progressive shift in focus of the GATT regime from border to internal measures. During the reign of GATT 1947, the principal impediments to international trade were border measures, in particular high tariffs. The underlying thrust of the GATT, at least as originally negotiated in 1947, was to rule out all types of border measures except for tariffs, while at the same time binding the level of tariffs. Thus, the preoccupation of the GATT 1947 regime was on GATT Contracting Parties negotiating gradual reductions in tariffs under Article II of the GATT, which operate on a MFN basis. This left only a minor and merely supplementary role for the NT principle in preventing tariff reduction commitments from circumvention by means of discriminatory internal measures – as a disparate tax or regulation would have the same effect as a tariff. However, with the success of GATT 1947 in reducing tariffs to very low levels by the 1980s, the NT principle began to emerge as the important instrument for disciplining protectionism or discrimination in international trade that lay beyond or within the Member country's borders in the form of internal non-tariff, that is, tax or regulatory barriers to trade. Just when economics arose in the discussion for the interpretation of likeness and DCS, the Appellate Body remarked that the original purpose of the NT obligation should not be over-emphasized because the sheltering scope of the provision also applied to products not bound by tariff commitments.[254] Instead, it recognized that "the broad and fundamental purpose of Article III is to avoid protectionism in the application of internal tax and regulatory measures," to which end it recognized NT as a more general obligation that provides "equality of competitive conditions for imports in relation to domestic products."[255]

A second aspect of the more sweeping application of the NT obligation is the extension of the provision's ambit to *de facto* discrimination. To the extent that there were trade disputes based on NT in the initial GATT 1947 phase of tariff reductions, they primarily involved cases of *de jure* discriminations and the protection of tariff commitments. These were rather simple cases, also in terms of product comparison, because likeness had in any case been presumed as a consequence of *prima facie* illegality of *de jure* discrimination. The change in focus on internal measures also

[254] Appellate Body Report, *Japan – Alcoholic Beverages II, supra*, Introduction, fn. 15, at 17.
[255] Appellate Body Report, *Japan – Alcoholic Beverages II, supra*, Introduction, fn. 15, at 16.

led to the more frequent encounter of *de facto* discriminations in trade disputes that require a thorough analysis of product comparability.

The increasing awareness for *de facto* discriminations occurred virtually in parallel to the generally increasing importance of the NT obligation.[256] Both provide the background – and perhaps to some extent the reasons – why the dispute settlement bodies performed their interpretative function more aggressively, and were thus induced to break free from the constraints of the traditional approach to product comparison and to break new ground turning to economic expertise and insights.

B "Supply-side" factors

On the "supply-side," there has been a considerable increase in economic input into antitrust law. Economists are increasingly involved in antitrust proceedings. The appearance of an economist as an expert testifying on behalf of the plaintiff or defendant is a common feature nowadays.[257] A whole industry of forensic economists has mushroomed and economic consultancy firms are increasingly involved in antitrust proceedings.[258]

Another aspect driving the economic input is the substantial presence of economists in the enforcement agencies. At the DoJ and the US Federal Trade Commission (hereinafter FTC), this has been the case for a long time.[259] Although once only "handmaidens to the lawyers, and rather neglected ones at that," their role within the agencies has evolved drastically over the years and is now firmly institutionalized.[260] In the European Commission, the creation of the Office of the Chief Competition

[256] See *supra*, Ch. 2, fn. 89.

[257] According to Gavil, "After Daubert: Discerning the Increasingly Fine Line Between the Admissibility and Sufficiency of Expert Testimony in Antitrust Litigation," *Antitrust Law Journal* 65 (1997), 663, 663, 666–667: "litigating an antitrust case absent the aid of an economist has become an increasingly perilous proposition" and it is "virtually impossible to proceed with an antitrust case without an economist."

[258] See Neven, "Competition Economics and Antitrust in Europe," pp. 748–749; Sievers, *Wettbewerbsgutachten: Ökonomen als Dienstleister*, p. 7 (2009).

[259] Stevens, "The Federal Trade Commission's Contribution to Industrial and Economic Analysis: The Work of the Economic Division," *George Washington Law Review*, 8 (1940), 545–580.

[260] Posner, "A Program for the Antitrust Division," *University of Chicago Law Review*, 38 (1971), 500, 532. For accounts see Barnett, "Competition Law and Policy Modernization: Lessons from the US Common-law Experience," Presentation to the Lisbon Conference on Competition Law and Economics, Lisbon, 2007, available at: www.justice.gov/atr/public/speeches/227755.htm and White, "Economics, Economists, and Antitrust: A Tale of Growing Influence," in Siegfried (ed.), *Better Living Through Economics*, pp. 226, 231–233 (2010).

Economist came only in 2003 – it was as late as 2007 when the German Federal Cartel Office followed – and fits into the more recent move toward economics in Europe.

One aspect for a push of economics from the "supply-side" in the WTO regime may have come with the admission of independent private legal counsel at dispute settlement proceedings. This occurred concomitantly with the ascent of economics in the context of Article III product comparison.

The DSU does not specifically address the issue of who may represent a party before Panels and the Appellate Body. Under GATT 1947, the practice had been that private legal counsel was not allowed. In 1997, the Appellate Body recognized the right of parties and third parties under the WTO legal regime to have independent private legal counsel appear on their behalf in hearings and become involved in the preparation of parties' written submissions.[261] Beyond the mere simultaneity, there is no apparent causal link between the appearance of legal counsel in dispute settlement proceedings and the increased use of economic evidence. But, as it has been explained, until 1996 proceedings were more "diplomatic" in nature. They did not have the character of court-room proceedings, where each party aggressively resorts to every bit of favorable evidence. The judicial process is now compulsory under the "juridified" dispute settlement procedure. This has increased the number of reluctant defendants, who are more inclined to dispute the facts and therefore also prepared to resort to all means of evidence, including that of an economic nature. Moreover, since the admissibility of independent private counsel to WTO disputes, lawyers who are experienced in litigation and proof-gathering have entered the stage. They are also leaning more toward bringing in economic evidence than government officials who are inexperienced in litigating cases in a trial format.[262] Moreover, those specialized law firms with a substantial presence in WTO litigation have the potent support of economists on their staff with the skills and capabilities of developing economic evidence. One may argue that since private law firms have discovered that it is possible to earn consulting fees in WTO dispute settlement, they will bring in more complex evidence (and more expensive experts). In any case, especially those parties relying on private law firms increasingly turn to economists for expert witness testimony

[261] Appellate Body Report, *EC – Bananas III*, *supra*, Ch. 2, fn. 81, paras. 10–12.

[262] For the "rule of lawyers" in the WTO regime see Weiler, "The Rule of Lawyers and the Ethos of Diplomats," pp. 197–200.

and economic studies as supporting evidence.[263] Thus, the appearance of private counsel and economic evidence on the stage of WTO litigation may not have been coincidental after all.

Lastly, several other improvements on the "supply-side" in general, that is, the technical tools and availability of data, have facilitated this transition in both legal fields. Computing technology has rapidly improved; advances in theoretical economics have produced a large variety of empirical methods; and there is greater availability of data on commercial transactions owing to, in particular, supermarket or point-of-sale scanner data. For these reasons, empirical analysis has become feasible and less expensive. Processing and analyzing large volumes of quantitative data has therefore become a rapid and accessible task. Overall, these developments allow economists to use and analyze data to answer the difficult questions, such as on the relevant market, more easily and readily.

C *Problems with the traditional approach*

As the case law overview already indicates, important criticism has been associated with the traditional approach. Four problems will be explained in more detail. First, the concern that the traditional approach, with its malleable criteria, becomes an issue of framing and thus produces arbitrary results. Second, the problem that the traditional approach does not provide an answer to the pertinent issue behind the market definition inquiry. Third, the risk that this approach can be manipulated to reach predetermined outcomes. Lastly, its failure to adequately reflect degrees of substitutability. Against this background, substantial doubt exists about the usefulness of the traditional approach, in particular, with regard to the transparency, predictability, and consistency of the market definition inquiry.

(i) Arbitrariness

Under the traditional approach, the legal profession attempted to convert the notion of a relevant market into a legal concept. By drawing up fixed legal criteria, lawyers sought to provide some degree of legal certainty. This is important from a legal perspective in order to bring about an element of predictability in defining the scope of intervention of international law

[263] Bown, "The WTO Secretariat and the Role of Economics in Panels and Arbitrations," in Bown and Pauwelyn (eds.), *The Law, Economics and Politics of Retaliation in WTO Dispute Settlement*, pp. 391, 400 (2010).

into domestic law. Hence the United States in *Japan – Alcoholic Beverages II* observed that: "time has shown that the only stable legal criteria in the GATT have been those which are based on qualitative factors, not on economic factors or market shares."[264]

Yet the opposite is true in practice. The traditional way of defining markets in fact leads to the decision maker being given unduly broad discretionary powers. It is thus susceptible to producing arbitrary results. Any market definition can be advanced simply by selectively appealing to certain product characteristics and end-uses. Depending on how closely products are analyzed, one may always find either similarities or differences in terms of physical characteristics. Alcoholic beverages are a recurring example, both in antitrust and trade case law. On greater scrutiny, one may find sufficient differences in ingredients (for example, grapes versus grains in the cases of whisky and cognac), while at a higher level of generality the similarities in base materials may be emphasized (for example, organic high starch materials leading to high alcohol content which are common to both).[265] Another example is *EC – Asbestos* where the Panel's general analysis found asbestos and asbestos-free material to be "like" each other in terms of physical characteristics, whereas the Appellate Body's close scrutiny at the molecular level found physical differences.

In order to apply the criterion of end-uses the relevant end-use has to be defined in the first place. For multifunctional products this may not be straightforward. What would be the relevant use? Any overlapping function or simply the typical one? Moreover, any specific definition of end-uses can simply be modified. It can be narrowed down by merely adding supplementary specifications and enlarged by omitting qualifications. For example, in *Nestlé/Perrier* the question was whether the appropriate end-use was, more generally, thirst quenching or, more specifically, thirst quenching from a healthy, natural source that provides minerals. In the whisky/cognac example, some may make a distinction between aperitif and digestif, while others may emphasize that both are bought for the purpose of drinking a beverage with a high concentration of alcohol.

[264] Appellate Submission by the United States to the Appellate Body, *Japan – Taxes on Alcoholic Beverages*, para. 99, August 23, 1996 (on file with author).

[265] See Wille, "Recapturing a Lost Opportunity: Article III:2 GATT 1994 Japan – Alcoholic Beverages 1996," p. 2 (objecting to reliance on physical characteristics, and descriptive criteria more generally, by asking: "But why does one physical characteristic determine likeness and another does not? Is the color of the alcohol most important or the distillation process? Does the type of sugar used in the process determine the likeness or is it more pertinent to know if the alcohol is usually diluted before consumption?").

The choice of relevant characteristics and end-uses, and the degree to which these characteristics and uses may vary, grants adjudicators a wide degree of discretion. This carries the risk that they single out characteristics and end-uses more or less at random. More to the point, the actual weight given to long lists of physical, technical, chemical, nutritional, or other characteristics is of little relevance. It should not be for adjudicators' personal inclinations to decide which characteristics are relevant, and to what extent. This diverts attention from the real issue of consumer preferences in the market, and thus actual demand substitutability.

In this respect the criterion of CTH may be more relevant, at least in order to ascertain demand-side substitution. Yet both legal regimes have handled the assessment of consumer patterns and perceptions, perhaps not always but at least at times, in a manner that abstracts from actual consumer preferences and develops an ideal-type consumer standard. The Appellate Body's emphasis of a rational and reasonable consumer perspective under the CTH criterion in *EC – Asbestos* exhibits striking parallels with what has been outlined as the reasonably prudent consumer standard in antitrust law.

The application of an abstract analysis of consumer preferences has substantial dangers.[266] The complexities of actual buyer perceptions are replaced by the adjudicators' subjective (and possibly biased) speculations on a rational purchaser's decision. One may object that adjudicators will also draw on well-founded life experience for their conclusions, and, naturally, this may be enough in clear-cut cases. But market definition will arise as a problem where cases are complicated and life experience may not provide an unambiguous picture. Even with respect to simple products, as the alcoholic beverages examples show, there is not one obvious reasonableness standard because reasonable people will usually disagree.

Moreover, the rational consumer standard ignores the point that customers are often utterly unreasonable and thus shape market boundaries differently. For example, with regard to the preference for branded over virtually identical non-branded products, consumers make purchasing decisions that can deviate considerably from what adjudicators would deem reasonable.[267] But market definition is not the normative issue of

[266] Remarkably, Englisch, *Wettbewerbsgleichheit im grenzüberschreitenden Handel*, p. 485 actually calls for abstraction from actual market conditions. Immenga and Körber, "Artikel 2 Beurteilung von Zusammenschlüssen," para. 32 advocate a plausibility standard.

[267] Note that the traditional economic tenets of the *homo oeconomicus* and the profit-maximizing standard have been increasingly questioned by new schools of

which products *should* be grouped together, but rather which products *are* in fact part of the same market. It is insufficient that – from a public policy perspective – consumers *should* make a distinction between products, if in fact they do not.[268] Relevant markets are not determined by judicial (normative) command; they are created by market perceptions. The adjudicator's task is not to tailor markets himself and thus to patronize consumers. He is merely to uncover and accept the real world factual circumstances.[269] Neither legal regime is in the business of protecting an idealized marketplace. Their objectives are to identify market power and to prevent protectionism – no matter how foolish the market participants are. To achieve these purposes it is irrelevant how a reasonable consumer in an ideal world might behave. Only the real market players are subject to the rules – and are also protected by them. When erroneously applied in this normative way the CTH criterion introduces subjectivity into the assessment of competitive relationships that cannot be tested empirically. Consumer preferences can then be applied as a criterion to support whatever market definition one wishes to support.

Overall, the traditional categories are hopelessly malleable. Their assessment risks producing arbitrary results; any market delineation may be advanced simply by selectively framing the criteria of product characteristics, indented end-use, or consumer perceptions.[270] On this basis

economic thinking referred to as "behavioral economics," "bounded rationality," and "experimental economics." They recognize that consumers and firms also act irrationally and not in a utility- and profit-maximizing way. For an introduction see, Office of Fair Trading (Armstrong and Huck), *Behavioural Economics as Applied to Firms: A Primer*, (2010), available at: www.oft.gov.uk/shared_oft/economic_research/oft1213.pdf and Office of Fair Trading, *What Does Behavioural Economics Mean for Competition Policy?* (2010), available at: www.oft.gov.uk/shared_oft/economic_research/oft1224.pdf.

268 For this reason, one must reject the concern that measuring actual buyer substitution would result in atomized micromarkets that, from a policy intuition, would "wrongly" and "unreasonably" group, e.g., physically identical goods in separate markets. For this erroneous concern see Ewald, "Paradigmenwechsel bei der Abgrenzung relevanter Märkte?" *Zeitschrift für Wettbewerbsrecht*, pp. 512, 531 (2004); Müller, *Abschied vom Bedarfsmarktkonzept bei der Marktabgrenzung?* pp. 82, 128 (2007); Immenga and Körber, "Artikel 2 Beurteilung von Zusammenschlüssen," para. 41.

269 Sandrock, "Grundprobleme der sachlichen Marktabgrenzung," in Merz and Schluep (eds.), *Recht und Wirtschaft heute: Festgabe zum 65. Geburtstag von Max Kummer*, pp. 449, 469 (1980) (market definition as a "*wertungsfreier Erkenntnisakt*" instead of a "*normatives Werturteil*"). But see Charnovitz, "Book Review: 'Like Products' in International Trade Law: Towards a Consistent GATT/WTO Jurisprudence," *American Journal of International Law*, 98 (2004), 610, 614, who warns that product likeness should not be viewed "as a market condition detectable with an economist's empirical scanner."

270 Tariff classifications, as used in GATT, are a criterion that should be disposed of entirely. It is an artificial criterion unrelated to any real world distinctions since tariff classifications are negotiated differentiations, see *supra*, Ch. 1, fnn. 32 *et seq*.

it will always be possible to construct a list of similarities or differences. But the real question is whether or not these similarities or differences are meaningful – an issue that needs to be settled by recourse to empirical observations.

(ii) Failure to respond to the pertinent question

Whether the criteria are meaningful depends on whether they respond to the question being asked. This leads to a second criticism relating to the relevance of the criteria with regard to the underlying objectives of market definition.

The first issue is that a purely legal interpretation of the market definition concept ignores the policy rationales behind the need for market definition. The traditional criteria have decorative rather than instructional value.[271] They do not respond to the question of whether market power exists, or whether a protectionist internal measure would be imposed. This is most manifestly demonstrated by the *Border Tax Report*. This *Report* has not been tailored to the individual purpose of Article III of the GATT, but applies – regardless of the specific purposes of the different provisions – to all sixteen instances of product likeness in GATT. More generally, some traditional criteria, such as tariff classifications, or industry or public recognition under the *Brown Shoe* criteria, are patently inapposite to the antimarket power or antiprotectionist purpose. Others, such as physical characteristics and end-uses, do not in themselves, without further explanation, indicate whether a SSNIP would be profitable or whether the products are in such a close relationship that a government is likely to impose a discriminatory protectionist measure.[272] Reinforcing the claim that the traditional criteria do not pertain to the ultimate issue of interest, the basic policy of Article III of the GATT would not be served by a definition of likeness limited to products that have nearly identical physical characteristics. Such a narrow definition would allow governments to give less favorable treatment to a foreign product that, although competitive with the domestic product, had some different physical characteristics.

As a second issue, even if physical characteristics and end-uses may be applied in a way that elucidates demand substitution, their traditional application has been misguided. The fundamental problem is that adjudicators have shied away from articulating a coherent mode of analysis,

[271] Säcker, *The Concept of the Relevant Product Market: Between Demand-side Substitutability and Supply-side Substitutability in Competition Law*, p. 24 (2008).

[272] Posner, *Antitrust Law: An Economic Perspective*, p. 129 (1976).

which indicates how the various factors might be integrated or balanced. With the *Brown Shoe* indicia and *Border Tax* criteria, they simply gave laundry lists of criteria. This led to an overly formalistic and mechanistic approach involving counting the number of criteria satisfied. The absence of one or more of the seven *Brown Shoe* indicia does not preclude a finding of a (sub)market as long as a majority of indicia point to delineate a certain market.[273] Similarly, in the case of the *Border Tax* criteria, adjudicators closely adhere to the list. In practice, no products have been considered unlike or not DCS where the majority of factors indicated the contrary. But whether or not the majority of criteria on the list goes for or against a single relevant market bears no relation to the underlying questions of interest.

(iii) Predetermined results

Where the criteria are so malleable that the boundaries of the market can be expanded or contracted at the discretion of the adjudicator there is a great risk of adapting biased *ad hoc* market definitions. This forms the basis of a third criticism. Rather than being an open-ended, independent inquiry, market delineation is susceptible to potential manipulation to correspond with a pre-defined and desired outcome ("gerrymandering" in US parlance).

Such concerns have been voiced with regard to a perceived "self-confirming bias" of the European Commission. Induced by the combination of prosecutorial and adjudicative functions, it is considered to frequently first determine that an infringement has occurred and then to define the market in such a way that market power becomes unquestionable.[274] Similar concerns have also been raised with regard to antitrust enforcement in the United States.[275] CPE of demand, reasonable interchangeability and the practical indicia are seen as a "smorgasbord

[273] *Harnischfeger Corp. v. Paccar, Inc.*, 474 F.Supp. 1151, 1155 (ED Wis. 1979): "It is clear that these seven criteria are litmus paper tests that must be held up against the proposed submarket in order to determine whether a relevant submarket exists. If a sufficient number of those indicia are present, a valid submarket has been established." See also Turner, "The Role of the 'Market Concept' in Antitrust Law," p. 1151: "The typical [jury] instruction sort of recite the Brown Shoe factors and say, now, fellows, the more of these you find, the more likely it is a market."

[274] Wils, "The Combination of the Investigative and Prosecutorial Function and the Adjudicative Function in EC Antitrust Enforcement: A Legal and Economic Analysis," *World Competition*, 27 (2004), 201–224; O'Donoghue and Padilla, *The Law and Economics of Article 82 EC*, p. 68.

[275] Simons and Williams, "The Renaissance of Market Definition," *Antitrust Bulletin* 38 (1993), 799, 805.

of tests."[276] They allow the test to be chosen according to the preconceived outcome the court or enforcers wish to reach.[277] It appears that courts and agencies upholding broad market definitions tend to rely on functional interchangeability of end-use, while de-emphasizing or simply overlooking the question of CPE of demand or the relevance of the *Brown Shoe* indicia. Conversely, courts can and do carve out narrow (sub)markets by treating CPE of demand as a requirement for placing products in the same market or relying on the *Brown Shoe* indicia.[278]

Equivalent concerns may be raised under GATT. Where dispute settlement bodies are convinced that protectionist intent lies behind a measure, there may be a temptation to draw the boundaries of "like" or DCS products so as to hold the respondent responsible. Hudec called this the "smell test": "Once the tribunal comes to a conclusion about who should win, it fashions an analysis, in terms of the meaningless criteria it has been asked to apply, that makes the case come out that way."[279] In *EC – Asbestos*, for instance, there was arguably never a serious doubt as to the material outcome of the case, that is, that France could legitimately protect its citizens from asbestos. It is suspected that the complainant Canada needed a WTO ruling against itself as a matter of domestic politics.[280] Thus, it appeared to be clear to everybody that Canada would lose, but not on what grounds – already on the "like" product issue or at the justification stage. The Appellate Body's attempt to delineate an idealized market may therefore have been guided by the predetermined and apparently politically correct result of the case. It could not bring itself to do what has been described as the "naming and shaming" of what public opinion

276 Keyte, "Market Definition and Differentiated Products: The Need for a Workable Standard," p. 705.

277 It is most telling that until 1974 the US government was successful in every case to reach the US Supreme Court under Section 7 of the Clayton Act, prompting Justice Stewart to state in his 1966 dissent in *United States* v. *Von's Grocery Co.*, 384 US 270, 301 (1966) that the "sole consistency" he could find in the Court's Section 7 decisions was that "the Government always wins." Critics maintain that this was due to the Court's "result-oriented approach to definition of the market, gerrymandering the boundaries so as to maximize the prospect of invalidating the challenged acquisition." The Supreme Court, 1963 Term, *Harvard Law Review*, 78 (1964), 143, 274–275 (internal quotation omitted).

278 Pitofsky, "New Definitions of Relevant Market and the Assault on Antitrust," pp. 1808, 1817; Werden, "The History of Antitrust Market Delineation," p. 172.

279 Hudec, "GATT/WTO Constraints on National Regulation: Requiem for an 'Aim and Effects' Test," p. 634.

280 See Horn and Weiler, "EC – Asbestos European Communities: Measures Affecting Asbestos and Asbestos-Containing Products," pp. 130–131.

would consider a legitimate measure banning life-threatening material in violation of the NT principle, and relegating it to the requirement of justification.[281]

(iv) Failure to reflect degrees of substitutability

The process of market definition involves judgments on "matters of degree" that can at times be "extremely difficult to measure."[282] To the same extent in GATT law discrete categorization of direct competitiveness or substitutability and likeness, as a definable subset of the former, is a matter of degree of substitutability. The traditional approach with its formalistic line-drawing is unsuitable for this purpose. As has been established in case law, there is a "spectrum of degrees of 'competitiveness' or 'substitutability.'"[283] As "part of a logical continuum," likeness is at one end of the spectrum and different products at the other, with DCS products somewhere along the spectrum.[284] Therefore, likeness requires the highest degree of substitutability. By contrast, only a lesser degree of propinquity is needed for the DCS category. Physical characteristics and end-uses seem unfit to form the sole basis on which to judge where two products are situated on this spectrum of competitiveness. The traditional approach is misleading in the sense that it is based on asking seemingly clear-cut questions of similarities and differences. It thereby gives the false impression that whether or not products are in a competitive relationship is simply a matter of yes or no instead of a matter of degree.

Product differentiation is a particular instance where the traditional approach is confronted with difficulty in determining how close a substitute must be in order to be included in a market. In most industries, particularly with regard to consumer goods, products are differentiated to some degree.[285] This can be in any number of ways, including physical differences, quality, pricing, sales and distribution methods, packaging, brand name, advertising, and marketing to name but a few.[286]

[281] Horn and Weiler, "EC – Asbestos European Communities: Measures Affecting Asbestos and Asbestos-Containing Products," p. 143.

[282] Pitofsky, "New Definitions of Relevant Market and the Assault on Antitrust," p. 1807.

[283] Appellate Body Report, *EC – Asbestos, supra*, Ch. 2, fn. 70, para. 99.

[284] Appellate Body Report, *EC – Asbestos, supra*, Ch. 2, fn. 70, para. 79.

[285] On the problem of product differentiation in antitrust law see ABA Section of Antitrust Law, *Market Power Handbook*, 2005, pp. 103–110; Lücking and Simon, "Definition of the Relevant Market," paras. 3.201–3.208.

[286] For example, brand differentiation between cigarettes was an important consideration in Panel Report, *Dominican Republic – Cigarettes, supra*, fn. 80, paras. 7.165, 7.331.

The issue with product differentiation arises most acutely when products have the same, or substantially the same, characteristics and end-uses, but are otherwise highly differentiated along a continuum, for example, in terms of branding or quality. With regard to product characteristics and end-use, products on each end of the spectrum, for example, luxury and budget brands, would constitute a single market. A SSNIP or marketplace test would arguably give a very different answer.[287] From a customer perspective, products at each end of the spectrum will often not be substitutable in terms of price or quality. But more importantly, despite a shared identity in terms of attributes and use, whether consumers perceive differentiated products as substitutable or not will significantly depend on whether and to what extent customers make a price/quality trade-off between premium and budget brands. If consumers do not trade up to the better value or down to lower when faced, for example, with a price increase, it seems appropriate to separate the markets regardless of similarities in characteristics or use.

Product differentiation can lead to narrow markets separating physically identical products serving the same use. In this view, the concern often encountered in antitrust scholarship is that of "unreasonably" atomized markets that lead to overstated market power, and thus to over-enforcement.[288] This reasoning has already been rejected for erroneously patronizing consumers. Likewise, there may be a concern over treating differentiated products as "unlike" or not DCS, although they would fall under the purview of Article III of the GATT when applying the traditional criteria. In this context, the concern would relate to under-enforcement. But this concern is equally unfounded. If consumers do not perceive physically identical products serving the same use as substitutable, there is no reason to accord them protection under Article III of the GATT. An exception may be, for example, when consumers do not currently view products as substitutable, but absent governmental

[287] For complications in the use of the SSNIP test in the case of highly differentiated products see Rubinfeld, "Econometric Issues in Antitrust Analysis," *Journal of Institutional and Theoretical Economics*, 166 (2010), 62, 63. The Panel Report, *Korea – Alcoholic Beverages*, *supra*, Introduction, fn. 36, paras. 10.51–10.60, confirmed by Appellate Body Report, *Korea – Alcoholic Beverages*, *supra*, Ch. 2, fn. 71, paras. 139–145, "grouped" together subcategories of spirits "for convenience in analysis." The Panel explicitly acknowledged the question of where to draw the line between the categories. But it was convinced that all imported types of alcoholic beverages were sufficiently similar under the traditional criteria, *ibid.*, paras. 10.59–10.60. This raises the issue of how those subcategories would be treated from the viewpoint of the consumer under a marketplace test.

[288] *Supra*, fn. 268.

discriminatory treatment may change their view. Yet this is a problem of "potential" and "latent" competition to be addressed later. It does not justify giving general precedence to identity in terms of attributes and uses over differentiation actually perceived by consumers.

3 Reasons for the transitory impact of economics in GATT

Although the criticism of the traditional approach does not in itself provide a positive argument in favor of an economic approach, it will become clear in Chapter 4 that some of the drawbacks associated with it can be addressed by an economic approach. But despite these problems, there has been a backlash from an economic to the traditional approach in WTO case law. While antitrust law has embraced an economic approach with lasting effect, it appeared – at least until the two most recent Panel Reports *Thailand – Cigarettes* and *Philippines – Distilled Spirits* in 2011 – to be only a temporary episode in GATT. The reasons remain obscure. One may be that in WTO law, a reverse tendency can be observed with regard to the objectives of the legal regime. Antitrust policy has seen the development from a multitude of competing goals to the crystallization of economic rationales, namely, efficiency and welfare, as the – commonly accepted – central objectives. In WTO law, this is mirrored by an opposite evolution, where the focus has been diffused from a more or less purely economic goal of trade liberalization toward a multitude of competing goals, such as human health, the environment, human rights, etc. Especially as the severe criticism of international trade and globalization in general has intensified in the public debate since the 1990s, the WTO has responded by opening up to non-trade considerations. It is in this general context that it can be seen that the WTO legal regime was less receptive to adopting a pronounced rule of economics.

Another reason may be that there has not been an institutionalization of economic expertise and capabilities as has been the case in antitrust law. Rather, what is presented as evidence in those proceedings depends mainly on what has been submitted by the parties and their counsel.[289] For various reasons, those may or may not choose to resort to economic evidence. This may also explain the somewhat surprising recurrence of economics and quantitative analysis in the most recent case law. The Philippines were the complainant in *Thailand – Cigarettes* as well as the defendant in *Philippines – Distilled Spirits*. In both cases, it was the

[289] See *infra*, Ch. 5, fn. 37.

Philippines that presented economic/quantitative evidence to the Panel.[290] Thus, it seems that it is one particular Member country that is apparently more leaning toward economic arguments that has been the driving force behind the most recent resurgence of economic arguments in Article III product comparison.

But crucially, the parties in the particular cases cannot be seen dissociated from the WTO membership. As will be outlined later, from a procedural point of view nothing in fact prevents economic testimony. And, at first glance, there does not seem to be any reason why a Panel would not consider expert economic testimony. So what is the problem? Much depends on the political willingness of WTO Members to open the proceedings to economics. It may be the very sensitivity of this area for the Members that explains the interpretative choices made by the dispute settlement bodies. It has been noted that the NT discipline intrudes severely upon domestic fiscal and regulatory autonomy. It can be observed in party submissions that particularly economics – for its "objective" nature – has been perceived as a serious assault on state sovereignty, especially by the most influential WTO members.[291] It cannot be disregarded that the WTO is a Member-driven intergovernmental organization. Major WTO Members have the ability to put pressure on the WTO institutions since the WTO remains the realm of international diplomacy where the international organization, the agent, can politically oppose its principals, the Members, only to a very limited degree.[292] The WTO being a forum for give and take between its Members, where some powerful Members oppose economics, as the United States did, other Members are likely to concede and refrain from raising economics in exchange for expected compromises in their favor in other areas. If not expressly stated by Members, it seems that after some trial and error fiddling with economics there has been a consensus – *sub silencio* – between the WTO Members not to pursue this highly contested avenue further – with the Philippines being somewhat of a "maverick" in antitrust terminology. Against this background, in a newly "judicialized"

[290] In *Philippines – Distilled Spirits*, the Philippines submitted a study that estimated CPE, while a study submitted by the EU and the United States was in fact "less" quantitative in that it was "not [in the Panel's view] an attempt to estimate and provide figures for the cross-price elasticity for the imported and domestic distilled spirits," Panel Report, *Philippines – Distilled Spirits*, *supra*, Introduction, fn. 23, para. 7.112.

[291] See *infra*, Ch. 5, fn. 191.

[292] See on the principal–agent relationship of WTO Members and the WTO Secretariat in Elsig, "Agency Theory and the WTO: Complex Agency and 'Missing Delegation'?" *European Journal of International Relations*, 17 (2011), 495–517.

dispute settlement process where Members' influence on the rulings has been minimized, the new WTO institutions and their newly established authority are particularly exposed to damaging criticism from national governments. Recognizing this very exposure, the Appellate Body may well have concluded that the safest refuge from political criticism is to stay as close as possible to the shelter of the legal texts and establish a practice for market definition accepted by governments, that is, the traditional *Border Tax* approach.

IV CONCLUSION

To conclude, the evolution of an economic approach toward market definition under antitrust law and Article III of the GATT can be understood as a move from a conception that perceived market definition as a goal in itself, detached from the objective of either field of law, to a concept that tied the delineation of the relevant market to the precise policy goals of the respective legal regime. It geared the delineation of the relevant market toward the identification of market power and, as will be expounded in greater detail in the following, the identification of protectionism, respectively.

It is important for this study to summarize the observation made above that there has been and still is a co-existence of the economic conceptual framework (SSNIP test and *competitive relationship in the marketplace* test) with the remnants of the traditional approach (that is, qualitative criteria). Even in antitrust law, the market definition inquiry has, and still does, commonly looked first and often exclusively to descriptive, qualitative evidence. In short, it is difficult to envisage the appraisal of characteristics and end-uses being in practice confined to the "first step" as suggested in the *Commission Notice on market definition*.[293] In fact, they apparently still form a considerable part of the European Commission's practice.[294] Therefore, in conclusion, it is noteworthy that the economic approach in both legal regimes does not mean that the traditional criteria have been abandoned nor does it imply an exclusive role of quantitative criteria, in particular of CPE of demand.[295] Instead, the economic

[293] Jones and Sufrin, *EC Competition Law*, para. 76.

[294] Coppi and Walker, "Substantial Convergence or Parallel Paths?," p. 104.

[295] For the persisting use of qualitative evidence in the United States see Coate and Fischer, "A Practical Guide to the Hypothetical Monopolist Test for Market Definition," pp. 1054–1055.

approach only opened the door to the use of empirical methods in order to implement the conceptual framework. Again, this invokes the distinction between the conceptual economic framework that addresses the issue as to what the market definition should ideally capture (in antitrust law those products that make a SSNIP unprofitable, and in trade law those products that are in a sufficiently close competitive relationship in the marketplace so as to make differential protectionist treatment possible), and the methodological issue of how to establish in practice whether a pair of products fulfills this definition (using either qualitative or quantitative evidence).

4

Conceptualizing an economic approach to market definition

I INTRODUCTION

The former president of the German Federal Cartel Office (Bundeskartellamt), Heitzer, recently noted that: "the discussion on the 'more economic approach' at least sometimes bears some resemblance to lawyers and economists sitting in the car of competition law enforcement fiercely fighting over the steering wheel."[1] He then addressed the role of economics and outlined that one of the core contributions of economics to antitrust law has been to provide a suitable conceptual framework. This is particularly true for market definition. To stick to the metaphor, economics "provide[s] the 'maps' to find the way through the facts of a case."[2] Specifically with reference to antitrust market definition, the SSNIP test as the conceptual idea allows for two things. First, it is a guide to the correct approach toward the issue of market definition and market power. Second, it maps the way for (ideally) embracing such qualitative and quantitative evidence that is responsive to the market power inquiry.

Likewise, a coherent theory of interpretation ensures a conceptually consistent view of market definition under Article III of the GATT. Article III's notion of a *competitive relationship in the marketplace* has been an epithet devoid of substance. Dispute settlement bodies never explained what type of analysis this standard entails. This chapter seeks to give substance to the *competitive relationship in the marketplace* standard. It sets out an over-arching conceptual framework based on economics. From this follow, on the methodological level, the appropriate methodological tools to establish in practice whether a pair of products fulfills the "like" or DCS requirement.

[1] Heitzer, *Economic Assessment in Competition Enforcement: Developments in France and Germany – Statement for the Panel*, p. 3.

[2] Heitzer, *Economic Assessment in Competition Enforcement: Developments in France and Germany*, p. 4 (emphasis omitted).

There are strong voices in the literature for a market-based approach to trade market definition.[3] But neither jurisprudence nor scholarship has adopted a similar two-level distinction between conceptual framework and methodological approaches. It is for this reason that the separate issues of whether or not to embrace a marketplace perspective and which criteria to adopt have usually not been discussed separately.

To devise an economics-based conceptual framework, section II takes the canon of treaty interpretation as the starting point. It will be the purposive modality of interpretation that provides the basis for a *competitive relationship in the marketplace* test. Section III will then elaborate on the content of this test, which will be designed so as to tie the market definition paradigm to the aim of Article III of the GATT. Sections IV, V, VI, and VII will address further aspects of the test. These are the need for a prospective analysis, the distinction from other "market" concepts, the consequences of the conceptual framework for the traditional criteria, and the relationship between Article III:2(1) and (2) of the GATT.

II MARKET DEFINITION FRAMEWORK: A MATTER OF TREATY INTERPRETATION

By nature, the definition of the GATT terms likeness and DCS are a matter of legal treaty interpretation. This section therefore addresses whether there is some hermeneutic foundation for an economics-based construction of the terms.

All agreements concluded under the WTO framework constitute public international law and are thus subject to customary international law on the law of treaty interpretation. Article 3.2 DSU even mandates WTO adjudicators to construe the provisions of the WTO agreements in accordance with the customary rules of interpretation of public international law. The Appellate Body recognized that the canons of treaty interpretation pursuant to Articles 31 and 32 of the VCLT have attained the status

[3] Bronkers and McNelis, "Rethinking the 'Like Product' Definition in WTO Antidumping Law," *Journal of World Trade*, 33 (1991), 73–91; Mattoo and Subramanian, "Regulatory Autonomy and Multilateral Disciplines: The Dilemma and a Possible Resolution," *Journal of International Economic Law*, 1 (1998), 303–322; Quick and Lau, "Environmentally Motivated Tax Distinctions and WTO Law," p. 433; Trebilcock and Giri, "The National Treatment Principle in International Trade Law," pp. 188, 224–225; Mavroidis, *Trade in Goods*, pp. 217–221, 234–236, 238–242 and 247–248 (2007).

of a rule of customary international law.[4] Article 31 of the VCLT stipulates as the general rule of interpretation that the provisions of international agreements shall be interpreted in good faith: (1) in accordance with the ordinary meaning to be given to the terms; (2) in their context; and (3) in the light of their object and purpose. Article 32 of the VCLT allows for recourse to supplementary means of interpretation, including the preparatory work of the treaty and the circumstances of its conclusion, in order to confirm the meaning resulting from the application of Article 31, or to determine the meaning when the interpretation according to Article 31 results in the meaning being ambiguous, or obscure, or leads to a result that is manifestly absurd or unreasonable.

This section addresses each aspect in turn. It begins with the ordinary meaning of the terms pursuant to Article 31:1, and, having found that the plain meaning gives no clear result, proceeds to examine whether, in the light of the other interpretative considerations in Article 31 (object, purpose, and context) and Article 32 (negotiating history), an economics-based meaning can be attributed to the terms.

1 Ordinary meaning of the words

Article III of the GATT does not define the terms "like" or DCS products. Moreover, they have no context-independent, technical meaning in economic theory. Hence, the starting point for dispute settlement bodies has been textual interpretation according to the ordinary meaning of the terms.[5] To put it bluntly, the adjudicators have been devoted to a textual fetish. On numerous occasions, they have displayed a tendency to follow closely the text of the provisions and to turn to dictionary definitions of the terms likeness or DCS.[6] From the dictionary meaning of "like," the adjudicators inferred the need for "identical" or "similar" characteristics or qualities. This seemed to be confirmed by a further textual argument. The comparison with the Spanish and French versions of GATT, which, as the

[4] See, e.g., Appellate Body Report, *Japan – Alcoholic Beverages II*, *supra*, Introduction, fn. 15, at 10–12. For the application of this canon of interpretation see, e.g., Bernhardt, "Interpretation of International Law," in Bernhardt (ed.), *Encyclopedia of Public International Law*, vol. II, pp. 1416–1426 (1999).

[5] Appellate Body Report, *Japan – Alcoholic Beverages II*, *supra*, Introduction, fn. 15, at 17: "The proper interpretation of the Article is, first of all, a textual interpretation."

[6] For the dictionary interpretation of likeness see Panel Report, *US – Gasoline*, *supra*, Ch. 3, fn. 97, para. 6.8 and Appellate Body Report, *EC – Asbestos*, *supra*, Ch. 2, fn. 70, paras. 90–92; on DCS see Appellate Body Report, *Korea – Alcoholic Beverages*, *supra*, Ch. 2, fn. 71, para. 114.

English text, are equally recognized as official, read "productos similares" and "produits similaires," respectively. Yet a pure semantic and lexicographic approach is dangerous, as the Appellate Body eventually acknowledged in *EC – Asbestos*.[7] The unreflected reliance on dictionary definitions does not resolve important interpretative issues for product comparison. Among the unresolved issues are which characteristics and qualities are important, the degree or extent to which products must share characteristics and qualities, and from whose perspective they should be judged. Thus, the precise contours of likeness and the concept of a DCS relationship cannot be determined according to the mere textual meaning of the terms.

2 Contextual modality

The textual interpretation being inconclusive, it is correct that "the term must be interpreted in light of the context, and of the object and purpose, of the provision at issue, and of the object and purpose of the covered agreement in which the provision appears."[8] Beginning with the contextual modality, the GATT terms need to be examined in context. Primarily, this refers to the context of the WTO Agreements. However, the contextual mode of analysis shall also be extended to the EU legal regime on the internal market. The TFEU contains nearly identical non-discrimination obligations and provides ample case law on the issue of product comparability. Although non-binding for WTO purposes, EU trade law may nevertheless provide helpful guidance for developing an interpretative approach in WTO law.[9] For this reason, the Panel in *Korea – Alcoholic Beverages* found that, notwithstanding differences in object and purpose of the treaties, there is relevance for the application of Article III:2 of the GATT in examining how the ECJ has defined markets for the purpose of the corresponding TFEU provision on the prohibition of fiscal discrimination (and of the EU antitrust rules).[10] Moreover, a glance at the TFEU

[7] Appellate Body Report, *EC – Asbestos*, *supra*, Ch. 2, fn. 70, para. 92.

[8] Appellate Body Report, *EC – Asbestos*, *supra*, Ch. 2, fn. 70, para. 88.

[9] See Slotboom, *A Comparison of WTO and EC Law: Do Different Objects and Purposes Matter For Treaty Interpretation?* pp. 73–96 (2007) and Demaret, "The Non-Discrimination Principle and the Removal of Fiscal Barriers to Intra-Community Trade," in Cottier and Mavroidis (eds.), *Regulatory Barriers and the Principle of Non-discrimination in World Trade Law*, pp. 171–189 (2000).

[10] Panel Report, *Korea – Alcoholic Beverages*, *supra*, Introduction, fn. 36, para. 10.81. The EU view on transposing the interpretative approach of the ECJ to Article III of the GATT is more reluctant, see Opinion of Advocate General van Gerven, Case 70/87, *Fediol* v. *Commission* [1989] ECR 1781, para. 23.

is of interest, as the same EU institutions have interpreted both antitrust and non-discrimination provisions – shaping them quite differently with regard to their respective product comparison requirements.

A Immediate context: the WTO legal regime

The WTO regime provides several instances that express different concepts of the relationship between products. Article 15:2(a) of the WTO Agreement on Implementation of Article VII of the General Agreement on Tariffs and Trade 1994 (Customs Valuation Agreement) defines the term "identical" goods as "which are the same in all respects including physical characteristics, quality and reputation. Minor differences in appearance would not preclude goods otherwise conforming to the definition from being regarded as identical." In contrast, that provision defines "similar" goods as those "which, although not alike in all respects, have like characteristics and like component materials which enable them to perform the same functions and to be commercially interchangeable. The quality of the goods, their reputation and the existence of a trademark are among the factors to be considered in determining whether goods are similar." Article 2.6 of the Agreement on the Implementation of Article VI of the GATT 1994 (Antidumping Agreement) even contains a definition of "like" products under that agreement, reading that this term "shall be interpreted to mean a product which is identical, i.e., alike in all respects to the product under consideration, or in the absence of such a product, another product which, although not alike in all respects, has characteristics closely resembling those of the product under consideration."[11]

These definitions seem to endorse a rather formalistic conception of product comparability. But seeking contextual assistance in the interpretation of the GATT terms meets significant limitations. Exporting the above definitions to GATT would presume that it is appropriate to draw an analogy. Interpretative consistency in the different trade law contexts would be an argument in support thereof.[12] Importantly, however, an analogy requires the need to fill an unintended lacuna. This, however, is not the case here, because the drafters have consciously eschewed efforts to define the meaning of the terms thus positively intending the omission

[11] Note 46 to Article 15.1 of the SCM Agreement has identical wording.

[12] See in this respect, Berg, "An Economic Interpretation of 'Like Product,'" *Journal of World Trade*, 30 (1996), 195 and Choi, *"Like Products" in International Trade Law*, pp. 49–90.

of any precise definition.[13] In addition, transplanting other provisions' definitions is inappropriate because the concept of likeness cannot be uniformly circumscribed and harmonized. As the Appellate Body stated: "there can be no one precise and absolute definition of what is 'like.'"[14] Using the famous accordion metaphor, it declared that there is no single meaning in GATT and beyond for the term of "like" products.[15] Thus, the meaning of the terms is relative to the context in which it appears and depends on the respective purpose of the provision.

It is for these reasons that a contextual analysis does not provide interpretative help. Notably, the flexibility in the product scope of the different provisions rules out a uniform definition for product comparison even within Article III of the GATT. But to clarify, the absence of a fit-for-all definition does not preclude what is at the heart of the quest here: devising a coherent economics-based conceptual framework – at least limited to Article III of the GATT – that allows for different "widths of the accordion" on a case-by-case basis.

B Broader context: the EU legal regime

With Articles 110 and 34 of the TFEU (ex Articles 90 and 28 of the EC Treaty) the EU legal regime provides provisions that correspond to Articles III:2 and III:4 of the GATT, respectively. For the present purpose, however, only Article 110 of the TFEU is of interest. The ECJ has adopted an interpretative approach toward Article 34 of the TFEU that moved beyond discrimination between imported and domestic products and that therefore obviates the need to compare products.[16]

The prohibition of fiscal discrimination pursuant to Article 110 of the TFEU is very similar in terminology, structure, and purpose to Article III:2 of the GATT. Its first paragraph prohibits taxation in excess of that imposed on "similar domestic products."[17] Its second paragraph refers to

[13] See *infra*, fn. 35.

[14] Appellate Body Report, *Japan – Alcoholic Beverages II, supra*, Introduction, fn. 15, at 21.

[15] Appellate Body Report, *Japan – Alcoholic Beverages II, supra*, Introduction, fn. 15, at 21: "The concept of 'likeness' is a relative one that evokes the image of an accordion. The accordion of 'likeness' stretches and squeezes in different places as different provisions of the *WTO Agreement* are applied" (emphasis in original).

[16] See Case 8/74, *Procureur du Roi* v. *Dassonville* [1974] ECR 837, para. 5 and Case 120/78, *Rewe-Zentrale* v. *Bundesmonopolverwaltung für Branntwein* [1979] ECR 649, para. 8.

[17] "No Member State shall impose, directly or indirectly, on the products of other Member States any internal taxation of any kind in excess of that imposed directly or indirectly on similar domestic products."

"other products."[18] In accordance with the wording, the ECJ has developed a two-test approach, first, testing products under the similarity standard before coming to the second paragraph.[19]

According to the ECJ, the notion of similarity does not require products to be precisely identical. Rather, it is established case law that similar products need to have analogous properties and similar or comparable usage from the perspective of the consumers.[20] For example, in a number of cases on alcoholic beverages in the early 1980s, the ECJ heavily relied on the analysis of "objective characteristics," such as their origin, method of manufacture, organoleptic properties, alcohol content, ingredients, etc., as well as an analysis of whether they respond to the same needs from the point of view of consumers.[21] Likewise, in a number of Article 110 cases on automobiles, the ECJ determined that:

> products, such as cars are similar for the purpose of the first paragraph of Article 95 of the Treaty [now Article 110 of the TFEU] if their characteristics and the needs which they serve place them in a competitive relation and, second, that the degree of competition between two models depends on the extent to which they meet various requirements regarding price, size, comfort, performance, fuel consumption, durability, reliability and other matters.[22]

In early case law, the ECJ sometimes also considered tariff classifications as a relevant criterion for the similarity of products.[23] But the ECJ has come to the opinion that this criterion must be treated with caution.[24]

[18] "Furthermore, no Member State shall impose on the products of other Member States any internal taxation of such a nature as to afford indirect protection to other products."

[19] Note, however, that the ECJ often does not distinguish in its analysis between the first and the second paragraph, see, e.g., Case 168/78, *Commission* v. *France* [1980] ECR 347, para. 39; Case 169/78, *Commission* v. *Italy* [1980] ECR 385, para. 33.

[20] Joined Cases C-367/93–C-377/93, *Roders* v. *Inspecteur der Invoerrechten* [1995] ECR I-2229 (hereinafter *Roders*), para. 27.

[21] See, e.g., *Commission* v. *France*, *supra*, fn. 19, paras. 5, 11; Case 106/84, *Commission* v. *Denmark* [1986] ECR 833 (hereinafter *Fruit Wine*), para. 12; Case 243/84, *John Walker* v. *Ministeriet for Skatter* [1986] ECR 875, para. 11.

[22] Case C-265/99, *Commission* v. *France* [2001] ECR I-2305, para. 43; see also the prior Case C-421/97, *Tarantik* v. *Direction des services fiscaux* [1999] ECR I-3633, para. 28. Generally on the alcoholic beverages and automobile cases, see: Kuyper, "Booze and Fast Cars: Tax Discrimination under GATT and the EC," *Legal Issues of European Integration* (1996), 129–144; Lubkin, "Is Europe's Glass Half Empty or Half Full? Alcoholic Beverage Taxation and the Development of a European Identity," *Columbia Journal of European Law*, 3 (1997), 357, 387–396.

[23] For example, Case 27/67, *Fink-Frucht GmbH* v. *Hauptzollamt München-Landsbergerstrasse* [1968] ECR 223, at 232; Case 45–75, *Rewe-Zentrale des Lebensmittel-Großhandels GmbH* v. *Hauptzollamt Landau/Pfalz* [1976] ECR 181 (hereinafter *Rewe*), para. 12.

[24] For example, *Fruit Wine*, *supra*, fn. 21, para. 17.

Finally, the ECJ at times also examines "consumer habits."[25] In striking similarity to the WTO approach on "abstract" CTH, the ECJ has adopted an artificial "uniform" standard of consumer habits in the EU that generalizes from what in the real world would be a heterogeneous pattern of different consumer habits in different regions of the EU.[26] On other occasions, this criterion has been relegated to secondary importance.[27]

The category of "other products" under Article 110(2) of the TFEU has been interpreted by the ECJ so as to encompass products that are not similar, but are nonetheless in a situation of competition, even if only in partial, indirect, or potential competition.[28] Thus, the ECJ assesses whether products imported from other EU Members are actually or potentially competing with domestic products. For this, the ECJ refers to the examination of whether products are actually or potentially substituted for one another.[29] Apparently, this depends on whether the products constitute an alternative choice for consumers.[30] However, in practice this only leads the ECJ to turn to the criteria already laid out under Article 110(1) of the TFEU.[31]

The ECJ has remained silent on the use of other, in particular economic and quantitative, criteria. For example, the Court did not reply to Denmark's submission in the *Aquavit* case to rely on CPE of demand.[32]

In conclusion, the ECJ's interpretative approach to "similar" and "other" products under Article 110 of the TFEU closely corresponds to what has been presented under the traditional interpretative approach of the WTO dispute settlement bodies to the concepts of "like" and DCS products under Article III:2 of the GATT. In particular, both regimes have relied on the four criteria of physical characteristics, end-uses, tariff

[25] Case 170/78, *Commission* v. *United Kingdom* [1980] ECR 417, para. 14; *Fruit Wine*, *supra*, fn. 21, para. 15 (in the context of the criterion of "meeting the same needs").

[26] Opinion of the Advocate General Reischl, Case 168/78, *Commission* v. *France* [1980] ECR 347, at 376, 382, accepted by the ECJ, e.g., in Case 216/81, *COGIS* v. *Amministrazione delle Finanze dello Stato* [1982] ECR 2701, para. 8.

[27] For example, Opinion of Advocate General Alber, Case C-302/00, *Commission* v. *France* [2002] ECR I-2055, para. 72.

[28] *Commission* v. *France*, *supra*, fn. 19, paras. 6 and 12; *Roders*, *supra*, fn. 20, para. 38.

[29] *Commission* v. *United Kingdom*, *supra*, fn. 25, para. 12.

[30] Case 356/85, *Commission* v. *Belgium* [1987] ECR 3299, para. 11.

[31] *Commission* v. *Belgium*, paras. 9–11; *Commission* v. *United Kingdom*, *supra*, fn. 25, paras. 13–19.

[32] Case 171/78, *Commission* v. *Denmark* [1980] ECR 447 (hereinafter *Aquavit*), para. 28. In a different case, the Court also ignored the Advocate General's suggestion to use CPE, though this was in the context of the assessment of the protective effect required under Article 110(2) of the TFEU, see Opinion of Advocate General Vilaça, Case 356/85, *Commission* v. *Belgium* [1987] ECR 3299, para. 122.

classifications, and CTH. Moreover, EU case law appears to have placed particular emphasis on physical characteristics.[33] In this regard, a comparison with Article 110 of the TFEU is of only limited usefulness for the development of an economic approach to Article III of the GATT. In the course of this book, the ECJ's interpretative approach can nevertheless provide some additional support for certain aspects of an economic approach to Article III of the GATT.

3 Historical modality

Although only a supplementary and subsidiary means of interpretation under Article 32 of the VCLT, the lack of interpretative guidance from the *travaux preparatoires* and the circumstances of the conclusion of either GATT 1947 or GATT 1994 shall be addressed briefly before turning to the most important and most informative part, the purposive interpretation.[34]

At both the 1946 and 1947 GATT Preparatory Conferences, the drafters consciously abstained from defining the terms of "like" and DCS products.[35] There were discussions on the definition of "like" at the preparatory conferences and delegates gave very specific, but no coherent examples. For example, one opinion was that cars weighing below 1.500 kilograms would not be "like" cars above this threshold. Other illustrations of DCS products were mentioned, such as tung oil and linseed oil, tramways and buses, coal and fuel oil, or apples and oranges.[36] The delegates did not commit themselves to any general definition or workable guidelines. At times, parties to dispute settlement proceedings attempted to make inferences for current cases from those specific historic examples.[37] But as the criteria and methods for product comparison remain obscure, the

[33] See, e.g., Opinion of Advocate General Tizzano, Case C-475/01, *Commission* v. *Greece* [2004] ECR I-8923, para. 89.

[34] This is in line with the practice of the dispute settlement bodies, which do not treat Article 32 considerations as strictly subsidiary to the textual, contextual, and purposive interpretation. See, e.g., GATT Panel Report, *Japan – Alcoholic Beverages I, supra*, Ch. 2, fn. 65, para. 5.6; Panel Report, *Chile – Alcoholic Beverages, supra*, Ch. 2, fn. 68, para. 7.140.

[35] For a recounting of the drafting history see Jackson, *World Trade and the Law of GATT*, paras. 11.4, 12.3 (1969) and Bhala, *Modern GATT Law*, paras. 1-015–1-018.

[36] Panel Report, *Korea – Alcoholic Beverages, supra*, Introduction, fn. 36, para. 10.38.

[37] First written submission of the European Communities to the Panel on *Japan – Taxes on alcoholic beverages*, p. 21, December 4, 1995 (on file with author); Panel Report, *Korea – Alcoholic Beverages, supra*, Introduction, fn. 36, paras. 6.174, 6.183, 6.187, 10.38.

reported discussions are of little help. As Bhala concludes, "their legacy is one of confusing, even implausible statements."[38]

4 Object and purpose

The terms "like" and DCS products are vague and undefined legal concepts, which cannot be rendered more precise by reference to textual, contextual, or historical interpretation. This is why a construction that accounts for the specific purpose of the provision and its larger teleological context is of paramount importance to justify an economics-based approach.

A *Introductory remarks*

It may seem common sense that, as the US Supreme Court stated in the antitrust context, the "definition of the relevant market must reflect economic and commercial realities."[39] There is also an instant intuitive appeal to the argument of Hudec that "since GATT is a commercial agreement, it seems reasonable to start with the assumption that 'likeness' is (or should be) a commercial concept meant to describe one or more market phenomena. The central commercial concept that comes to mind is competitiveness."[40]

Beyond this superficial reasoning, an emphasis on the doctrinal structure of the NT obligation will inevitably bring economics to bear in the quest for a trade market definition approach. The competitive relationship in the marketplace as the relevant test in the assessment of likeness and DCS can be fully understood from a legal methodology perspective when viewed as a marketplace comparator. Doctrinally, the flip side of Article III of the GATT's concept of non-discrimination is, positively formulated, the principle of equality before the law or the doctrine of equal protection, deeply rooted in many legal systems. It directs the government to accord the same or similar treatment to subjects in similar circumstances or belonging to the same class. Two principal legal elements are inherent in the concept of equality. First, there must be some form of differential treatment of one situation, person, or object with regard to

[38] Bhala, *Modern GATT Law*, para. 1–017.

[39] *Eastman Kodak*, *supra*, Ch. 2, fn. 32, at 467.

[40] Hudec, "'Like Product': The Differences in Meaning in GATT Articles I and III," p. 104. Highly critical, Regan, "Regulatory Purpose and 'Like Products' in Article III:4 of the GATT (With Additional Remarks on Article III:2)," p. 453.

another. This requires a comparison of the treatments accorded. In the case of Article III of the GATT, this presupposes the presence of discrimination against the imported product. Second, is the element of sufficient comparability of the situations, persons, or objects that are treated differently. Under Article III of the GATT, this requires the two products to be "like" or DCS, with the exception of the one difference that provides for the basis of the explicit or implicit discrimination, here the origin of the products. With regard to this second element, the comparison is made in relation to a point of comparison, a comparator or *tertium comparationis*. The comparator is the quality or element that two situations, persons, or objects that are being compared have in common for a conclusion of likeness or DCS. The two elements, the standard of discrimination, and the relevant comparator will be addressed in the following. The analysis of the standard of discrimination reveals that Article III of the GATT is premised on an economic notion of protectionism based on the modification of the conditions of competition. The analysis of the second element addresses the choice of the appropriate comparator. Its identification is a value judgment that is determined by the values and principles of the particular legal order and the purpose for which the comparison is made. The choice of the pertinent comparator under a purposive interpretative approach draws on the economic understanding of protectionism and the economic purpose of the NT obligation and of the WTO/GATT regime more generally.

B The standard of discrimination and the interpretation of protectionism

The underlying principles of discrimination and protectionism guide the legal analysis of likeness and DCS.[41] Differential treatment, "taxation in excess," or "less favorable treatment" under Articles III:2(1) and III:4 of the GATT, is the essence of discrimination and one of two legal elements that constitute the concept of equality. The Article III requirement for differential treatment also echoes the principle set forth in Article III:1 of the GATT. As the Appellate Body in *EC – Asbestos* noted, "the term 'less favorable treatment' expresses the general principle, in Article III:1, that internal regulations 'should not be applied … so as to afford protection

[41] Note that this analysis is primarily concerned with *de facto* discrimination, given that there is no need to prove the existence of likeness in the case of *de jure* discrimination, *supra*, Ch. 2, fn. 91.

to domestic production.' If there is 'less favorable treatment' of the group of 'like' imported products, there is, conversely, 'protection' of the group of 'like' domestic products."[42] Hence, a showing of discrimination ("less favorable treatment") serves to demonstrate the presence of protection.

The question of which type of measure amounts to "less favorable treatment," or what constitutes differential treatment in general, is not defined in GATT.[43] Therefore, the concept of protection also remains an elusive notion.[44] GATT 1947 and WTO jurisprudence have long embraced an objective standard of discrimination and therefore an objective interpretation of what is meant by protectionism.[45] They endorsed the standard of "conditions of competition" as the guiding principle for the interpretation and application of differential treatment, in particular, "less favorable treatment." The Appellate Body confirmed this reading, holding that "less favorable treatment" requires an examination of "whether a measure modifies the *conditions of competition* in the relevant market to the detriment of imported products."[46] Under this interpretative approach, discrimination, or the analogous notion of protection, is analyzed by reference to the conditions of competition. Differential treatment qualifies as "less favorable treatment" under Article III of the GATT only if it modifies the conditions of competition. Consequently, a measure needs to result in a competitive disadvantage for the imported product or competitive

[42] Appellate Body Report, *EC – Asbestos*, *supra*, Ch. 2, fn. 70, para. 100.

[43] By contrast, note the definition provided by Article XVII:3 of the GATS: "different treatment shall be considered to be less favourable if it modifies the conditions of competition."

[44] The "considerable intellectual difficulty in translating the term protection in operational terms" has left the issue unresolved, Mavroidis, *The General Agreement on Tariffs and Trade: A Commentary*, p. 178.

[45] There is also a subjective approach to the definition of protectionism which has not received much attention in scholarship, and which has not been acknowledged by WTO jurisprudence. Under a subjective theory of protection, an anticompetitive effect of a measure would not be in itself sufficient to qualify as "less favorable treatment." In addition, a subjective component of protectionist purpose would also be necessary. The measure would need to be adopted with the actual purpose to modify the conditions of competition in the domestic market. Measures with an objective unrelated to trade which nonetheless modify the conditions of competition would not qualify as "less favorable treatment." See, e.g., Pauwelyn, "Recent Books on Trade and Environment: GATT Phantoms Still Haunt the WTO," *European Journal of International Law*, 15 (2004), 575, 583–584.

[46] Appellate Body Report, *Korea – Measures Affecting Imports of Fresh, Chilled and Frozen Beef*, WT/DS161/AB/R, WT/DS169/AB/R, adopted January 10, 2001, para. 137 (emphasis in original). The first report to adopt this standard was GATT Panel Report, *Italian Discrimination Against Imported Agricultural Machinery*, *supra*, Ch. 2, fn. 88, para. 12.

advantage for the domestic product to constitute prohibited discrimination and protectionism.

Under this objective approach to protectionism, the modification of the conditions of competition can be due to actual or potential effects of the differential treatment. Actual effects can manifestly result in case of a discriminatory impact of the measure to the detriment of the imported product or the benefit of the domestic product.[47] Potential effects are also sufficient to modify the competitive conditions. As the Appellate Body held, the examination of "less favorable treatment" "cannot rest on simple assertion, but must be found on a careful analysis of the contested measure and of its implications in the marketplace. At the same time, however, the examination need not be based on *actual effects* of the contested measure in the marketplace."[48] The rationale for this approach goes back to the fact that the Appellate Body found that Article III of the GATT protected the legitimate expectations of competitive conditions and thus did not require actual trade effects to be shown to find a violation of Article III of the GATT ("trade effects test").[49]

In conclusion, under an objective approach, the analysis focuses on the actual or potential effects of differential treatment on the competitive relationship in the market. The formulation of Article III:1 of the GATT ("so as to afford protection to *domestic* production") stresses the protection that is granted to domestic products and makes no reference to the disadvantage imposed on foreign products. Consequently, as a general rule, protection can be thought of as some kind of (actual or potential) commercial or competitive advantage attributed to the domestic product.[50]

[47] See Davey and Pauwelyn, "MFN Unconditionality," pp. 38–40 ("discriminatory effects test"); Ehring, "De facto Discrimination in World Trade Law," p. 924 ("asymmetric impact"); Regan, "Further Thoughts on the Role of Regulatory Purpose Under Article III of the GATT," pp. 741, 756 ("disparate impact"). On the related question of whether "less favorable treatment" and, therefore, a modification of the conditions of competition should already be found to exist if a measure treats only *one* imported product disfavorably (failure to accord best treatment) or rather if the *group* of imported products is disproportionately disadvantaged vis-à-vis the corresponding group of domestic products see *supra*, Ch. 2, fn. 94 and Ehring, "De facto Discrimination in World Trade Law.

[48] Appellate Body Report, *United States – Tax Treatment for "Foreign Sales Corporations" – Recourse to Article 21.5 of the DSU by the European Communities*, WT/DS108/AB/RW, adopted January 29, 2002, para. 215 (emphasis in original).

[49] Appellate Body Report, *Japan – Alcoholic Beverages II*, *supra*, Introduction, fn. 15, at 16; Appellate Body Report, *Korea – Alcoholic Beverages*, *supra*, Ch. 2, fn. 71, paras. 128–131.

[50] For a formulation that describes protectionism as treatment that imposes a competitive disadvantage on *foreign* products see Hudec, "'Like Product': The Differences in Meaning in GATT Articles I and III," p. 104.

C The marketplace comparator

The second element of the concept of equality is the relevant comparator. The Appellate Body introduced a marketplace comparator when it based the purposive construction of likeness and DCS on the "general principle" of the Chapeau of Article III:1 of the GATT and its antiprotectionist goal.[51] It interpreted Article III:1 of the GATT to include not only products in case a measure has a protectionist motive, but to encompass the much broader category of all products where the measure has a discriminatory effect on imported products. Thereby, the Appellate Body elevated equal competitive conditions, and even the mere expectations of equal competitive conditions, to constitute the core interpretative tenet for likeness and DCS. It developed the single and uniform notion of a *competitive relationship in the marketplace* as the appropriate test for all non-discrimination obligations under Article III of the GATT.[52] The reasons why the dispute settlement bodies suddenly endorsed the marketplace comparator have remained a mystery. But there are two arguments that justify the marketplace comparator from a purposive perspective.

The first argument is linked to the immediate function of Article III of the GATT in the interplay with other GATT obligations. Here the purposive interpretation is guided by the general principle articulated in Article III:1 of the GATT, as well as the objective interpretation of protectionism outlined under the standard of discrimination. It goes back to the NT's evolution from its complementary role as a reinforcement of reductions in tariffs to an instrument of independent significance for the protection of equal competitive conditions. This has already been put into perspective by the rise of the economic approach in WTO case law.[53] To recall, the original purpose of Article III of the GATT was confined to defending the value of tariff concessions negotiated in the GATT rounds. Since tariffs have been substantially reduced, emphasis is now

[51] *Supra*, Ch. 3, fn. 189. Importantly, this interpretative approach by the dispute settlement bodies revolves around the construction of SATAP, and thereby around the notion of "protection." In conformity with the notion of protection under the interpretation of the standard of discrimination just outlined, the notion of protection has been interpreted objectively, rejecting a subjective aims-and-effects reading; see *supra*, Ch. 2, fn. 67 and Ch. 3, fn. 156.

[52] Although less obvious, the ECJ may also be understood to have opened the door to a market-based interpretation of Article 110 of the TFEU, see, e.g., *Commission* v. *France*, *supra*, fn. 19, para. 13 (the Court deeming it "necessary to examine within this framework the economic relationships between the products concerned").

[53] *Supra*, Ch. 3, fn. 257.

on the creation and maintenance of competitive conditions and opportunities with regard to internal measures. That is why the marketplace orientation finds its origin in the modern role of NT as a guarantee of a level playing field with regard to internal measures on the domestic market, protecting the generally weaker-placed foreign products from discriminatory governmental intervention. With this change in function of Article III of the GATT, there was thus a concurrent change in teleological understanding, stressing the "general principle" that informs the Article's operative provisions. The notion of competitive conditions was not altogether new,[54] but it was now anchored doctrinally in Article III:1 of the GATT and came to the fore with the emphasis on the principles of equality of competitive conditions and the protection of expectations of equal competitive relationships.

Under the modern understanding of the role of Article III of the GATT, the marketplace test is logical because the corollary of outlawing internal protectionist measures, where protectionism is understood objectively as the modification of conditions of competition, is the commitment to equal competitive conditions and opportunities once the border has been passed by the imported product. Put differently, as the Appellate Body correctly noted: "if there is – or could be – no competitive relationship between products, a Member cannot intervene, through internal taxation or regulation, to protect domestic production."[55] There is simply no question of protecting a domestic product against competition from a foreign product, unless the two are actually in competition. Protectionism defined as the modification of conditions of competition in favor of a domestic product only makes sense with regard to a foreign product that is in a competitive relationship in the marketplace with former. This means that the relevant comparator to product comparison under Article III of the GATT is the *competitive relationship in the marketplace*.[56] Under

[54] See already GATT Panel Report, *Italian Discrimination Against Imported Agricultural Machinery*, *supra*, Ch. 2, fn. 88, para. 13: "The intent of the drafters [of Article III] was to provide equal conditions of competition once goods had been cleared through customs"; GATT Panel Report, *US – Superfund*, *supra*, Ch. 3, fn. 95, para. 5.1.9: "Article III:2, first sentence, obliges contracting parties to establish certain competitive conditions for imported products in relation to domestic products."

[55] Appellate Body Report, *EC – Asbestos*, *supra*, Ch. 2, fn. 70, para. 117.

[56] Tietje, *Normative Grundstrukturen der Behandlung nichttarifärer Handelshemmnisse in der WTO-GATT-Rechtsordnung*, pp. 237–238 (who argues for the aims-and-effects test); Horn and Weiler, "EC – Asbestos European Communities: Measures Affecting Asbestos and Asbestos-Containing Products," paras. 138–141; Raible, *Protektionismusverbote im Recht der Wirtschaftsintegration*, pp. 51–52.

this reasoning, this economically determined comparator is the only valid comparator which leads to a purely objective analysis.[57]

The second argument relies on the fundamental economic purpose of NT and GATT as a whole. As interpretative guidance, it emphasizes the fundamental economic theory of international trade law that has been described at the outset of this study. The argument is that where economic welfare and efficiency play a role, likeness and DCS will necessarily be framed in terms of an economic marketplace comparator.

The theory of comparative advantages is premised on supply and demand to operate so as to determine the optimal allocation of resources through the process of specialization and labor division. This presupposes the existence of an untainted international competitive process in which both supply and demand remain undistorted and interact freely. In an unregulated failure-free market, consumers' choices in response to sellers' offers generate results that are efficient for both consumers and sellers. Only then can foreign producers make use of their individual competitive (and comparative) advantages which they gain through the more efficient use of resources. It is under these circumstances that the choices of rational and profit-maximizing market participants lead to an allocation of resources that is economically optimal and, by way of specialization effects, result in overall welfare maximization. In contrast, in economic terms, rampant discrimination leads to inefficiencies and a reduction in global welfare. Products would be produced and sold not because they are superior in terms of their pricing or quality, but because of their origin.

The NT obligation prevents market distortions between imported and domestic products brought about by governmental intervention. Its aim is to create and maintain a level playing field with respect to governmental fiscal and other regulatory conditions under which imported and domestic products are distributed and sold. It ensures that supply and demand can operate freely so that the selection between products is made only by means of a competitive process. These are the structural characteristics of markets that international trade requires for the proper operation of comparative advantages. The NT obligation guarantees the basic parameters for the competitive conditions necessary for achieving an optimal allocation of resources.

Regan submits that the framers of GATT (and later the WTO) meant to prohibit only one particular sort of inefficient measure, purposeful

[57] This precludes a subjective comparator provided by the regulatory purpose and thus an aims-and-effects test.

protectionism.[58] He argues that they did not seek to outlaw another type of inefficient measure: one which is *bona fide* but with an incidental disparate impact. In his view, measures without a protectionist purpose that a government decides to be in the collective interest of its citizens for non-trade purposes, such as environmental protection or human rights, are (globally) efficient, even if the measure has a disparate impact on imports. He presumes that a non-protectionist measure with an incidental discriminatory effect to be optimal from the point of view of the domestic interests of the regulating state. However, against the background of special interest capture, it is already doubtful when equating the government's decision with what is most efficient for the collective. Moreover, what is most efficient locally cannot be equated with what is globally most efficient. But most importantly, for what is economically efficient deference must be given to the actors in the marketplace (and thus the competitive system or process) and not to the regulating government – except in cases of clear market failure.

As the fundamental economic theory applies to its full extent, it can be read into the judicial emphasis of equality of competitive conditions. The "like" and DCS product determination must identify those foreign products which would, as a result of comparative advantages and absent the discriminatory measure, match or outperform domestic products and, hence, achieve the optimal allocation of resources. In this respect the fundamental economic rationale behind NT supports the choice of a marketplace comparator.

To conclude, there are two important arguments, Article III's function to ensure a level playing field and the economic logic of comparative advantages, that provide the basis for a marketplace analysis of the competitive relationship between products, and thus for a marketplace comparator.

III THE CONTENT OF A MARKETPLACE TEST

So far, dispute settlement bodies have provided no substantive information on how to perceive the standard of the competitive relationship in the marketplace. It has been shown above that it depends on the purpose for which market definition is used in order to properly draw the boundaries

[58] Regan, "Regulatory Purpose and 'Like Products' in Article III:4 of the GATT (With Additional Remarks on Article III:2)," p. 452.

of a market. But for a long time in antitrust law – and remains so under Article III of the GATT – market definition has been assessed in a vacuum, unmoored from the underlying purposes for which it is used. Devoid of a theory that links market definition to its purpose, it tended to embrace evidence, in particular of qualitative nature, which was not meaningful with respect to the underlying aim of the inquiry.

An important lesson learned from the antitrust experience is that the concept of market definition needs to be closely related to the underlying objectives pursued under the legal regime in which it is conducted.[59] This insight will be applied here to Article III of the GATT. The aim is to gear Article III market definition toward the underlying purpose of identifying and eliminating discriminatory, protectionist governmental measures. First, demand-side substitution will be identified as the critical factor for the marketplace test. Then, a price increase test along the lines of the SSNIP test will be proposed for Article III purposes.

1 The relevant economic force: demand-side substitutability

The marketplace is where buyers and sellers meet.[60] Conditions in the marketplace may therefore be analyzed both by looking at the demand-side, the buyers, and at the supply-side, the sellers. This is the approach in antitrust law. Antitrust market definition is an instrument for determining the effectiveness of competitive constraints in a market. A relevant antitrust product market hence comprises all those products that impose a competitive constraint on the product of the firm in question. To determine the competitive constraints that impact on the undertaking concerned, it is necessary – as the General Court stated – to analyze "the structure of supply and demand on the market."[61]

[59] The *Commission Notice on market definition*, para. 10 explicitly recognizes this fact.

[60] Appellate Body Report, *Korea – Alcoholic Beverages*, *supra*, Ch. 2, fn. 71, para. 114: "The context of the competitive relationship is necessarily the marketplace since it is the forum where consumers choose between different products." See also the French competition authority's explanations of the relevant market concept, Conseil de la concurrence, *Rapport annuel* 2001, Deuxième partie, Titre I, Le marché pertinent, Introduction, available at: www.autoritedelaconcurrence.fr/user/standard.php?id_rub=31&id_article=58#p2t: "Le marché, au sens où l'entend le droit de la concurrence, est défini comme le lieu sur lequel se rencontrent l'offre et la demande pour un produit ou un service spécifique."

[61] *Tetra Pak* v. *Commission*, *supra*, Ch. 3, fn. 176, para. 63; Case T-219/99, *British Airways* v. *Commission* [2003] ECR II-5917, para. 91.

The SSNIP test has merit in that it formalizes what the inquiry into the competitive constraints must focus upon. It makes the profitability of a price increase, and hence the existence of market power, the yardstick which can be constrained by three possible reactions of customers and competitors. Customers may stop buying altogether and exit the market, or switch to a different product, and firms in neighboring markets may start producing the product. Disregarding the first possibility, the SSNIP test gives a theoretical underpinning for what already intuitively appears to be dispositive: demand and supply substitution as the main economic forces for antitrust market definition.

Continuing along those lines, the *Merger Guidelines* and the *Commission Notice on market definition* identify three main sources of competitive constraints.[62] All of them are based on the concept of substitutability. Demand-side substitution is considered the most important competitive constraint, because it is the most immediate and effective disciplinary force. If a sufficient number of customers can easily switch to available products they regard as substitutable or to suppliers located elsewhere, then the firm cannot exercise market power and raise price if it does not want to lose customers.[63] A second, but less immediate and therefore less important, constraint is exerted by those firms that can quickly switch their production to those products of the firm under investigation because they will be attracted by the higher prices (supply-side substitution). Supply-side substitution has a constraining effect on the pricing decisions of the firms already in the market. If a firm in a neighboring market can switch its production in case of a price rise of another firm without incurring significant additional costs from investment in production facilities and channels of distribution, its competitive influence will already be reflected in the current market price. The price will then be set as high as possible, but still so low as to discourage supply substitution.

In antitrust analysis, a third type of competitive constraint is "potential competition" (the term used more frequently in Europe) or ease of "entry" (the term commonly used in the United States). Supply-side substitution concerns the ability of firms to switch production in the short term (no more than one year) and without incurring large sunk costs

[62] *Commission Notice on market definition*, para. 13; *1992 Merger Guidelines*, para. 1.0.

[63] The fact that demand is lost is not *per se* sufficient to ascertain whether a price increase will be unprofitable. The key issue is whether the loss of sales will be sufficient to offset the increased profits that will be made from the retained sales; see *infra*, Ch. 5, fn. 152.

("uncommitted entry" in US antitrust jargon).[64] By contrast, potential competition denotes the situation in which a firm is required to make substantial investments in production and distribution, and for this reason can enter the market only in the mid- or long term ("committed entry").[65]

Whether or not to include supply-side substitution in the market definition analysis remains controversial. From a purely economic perspective, supply-side substitution may be a less immediate, but equally relevant, competitive constraint.[66] While the *Commission Notice on market definition* emphasizes demand substitution, but also permits supply-side considerations, the *Merger Guidelines* focus on demand-side substitution at the market definition stage and take supply-side substitution into account at a later stage of the analysis.[67] In practice, however, regulators and courts on both sides of the Atlantic stress demand-side substitutability, and sometimes also take supply-side substitution into account.[68] But most importantly, despite the difference in approaches, the same conclusion will be reached as to market power, as long as supply-side substitution is accounted for at some stage in the analysis. By contrast, neither antitrust jurisdiction includes potential competition in the market definition analysis.[69] The reason for including supply-side substitution rather than potential competition in the market definition analysis, is that the latter is considered not to pose a sufficiently close competitive constraint so as

[64] A sunk investment is one that is irreversible and therefore cannot be recovered, i.e., assets that cannot be sold on exit such as advertising expenditures or machinery that cannot be resold.

[65] For the further requirements of timeliness, likelihood, and sufficiency of market entry see *2010 Merger Guidelines*, at pp. 28–29 and *Guidelines on horizontal mergers*, paras. 68–75.

[66] On the basis of pure economic theory, a sound market definition should always take supply substitution into account. This is because the profitability of a price increase depends on both demand and supply substitution. This is the so-called residual demand model, which accounts for own-price elasticity of demand (demand-side substitution) and the reactions of competitor firms (supply-side substitution), van den Bergh and Camesasca, *European Competition Law and Economics*, pp. 113, 128.

[67] *Commission Notice on market definition*, paras. 13–14, 20–23 and *2010 Merger Guidelines*, at 7.

[68] For EU jurisprudence see, e.g.: *Continental Can*, *supra*, Ch. 2, fn. 19, para. 32; *United Brands*, *supra*, Ch. 2, fn. 30, para. 12; Case T-340/03, *France Télécom* v. *Commission* [2007] ECR II-107, para. 78. For references to US case law see ABA Section of Antitrust Law, *Antitrust Law Developments*, 2007, p. 557 fn. 37.

[69] *Commission Notice on market definition*, para. 24; *1992 Merger Guidelines*, paras. 1.0, 3.0; *2010 Merger Guidelines*, at 27–29.

to be treated as part of the relevant market, while still forming part of the substantive competitive assessment.

A *competitive relationship in the marketplace* test must be designed to identify the main competitive force for purposes of Article III of the GATT. As the ultimate aim of Article III of the GATT is to create maximum efficiency and welfare through specialization effects in accordance with the nations' comparative advantages and as this is achieved through the interplay of demand and supply, product comparability under this provision may, in theory, be based on both demand- and supply-side substitutability.

Case law under Article III of the GATT has not so far taken a clear position on the role of supply-side factors. The Appellate Body in *EC – Asbestos* addressed the question of whether or not to include supply-side substitutability by noting that the "dictionary definition of 'like' does not indicate *from whose perspective* 'likeness' should be judged. For instance, ultimate consumers may have a view about the 'likeness' of two products that is very different from that of the inventors or producers of those products."[70] Yet it did not give an answer, although its CTH analysis ultimately relied on the examination of final and intermediate consumer reactions – under an idealized market scenario – and thus *de facto* adopted an exclusive demand-side approach. This is in line with case law generally, which has adopted a demand-side analysis.[71] This focus has been inherent in the definitions of likeness and DCS provided by the dispute settlement bodies. It was held that likeness "must be examined taking into account not only objective criteria (such as composition and manufacturing processes of products), but also the more subjective *consumers'* viewpoint (such as consumption and use by *consumers*)."[72] The same perspective was implicitly incorporated in the definition of DCS products as being "alternative ways of satisfying a particular need or taste."[73] The Panel in *Mexico – Soft Drinks* reiterated this phrase and continued that this "connotes a relationship between imported and domestic products at issue that can be

[70] Appellate Body Report, *EC – Asbestos*, *supra*, Ch. 2, fn. 70, para. 92 (emphasis in original).

[71] For a different reading, especially regarding *Japan – Alcoholic Beverages II*, see Hogg and Nawaz, "Japan – Alcoholic Beverages, Report of the Panel, 11 July 1996 and of the Appellate Body, 4 October 1996," p. 350.

[72] GATT Panel Report, *Japan – Alcoholic Beverages I*, *supra*, Ch. 2, fn. 65, para. 5.7 (emphasis added). This is in line with the ECJ's analysis of Article 110 of the TFEU, see, e.g., *Rewe*, *supra*, fn. 23, para. 12: "meet the same needs from the point of view of the consumer," and *supra*, fnn. 20 and 30.

[73] Appellate Body Report, *Korea – Alcoholic Beverages*, *supra*, Ch. 2, fn. 71, para. 115.

essentially described as 'in competition' in the marketplace."[74] This latest statement overtly links the concept of demand-side substitutability with the marketplace test. Moreover, demand-side considerations have been an integral part of the *Border Tax* criteria in the form of the CTH and end-uses. In particular, the latter has been understood as evidence "to the extent to which consumers are – or would be – willing to choose one product instead of another."[75] This squarely equates to demand-side substitutability.

But some instances may also be interpreted to point toward dispute settlement bodies crediting supply-side considerations. In *Chile – Alcoholic Beverages* the Panel seemed to criticize the lack of supply-side considerations in econometric studies submitted to it when stating: "We note at the outset, that both this study and the Chilean data lack a model incorporating the supply side, and as such all the variation in the data is interpreted as movements along, or shifts of, the demand curve."[76] Supply-side considerations were made in some other cases in the context of Article I:1 of the GATT or in relation to the question of whether the tax was discriminatory.[77] Further, in *Korea – Alcoholic Beverages*, the Panel looked at changes in supply patterns by domestic soju producers as evidence of a competitive relationship. In order to meet the potential threat of imports, domestic producers had changed the physical characteristics of soju in a way that made it more similar to Western-style beverages.[78] This last instance implies that the notion of supply-side analysis under Article III of the GATT may also differ from that in the antitrust context. Here, it may not only turn to third-party supply-side reactions, but may take account of supply substitution by the domestic and/or foreign producer(s) involved in the dispute.

Even though some in the literature argue for supply-side substitution, concentrating solely on the demand-side seems correct.[79] Textually,

[74] Panel Report, *Mexico – Soft Drinks*, *supra*, Ch. 2, fn. 80, para. 8.68.

[75] Appellate Body Report, *EC – Asbestos*, *supra*, Ch. 2, fn. 70, para. 117.

[76] Panel Report, *Chile – Alcoholic Beverages*, *supra*, Ch. 2, fn. 68, para. 7.63.

[77] In the context of Article I:1 of the GATT, the Panel Report, *Indonesia – Autos*, *supra*, Ch. 2, fn. 92, para. 14.141 credited the argument that foreign producers could switch production to manufacture parts and components for vehicles that are currently produced by domestic producers. See also Fauchald, "Flexibility and Predictability Under the World Trade Organization's Non-Discrimination Clauses," *Journal of World Trade*, 37 (2003), 443, 458.

[78] Panel Report, *Korea – Alcoholic Beverages*, *supra*, Introduction, fn. 36, para. 10.79.

[79] Zedalis, "A Theory of the GATT 'Like' Product Common Language Cases," *Vanderbilt Journal of Transnational Law* 27 (1994), 33, 69; Hogg and Nawaz, "Japan – Alcoholic Beverages, Report of the Panel, 11 July 1996 and of the Appellate Body, 4 October 1996,"

Article III of the GATT remains silent on whose viewpoint, buyer or seller, to include in the market definition test.[80] A first argument against supply-side considerations may be drawn from a comparison with the GATS. Unlike Article III of the GATT, which only mandates "products" to be alike, its NT counterpart in Article XVII:1 of the GATS explicitly mentions the supply-side.

But the purposive interpretation of Article III of the GATT argues most convincingly against supply-side substitution. To begin with, one may assume that a government imposes a discriminatory tax on a foreign product A in order to protect the domestic product B. The analysis of supply-side substitution would direct the adjudicator's attention to the question of whether the foreign producer switches production from A to B, thereby attempting to share the increased producer surplus from the protection afforded to product B. This, however, is not a relevant consideration. First of all, as described above, Article III of the GATT is not concerned with *producers*. Its sole beneficiaries are the specific *products* as such.[81] The trade regime is about trade opportunities and not individual rights of foreign producers. Governments make the exchange of competitive opportunities for products not only, or even in the main, to benefit individual exporters. Instead, their aim is to enable freer trade policies in the overall interest, including, most specifically, the interest of consumers. This seems to confirm the rejection of the supply-side perspective because an argument for supply-side substitution would, as Diebold noted, require extending the "explicit protection of competitive opportunities for products to an implicit protection of producers."[82]

Moreover, a focus solely on the demand-side makes sense under the economic rationale of the NT obligation. As Emch convincingly argues, Article III of the GATT establishes a level playing field for *products*. The supply-side, that is, the products in the dispute at hand, here A and B,

p. 350; Neven, "How Should 'Protection' be Evaluated in Article III GATT Disputes?" 17 *European Journal of Political Economy*, 17 (2001), 421, 438; Horn and Mavroidis, "Still Hazy after all These Years," pp. 59, 61; Melloni, *The Principle of National Treatment in the GATT*, p. 127; Shadikhodjaev, "National Treatment under GATT Article III:2 and its Applicability in the Context of Korea's FTAs," *Journal of International Economic Studies*, 12 (2008), 65, 69, 84; more cautiously Fauchald, "Flexibility and Predictability Under the World Trade Organization's Non-Discrimination Clauses," pp. 458–459.

80 Differently, Choi, *"Like Products" in International Trade Law*, pp. 16–18, 35–36, 66–71 who, based on an out-of-context dictionary interpretation, unconvincingly suggests that the term "competitive" in DCS is a producer-oriented concept and "substitutable" connotes demand views.

81 See *supra*, Ch. 2, fn. 83.

82 Diebold, *Non-Discrimination in International Trade in Services*, p. 320.

must therefore be taken as a constant, while the effect of the discriminatory measure on the *given* product must be assessed with regard to the variable, that is, demand.[83] To clarify, supply-side substitution identifies other firms that are not yet competitors from the demand-side point of view, but that should be included in the relevant market because they already pose a competitive constraint. In contrast to the antitrust market power inquiry, it is not pertinent under Article III of the GATT to identify all possible competitive constraints, but only to determine the actual competitive relationship between the two specific and predefined products at issue.[84]

The product categorization as "like" or DCS is not, as has been said, an end in itself, but a tool to achieve the specific objective of identifying products subject to a protectionist measure. The Article III market definition inquiry is about whether there is the *kind* of competitive relationship between the imported product and the domestic product that could lead to a conclusion of protectionism. As outlined, the concept of protectionism has been perceived objectively by the dispute settlement bodies. It can be thought of as some kind of competitive advantage attributed to the domestic product with which the foreign product competes for sales, that is, which are demand substitutes. Typically, this will be in the form of directing demand for a foreign to a domestic product or of preventing demand from switching from a domestic to a foreign product. In both instances, the most direct way to achieve this effect is by increasing the price of the foreign product with respect to the domestic product. If there is no demand substitutability between the products, and regardless of the existence of supply-side substitutability, there is no question of state intervention to protect a domestic product with respect to the specific foreign product. Consumer choice between the two products could not be interfered with and demand for both products would remain unchanged. Whether the foreign producer can switch, for example, from A to B, is irrelevant to the issue of protectionism because, regardless of whether the producer could or not, the protectionist measure would achieve its goal of giving a competitive advantage to the specific product B. If there were no demand-side but existing supply-side substitution, the foreign producer could switch from A to B, but this would not shed light on the question of whether A is a product which is so comparable to B that it would make

[83] Emch, "Fiscal Discrimination in WTO Law and EU Law," p. 373.

[84] Similarly, Englisch, *Wettbewerbsgleichheit im grenzüberschreitenden Handel*, pp. 297, 482–483, 485.

sense to impose a protectionist measure in order to afford protection to B. Only if consumers, for whatever reason, do not see the products as substitutable, will there be no protective effect of, say, lower taxation for sales of the domestic product compared with the foreign product. Put differently, the need for protectionist governmental intervention typically arises from the fact that consumers do not distinguish between foreign and domestic products when, in the government's eyes, they should. Thus, Article III of the GATT aims to prohibit state interference with consumer preferences. More precisely, it seeks to prevent a tax or regulation having the effect (in particular, through price differentials) of changing consumer choice to a preference for domestic product over an import. In line with the logic of comparative advantages, states are to refrain from altering consumer attraction to a certain good. Only if consumer attraction is not diverted to a product of a less efficient (domestic) producer, will the most efficient (global) producer prevail in competition.

From this teleological interpretation, it follows that consumer choice lies at the heart of the *competitive relationship in the marketplace* test. It is ultimately the consumer who must be regarded as the final arbiter over the question of which products are in a competitive relationship. Thus, under any analytically useful market definition test, demand-side substitution is the determining factor for what are understood as "like" or DCS products. Not only does this rule out supply-side considerations, it is also hard to see how any alternative approach, for example, regulatory purpose, could be consistent with the basic requirement to assess competition between products.

If demand-side substitutability is at the center of attention, the question follows as to which kind of buyers to turn in the assessment. Depending on the distributional level or the social or cultural background, various consumer groups have different attitudes toward the importance of price and product characteristics. Therefore, they may have differing opinions about the substitutability of products. For this reason, much depends on defining the relevant buyer group. This issue has been resolved in antitrust law, but ignored under Article III of the GATT.

In antitrust law, it is acknowledged that products in a market need not be perfect substitutes based on complete substitutability.[85] Further, it is not necessary for a reasonable consumer, often taken as the average consumer, or for a certain customer group, or for all or even a majority

[85] Bishop and Baldauf, *Theoretische Grundlagen und praktische Anwendung wettbewerbsökonomischer Methoden*, pp. 34–36.

of customers to switch between products. What is determinative for the extent of demand-side substitutability is the reaction of the so-called "marginal consumers": those who generally value the product at the price paid but not much more, and who therefore are the first to switch. For antitrust purposes under the SSNIP test, it is necessary that the proportion of customers at the margin who shift their demand from one product to another in response to a price increase is sufficiently large relative to the other customers (termed the "infra-marginal customers") for the price increase to be unprofitable.[86]

For Article III of the GATT, case law has been somewhat confusing on the requisite extent of substitution. The Appellate Body stated that: "while perfectly substitutable products fall within Article III:2, first sentence, imperfectly substitutable products can be assessed under Article III:2, second sentence."[87] Yet, to make economical sense, perfect substitution cannot be understood to require an illusory 100 percent rate of substitution. Restricting a market to perfect substitutes equates to a market served by a single firm, since even homogeneous products are differentiated in some way, for example, by location, availability, or image. Thus, rather a high degree of interchangeability must be mandated for an economic market definition approach. More in this line, the Panel in *Chile – Alcoholic Beverages* stated that: "products do not have to be substitutable for all purposes at all times to be considered competitive. It is sufficient that there is a pattern that they may be substituted for some purposes at some times *by some consumers*."[88] The Panel in *Thailand – Cigarettes* addressed the above-cited passage by the Appellate Body directly, holding that the statement should not be read in an overly restrictive manner limiting the "scope of like products to *identical* products. While this interpretation may be consistent with the economic definition of 'perfectly substitutable,' it would render a finding of likeness under Article III:2, first sentence, almost impossible."[89] Yet the question remains as to who those "some consumers" are. In fact, any determination of a specific group of

[86] This is true in the absence of price discrimination among customer groups, thus barring arbitrage between infra-marginal and marginal customers, Faull and Nikpay, *The EC Law of Competition*, para. 1.140.

[87] Appellate Body Report, *Korea – Alcoholic Beverages*, *supra*, Ch. 2, fn. 71, para. 118; see prior Appellate Body Report, *Canada – Periodicals*, *supra*, Ch. 2, fn. 50, at 28.

[88] Panel Report, *Chile – Alcoholic Beverages*, *supra*, Ch. 2, fn. 68, para. 7.43 (emphasis added).

[89] Panel Report, *Thailand – Cigarettes*, *supra*, Introduction, fn. 23, para. 7.436 (emphasis in original). See also Appellate Body Report, *Philippines – Distilled Spirits*, *supra*, Ch. 2, fn. 44, para. 149.

("captive" or infra-marginal) consumers, as implied by the Panel, would be misguided. For the assessment of demand-side substitution under Article III of the GATT the proportion of the customers who switch must be sufficiently large for a protectionist measure in favor of the domestic product to make sense. Only in case of substitution by a critical mass of consumers would the imported product constitute a competitive threat to the domestic product. Therefore, it is equally immaterial under Article III of the GATT whether a large majority, the average and reasonable, or a certain consumer group does or does not switch between the products at issue.[90] Instead, Article III market definition turns on the aggregate of decisions of all consumers as a whole and, more precisely, focuses on the role of marginal customers, in particular, since, as proposed in the following, the marketplace test is guided by precepts of a price increase test.

2 A price increase test for Article III of the GATT

It may be tempting to just carry the SSNIP test into the trade law context.[91] Yet this has largely been rejected in scholarship.[92] It has been understood as readily apparent that the SSNIP test is inappropriate in the trade law context, since the profitability of a price increase above the competitive level is not an issue in the trade law analysis. Indeed, Article III of the GATT is not concerned with measuring market shares and thus ascertaining market power of private firms, the concept behind the question of whether a SSNIP may be profitable.

This outright and intuitive rejection of a price increase test may be shortsighted. It may be based on the failure to distinguish between, as explained above, the economic concept of market power and the function

[90] This is what Quick and Lau, "Environmentally Motivated Tax Distinctions and WTO Law," p. 432, misunderstand when they ask the question of which is the relevant customer group.

[91] Suggestions to import some version of the SSNIP test into Article III of the GATT have been made by Neven, "The Economic Evaluation of Protection under Art III: Some Principles and Suggestions for the Definition of a Trade Relevant Market," in Cottier and Mavroidis (eds.), *Regulatory Barriers and the Principle of Non-discrimination in World Trade Law*, pp. 331, 332 (2000); Neven, "How Should 'Protection' be Evaluated in Article III GATT Disputes?" p. 438; Choi, *"Like Products" in International Trade Law*, p. 57; Trebilcock and Giri, "The National Treatment Principle in International Trade Law," p. 224; Keck, "WTO Dispute Settlement: What Role for Economic Analysis? A Commentary on Fritz Beuss," *Journal of Industry, Competition and Trade*, 4 (2004), 365, 370.

[92] Emch, "Fiscal Discrimination in WTO Law and EU Law," p. 388; Diebold, *Non-Discrimination in International Trade in Services*, pp. 282, 285, 290.

of market shares as a proxy for the determination of market power. Market shares are indeed of no importance to Article III of the GATT. Yet the ability of pricing above the competitive price level, and thus the economic concept of market power, may actually prove to be informative for conceptualizing a trade market definition test. Even more intriguingly, the following will explain why the SSNIP test may in fact provide more guidance for the Article III test than one might think at first glance.

In order to ensure that the market definition test is meaningful, it is imperative to attune the market definition exercise to the underlying question being asked, that is, for Article III of the GATT whether a measure is protectionist. This means that the concepts of likeness and DCS are meant to capture such products which it would make sense to subject to a protectionist measure. Similar to the hypothetical monopolist test in antitrust analysis, it can make sense to delineate the market in a manner in which, in the absence of competition, domestic firms would benefit from the existence of a trade barrier.[93] This means that products should be considered "like" or DCS when in the presence of a protectionist measure the domestic product would obtain a certain degree of protection.

As described above, protectionism can be thought of as some commercial or competitive advantage conferred on the domestic product. This can be translated to mean that a domestic governmental measure directly or indirectly confers the ability to a domestic firm to maintain or even to increase sales in contrast to what it would sell under competitive conditions. To generalize, in most instances the effect of a protectionist measure will be to create an artificial price differential. As the most extreme form of protectionism, this leaves aside instances of an outright ban on an imported product because, as they will usually take the form of origin-specific discrimination, WTO/GATT jurisprudence would assume likeness anyway. So, in a simplified model, price can be taken as a measure of protection. Two situations of protection can be distinguished.

First, an imported product can be burdened by a tax or a regulatory measure which – holding all else equal – will lead to the imported product's price rising. A parallel may be drawn with the antitrust concept of raising rivals' costs.[94] It describes a firm's strategic behavior which raises the costs of its rivals relative to its own with the aim of excluding or marginalizing

[93] Neven, "The Economic Evaluation of Protection under Art III," p. 336; Neven, "How Should 'Protection' be Evaluated in Article III GATT Disputes?" pp. 421, 438.

[94] Krattenmaker and Salop, "Anticompetitive Exclusion: Raising Rivals' Costs to Achieve Power over Price," *Yale Law Journal*, 96 (1986), 209–293.

the rivals. It usually requires some degree of market power and includes interfering with the production or selling methods of rivals – not only by tying, exclusionary dealings with suppliers, increasing the price of inputs, etc., but also by way of instigating government regulation that has a differential impact on rivals' costs. Quite similar to this last instance, in an international trade law context the inquiry would condemn domestic governmental measures that raise the (marginal) costs of the foreign firm relative to the (marginal) costs of the domestic firm.[95]

Second, a domestic product can benefit from an exemption or reduction in fiscal or regulatory treatment which engenders a price decrease of the domestic product relative to the imported product. In this case, the inquiry would condemn a governmental measure that decreases the (marginal) costs of the domestic firm relative to the (marginal) costs of the foreign firm.

Thus, either the effect of a protectionist measure is an increase in the marginal costs of the imported product, or a decrease in the marginal costs of the domestic product. In both scenarios, the fiscal or regulatory measure will usually favor the domestic product in terms of more stable or even increased sales volume, because either the imported product is made more expensive or the domestic product becomes cheaper relative to the foreign product. Therefore, both instances have in common the creation of an artificial price differential in favor of the domestic product and to the detriment of the import.

For the purpose of identifying protectionism understood as creating an artificial price differential to the benefit of the domestic product, one could turn the analysis to the price distortions associated with domestic discriminatory measures.[96] By virtue of the discriminatory measure, the domestic profit-maximizing firm can, regardless of its market share, increase its price relative to the level that it would have to charge without the increase in marginal cost of the foreign firm or the decrease in its own marginal cost. Therefore, the extent to which the domestic firm can raise the price could serve as proxy for the protection conferred to the domestic firm.

[95] The distinction must be made, however, with regard to the fact that there is no profit sacrifice on the part of the domestic producer in order to raise its rival's costs. The competitive advantage by way of the discriminatory state measure is conferred on the domestic producer free of charge.

[96] See Neven, "How Should 'Protection' be Evaluated in Article III GATT Disputes?" p. 430.

The possibility of raising prices in the first instance is obvious. In this situation, as in the case of raising rivals' costs, the price of the import has been increased. That is why the domestic product's price can be increased profitably and without provoking considerable substitution away to the – still sufficiently more expensive – foreign product.

In the second instance, there might not in fact be an increase in the domestic product's absolute price above its previous price level. But since its marginal costs have been decreased artificially by the governmental measure, even maintaining its previous price level allows for additional profit maximization and thus has the same effect as a straightforward price increase.

Under this perspective, the effect of protection afforded to a domestic firm displays striking similarities to that of a firm that possesses market power. Under both situations, the firm has the competitive advantage of pricing higher than it could under competitive conditions.[97] The difference is that the ability to raise prices does not stem from restricting output, but from the governmental trade barrier. Economically speaking, market definition under Article III of the GATT would entail finding a set of products over which, in the absence of competition (or, in other words, given the presence of the discriminatory measure) a domestic producer would be able to raise prices profitably above the competitive level that would prevail in the absence of the discriminatory measure.[98]

This proposed market definition paradigm has the great virtue of focusing the very process directly on the issue that goes to the heart of the matter of most protectionist cases: the creation of an anticompetitive, protectionist price differential. It uses a test expressed in terms of the major variable of interest in this respect, the ability to price above the competitive level that would prevail absent the protectionist measure. It implicitly focuses upon the relevant economic force, demand-side substitutability,

[97] This would even apply to the above-mentioned instance of an outright ban on the foreign product.

[98] This approach is also in line with the above endorsed view that any inquiry into the regulatory purpose of the governmental measure has no place in the likeness analysis. This is because the proposed approach leaves to a later stage the issue of whether or not the measure is based on a legitimate or protectionist rationale (e.g., under a SATAP test as a separate substantive element independent of the product comparison or under Article XX of the GATT). Although the proposed approach and the regulatory purpose approach both raise the issue of (protectionist) rationale, one must distinguish the suggested likeness test devised according to the *antiprotectionist rationale* of Article III of the GATT from the inquiry into the presence or absence of a *protectionist rationale* (regulatory purpose) of the governmental measure.

measured in response to the creation of a price differential. This market definition approach is useful for GATT purposes, because it establishes the product range over which the imposition of a protectionist measure would make sense and therefore over which the application of such a measure should be prohibited.

Importantly, the inquiry under this test is focused on the assessment of the *hypothetical* ability to increase the price profitably. It is therefore not a measure of *actual* trade effects of the contested measure which the Appellate Body has rejected as necessary to the finding of an Article III violation.[99] Moreover, there exist complications when implementing this test solely on the basis of quantitative measurements of demand-side substitution following a hypothetical price increase.[100] However, it is important to note that these complications do not undermine the conceptual test as such, but only restrict the estimation methods on the methodological level.[101] Admittedly, there is no single completely satisfactory answer to the trade market definition framework. This price increase paradigm is, however, an adequate and workable simplification because, overall, it allows for the inquiry to be conducted on an informed basis which is related to the antiprotectionist aim.

IV POTENTIAL COMPETITION

In antitrust analysis, firms are not only restrained by demand and supply substitution, but also by potential competition. It has already been explained that potential competition does not feature at the antitrust market definition stage. Despite an identical terminology, the notion of "potential competition" for international trade law purposes must be distinguished from the antitrust concept. Under Article III of the GATT, the inquiry does not look at the likely supply-side responses, but at the demand-side. The dispute settlement bodies have usually indiscriminately referred to "potential" or "future competition," as well as to "latent demand." In the interests of analytical rigor and clarity, one may, however,

[99] *Supra*, fn. 50. Even more importantly, the (quantitative) measurement of the competitive relationship between products is analytically distinct from the assessment of actual or potential effects of differential treatment.

[100] See *infra*, Ch. 5, "Potential estimation problems under GATT."

[101] *Contra* Diebold, "Assessing Competition in International Economic Law: A Comparison of 'Market Definition' and 'Comparability,'" *Legal Issues of Economic Integration*, 38 (2011), 115, 127.

distinguish between them more finely. On the one hand, latent demand may be understood as the notion of *present* competition that would, hypothetically, exist but for the trade barrier.[102] This can be understood to connote that some true underlying, yet suppressed, demand patterns exist as a potential and only need to be activated by removing the domestic discriminatory measure. On the other hand, potential or future competition may be taken to refer to competition that will come into being in the *future*.[103] Also hypothetically, it looks at the likely evolution of demand.

Without making any similar conceptual distinction, the Appellate Body in *Korea – Alcoholic Beverages* endorsed the Panel's approach to examine not only extant, but also latent demand and to appraise potential future competition: "Competition in the market place is a dynamic, evolving process. [This] implies that the competitive relationship between products is *not* to be analyzed *exclusively* by reference to *current* consumer preferences."[104] This echoes the approach that has been developed by the ECJ for purposes of Article 110 of the TFEU. The Court recognized that for the purpose of measuring the degree of substitution consumer habits are "variable in time and space … and cannot be considered a fixed rule."[105] It adopted an approach that explicitly takes account of "potential competition."[106] In making this assessment, the ECJ looks at the evolution of competition, in particular, at the evolution of the consumption of the products.[107] The ECJ therefore endorses a prospective analysis of demand substitution.

Extending the scope of the analysis to future demand substitutability is in sharp contrast to antitrust law where the inquiry is not future-oriented. Inquiries into anticompetitive agreements and monopolization or dominance are concerned with the current competitiveness of the markets in

[102] See Diebold, *Non-Discrimination in International Trade in Services*, p. 329 ("potential competition in the narrow sense").

[103] Diebold, *Non-Discrimination in International Trade in Services*, p. 331 ("demand-side future competition").

[104] Appellate Body Report, *Korea – Alcoholic Beverages*, *supra*, Ch. 2, fn. 71, para. 114 (emphasis in original); see also *ibid.*, para. 124.

[105] *Commission* v. *United Kingdom*, *supra*, fn. 25, para. 14.

[106] See *supra*, fn. 23.

[107] *Fruit Wine*, *supra*, fn. 21, para. 15 (the question as to whether products "meet the same needs must be assessed on the basis not of existing consumer habits but of the prospective development of those habits"); *Commission* v. *United Kingdom*, *supra*, fn. 25, para. 6: "it is necessary to consider not only the present state of the market but also the possibilities for development within the context of free movement of goods at the Community level and further potential for the substitution of products for one another which may be revealed by intensification of trade."

question. The market definition assessment is consequently directed at past and present customer behavior.[108] Only merger inquiries, looking at future anticompetitive effects of concentrations, are different. The competitive concern is whether the merger will create or strengthen a position of market power and ultimately raise prices above the prevailing level. Hence, the merger inquiry allows for a limited prospective perspective, particularly in the context of the assessment of the competitive effects of the merger, but also to some extent in the market definition exercise. But the general rule is that different moments in time must be analyzed separately. To permit consistency between the legal regimes, the same approach has been advocated for Article III of the GATT.[109] Yet deviating from the general antitrust rule and more in consonance with merger control, there are good reasons for the analysis in international trade law to look at present and also future markets.

First, a positive legal argument for a future-oriented market definition may be inferred from the terminology of "directly competitive *or* substitutable." Normally, substitutability is a measure for competitiveness. Where products are substitutable, this is what brings them into competition with each other. Still, the legal text explicitly contemplates a situation in which products are substitutable while not in competition. Most probably, this textual distinction was an error in the legal drafting and the terms were actually meant as synonyms.[110] Nevertheless, the strict textual argument may be made that if "directly competitive" is measured by actual demand-side substitutability, "substitutability" may stand for a situation in which there is not (yet) demand-side substitutability, but where products will become "directly competitive" in the future because they are potential demand substitutes.[111] This is in fact the interpretation that the Appellate Body itself professes: "In our view, the word 'substitutable' indicates that the requisite relationship *may* exist between products that are not, at a given moment, considered by consumers to be substitutes but which are, nonetheless, *capable* of being substituted for one another."[112] In this passage, the Appellate Body explicitly acknowledged

[108] See *supra*, Ch. 2, fn. 23.

[109] Emch, "Fiscal Discrimination in WTO Law and EU Law," p. 378.

[110] See *supra*, Ch. 2, fn. 59.

[111] Such a distinction is also suggested by Horn and Weiler, "EC – Asbestos European Communities: Measures Affecting Asbestos and Asbestos-Containing Products," p. 7 fn. 5.

[112] Appellate Body Report, *Korea – Alcoholic Beverages*, *supra*, Ch. 2, fn. 71, para. 114 (emphasis in original).

that the product comparison has to be assessed not only with respect to current consumer preferences, but also in a prospective manner.

Second, teleological considerations are in favor of a future-oriented, "potential competition" analysis. In the international trade law context, scenarios exist in which there is not (thus far) competition between an imported and a domestic product from the consumer perspective at present. But once untampered competitive conditions have been established, consumers may regard those products as substitutes. Such a trade-specific situation may justify accounting for "potential competition."

A first instance that may be thought to call for such an approach is the case where a domestic and an imported product are already in the market, but consumers do not consider them as substitutable because the discriminatory governmental treatment in question has entrenched consumer perceptions over time. For example, a discriminatory tax on imported whisky may have shaped the view of consumers over decades. Due to the price differential they might have internalized that whisky and a certain type of domestic spirit are not substitutes. According to a demand-side analysis, the products in such a case would not stand as being "like" or DCS. This is the scenario with which the Panel and the Appellate Body in *Korea – Alcoholic Beverages* legitimized their support of a potential demand inquiry under the heading of "potential competition."[113] But in order to ensure that the products fall under the ambit of Article III of the GATT despite demand distortion, a simple "but for" test would be sufficient, looking at the *present* demand "but for" the discriminatory measure.[114] This line of argument in fact supports what has been circumscribed above as latent demand, that is, the notion of competition that would exist but for the trade barrier, and not the future-oriented potential competition concept. For a counterfactual version of the market in the absence of the discriminatory domestic measure (the "but for" world) the relevant question is whether the products would be in competition *now*, if the discriminatory measure had never been adopted. This is a different question to the one of whether products may be perceived as substitutes by consumers in the *future* and therefore will be in competition with each other at a later stage. Consequently, entrenched demand is not in itself a reason to adopt a "potential competition" approach for Article III of the GATT.

[113] Appellate Body Report, *Korea – Alcoholic Beverages*, *supra*, Ch. 2, fn. 71, para. 120.

[114] Such approach has been suggested by Korea in Panel Report, *Korea – Alcoholic Beverages*, *supra*, Introduction, fn. 36, para. 10.47. See also Emch, "Fiscal Discrimination in WTO Law and EU Law," p. 379 who argues for a "but for" test.

A better argument for a future-directed inquiry under the notion of "potential competition" is based on a different trade-specific scenario. It relates to the situation where competition between the imported and the domestic products does not (yet) exist from the consumer perspective. This is the case in which an import has just been introduced as a new product on the domestic market. Initially, both the domestic and the imported product may not be considered substitutable by consumers due to their lack of familiarity with the import. Only slowly, after a learning process, would consumers regard them as substitutes. Under antitrust logic, exclusively taking current consumer perceptions at the time of the market introduction as the yardstick, the products would be qualified as "unlike" or not DCS. An importing state would be free to discriminate between the products, hereby shaping consumer preferences and thus preventing any initial competition arising. Such a result would seriously undermine Article III of the GATT: while competition law is primarily concerned with maintaining already existing competitive conditions (usually in markets where consumers are already familiar with the competing products), international trade law – and hence the NT provision – is two-dimensional. On the one side, it is about upholding a level playing field under equal competitive conditions on these markets. This thrust of WTO law is evident since an optimal allocation of resources requires competitive conditions in which supply and demand remain undistorted by governmental intervention. But, on the other side and at a prior stage, it is about the creation of competitive conditions in the first place by opening up markets to new products (in markets where consumers are not yet familiar with the imported products).[115] Thus, WTO law is also concerned with creating contestable markets and preventing market foreclosure as a precondition to the maintenance of actual competitive conditions. It is against this background that it can be understood that the Appellate Body held that Article III of the GATT already protects the "expectations" of an equal competitive relationship between imported and domestic

[115] The WTO core concept of "market access" refers to the access of each Member to the market of other Members. The WTO/GATT regime does not, however, contain a general right to market access. It preserves the liberty of individual Members to regulate market access, subject to specific constraints, such as non-discrimination obligations. Thus, GATT creates only a negative right that access should not be denied by discriminatory rules. On the topic of market access, see Waincymer, *WTO Litigation: Procedural Aspects of Formal Dispute Settlement*, p. 444 (2002) and Puth, "Zölle und allgemeine Fragen des Marktzugangs," in Hilf and Oeter (eds.), *WTO-Recht: Rechtsordnung des Welthandels*, § 10, para. 1 (2005).

products and not any particular actual trade volume.[116] It thus extends its static focus beyond the mere correction of current market distortions to the protection of *future* economic opportunities. In this way the scope of protection under Article III of the GATT encompasses not only present, but also potential competitive relationships. Were Article III of the GATT to disregard potential or future demand, it would be an easy task for states to circumvent the provision in cases of new products with which consumers are still unfamiliar. The goal of opening markets to international trade would be jeopardized. This is why the need to assess market dynamics under Article III of the GATT requires a prospective and dynamic approach to defining markets.

Instead of educated guesswork and speculation, the inquiry into potential competition should then rely on a qualified exercise of discretion based on hard evidence, such as empirical surveys.[117] For the relevant time frame, the Panel in *Korea – Alcoholic Beverages* attempted to draw the line on a "case-by-case basis," promising not to "speculate on what could happen in the distant future," and rather to consider the "near future" or "near term."[118] From an economic standpoint, there is no clear-cut answer to the question of how far into the future such inquiry must project. What can be said is that substitutability of products is always greater the longer the time span.[119] Considering the relevant time horizon on a flexible basis appears appropriate because the period of interest depends, among other things, on how promptly a substantial number of potential buyers learn of the higher prices of a reference good, the presence of long-term contracts in the market or other economic arrangements that would make it expensive to shift to the new supplier, the cost involved in switching to a new product, and the perceptions as to whether the higher price levels are permanent.

While it has thus been established that an inquiry into potential competition is necessary for Article III market definition purposes, it remains

[116] Appellate Body Report, *Japan – Alcoholic Beverages II*, *supra*, Introduction, fn. 15, at 16; see prior GATT Panel Report, *US – Superfund*, *supra*, Ch. 3, fn. 95, para. 5.1.9 and GATT Panel Report, *Japan – Alcoholic Beverages I*, *supra*, Ch. 2, fn. 65, para. 5.11.

[117] The logic that future-oriented analyses necessitate a prospective but facts-based inquiry can be discerned in Panel Report *Korea – Alcoholic Beverages*, *supra*, Introduction, fn. 36, paras. 10.90, 10.91, where the Panel acknowledged the usefulness of hypothetical survey questions on potential competitiveness instead of an inquiry into current consumer behavior.

[118] Panel Report, *Korea – Alcoholic Beverages*, *supra*, Introduction, fn. 36, paras. 10.48, 10.50.

[119] Turner, "The Role of the 'Market Concept' in Antitrust Law," p. 1148.

unresolved what role this analysis plays alongside the analysis of present competition. Should it be of independent substantive significance? Or should it only be complementary in order to confirm the validity of the contemporary analysis? In accordance with the reasoning underlying the inclusion of potential competition, that is, preventing the circumvention of Article III of the GATT, one has to say that the concept of potential competition is to extend the protection conferred to foreign products. At the same time, it should not operate so as to abridge this protection.

What this means can be exemplified. Suppose a future-directed inquiry reveals that competition exists now, but that no future competition is foreseeable. Such a scenario may arise in rapidly evolving industries such as information technologies. Unmistakably, Article III of the GATT would apply, even if products may not be substitutable in the future, because currently competitive products are entitled to the protection of Article III of the GATT regardless of future developments. Thus, present competition must be sufficient in order to find products to be "like" or DCS. In the converse scenario, a pair of products is not presently in competition. Under this reasoning, a finding of likeness or of a DCS relationship could be based largely, or even wholly, on potential competition because the purpose of Article III of the GATT requires the protection of the expectation of competitive conditions for new products on the market.

V THE RELEVANT "MARKET" CONCEPT

Naively, one could think that everybody knows what a market is. The term is omnipresent in everyday parlance, as well as in economics, business life, and politics. However, it is also a highly elusive concept. As the US Supreme Court stated: "a market, as most concepts in law or economics, cannot be measured by metes and bounds."[120] In common usage, a market may at best be thought of as a physical or virtual place where there is a meeting of supply and demand as well as a meeting of the minds of the parties, based on offer and acceptance and related to market transactions.[121] It usually denotes a group of products that are in some way or another related to each other within some geographical confines. But there is not one generally accepted definition for what a market is. As is the case in antitrust and international trade law, even the individual disciplines have

[120] *Times-Picayune Publishing Co.* v. *United States*, 345 US 594, 611 (1953).

[121] Behrens, "Markets," in Clark (ed.), *Encyclopedia of Law & Society*, vol. II, pp. 985, 985 (2007).

trouble coming to a workable definition. In fact, the concept of a market differs significantly between the contexts in which it is discussed. Thus, there are many different ways to define markets, which do not necessarily lead to coinciding results.[122] Yet when looking at antitrust and WTO/GATT precedent adjudicators have (most probably unconsciously) relied on different market concepts. Therefore, the following is to elucidate those different concepts and to analyze whether they are informative in the Article III context. What becomes clear is that market conceptions of other disciplines will not reflect the understanding of antitrust or international trade principles. Consequently, markets defined for the purpose of antitrust and international trade law might differ significantly from each other and from those defined for other purposes. In particular, antitrust markets need to be distinguished from other commonly used market classifications: economic markets, industries, and strategic markets. In contrast, the notion of industries and strategic markets may be informative for market delineation purposes under Article III of the GATT.

In economic theory, the traditional definition of a market has its origin in the work of Cournot and Marshall, later refined by Stigler, who defined a market as a group of products for which, and an area in which, prices "tend to uniformity, allowance being made for transportation costs."[123] This is the set of products and the area over which "the law of one price" holds.[124] Put differently, a classically defined market is that set of products and area within which prices are linked to one another by supply- and demand-side arbitrage. Supply and demand lead to an equilibrium price as arbitrage operates through the free interaction between buyers and sellers to eliminate price differences between products in a market over time.[125] Thus, the single-price property of a market is based on demand and supply substitution.

Courts and agencies in antitrust law have, at times, relied on the analysis of prices, usually in terms of a descriptive comparison of absolute prices.[126] Yet it has only been since the 1980s that the single-price property

[122] Geroski, "Thinking Creatively About Markets," *International Journal of Industrial Organization*, 16 (1998), 677–695.

[123] Stigler, *The Theory of Price*, p. 85 (1966).

[124] Geroski, "Thinking Creatively About Markets," p. 679.

[125] Arbitrage is the opportunity to buy an asset at a low price and to resell it to others at a higher price.

[126] Note that the price criterion has already been part of the traditional tripartite test along with product characteristics and end-uses in both the United States and the EU; see *supra*, Ch. 3, fnn. 13, 18, and 43.

of a market has been converted into more sophisticated (quantitative) tests for antitrust market delineation.[127] The rationale is to group together into the relevant market products that are sufficiently close substitutes in demand and supply to mutually "price discipline" each other. Thus, the comparison of absolute prices (the inquiry into whether the prices of two candidate products tend to unity in absolute terms) and price correlation analysis (the evaluation of the extent to which the movements in the price of one product are associated with the movements in the price of another) have been employed, the latter with particular popularity in Europe even in recent cases.[128] Similarly, those tools have been used, or at least referenced to, in the context of Article III market definition.[129] The Appellate Body very recently issued the clear statement that:

> Price is very relevant in assessing whether imported and domestic products stand in a sufficiently direct competitive relationship in a given market. This is because evidence of price competition indicates that the imported product exercises competitive constraints on the domestic product, and *vice versa*. In this respect, we agree ... that evidence of major

[127] For empirical methods based on price equality see Shrives, "Geographic Market Areas and Market Structure in the Bituminous Coal Industry," *Antitrust Bulletin*, 23 (1978), 589–625; Horowitz, "Market Definition in Antitrust Analysis." For a test based on price correlation see Stigler and Sherwin, "The Extent of the Market," *Journal of Law & Economics*, 28 (1985), 555–585.

[128] For absolute price comparisons in US and EU law see, e.g., *United States* v. *Aluminum Co. of America*, 377 US 271, 276–277 (1964); *United States* v. *Gilette Co.*, 828 F.Supp. 78, 81–83 (DDC 1993); Case IV/M.113, *Courtaulds/SNIA* [1991] OJ C333, paras. 13–14; Case IV/M.1524, *Airtours/First Choice* [2000] OJ L93 1, paras. 22–25; Case COMP/M.3056, *Celanese/Degussa/JV* [2003] OJ L38 47, para. 25. For price correlation analysis in US and EU law see, e.g., *Avnet, Inc.* v. *FTC*, 511 F.2d 70, 77 (7th Cir. 1975); *RSR Corp.* v. *FTC*, 602 F.2d 1317, 1322 (9th Cir. 1979); Case IV/M.308, *Kali+Salz/MdK/Treuhand* [1994] OJ L186 38, paras. 25–28; Case IV/M.1939, *Rexam/American National Can* [2001] OJ C325 11, paras. 10–12; Case COMP/M.4439, *Ryanair/Aer Lingus* [2007] OJ C10 06, para. 34, Annex III; Case COMP/M.4513, *Arjowiggins/M-real Zanders Reflex* [2008] C301 03, paras. 47–59, Annex I; Case COMP/M.5153, *Arsenal/DSP* [2009] C227 10, paras. 38, 79.

[129] The comparison of absolute price differences has been used in Panel Report, *Korea – Alcoholic Beverages*, *supra*, Introduction, fn. 36, para. 10.94; Panel Report, *Chile – Alcoholic Beverages*, *supra*, Ch. 2, fn. 68, para. 7.75 and Panel Report, *Dominican Republic – Cigarettes*, *supra*, Ch. 3, fn. 80, paras. 7.331, 7.333, 7.336. Price correlations have not been used so far, but Panels have hinted at the potential role of the analysis of price movements: Panel Report, *Korea – Alcoholic Beverages*, *supra*, Introduction, fn. 36, para. 10.94: "absolute price differences are less important than behavioural changes that occur due to relative price movements"; and Panel Report, *Chile – Alcoholic Beverages*, *supra*, Ch. 2, fn. 68, para. 7.75: "What is important is the effect of relative price movements, since it is relative prices and their changes that influence consumer behaviour in the dynamic situation of changes in the demand for directly competitive or substitutable products."

> price differentials could demonstrate that the imported and domestic products are in completely separate markets.[130]

However, the unitary price that circumscribes what is termed in antitrust literature as the "economic market" has very limited conceptual usefulness for both antitrust and trade market definition.[131] With regard to antitrust law, economic markets are not designed to answer the relevant question of whether a SSNIP would be profitable, that is, whether a market is worth monopolizing. They merely identify the products and areas for which arbitrage keeps prices linked. An economic market may be of interest for antitrust market definition because arbitrage is relevant in the assessment of market power. As it has been observed, "arbitrage tempers but does not necessarily eliminate market power," since it is only one out of many factors.[132] In fact, antitrust markets can match, but can also be smaller or larger than an economic market.[133]

Moreover, economic and international trade markets are conceptually different. Since an economic market is based on the concepts of arbitrage and an equilibrium price, which rely on the interaction of demand and supply, it cannot be seen as in harmony with a trade-relevant market that is based, as conceived above, solely on demand-side substitution. Whether or not a uniform price prevails is not necessarily an indicator of the existence or absence of demand substitutability between two products. This is particularly true in the case of product differentiation. Grouping all products with a unitary price may fit an economic market model. Yet allocating products to different economic markets may fail to account for potential buyer substitution to other products outside this price range on the basis of a price/quality trade-off. For instance, consumers may switch

130 Appellate Body Report, *Philippines – Distilled Spirits*, *supra*, Ch. 2, fn. 44, para. 215.

131 For the distinction between "economic" and antitrust markets see, e.g., Scheffman and Spiller, "Geographic Market Definition Under the US Department of Justice Merger Guidelines," *Journal of Law & Economics*, 30 (1987), 123, 127; Simons and Williams, "The Renaissance of Market Definition," p. 849; Church and Ware, *Industrial Organization: A Strategic Approach*, pp. 601–603 (2000), available at: http://works.bepress.com/cgi/viewcontent.cgi?article=1022&context=jeffrey_church.

132 Scheffman and Spiller, "Geographic Market Definition Under the US Department of Justice Merger Guidelines," p. 127.

133 For example, a SSNIP may be profitable in an economic market if other producers are capacity constrained (in case of low supply elasticity), and hence cannot take up consumers who would want to switch away. In such a case, the antitrust market would be smaller than the economic market. Conversely, Scheffman and Spiller, "Geographic Market Definition Under the US Department of Justice Merger Guidelines," observed that "producers outside an economic market might be included in an antitrust market if their supply elasticity is sufficiently large at prices slightly above the prevailing price."

from expensive high quality products to lower priced substitutes of lower quality following a price increase of the former product.[134]

Therefore, the use of price comparison tests in antitrust and trade market definition blurs the analytical distinction between different market concepts, and ignores the point that antitrust and trade relevant markets may not coincide with economic markets.

Harvard School economists, in particular Bain, developed the notion of "industries," defined as a group of products featuring high CPE with each other, but low CPE with other products.[135] Bain's concept of an industry highlights the idea of interdependence between products. In particular, it is premised on the realization that in the real world products are seldom perfect substitutes for each other and that substitutability is a matter of degree. He reinforced the notion of CPE in order to distinguish significant from insignificant interdependence.

The Bainian emphasis on CPE was explicitly taken up by the US Supreme Court in *Cellophane*, and also found its way into the ECJ case law. However, as will be outlined later, CPE of demand alone is, contrary to widely-held belief, insufficient to define antitrust markets. Therefore, for antitrust purposes, the notion of industries is misleading and would generate overly broad markets. It suffices here to indicate that CPE of demand may play a more important role in international trade law than in antitrust law; for which reason the notion of industries may be more of a guiding concept for the trade market definition.

Strategic markets, a concept prevalent in marketing literature,[136] comprise product groups (or geographic areas) in which similar marketing strategies, sales methods, distribution techniques, promotional schemes, or advertising efforts are employed.[137] In particular, different distribution channels have repeatedly figured in antitrust market analysis.[138] A

[134] Motta, *Competition Policy: Theory and Practice*, p. 109.

[135] See Bain, "Relation of Profit Rate to Industry Concentration: American Manufacturing, 1936–1940," fn. 6, which contains this definition. See also Bain, *Price Theory*, p. 52 (1952): "The magnitude of [the] cross-elasticity indicates the degree of substitutability. A low cross-elasticity indicates poor substitutes; a high cross-elasticity indicates close substitutes."

[136] Nevo-Ilan, "Definition of the Relevant Market: (Lack of) Harmony between Industrial Economics and Competition Law," p. 61 (2007) (on file with author). See generally, Kotler *et al.*, *Marketing Management*, pp. 12–16 (2009).

[137] Geroski, "Thinking Creatively About Markets," pp. 683–691; van den Bergh and Camesasca, *European Competition Law and Economics*, p. 118.

[138] Lücking and Simon, "Definition of the Relevant Market," paras. 3.167–3.172; Schwalbe and Zimmer, *Kartellrecht und Ökonomie*, pp. 135–137.

strategic perspective accounts for consumer buying patterns, but does not ask the question of how buying behavior changes in response to changes in price. Therefore, strategic markets need not be identical to antitrust markets.[139] In several international trade law cases, however, the analysis of marketing strategies and distribution channels has been understood as quite informative in order to confirm conclusions drawn from other evidence.[140]

However, there are important pitfalls. For instance, the use of distinct channels of distribution as an indicator that products belong to separate markets may be misleading if products sold through different channels compete with each other further downstream, closer to the level of the user or consumer.

Inquiring into marketing strategies may provide valuable information on demand patterns. Yet it does not directly provide information on demand-side substitutability, but only on the strategy of a company to capture consumers. It may therefore not only respond to, but is also aimed at creating consumer patterns. Marketing and distribution may be employed to actually cause distinctions in order to differentiate a product from its competitors. The Panel equated this scenario to cases in which a discriminatory governmental treatment shapes consumer perceptions. In such cases, the Panel concluded that it was necessary to disregard information derived from the analysis of marketing strategies under certain conditions. In particular, in cases of physically similar products, this should apply if the analysis of such strategies comes to the conclusion that consumers do not consider these products to be substitutes, although they would do so had they not been influenced by the marketing strategy.[141] Consequently, the dispute settlement bodies formulated a rule according to which evidence from the analysis of marketing strategies would have probative value only if it points to products being demand substitutes, for example, when they both target the same consumer group, but not in the opposite case where they create perceptual distinctions between

[139] For an approach advocating the use of marketing principles and techniques to define relevant antitrust markets see Karp, "A Consumer Oriented Approach to Market Definition Under the Antitrust Laws," *University of San Francisco Law Review*, 18 (1983), 221–251.

[140] See *supra*, Ch. 3, fnn. 218–220.

[141] Panel Report, *Korea – Alcoholic Beverages*, *supra*, Introduction, fn. 36, paras. 10.65, 10.66: "If two products are physically identical or nearly so, it is highly probable that they are 'like.' They should not then be found to be not directly competitive or substitutable because marketing campaigns (or government tax regimes) have created a distinction in consumer perceptions."

products.[142] However, it does not seem appropriate to treat the situation of a governmental measure and the marketing activities of firms similarly. While the former creates distorted consumer perceptions in order to prevent competition, the latter is an expression of competition itself. In a competitive environment, firms are free to advertise their products. A new product to the marketplace would not be able to make a successful market entry if it could not generate demand by way of heavy advertising. To categorically treat demand created or influenced by marketing strategies as "distorted," and therefore irrelevant, is plainly wrong. A comparison with antitrust law makes this clear, where consumer perceptions subject to and formed by marketing and promotional activities are not disregarded, but are taken as the manifestation of the competitive relationship.[143] The underpinning of the Panel's erroneous logic seems to be that there is some underlying form of untainted consumer perceptions, which alone shall be determinative for market definition. Yet this is not only unrealistic, but disregards the real world, where demand for most products is stimulated and shaped by marketing and product differentiation.

Finally, the question remains as to what extent the trade market definition can be informed by relevant antitrust markets. In view of perceived differences in the regimes' policy objectives (protection of competitive opportunities versus protection of actual mechanisms of competition), the Panel in *Korea – Alcoholic Beverages* distinguished the trade market concept from the antitrust one. It stated that: "while the specifics of the

[142] Panel Report, *Korea – Alcoholic Beverages*, *supra*, Introduction, fn. 36, para. 10.95: "Marketing strategies alone should not be the basis for finding products not potentially competitive ... On the other hand, when two products ... begin to be marketed in similar fashions ... it is strong evidence of potential competition." Yet differently and obviously oblivious of possible distorted demand, Panel Report, *Chile – Alcoholic Beverages*, *supra*, Ch. 2, fn. 68, para. 7.45: "Marketing strategies that highlight *fundamental product distinctions* or, alternatively, underlying similarities may be useful tools for analysis" (emphasis added); and *ibid.*, para. 7.59: "In our view, if products have quite distinct channels of distribution that could be a negative indicator with respect to substitutability".

[143] See as a good example *Nestlé/Perrier*, *supra*, Ch. 3, fn. 51, para. 13: "The market of bottled source water in France is characterized by strong marketing and promotional activities, with high advertising budgets for the three main suppliers. As a consequence of the resulting image of natural, pure and healthy product associated with source waters consumers do not recognize soft drinks as a substitute of bottled source water for daily use at home. The general image directly associated by consumers with branded source water as a consequence of the common axes of the publicity of each brand, and their additional attachment to each particular brand reduce the importance of price as purchasing criteria (small elasticity of demand). Therefore, a small increase in the price of source waters is not likely to induce a reaction of consumers resulting in a significant substitution of bottled source water by soft drinks."

interaction between trade and competition law are still being developed, we concur that the market definitions need not be the same."[144] The findings of the Panel are confirmed when looking at EU trade law. On one occasion, the ECJ ignored the claim that Article 110 market definition should be undertaken according to antitrust law rules.[145] On another occasion, Advocate General Alber found that the "assessment … for competition-law purposes can only be of limited importance … Each area of law is subject to its own rules, the application of which must be examined separately."[146] Although the TFEU contains both antitrust and non-discrimination provisions, which are applied and interpreted by the same institution and court, the ECJ has – quite surprisingly – never made reference to antitrust market definition in the context of Article 110 of the TFEU.

It has been argued above that on close examination the policy rationales of the two regimes have, in fact, more in common than what separates them. But although they share as their common denominators the concept of competitive conditions, as well as the welfare and efficiency goals, it will become clear that the Panel's observation remains correct, but for different reasons. Nevertheless, on the occasions of *Chile – Alcoholic Beverages* and *Mexico – Soft Drinks*, Panels referred to decisions by national antitrust authorities in order to corroborate their conclusions about products being DCS.[147] In *Chile – Alcoholic Beverages* the Panel justified its reliance on the antitrust market definition as additional evidence with the observation that antitrust markets would generally utilize narrower market definitions than those used when analyzing markets pursuant to Article III:2(2) of the GATT.[148] On this premise, "it seems logical that competitive conditions sufficient for defining an appropriate market with respect to antitrust analysis would *a fortiori* suffice for an Article III analysis."[149]

Two points must be made here. First, Panels inferred from the alleged differences in policy objectives that the markets must be defined more

[144] Panel Report, *Korea – Alcoholic Beverages, supra*, Introduction, fn. 36, para. 10.81.

[145] *Aquavit, supra*, fn. 32, para. 28.

[146] Opinion of Advocate General Alber, *Commission* v. *France, supra*, fn. 27, para. 63.

[147] Panel Report, *Chile – Alcoholic Beverages, supra*, Ch. 2, fn. 68, paras. 7.86, 7.87; Panel Report, *Mexico – Soft Drinks, supra*, Ch. 2, fn. 80, para. 8.77. Similarly, but not in the context of Article 110 of the TFEU, the ECJ acknowledged that market definition arguments in a tax case were in accordance with EU antitrust law, Case C-481/98, *Commission* v. *France* [2001] ECR I-3369, para. 29.

[148] Panel Report, *Chile – Alcoholic Beverages, supra*, Ch. 2, fn. 68, para. 7.87.

[149] Panel Report, *Chile – Alcoholic Beverages, supra*, Ch. 2, fn. 68, para. 7.87.

broadly under international trade law than under antitrust law.[150] This reasoning has been reiterated by commentators.[151] Again, EU case law appears to confirm the assertion that markets defined for the purposes of non-discrimination provisions are indeed broader than those defined for antitrust law purposes. For example, in two cases the ECJ held bananas to be "in competition" with other fruit under Article 110(2) of the TFEU, while the Court considered bananas to constitute a separate relevant market under Article 102 of the TFEU.[152] Similarly, in a number of cases concerning alcoholic beverages, the ECJ found whisky to be "similar" or "in competition" with other spirits for the purpose of Article 110 of the TFEU.[153] In contrast, the European Commission defined the relevant market in an Article 101 and in a merger case in a way that whisky constitutes a market separate from that of other spirits.[154]

Yet the distinction that the theory of broad trade versus narrow antitrust markets purports to justify does not exist in reality. The assumption that market boundaries need to be drawn to different extents in antitrust and international trade law actually underscores the identical thrust of both legal regimes. A broader trade-relevant market and a narrower antitrust market are actually in line with the common goal of ensuring competitive relationships in the marketplace. The former results in a broader range of products falling under Article III of the GATT, and thus reflects a more extensive application of the NT discipline. The latter makes a finding of market power more likely, and for this reason leads to a stricter application of the antitrust rules. Thus, in terms of pursuing a procompetitive goal, the GATT NT agenda and the antitrust agenda actually come close to each other.

The second – more fundamental – point is, however, that this purported relationship between trade and antitrust markets does not in fact

[150] Panel Report, *Korea – Alcoholic Beverages*, *supra*, Introduction, fn. 36, para. 10.81: "It is not illogical that markets be defined more broadly when implementing laws primarily designed to protect competitive opportunities than when implementing laws designed to protect the actual mechanisms of competition."

[151] See, e.g., Goco, "Non-Discrimination, 'Likeness,' and Market Definition in World Trade Organization Jurisprudence," p. 333.

[152] Case 184/85, *Commission* v. *Italy* [1987] ECR 2013, para. 12; Case 193/85, *Co-Frutta* v. *Amministrazione delle finanze dello Stato* [1987] ECR 2085, para. 21; *United Brands*, *supra*, Ch. 2, fn. 30, para. 35.

[153] For example, Case 169/78, *Commission* v. *France*, *supra*, fn. 19, para. 40; *Aquavit*, *supra*, fn. 32, para. 34.

[154] 85/562/EEC, *Sole Distribution Agreement for Whiskey and Gin* [1985] OJ L369 19, para. 24; Case IV/M.938, *Guinness/Grand Metropolitan* [1998] OJ L288 24, paras. 23, 82.

exist and that therefore any *a fortiori* argument is erroneous. The market concepts in antitrust and international trade law are different. Both take different economic forces into account, (actual) demand and supply in antitrust, and actual and potential demand in trade market definition. The antitrust market definition answers the question of whether the market is worth monopolizing, that is, whether a SSNIP would be profitable. For trade market definition, as applied by the Panel, this has been irrelevant. With respect to the trade market, an antitrust market is therefore not in *a minore ad maius* relationship. An antitrust market – even if smaller in scope – is not necessarily part of a broader trade market. In fact, the practical experience shows that the relationship between antitrust and trade markets is more complicated than what has been claimed by WTO adjudicators. For example, in *Mexico – Soft Drinks* the Panel found that high-fructose corn syrup (HFCS) and cane sugar were DCS for the purposes of Article III:4 of the GATT.[155] To come to this conclusion, it relied, among other things, on a decision by the Mexican antitrust agency that buttressed the Panel's findings of a broad market. Yet there is also antitrust case law (on another geographical market) pointing in the other direction. In a Section 7 Clayton Act case, the US Court of Appeals for the Eighth Circuit in fact found a HFCS market separate from that of sugar.[156]

In conclusion, although both antitrust and Article III market definition rely on similar theoretical underpinnings, market delineations for the same products are not necessarily identical in the two disciplines and, therefore, are not interchangeable. They are the result of a case-by-case analysis and may differ within any one of the two legal fields. For example, antitrust market definitions themselves do not constitute a coherent body of case law even if the same products and the same substantive test are involved.[157] This is not a deplorable state of incoherence, but necessarily flows from the fact that markets change across time and space, and that the exercise of delineating markets can change depending on whether it is conducted for monopolization, cartel, or merger analysis. Similarly, recalling the image of the accordion of likeness that stretches differently

[155] Panel Report, *Mexico – Soft Drinks*, *supra*, Ch. 2, fn. 80, para. 8.78.

[156] *United States* v. *Archer-Daniels-Midland Co.*, 866 F.2d 242, 246 (8th Cir. 1988).

[157] For reasons why antitrust markets can differ, see Vogel and Vogel, "Demand and Elasticities: How to Assess the Relevant Market," *Concurrences*, 4 (2009), paras. 10–15. For divergences between the US and EU jurisdictions see Coppi and Walker, "Substantial Convergence or Parallel Paths?" p. 106.

in the various provisions of GATT, trade market definitions can vary in the different contexts.

Therefore, turning to specific prior antitrust market definitions for Article III purposes is uninformative at best and misleading at worst. For the purpose of this comparative analysis, however, it is important to emphasize that this is not the aim of importing antitrust market definitions into international trade law. Rather, the method employed for delineating relevant antitrust markets, an economic approach, may provide guidance for developing a specific economic methodology for trade relevant markets.

VI THE ROLE OF THE TRADITIONAL CRITERIA

The above conceived conceptual framework for a marketplace test opens the door to an informed choice and application of relevant evidence. Under the economics-based framework, evidence is only relevant if it sheds light on demand substitution. Relevant evidence can be quantitative or qualitative in nature, with both types reflecting different modes of direct and indirect analysis of demand substitution.

Quantitative criteria represent direct evidence of demand substitution. As evidence of actual switching it carries more weight because it registers "revealed preferences."

In contrast to how they have been employed under the traditional approach, qualitative criteria may be of probative value only if they serve as proxy for demand-side substitutability. They amount to indirect evidence of demand substitution because they do not provide evidence of actual demand-side substitutability, but allow for inferences to be made about the likelihood of demand-side substitutability. Under this framework, it is not the commonality or divergence in physical characteristics or end-uses *per se* that are important, but the consumer *perceptions* of qualitative factors. What matters is whether these qualitative differences influence demand for the products. There are some rare and exceptional instances where case law has been receptive to this conception.[158] More economically speaking, examining qualitative factors is to assess whether they are capable of satisfying an inelastic customer need. In making this assessment regard must be had to the needs of marginal consumers in particular. As a major consequence, it is not necessary for products to be

[158] See *supra*, Ch. 3, fn. 214.

actually identical or substantially similar in physical characteristics – as suggested by adjudicators for Article III:2(1) of the GATT – in order for them to be considered substitutable.

As with the most common qualitative criteria, physical characteristics and end-uses, other qualitative criteria play a role to the extent that they help to ascertain demand substitutability. Thus, contrary to what has been held by WTO adjudicators, PPMs can come under the purview of Article III of the GATT, but only when differences or commonalities in PPMs influence (marginal) consumer behavior.[159] In contrast, tariff classifications that are still prevalent in modern WTO case law would need to be discarded from the analysis. As Hudec summarized: "the tariff distinction was a classic example of an objectively-based distinction of virtually no commercial significance."[160] The classifications of products in the tariff nomenclatures do not bear upon the market and it is inconceivable that they can shed light on demand patterns.

Under this approach the *Border Tax* criteria are functionally subordinate and instrumental to the market-based framework. A doctrinal basis for this approach may be found in the Appellate Body's statement that "whether the Border Tax Adjustments framework is adopted or not, it is important under Article III:4 to take account of evidence which indicates whether, and to what extent, the products involved are – or could be – in a competitive relationship in the marketplace."[161]

Moreover, there are two ways of thinking about the relationship between the indirect and direct mode of analysis. Either an indirect assessment is complementary but subsidiary to the direct assessment, then qualitative evidence would be used only if a quantitative analysis is not feasible; or, as contemplated in the *Commission Notice on market definition*, a qualitative analysis could be conceived as a first-step screening device. The latter approach has already been criticized for the risk of delineating markets too narrowly. Customers may regard products as substitutes despite different attributes. Moreover, it seems even less appropriate in the area of GATT law. Article III proceedings are concerned with the comparison of

[159] See similarly Thaggert, "A Closer Look at the Tuna-Dolphin Case: 'Like Products' and 'Extrajurisdictionality' in the Trade and Environment Context," in Cameron *et al.* (eds.), *Trade & the Environment: The Search for Balance*, vol. I, pp. 69, 72, 85 (1994).

[160] Hudec, "'Like Product': The Differences in Meaning in GATT Articles I and III," p. 116.

[161] Appellate Body Report, *EC – Asbestos*, *supra*, Ch. 2, fn. 70, para. 103. The ECJ may have a similar application of the traditional criteria under Article 110 of the TFEU in mind, see, e.g., *Fruit Wine*, *supra*, fn. 21, para. 15: "objective characteristics which ensure that a product is capable of meeting the same need as another product from the point of view of certain categories of consumers."

two specific predetermined products only.[162] There is no need, as in antitrust proceedings, and in particular in merger cases, to limit the scope of the investigation in view of numerous possible substitutes.

Evidently, direct evidence of substitution patterns is preferable. But there is no formal hierarchy. Indeed, flexibility is required as a practical matter, since qualitative evidence, such as information on the physical characteristics and intended uses, will always – and for lack of empirical data often exclusively – be available. And after all, it would be to ignore reality if one were unaware that adjudicators in general are intuitively guided by a first impression based on physical attributes and end-uses.

Under the proposed framework, the question of weight among the traditional criteria becomes easily soluble. Instead of a general rule, it is a matter of how much weight consumers attribute to a certain factor in their specific purchasing decision. Moreover, under the marketplace test adjudicators cannot patronize consumers any longer. If (marginal) consumers disregard, for example, health risks or environmental hazards as determinative for their purchasing decision, these considerations will be irrelevant, even if this leads to "unreasonable" results from the perspective of the adjudicators. By contrast, when considerations other than the perception of physical characteristics or end-uses impact on demand patterns, they are relevant to an equal degree at the product comparison stage and must not be relegated to the stringent justification requirement under Article XX of the GATT.

Where demand perceptions guide the application of qualitative criteria, CTH takes a key role in the analysis. In fact, the proposed focus on demand substitutability would seem to be nothing besides an inquiry into the CTH.[163] Whereas it is a stand-alone substantive element under the *Border Tax* framework, CTH are the guiding principle against which to assess physical characteristics, end-uses, and all other relevant evidence under the proposed approach. Thus, CTH as a separate criterion has no independent significance under an economic approach. Rather, it

[162] This is at least true for the "like" products definition. Whether the subsequent step of determining the existence of differential treatment requires a comparison of the treatment of the broader group of domestic and imported products is open to debate; see *supra*, Ch. 2, fn. 94 and *supra*, fn. 47.

[163] Panel Report, *Philippines – Distilled Spirits*, *supra*, Introduction, fn. 23, paras. 7.104 *et seq.* in fact equated the assessment of "the competitive relationship between the products" on the basis of a quantitative measurement of demand-side substitutability with the inquiry into CTH.

is merged with the examination of the other criteria.[164] Admittedly, this is in contradiction to the Appellate Body in *EC – Asbestos*, which explicitly held that each criterion must be examined separately and that CTH is not, on its own, a sufficient aspect of the likeness determination.[165] However, it also resolves the inherent inconsistency that results from requiring, on the one hand, a market-detached, mechanical examination of the criteria in the abstract and, on the other hand, stipulating an inquiry into the competitive relationships in the marketplace.

VII MAKING SENSE OF THE DIFFERENT ARTICLE III PROHIBITIONS

The distinction between "like" and DCS products has no basis in economic theory. But to make sense of it and to render the provisions operative, the proposed approach can contribute to a more coherent understanding of the interrelation between the three instances of product comparison under Article III of the GATT, and, in particular, the relationship between the first and second sentence of Article III:2. The different scopes of application of Article III prohibitions can be reconciled with the unifying concept of competitive relationships in the marketplace and differing degrees of demand substitutability.

Case law has distinguished Article III:2(1) from Article III:2(2) by the additional requirement for the former that products must share most physical characteristics. To recall, the Appellate Body also described the relationship between the first and the second sentence as a logical continuum in which the concepts of likeness and DCS represent different points on the spectrum of degrees of competitiveness or substitutability.[166] As the Appellate Body indicated with its distinction between perfect and imperfect substitutability, it seems that the degree of competitiveness, and thus substitutability, must be very high for the first sentence and somewhat lower for the second.[167] Confirmation can be found

164 A slightly different way of putting it is to declare CTH the decisive criterion under which all the other evidence should be considered; see Diebold, *Non-Discrimination in International Trade in Services*, p. 263.

165 Appellate Body Report, *EC – Asbestos*, *supra*, Ch. 2, fn. 70, para. 139.

166 See *supra*, Ch. 2, fn. 70 and Ch. 3, fn. 283.

167 Appellate Body Report, *Canada – Periodicals*, *supra*, Ch. 2, fn. 50, at 28; Appellate Body Report, *Korea – Alcoholic Beverages*, *supra*, Ch. 2, fn. 71, para. 118. See also Appellate Body Report, *Philippines – Distilled Spirits*, *supra*, Ch. 2, fn. 44, para. 148.

in the Appellate Body's statement that: "like products are, necessarily, in the highest degree of competitive relationship in the marketplace."[168] Although this passage was made in the context of the definition of "like" products under the safeguard provision of Article 2.6 of the Agreement on Textiles and Clothing, it is clear from the accompanying footnote that this statement also applies to the relationship between likeness and DCS under Article III of the GATT.[169] Therefore, it is a matter of degree of closeness in the competitive relationship, or degree of (demand) substitutability, that distinguishes the two sentences. Since the DCS concept is practically co-extensive with the scope of Article III:4 of the GATT, it also distinguishes Article III:2(1) from Article III:4. Consequently, the Appellate Body's approach of making physical similarity an additional criterion for the first sentence does not make economic sense, because a high degree of competitiveness, or demand substitutability, can exist regardless of physical similarity.

Support for the suggestion that the intensity of competition makes the difference between likeness and DCS can be found in the architecture of Article III:2(1) and (2) of the GATT. Under the first sentence, "like" products have to be treated identically, whereas a *de minimis* standard for differential treatment applies to DCS products. This logic can be explained with reference to the difference in competitive proximity. The strict standard applied to the first sentence seems to be based on the following assumption. If two products are highly competitive and substitutable, that is, if they are "like," any difference in the fiscal treatment applied to them, even the smallest, will translate into a significant competitive advantage for the domestic product. In contrast, it can be thought that a mere *de minimis* difference in fiscal treatment of DCS products, which are substitutable to a lesser degree, would affect consumer demand only marginally. Hence, it would not affect the competitive relationship between the products in any significant way.

Against this background, it makes sense to group products under the first or second sentence according to whether or not they are so highly competitive that even a minimal differential treatment would have a noticeable impact on the competitive conditions.[170]

[168] Appellate Body Report, *US – Cotton Yarn*, *supra*, Ch. 2, fn. 61, para. 97.

[169] The footnote explicitly refers to GATT and remarks that: "in these cases, [the Appellate Body] stated that 'like' products are perfectly substitutable and that 'directly competitive' products are characterized by a high, but imperfect, degree of substitutability." *US – Cotton Yarn*, *supra*, Ch. 2, fn. 61, para. 87 fn. 68.

[170] One could also think of the distinction from a different angle. Likeness could be understood as "market" *plus* "policy." The former would be understood in terms of the high

After all, the difference in demand substitutability between likeness and DCS is a matter of different benchmarks on the spectrum of competitiveness. This marks the importance of economic analysis, on the one hand, but also its limits, on the other. Despite the conceptual clarity and appropriateness of measuring demand substitutability, there remains considerable uncertainty and discretion in the concrete analysis to the extent that "it is difficult, if not impossible, in the abstract, to indicate precisely where on this spectrum" likeness and DCS fall and to explain why two products are DCS, but not "like."[171] Not every degree of substitutability is sufficient, and economics does not provide an answer as to which degree of substitutability is necessary.[172] Economics can provide the guiding framework for the analysis and describe what the gaps in substitutability are between products. Whether or not the gaps are sufficiently large then warrants a legal conclusion. The difficulty of this problem is well illustrated in antitrust analysis. Under *Brown Shoe*, submarkets can exist within broader markets. In essence, this means that different degrees of substitutability should be considered, and that any market reasonably defined is acceptable under the law. Therefore, the critical matter of degree is a policy issue and requires a value judgment as to the adequate threshold that is left outside the realm of economics.[173] In this respect the concept of the market under Article III of the GATT will always remain "normative" and "legal" in nature. This discussion will resurface again with regard to the estimation of CPE of demand as one common measure for demand substitutability. The difficult question will be how high the level of CPE needs to be for products to be DCS or even "like."

intensity of competition. The latter would not connote the regulatory purpose approach, but would be understood in the sense that the product's functionality should be that there is no reason at all to differentiate treatment between the two "like" products. In contrast, there might be a reason, for example, because of an informational advantage of the government vis-à-vis its citizens on trade hazards, to differentiate – within the *de minimis* tolerance level – between two DCS products. For example, if a government says that all cars must carry catalyst X because only this catalyst guarantees Z percent emissions of gas, then all cars with this catalyst must be given *exactly* the same treatment – and are therefore "like." An imported car with catalyst Y which attains the Z percent emissions standard could be in intense competition, but (for example, by virtue of some informational advantage) the government could have reason to treat it slightly differently under the DCS standard.

171 Appellate Body Report, *EC – Asbestos, supra*, Ch. 2, fn. 70, para. 99.

172 In fact, the profitability threshold above which a price increase is profitable presents an economic answer to this question in antitrust analysis.

173 Brinker, "Praktische Probleme der Marktabgrenzung aus rechtlicher Sicht," p. 44; Turner, "The Role of the 'Market Concept' in Antitrust Law," p. 1147.

VIII CONCLUSION

To close this chapter, the main insights are reiterated briefly. First, the meaning of "like" or DCS products depends on the purpose of Article III of the GATT. Second, the economic rationale of the antiprotectionist objective requires an inquiry into the competitive relationship of two products in the marketplace based on demand-side substitutability and guided by the question of whether the domestic producer can profitably increase the price above the competitive level in the presence of the trade barrier. Third and fourth, the inquiry is prospective and must be distinguished from other "market" concepts. Fifth, evidence under this framework is relevant to the extent that it informs on demand-substitutability. Lastly, the difference between likeness and DCS in Article III of the GATT is a matter of degree in competitiveness and therefore in demand-side substitutability.

5

The implementation of an economic approach: quantitative methods

I INTRODUCTION

The implementation of an economic approach, in particular, the issue of generating economic evidence, is usually left to economists. Yet an informed legal discussion of an economic approach cannot stop at this point. It has to address the merits and limitations of economic evidence itself. Economic evidence encompasses a wide spectrum of techniques and information of varying complexity, ranging from merely organizing and presenting simple descriptive statistics of quantitative data (for example, on prices and demand) to performing in-depth quantitative analyses.[1]

In a way that is accessible to the legal community, this chapter examines the role that more sophisticated economic (quantitative) evidence can play in implementing an economics-based approach to market definition. The main benefit of quantitative evidence is that it can be instrumental to legal decision making by providing the quantification of legal issues. This is relevant where legal decisions must be informed by conclusions from hard and real world data, and that require the measurement of the relationship between different influences or events. Thus, quantitative economics is useful where an effects-based legal analysis is necessary

In antitrust law, the extent to which quantitative techniques are used differs on the two sides of the Atlantic. The "empirical revolution in antitrust analysis" began in the United States in the mid 1980s concurrently with the rise of an effects-based approach to antitrust analysis.[2] Before the issuance of the *1982 Merger Guidelines*, courts had usually been hostile

[1] For an overview of, and non-technical introduction to, quantitative methods used in competition law see Lexecon, *An Introduction to Quantitative Techniques in Competition Analysis*, (u.d.), available at: www.crai.com/ecp/assets/quantitative_techniques.pdf.

[2] Baker and Bresnahan, *Economic Evidence in Antitrust: Defining Markets and Measuring Market Power*, p. 2 fn. 4 (2006), available at: http://ssrn.com/abstract=931225.

to quantitative evidence.[3] Nowadays, by contrast, courts find it helpful or even a necessary prerequisite for establishing a relevant antitrust market.[4]

In Europe, the European Commission declared in 1994 that it would make use of quantitative methods for the purpose of analyzing demand substitutability.[5] The role of quantitative analysis has been elevated by the *Commission Notice on market definition*, which referenced several quantitative techniques. Still, rigorous quantitative analysis is not the hallmark of market definition. It is still less common than it is in the United States, encountered mostly in merger cases, and then usually in the form of less complex empirical instruments, such as price comparisons.[6]

As already summarized, the use of statistical evidence and quantitative techniques by WTO dispute settlement bodies has evolved from general reluctance to an increasing use in recent times.[7] Quite recently, in fact, the Appellate Body gave a clear mandate to the use of econometrics: "[Econometric] modelling exercises are likely to be an important analytical tool that a panel should scrutinize. The relative complexity of a model and its parameters is not a reason for a panel to remain agnostic about them."[8] Quantitative methods have also come to the fore for purposes of Article III product comparison. They premiered in *Japan – Alcoholic Beverages II* under Article III:2(2) of the GATT in order to assess DCS, and were then used in this context in *Korea – Alcoholic Beverages* and *Chile – Alcoholic Beverages*. More than ten years later, quantitative methods have unexpectedly reentered the stage in the two Panel Reports in *Thailand – Cigarettes* and *Philippines – Distilled Spirits*. Most importantly, these two cases have now extended the scope of application of quantitative evidence and of the estimation of CPE to Article III:2(1) of the GATT and therefore the "likeness" issue.[9]

[3] *United States* v. *Columbia Pictures Corp.*, at 185: "Statistical evidence can rarely, if ever, supply all the facts needed for a definitive judgment"; *McClesky* v. *Zant*, 580 F.Supp. 338, 350 (ND Ga. 1984): "Statistical evidence, of course, is nothing but a form of circumstantial evidence."

[4] See *infra*, fnn. 314–319.

[5] European Commission, *XXIVth Report on Competition Policy 1994*, p. 280.

[6] Reasons may include the reduced availability of high quality data in Europe and the traditional focus in Europe on commonality of characteristics and prices, rather than on a strict application of the SSNIP test.

[7] See *supra*, Introduction, fnn. 18–20.

[8] Appellate Body Report, *United States – Subsidies on Upland Cotton – Recourse to Article 21.5 of the DSU by Brazil* (hereinafter *US – Subsidies on Upland Cotton (Article 21.5 of the DSU)*), WT/DS267/AB/RW, adopted June 20, 2008, para. 357.

[9] Panel Report, *Thailand – Cigarettes, supra*, Introduction, fn. 23, paras. 7.742–7.415; Panel Report, *Philippines – Distilled Spirits, supra*, Introduction, fn. 23, paras. 7.52–7.57.

The Appellate Body has, however, always appeared quite reserved and has never unconditionally adopted quantitative methods. The Appellate Body has repeatedly underscored that there should be no "undue emphasis on quantitative analyses of the competitive relationship."[10] They were only accepted as one among a number of means of identifying markets. Therefore, "quantitative analysis is helpful, but not necessary."[11]

The Appellate Body, in fact, even precluded greater emphasis on quantitative analyses of competitive relationships between products for market definition purposes. It ruled that there must not be an effects-based inquiry in Article III of the GATT. The Appellate Body rejected the showing of a particular quantitative degree of competition with the argument that Article III of the GATT does not require that a contested measure must be shown to have a certain impact on trade ("trade-effects test").[12] In other words, the Appellate Body's concern is that a quantitative benchmark for likeness and DCS, for example, in the form of a certain CPE threshold to be satisfied, would amount to the requirement of proving that an internal tax or regulatory measure has a particular effect on trade.[13] As quantitative methods serve an effects-based analysis and, in the reading of the Appellate Body, Article III of the GATT does not require this type of analysis, quantitative methods would not be instrumental to the determination of likeness and DCS.

This reasoning, and thus the conclusion that quantitative methods have no (substantial) role to play in the market definition exercise, is flawed. It confounds the (quantitative) measurement of the effect of a policy measure on trade flows and the (quantitative) measurement of the reciprocal competitive effects that imported and domestic products may have on each other. It should be accepted that no impact on trade in precise trade volumes is necessary in order to find a violation of Article III of the GATT.[14] But the quantitative determination of the degree of

[10] Appellate Body Report, *Korea – Alcoholic Beverages*, *supra*, Ch. 2, fn. 71, para. 129.

[11] Panel Report, *Korea – Alcoholic Beverages*, *supra*, Introduction, fn. 36, para. 10.92.

[12] *Supra*, Ch. 4, fn. 50.

[13] Quite surprisingly, the Appellate Body very recently just did that when holding that the Panel in *Thailand – Cigarettes* "did not err in relying upon … econometric evidence [on significant CPE between imported and domestic cigarettes evidencing a close competitive relationship for purposes of the 'like' and DCS definition] for its finding of less favourable treatment under Article III:4," Appellate Body, *Thailand – Cigarettes*, WT/DS371/AB/R, adopted July 15, 2011, paras. 137, 138 upholding Panel Report, *Thailand – Cigarettes*, *supra*, Introduction, fn. 23, para. 7.735.

[14] See *supra*, Ch. 4, "The standard of discrimination and the interpretation of protectionism" for the definition of protectionism as the actual or potential effects of differential treatment on the conditions of competition.

competition is a preceding analytical step in the process of determining an infringement. Once it is (quantitatively) established that the products are in competition, the finding of a violation of Article III of the GATT, that is, of discriminatory treatment of the products, may be made without any precise assessment of the trade effects that this discriminatory treatment might have on actual trade flows. As the Panel correctly observed in *Japan – Alcoholic Beverages II* that: "a factual determination of whether two products are directly competitive or substitutable is a necessary precondition in order to apply the legal test of dissimilar taxation. In the Panel's view, this determination takes place in the marketplace and does not mean at all that Article III has been made subject to an effects test."[15]

Nevertheless, the dispute settlement bodies had until very recently renounced a pronounced market-based approach. Between 2000 and 2011, they have embraced once again an abstract and market-detached analysis of the *Border Tax* criteria. In this sense, as Trebilcock and Howse observed, having already

> relegated econometric criteria (cross-price elasticity) to second-order relevance ... the [Appellate Body] appears, since [*Japan – Alcoholic Beverages II*] to have effected a subtle shift from an economic notion of substitutability to a juridical conception of competitive equality, which ... views the issue of competition as a normative question about whether consumers *ought* to look at two products as substitutable given their preferences and needs, rather than as an empirical economic question about revealed consumer behaviour.[16]

As we stand today, however, the dispute settlement bodies appear to have opted for a pragmatic approach between the traditional *Border Tax* approach and an economic approach. *A priori*, they stick to the *Border Tax* criteria while ignoring the whole (academic) discussion on a sound economic conceptual framework. But where confronted with quantitative evidence submitted by the parties, they also engage in an economic and quantitative analysis.

The corollary of an economic approach is the issue of how economics is channeled into the legal decision-making process. Therefore, section II will turn to the institutional and procedural frameworks for expert economic testimony. Section III, will then present CPE of demand as direct economic evidence of demand-side substitutability. Its estimation by way

[15] Panel Report, *Japan – Alcoholic Beverages II*, *supra*, Ch. 3, fn. 73, para. 5.12.

[16] Trebilcock and Howse, *The Regulation of International Trade*, p. 95 (emphasis in the original).

of the statistical method of multiple regression analysis will be outlined. Article III case law will provide insights on how CPE of demand and multiple regression analysis have been dealt with by Panels. From this experience, conclusions can be drawn on the role of such measures and methods for implementing an economic approach to Article III market definition.

In fact, WTO case law on the market definition issue has employed three types of quantitative methods, which are also part of the toolkit for antitrust market definition purposes: the estimation of price elasticities of demand (on the basis of multiple regression analysis); tests based on price comparisons; and shock analysis.[17] Section III will concentrate only on the first method because the estimation of price elasticities of demand is the most important economic measure for buyer substitution, and multiple regression analysis is the statistical technique which has increasingly gained importance in legal decision making generally. Price comparison and shock analysis will not be addressed in further detail. Price comparisons in the forms of the comparison of absolute prices or price correlation analysis have already been presented as based on the notion of economic markets and are therefore conceptually distinct from antitrust or trade relevant markets.[18] Shock analysis can be understood as a method which provides direct evidence of substitution between products on the basis of past consumer switching in reaction to historical events ("shocks") in the market.[19] Each is a very simple technique with intuitive appeal and is therefore frequently used in EU antitrust practice. However, the two techniques both suffer from the problem that there may be unknown intervening, or confounding influences such as inflation, demographic changes, or other macroeconomic changes that can remain unaccounted for and thus impair their probative value. The problem of identifying the proper causal relationship (and avoiding what is called a "spurious" relationship or correlation) requires more sophisticated econometric techniques, in particular, multiple regression analysis. This is crucial for the issue of the probative value of quantitative evidence and therefore absolutely relevant in the courtroom, as the Panel Report in *Thailand – Cigarettes* highlights,

[17] See, e.g., the *Commission Notice on market definition*, paras. 38, 39.

[18] See *supra*, Ch. 4, fn. 128. For WTO case law reference see *supra*, Ch. 4, fn. 129.

[19] This type of analysis has been used in Panel Report, *Japan – Alcoholic Beverages II*, *supra*, Ch. 3, fn. 73, paras. 4.1, 4.82, 6.30 and Panel Report, *Korea – Alcoholic Beverages*, *supra*, Introduction, fn. 36, paras. 5.139–5.142, where the impact of changes in the tax regimes on the market shares of domestic and foreign alcoholic beverages was considered as probative of substitutability between domestic and imported spirits. In Panel Report, *Mexico – Soft Drinks*, *supra*, Ch. 2, fn. 80, para. 8.73, the relevant shock was the market entry of a product.

where some quantitative evidence was dismissed precisely on this issue.[20] Therefore, the estimation of price elasticities of demand using multiple regression analysis is of utmost practical relevance for legal decision making, and is an ideal example for a critical comparative antitrust/trade analysis with the aim of establishing what role quantitative techniques can play in an economics-based approach to Article III market definition.

II THE LAW AND ECONOMICS OF EXPERT ECONOMIC TESTIMONY

When exploring the potential for an economic approach to Article III market definition, it is one thing to talk about the nature of the evidence required under an economic framework and what it can and cannot establish. But the institutional framework containing the economic approach also affects the use and significance of economic evidence in the adjudicatory process.

A further aspect is that quantitative analysis can take many highly technical and complex forms that are inaccessible to laymen. Lawyers are usually ignorant of formal statistical thinking. In fact, quantitative evidence "typically has been a source of bewilderment to the legal profession."[21] Therefore, possibly the biggest practical hurdle for quantitative evidence lies in explaining the methodologies and their conclusions in terms that lawyers and judges can comprehend.

Against this background, this section raises the serious question of whether the WTO adjudicatory system, as an international judicial institution, is well placed to tackle complex economic, or otherwise scientific or technical, issues. It will therefore address the following questions. Do WTO dispute settlement procedures provide the procedural and evidentiary tools necessary to respond to the demands of economic evidence? Is the WTO institutionally equipped to enable adjudicators to obtain, handle, and incorporate reliable quantitative evidence into their legal decision making?

[20] Panel Report, *Thailand – Cigarettes, supra*, Introduction, fn. 23, paras. 7.448–7.449.

[21] Kaye, "The Limits of the Preponderance of the Evidence Standard: Justifiably Naked Statistical Evidence and Multiple Causation," *American Bar Foundation Research Journal*, 7 (1982), 487, 487; Kaye, "Naked Statistical Evidence," *Yale Law Journal*, 89 (1980), 601, 601, noting that "it is an unusual lawyer who knows that regression analysis is not available from his psychoanalyst."

The usual channel for economic evidence to enter the substantive analysis in litigation is through the testimony of economic experts. In contrast to lay witnesses, they offer their opinion based on expert knowledge.[22] This section will therefore: (1) examine how the institutional and procedural frameworks determine the form of expert testimony; (2) address the problems that arise from party-commissioned expert testimony characteristic of the adversarial mode of proof-taking; and, finally, (3) consider several remedial options for eliciting reliable expert economic testimony in the WTO. This comparative analysis will combine perspectives on expert economic testimony in WTO adjudication with experience from antitrust litigation in order to demonstrate that quantitative evidence can play a useful and constructive role in Article III market definition.

1 Institutional and procedural frameworks for expert testimony

Fact-finding by recourse to economic experts takes place in, and is determined by, a judicial system's specific institutional and procedural frameworks. The archetypal common law and civil law models of adjudication are distinguished by the dichotomy between the adversarial and inquisitorial modes of proof-taking.[23] The main characteristic of an adversarial jurisdiction is the passive reliance of adjudicators on opposing advocates to provide them with relevant evidence. Adjudicators limit themselves to basing their assessment on the factual record presented by the parties. Typically with inquisitorial systems, adjudicators have the power to seek information they deem necessary beyond that which the parties have presented. Adjudicators therefore take a more direct and active role, engaging in independent factual investigations.

Broadly speaking, in terms of expert economic testimony the adversarial mode of proof-taking appears to favor party-appointed experts, while the inquisitorial system is open to court appointed ones. Indeed, the adversarial system is considered to incentivize parties into conducting thorough searches for evidence and investing in economic expertise to support their pleadings.[24] Party-appointed expert testimony is more

[22] Article 13.2 of the DSU; Article 25 of the Statute of the Court of Justice of the European Union [2008] OJ C115 210 (hereinafter ECJ Statute); Rule 702 of the US Federal Rules of Evidence (hereinafter FRE).

[23] This analysis is necessarily operating on a high level of generality and disregards, e.g., that inquisitorial civil law systems have adversarial common law elements and vice versa.

[24] Bernstein, "Expert Witnesses, Adversarial Bias, and the (Partial) Failure of the Daubert Revolution," *Iowa Law Review*, 93 (2008), 451, 457–458.

often required in a litigious context where the adversarial process pitches expert against expert and each party tries to expose the weaknesses in the other party's case. For example, the long and widespread tradition of party-sponsored expert testimony in US antitrust litigation, and the prolific academic work on expert economic testimony in the United States, can be explained by the adversarial nature of the US common law judicial system in which federal antitrust enforcement largely takes place by judicial adjudication.[25] By contrast, case law and literature on expert testimony are largely absent in Europe, where proceedings before the EU courts, influenced by the common and civil law traditions, are characterized by a dual adversarial and inquisitorial nature.[26] This inquisitorial character is manifest in the power of the courts to request the production of evidence and, in particular, to order court-appointed expert testimony.[27] In practice, though, they rarely appoint economic experts.[28] The European Commission's process for enforcing EU antitrust law is characterized by a combination of investigative, prosecutorial, and adjudicative powers. The system of proof-taking implemented by the European Commission is mostly inquisitorial.[29] It is against this background that expert testimony in general, and partisan expert testimony specifically, has played a less significant role in Europe than it has in the United States.

The WTO dispute settlement procedure possesses features that give rise to a hybrid inquisitorial/adversarial structure.[30] While *de jure* the

[25] Generally enforcement agencies have to litigate cases in federal courts, which then take enforcement decisions. FTC actions are an exception: initially adjudicated by an administrative law judge, whose decision can be appealed to the FTC Commission, only the subsequent FTC decision can then be appealed before a federal court. The FTC thus combines prosecutorial and adjudicative functions.

[26] MacLennan, "Evidence, Standard and Burden of Proof and the Use of Experts in Procedure Before the Luxembourg Courts," in Weiss (ed.), *Improving WTO Dispute Settlement Procedures: Issues and Lessons from the Practice of Other International Courts and Tribunals*, pp. 265, 266, 288 (2000).

[27] Articles 24 and 25 of the ECJ Statute; Articles 45, 47, and 49 of the Rules of Procedure of the Court of Justice [2010] OJ C177 1 (hereinafter ECJ Rules); Articles 65, 68, and 70 of the Rules of Procedure of the General Court [2010] C C177 37 (hereinafter GC Rules). Note that the possibility of court-appointed experts also exists in the US adversarial system pursuant to Rule 706 of the FRE.

[28] De la Serre and Sibony, "Expert Evidence before the EC Courts," *Common Market Law Review*, 45 (2008), 941, 949 count a total of twenty-five cases. One of the few examples in the antitrust context is Joined Cases C-89/85, etc., *Ahlström Osakeyhtiö and others* v. *Commission* [1993] ECR I-1307, paras. 75–127.

[29] Neven, "Competition Economics and Antitrust in Europe," p. 747.

[30] Cass, "The 'Constitutionalization' of International Trade Law: Judicial Norm-Generation as the Engine of Constitutional Development in International Trade," *European Journal*

process resembles more that of the civil law inquisitorial model of adjudication, at least in cases of expert economic testimony it is *de facto* an adversarial process.

One reason for its inquisitorial nature is that adjudicators have been conferred an active role in the fact-finding process. Panels examine and decide both questions of fact and law. According to Article 11 of the DSU, Panels must "make an objective assessment of the matter before [them], including an objective assessment of the facts of the case and the applicability of and conformity with the relevant covered agreements." In carrying out this mandate, the Appellate Body stated that "a Panel has the duty to examine and consider all the evidence before it, not just the evidence submitted by one or the other party, and to evaluate the relevance and probative force of each piece thereof."[31] Article 13.1 of the DSU goes further and grants each Panel the "right to seek information and technical advice from any individual or body which it deems appropriate," and, pursuant to Article 13.2 of the DSU, to "consult experts to obtain their opinion on certain aspects of the matter" or to "request an advisory report … from an expert review group" in accordance with the procedures enshrined in Annex 4 of the DSU.[32] Panels are thus not confined to the evidence presented by the parties. Article 13 of the DSU endows each Panel with a "significant investigative authority" of a "comprehensive nature" to actively seek relevant factual information from external sources.[33] In this regard, WTO Panels have fact-finding powers that resemble the inquisitorial practice of courts in the civil law system.[34]

In practice, however, Panels have consulted experts only exceptionally, mostly in cases involving scientific and technical expertise regarding risk assessments relating to the protection of human, animal, or

of International Law, 12 (2001), 39, 60–61; Oesch, *Standards of Review in WTO Dispute Resolution*, p. 108 (2003).

31 Appellate Body Report, *Korea – Definitive Safeguard Measure on Imports of Certain Dairy Products*, WT/DS98/AB/R, adopted January 12, 2000, para. 137.

32 The authority to seek external expert advice is reaffirmed, e.g., in Article 11.2 of the SPS Agreement, Article 14.2 and Annex 2 of the TBT Agreement, Article 4.5 of the SCM Agreement, and Article 19.4 of the Agreement on the Implementation of Article VII of the General Agreement on Tariffs and Trade.

33 Appellate Body Report, *Japan – Measures Affecting Agricultural Products* (hereinafter *Japan – Agricultural Products*), WT/DS76/AB/R, adopted March 19, 1999, paras. 127, 129; Appellate Body Report, *Canada – Measures Affecting the Export of Civilian Aircraft*, WT/DS70/AB/R, adopted August 20, 1999, para. 185: "Article 13.1 imposes *no conditions* on the exercise of this discretionary authority" (emphasis in original).

34 Palmeter and Mavroidis, *Dispute Settlement in the World Trade Organization: Practice and Procedure*, p. 144 (2004).

plant life and health under the SPS Agreement.[35] Predominantly, this is because the SPS Agreement limits the Panels' discretion on the consultation of experts, stipulating that recourse "should" be had to experts.[36] In the remaining cases, Panels relied on the parties to engage in fact-finding and to provide them with all the relevant factual evidence. Parties then retained experts on their delegations, who participated through contributions to the party submissions or appeared at the substantive Panel hearings to provide expert opinions. This has been the case specifically where economic testimony was submitted on market definition questions under Article III of the GATT, but also in other cases where expert economic testimony has been involved.[37] Thus, the adversarial mode for proof-taking has been predominant in dispute settlement practice, and economic testimony has usually been introduced by way of party-retained experts.[38]

[35] See Panel Report, *European Communities – Measures Concerning Meat and Meat Products (Hormones) (Complaint by Canada)* (hereinafter *EC – Hormones (Canada)*), WT/DS48/R/CAN, adopted February 13, 1998 and Panel Report, *European Communities – Measures Concerning Meat and Meat Products (Hormones) (Complaint by the United States)* (hereinafter *EC – Hormones (US)*), WT/DS26/R/USA, adopted February 13, 1998, each at paras. VI.1 *et seq.* and paras. 8.5 *et seq.*; Panel Report, *Japan – Measures Affecting the Importation of Apples* (hereinafter *Japan – Apples*), WT/DS245/R, adopted December 10, 2003, paras. 6.1 *et seq.*; Panel Report, *Japan – Measures Affecting the Importation of Apples – Recourse to Article 21.5 of the DSU by the United States* (hereinafter *Japan – Apples (Article 21.5 of the DSU)*), WT/DS245/R, adopted July 20, 2005, paras. 6.1 *et seq.*; Panel Report, *European Communities – Measures Affecting the Approval and Marketing of Biotech Products* (hereinafter *EC – Biotech*), WT/DS291/R, WT/DS292/R, WT/DS293/R, adopted November 21, 2006, paras. 7.12 *et seq.*; Panel Report, *United States – Continued Suspension of Obligations in the EC – Hormones Disputes* (hereinafter *US – Continued Suspension (Hormones)*), WT/DS320/R, adopted November 10, 2008, paras. 7.55 *et seq.*; Panel Report, *Canada – Continued Suspension of Obligations in the EC – Hormones Dispute* (hereinafter *Canada – Continued Suspension (Hormones)*), WT/DS321/R, adopted November 10, 2008, paras. 7.53 *et seq.*

[36] Article 11.2 of the SPS Agreement. A broad discussion exists on the tension between judicial risk assessment guided by experts and the constraint of democratic national regulatory choices; see, e.g., Howse, "Democracy, Science, and Free Trade: Risk Regulation on Trial at the World Trade Organization," *Michigan Law Review*, 98 (2000), 2329–2357.

[37] For party-sponsored expert economic testimony under Article III market definition, see Panel Report, *Japan – Alcoholic Beverages II*, *supra*, Ch. 3, fn. 73, para. 4.88 and Panel Report, *Korea – Alcoholic Beverages*, *supra*, Introduction, fn. 36, para. 10.26. For a different context see, e.g., Panel Report, *United States – Subsidies on Upland Cotton*, *supra*, Introduction, fn. 19, para. 7.1202 fn. 1323.

[38] Christoforou, "WTO Panels in the Face of Scientific Uncertainty," in Weiss (ed.), *Improving WTO Dispute Settlement Procedures: Issues and Lessons from the Practice of Other International Courts and Tribunals*, pp. 243, 258 (2000).

2 Problems with party-proffered expert testimony

A Introductory remarks

When analyzing the differences between adversarial and inquisitorial legal systems, research traditionally focuses on the question of which of the two is more effective in eliciting relevant evidence and in reaching a fully-informed decision. The important consideration is the relative merit of having one piece of unbiased information unearthed by an inquisitorial adjudicator or two pieces of partial, biased, and incomplete information provided by self-interested parties. This poses a pertinent question for expert testimony; namely, whether an inquisitorial court-appointed expert or two adversarial partisan experts retained by each litigant are more apt to elicit reliable economic evidence. On the one hand, the inquisitorial system can rely on an impartial court-appointed expert for proof-gathering. It therefore seems superior in terms of the quality, that is, neutrality, of expert testimony.[39] On the other hand, it appears that overall the adversarial system generates more expert testimony and ensures the elucidation of arguments on both sides.[40] However, the adversarial system is viewed to be poorly adapted for expert testimony, in particular, for resolving conflicts between expert testimonies.[41] It is characterized by its reliance on direct and cross-examination as the main methods of eliciting the facts of the case, its premise being that a trial is a contest and that the adjudicators' role is an umpireal one. Consequently, witnesses are all too frequently coached by the lawyers to align their testimony with the party's position. For adversarial partisan experts this means that they are either pushed to slant their testimony to favor their client's position, or that they do so due to opportunistic motivation.

The present study need not decide as to which legal system is better suited for expert economic testimony. What matters is the fact that the

[39] Timmerbeil, "The Role of Expert Witnesses in German and US Civil Litigation," *Annual Survey of International and Comparative Law*, 9 (2003), 163, 182.

[40] The literature seems to provide some validation for the statement that the adversarial system, through the competitive and selective production of favorable evidence by each side and the dialectic mode of assertion and refutation by the parties, leads to the revelation of more complete information and ultimately the truth; see, e.g., Shin, "Adversarial and Inquisitorial Procedures in Arbitration," *RAND Journal of Economics*, 29 (1998), 378–405; Froeb and Kobayashi, "Evidence Production in Adversarial vs. Inquisitorial Regimes," *Economic Letters*, 70 (2001), 267–272.

[41] Posner, *Catastrophe: Risk and Response*, pp. 212–213 (2004).

WTO dispute settlement procedure appears to be highly compatible with expert testimony. Since it is of a hybrid nature, it combines the merits of adversarial partisan expert testimony conductive to producing a fully-informed decision, and the active role of inquisitorial adjudicators in assessing and evaluating party-proffered expert evidence.

The following describes in greater detail the problems encountered in the case of party-hired experts. There are several recurring criticisms of the use of party (economic) expert witnesses.[42] Focus will be given to the main problem identified in the literature; namely, the risk that arises from the potential partiality of party-appointed experts. It may be better understood through the view of the economic theory of "agency costs."[43]

B *Asymmetric information and principal–agent conflict of interests*

Antitrust enforcement agencies have an increasingly well-developed institutional capacity to handle economic thinking. By way of contrast, fact-finders in court-settings – judges and particularly jury members – have only limited cognitive and institutional capabilities. Most are economically illiterate, resulting in a discrepancy between the task judges are called upon to fulfill (that is, evaluating or even undertaking economic reasoning) and their ability to do so. The concern is that scientific evidence generally, and expert economic testimony in particular, may overwhelm or mislead adjudicators.[44] Presentation by an expert gives greater probative force than a layman's effort. At the same time, with little ability to understand the technical language and the concepts presented, adjudicators are not generally in a position to give an independent assessment of the expert's opinion. At the heart of the problem lies an asymmetry of

[42] For a summary see T. V. Lee, "Court-Appointed Experts and Judicial Reluctance: A Proposal to Amend Rule 706 of the Federal Rules of Evidence," *Yale Law and Policy Review*, 6 (1988), 480, 482–484.

[43] See Pindyck and Rubinfeld, *Microeconomics*, pp. 617–636.

[44] In other words, "the expert witness can mislead judges and juries more readily than lay witnesses can because they are more difficult to pick apart in cross-examination – they can hide behind an impenetrable wall of esoteric knowledge," Posner, "The Law and Economics of the Economic Expert Witness," *Journal of Economic Perspectives*, 13 (1999), 91, 93.

information[45] or "epistemic asymmetry";[46] it is only natural that the expert possesses knowledge, for example, about econometric methods, that the adjudicator does not have, and that the adjudicator lacks the information and expertise to evaluate the quality of the expert's testimony.

A principal–agent conflict of interest arises from the asymmetry of information. Party-introduced expert testimony is characterized by a triangular relationship. The expert is professionally bound to the party that employs him. At the same time, an overriding duty exists to provide unbiased testimony to the adjudicator.[47] In the relationship between the adjudicator and the party-retained expert there may be a misalignment of interests. The former expects rigorous and impartial testimony, while the latter has the two – potentially conflicting – interests of pleasing his client by supporting his case, and conforming to his obligation to provide independent and impartial testimony to the adjudicator (risk of "moral hazard"). The discrepancy of interests, incomplete information and the difficulty for the adjudicator to monitor the expert's performance give rise to a situation which is similar to a principal–agent conflict of interest. The adjudicator can be seen as the principal able to demand impartial and independent testimony, and the expert as the agent under an obligation to provide this type of testimony.[48] The unobserved agent may succumb to the self-interest of advancing his party's cause, which may be inimical to the adjudicator's truth-finding quest.

[45] Solow and Fletcher, "Doing Good Economics in the Courtroom: Thoughts on Daubert and Expert Testimony in Antitrust," *Journal of Corporation Law*, 31 (2006), 89, 490; Gutiérrez-Rodríguez, *Expert Economic Testimony, Economic Evidence and Asymmetry of Information in Antitrust Cases*, para. 4.1 (2007), available at: http://ssrn.com/abstract=1023494.

[46] Lianos, "'Judging' Economists: Economic Expertise in Competition Law Litigation: A European View," in Lianos and Kokkoris (eds.), *The Reform of EC Competition Law: New Challenges*, pp. 185, 189 (2010).

[47] For the expert's duty of independence and impartiality in the United States, see: *Kirk* v. *Raymark Indus.*, 61 F.3d 147, 164 (3d Cir. 1995): "despite the fact that one party retained and paid for the services of an expert witness, expert witnesses are supposed to testify impartially in the sphere of their expertise"; *Selvidge* v. *United States*, 160 FRD 153, 156 (D Kan. 1995): "An expert witness should never become one party's expert advocate. An expert witness should be an advocate of the truth with testimony to help the court and the jury reach the ultimate truth ... which should be the basis of any verdict." For EU law, see: Articles 47(6) and 49(6) of the ECJ Rules and Articles 86(5), 70(6) and 71 of the GC Rules. For WTO law, see: paras. II, III and IV of the Rules of Conduct for the Understanding on Rules and Procedures Governing the Settlement of Disputes, WT/DSB/RC/1.

[48] Gutiérrez-Rodríguez, "Expert Economic Testimony in Antitrust Cases: A Comparative Law and Economics Study," *International Law, Revista Colombiana de Derecho*

C Adversarial bias (partisanship)

The testimony of party experts is vulnerable to witness bias due to asymmetric information and moral hazard, creating the risk of erroneous judgments. This "adversarial bias" has at least two sources: the conscious bias of "hired guns" and the selection bias.[49]

The problem of conscious bias arises when "hired gun" experts behave opportunistically.[50] A party-retained expert can be tempted to align his testimony with his client's interests and to consciously adapt his opinion to favor his employer's position; a desire that the clients have little reason to discourage.[51] This risk is acute for several reasons. A party can shop from a large pool of expert witnesses, while there are normally only a limited number of ordinary fact witnesses in any given case. Moreover, unlike a lay witness, a party expert is paid for his testimony by the party that has retained him. He may therefore be enticed to act as a partisan expert, or "witness for hire." Moreover, an expert witness who is a repeat player for the provision of expertise in litigation ("forensic expert"), will strive to be hired in future judicial proceedings. The payoff for winning the case, demonstrating a good "track record" leading to likely future business, offers the economic expert a tempting incentive to slant his testimony. He may be inclined, for example, to select data and to make modeling choices regarding the relevant facts, variables, and methodologies that favor the client's position, or to misrepresent the accuracy and explanatory power of the chosen methodology.

A selection bias can arise because lawyers will search among a large pool of potential experts before hiring one whose testimony is likely to be compatible with their view of the case.[52] The selection of the expert is thus

Internacional, 14 (2009), 221, 224. The long-term contractual relationship and the possibility of recontracting typical for a principal–agent relationship can be seen in the fact that expert witnesses often appear as repeat players before courts.

49 Bernstein, "Expert Witnesses, Adversarial Bias, and the (Partial) Failure of the Daubert Revolution," p. 454. Note that bias can also arise "unconsciously," see already W. L. Foster, "Expert Testimony: Prevalent Complaints and Proposed Remedies," *Harvard Law Review*, 11 (1897), 169, 170–171.

50 Hovenkamp, *The Antitrust Enterprise: Principle and Execution*, p. 78 (2005).

51 Note, however, that "reputation costs" associated with producing biased testimony may limit such incentives, see Edmond and Mercer, "Trashing 'Junk Science,'" *Stanford Technology Law Review*, 3 (1998), para. 22. available at: http://stlr.stanford.edu/STLR/Articles/98_STLR_3; Posner, "An Economic Approach to the Law of Evidence," *Stanford Law Review*, 51 (1999), 1477, 1537. Critical of this disciplining mechanism, see Lianos, "'Judging' Economists," pp. 196–197.

52 Gross, "Expert Evidence," *Wisconsin Law Review*, (1991), 1113, 1129–1133.

made according to the expert's inclination for a certain viewpoint. Even if the expert is sincere, the court will be presented with a preselected opinion. This system is seen as favoring the selection of experts with extreme views that are unrepresentative of what the majority of experts would opine.[53]

D *Conflicting expert testimony*

As a result of the adversarial nature of party-proffered expert testimony, adjudicators will often be confronted with conflicting opinions ("battle of experts"), which the adjudicator is then called upon to resolve. To the untrained eye, contradictory results often lead to skepticism about the usefulness of economic analysis. This skepticism is often unjustified. It is based on the incorrect belief that science should always produce unambiguous and consistent results. It can be traced back to fundamental differences between scientific or economic analysis and legal analysis.

First, there is a difference between the legal and scientific notions of "objectivity" and "truth."[54] All scientific assertions are subject to the possibility of being discarded once proven false. Consequently, there is constant revision of scientific conclusions through a process of falsification. According to the philosopher of science Popper, this is the central characteristic of scientific knowledge.[55] Against this background, scientific objectivity is process-oriented. It is equated with independence, impartiality, and neutrality in the problem-solving process.[56] This conception of "truth" is compatible with different conclusions being valid at the same time. By contrast, objectivity in legal terms is result-oriented. It relates to a final and binding judicial decision, based on true and proven facts, that reaches the ultimate truth.

Second, economic theory and econometric analysis are imbued with judgments of relativity and tendencies.[57] For example, the concept of

[53] Sanders, "The Merits of the Paternalistic Justifications of Restrictions on the Admissibility of Expert Evidence," *Seton Hall Law Review*, 33 (2003), 881, 921.

[54] See *Daubert* v. *Merrell Dow Pharmaceuticals*, 509 US 579, 596–597 (1993) (hereinafter *Daubert*): "There are important differences between the quest for truth in the courtroom and the quest for truth in the laboratory. Scientific conclusions are subject to perpetual revision. Law, on the other hand, must resolve disputes finally and quickly."

[55] Popper, *Logik der Forschung*, pp. 16–19 (2005).

[56] Edmond, "After Objectivity: Expert Evidence and Procedural Reform," *Sydney Law Review*, 25 (2003), 131, 134.

[57] Vogel, "Le juriste face à l'analyse économique," *Revue de la Concurrence et de la Consommation*, 134 (2003), 812–813.

substitutability is an inherently relative one, because products are always *more or less* substitutable. This seems to conflict with the adjudicator's task of making an absolute and unequivocal determination. A product under Article III analysis can be only like or not like, but not a little bit like another product. In other words, the tension exists because adjudicators expect a "single right answer," which in science does not necessarily exist.

In context, even when both sides' experts refrain from scientific malpractice they may arrive at different yet scientifically "objective" conclusions because of differences in data, technique, or modeling. It would not be scientifically appropriate, nor would it serve the objective of sound legal decision making, to discard these conflicting studies as incorrect or unscientific. The adjudicator should rather investigate and weigh their relative merits. This may be a daunting task. Usually, adjudicators are not competent to assess the quality and technical differences. In addition, any conflict can further obscure the issues and leave the decision-maker in confusion and uncertainty.[58]

In such situations, there is a danger that adjudicators could treat conflicting expert testimony as canceling each other out. The use of experts would then create added costs without creating any benefits. Alternatively, adjudicators might be swayed by the expert who, as the better communicator, is easier to understand, or who is more appealing and charismatic. As a fall-back, adjudicators may resort to the burden of proof.[59] The burden of proof rests on the plaintiff, for example, on the claimant to prove the inconsistency of a measure with WTO law. If the experts are at odds, a Panel may be (too quickly) inclined to show deference to the respondent's expert position and find that the claimant has not met the burden of proof and thus cannot prevail.[60]

E Validity of these concerns

It has not been empirically proven that an asymmetry of information and the principal–agent relationship give rise to biased expert testimony being presented in WTO cases. Yet its presence in antitrust litigation confirms

[58] Vogel and Vogel, "Demand and Elasticities," para. 8 (noting "le désarroi du juriste" in those situations).

[59] For WTO law, see Pauwelyn, "The Use of Experts in WTO Dispute Settlement," *International & Comparative Law Quarterly*, 51 (2002), 325, 359–360. For antitrust law, see: Solow and Fletcher, "Doing Good Economics in the Courtroom," p. 490.

[60] Admittedly, however, if contradictory economic evidence on both sides is equally scientifically valid and none can be considered superior, the only legally legitimate conclusion is that the available evidence neither supports nor refutes a given proposition and that the claim has not been established by the complainant.

the existence of these problems in the real world. The "hired gun" problem and the risk of moral hazard have been mentioned in case law,[61] and have also been ascertained in empirical studies.[62] Adjudicators have all too often been confronted with the dilemma of choosing between conflicting testimonies.[63]

3 Remedial options

Different options can be considered to remedy the problems associated with party-selected expert economic testimony, and to specifically inject more economic and econometric analysis into WTO adjudication at the Panel stage. The forthcoming analysis of the proffered remedial options draws on the extensive discussion in antitrust law.[64]

A Introductory remarks

All suggested remedial options seek to improve the institutional structure in a way that enables an analysis in which adjudicators are willing and

[61] For instance in *In re Aluminum Phosphide Antitrust Litig.*, 893 F.Supp. 1497, 1500, and 1506–1507 (D Kan. 1995) (describing an expert as "an expert for hire" and "driven by a desire to enhance the measure of plaintiffs' damages, even at the expense of well-accepted scientific principles and methodology"); *Lantec, Inc.* v. *Novell, Inc.*, 146 F.Supp. 2d 1140, 1154 (D Utah 2001): "[The witness] is clearly a hired gun and any semblance of objectivity is lacking. His opinions lack all indicia of reliability and as such can only confuse and mislead the jury."

[62] In a survey, US judges and attorneys have identified these issues as most acute, Krafka *et al.*, "Judge and Attorney Experiences, Practices, and Concerns Regarding Expert Testimony in Federal Civil Trials," *Psychology, Public Policy, and Law*, 8 (2002), 309, 328. ABA Economic Evidence Task Force, *Final Report of Economic Evidence Task Force*, Appendix II (2006), available at: www.abanet.org/antitrust/at-reports/01-c-ii.pdf, which found that of the experts surveyed, 57 percent stated that unprofessional and confusing (defined as not *bona fide*) testimony occurred "sometimes." See also Lord Woolf, *Access to Justice*, Interim Report to the Lord Chancellor on the Civil Justice System in England and Wales, ch. 23, para. 5 (1995), available at: www.dca.gov.uk/civil/interim/woolf.htm: "Most of the problems with expert evidence arise because the expert is initially recruited as part of the team which investigates and advances a party's contentions and then has to change roles and seek to provide the independent expert evidence which the court is entitled to expect. … [In many cases, the expert has become] 'a very effective weapon in the parties' arsenal of tactics.'"

[63] See, e.g., Advocate General Mayras, lost between two diametrically opposed expert testimonies, was left to rely on his "impression" only, Joined Opinion of Advocate General Mayras, Case 48–69, *Imperial Chemical Industries Ltd.* v. *Commission of the European Communities* [1972] ECR 619, 679–680.

[64] See, e.g., OECD, *Presenting Complex Economic Theories to Judges* (2008), available at: www.oecd.org/dataoecd/39/59/41776770.pdf.

capable to weigh and consider possibly conflicting economic evidence. To this end they attempt to reduce the information asymmetry between the adjudicator and the economic expert, to mitigate the adversarial bias, and thus to diminish the risk of partial testimony. One approach is to emphasize inquisitorial characteristics and to resort to options that are already rooted in the DSU procedure. One such option is an increase in the use of intrusive investigative authority, or of institutional resources and capabilities. The rationale behind this approach is that a thorough examination of economic evidence requires adjudicators to be equipped with the necessary (either their own or external) economic capacity to seek information and explanation to facilitate active engagement in the assessment of the strengths and weaknesses of economic arguments. Moreover, the aim is to improve an adjudicator's capability to interpret and weigh the relative merits of conflicting economic testimony and to develop his own economic analysis in order to independently discern relevant evidence. Another approach is to emphasize the adversarial elements of the system, and to rely on admissibility rules and increased cross-examination to ensure that the dialectic method of assertion and refutation between the parties and their experts leads to the revelation of reliable evidence.

B Expert panelists

The most direct point of entry for economic expertise into the courtroom is the appointment of expert adjudicators. Such proposals have in fact been made with regard to the institution of "science courts" in general, specialized courts in antitrust law, and the appointment of expert panelists in the WTO.[65] Sweden, for example, includes economic experts to serve alongside legally qualified judges as members of the courts in antitrust matters.[66]

Panels are composed on an *ad hoc* basis and, according to Article 8.5 of the DSU, consist customarily of three, or if the parties so agree, five members. The WTO Secretariat proposes nominees to the parties

[65] In the order of the proposals: Posner, *Catastrophe: Risk and Response*, pp. 212–213; Bellamy, "An EU Competition Court: The Continuing Debate," in Lianos and Kokkoris (eds.), *The Reform of EC Competition Law: New Challenges*, pp. 33–52 (2010); Iynedjian, "The Case for Incorporating Scientists and Technicians into WTO Panels," *Journal of World Trade*, 42 (2008), 279–297.

[66] Chapter 8, Article 8 of the Swedish Competition Act, available at: www.kkv.se/upload/Filer/ENG/Publications/The_Swedish_Competition_Act.pdf.

who can object to any or all of the nominees. In the case of a failure to agree upon the panelists, the WTO Secretariat Director-General determines their composition.[67] Under Article 8.1 of the DSU, panelists must be "well-qualified governmental and/or non-governmental individuals, *including* persons who have ... taught or published on international trade law or policy, or served as a senior trade policy official of a Member."[68] Article 8.2 of the DSU further provides that "Panel members should be selected with a view to ensuring ... a sufficiently diverse background and a wide spectrum of experience." Panelists are therefore chosen for their qualifications and expertise in the subject matter under dispute.

Thus, the WTO adjudicatory system does not preclude – in fact, it even encourages – non-legal experts to be appointed as panelists. This is in stark contrast to ordinary domestic courts. There, professional judges or lay juries, usually without economic backgrounds, act as decision-makers ruling on economic evidence and issues. WTO adjudication, however, has the distinctive feature of including experts "on the bench." For instance, one of the customary three panelists, or the two additional panelists out of the possible total of five, could be an economic expert.

The possibility of appointing economic experts to a Panel already exists, and there are a number of disputes in which economists have already served on Panels. Nevertheless, it has been shown empirically that in most instances trade diplomats and lawyers are appointed, with economists only rarely being chosen.[69] When economists are appointed, although they possess university degrees in economics, they are not expert economists with sufficiently high qualifications indicative of an ability to solve the specific economic issues in question, in particular, to handle sophisticated quantitative evidence. Rather, it appears that the parties and the WTO Secretariat, who together determine the composition of each Panel, have not so far considered it necessary to have specific economic expertise on the Panel.

[67] Articles 8.6 and 8.7 of the DSU. [68] Emphasis added.

[69] Bown, "The WTO Secretariat and the Role of Economics in Panels and Arbitrations," pp. 404–409. Moreover, even those adjudicators who are appointed to serve on the WTO dispute settlement bodies may not always be chosen on the basis of their legal and policy expertise and experience. Specifically with regard to Appellate Body members, scholars have recently found an increased politicization of the nomination and appointment procedure, Elsig and Pollack, *Agents, Trustees, and International Courts: The Politics of Judicial Appointment at the World Trade Organization* (2011), available at: http://ssrn.com/abstract=1861443.

C *Institutional support of panelists*

Another option worth highlighting is the development of sources of internal economic expertise or measures to enhance the economic understanding of non-expert adjudicators.

(i) Economic expertise in the WTO secretariat

One way of building capacity is to improve the institutional design of the WTO itself. Taking the evolution toward an increased in-house economic capacity in antitrust enforcement agencies as a model, WTO adjudicators could benefit from an increase in the role of economic support staff in obtaining and dealing with economic input. In contrast to domestic courts, panelists already have access to permanent internal support located at the WTO Secretariat. So far, this internal support mainly assists with legal or factual questions and secretarial or technical support pursuant to Article 27.1 of the DSU.[70] In practice, this means that a legal officer from the Legal or Rules divisions and a second officer from whichever specialized division is most relevant to the dispute are assigned to each Panel. However, case support teams have rarely been staffed "horizontally," that is, across functions, with a Secretariat-provided economist.[71] Economic expertise is housed in the Economic Research and Statistics Division, which with eight economists with (what has been observed as) inadequate qualification, is far too small and improperly staffed to provide effective economic support.[72] It is against this background that the proposal can be made that existing support structures should be enhanced to provide (more) economic expertise.[73] Specifically, the staff of the Economic Research Division could be expanded upon to include more adequately qualified economic experts, who may then, on a regular basis, be assigned to serve on the WTO Secretariat support team to aid Panel adjudicators.[74]

[70] On the role of the WTO Secretariat see Nordström, "The World Trade Organization Secretariat in a Changing World," *Journal of World Trade*, 39 (2005), 819, 827–829.

[71] Bown, "The WTO Secretariat and the Role of Economics in Panels and Arbitrations," p. 411.

[72] Bown, "The WTO Secretariat and the Role of Economics in Panels and Arbitrations," pp. 394, 413.

[73] For aspects of organizational design to achieve the effective integration of economic analysis (and economic agency staff) in agency decision-making, see Froeb *et al.*, "The Economics of Organizing Economists," *Antitrust Law Journal*, 76 (2009), 569–584.

[74] Bown, "The WTO Secretariat and the Role of Economics in Panels and Arbitrations," p. 412.

(ii) Education and guidance of panelists

Systematic training and education may not render adjudicators experts in a given area, but could, to a certain extent, "facilitate the process of identifying and narrowing issues concerning scientific evidence by outlining for judges the pivotal issues in the areas of science that are often subject to dispute."[75]

For example, in the US guidance is provided to judges through the publication of the *Reference Manual on Scientific Evidence*.[76] Antitrust regulators have made additional efforts to ensure transparency in the proper handling of economic evidence by publishing Best Practice guides. Again, US regulators took the lead in this respect several years ago, while the European Commission and the major national European enforcement agencies have only very recently, in 2009 and 2010, provided more guidance on expert economic evidence.[77] These Best Practices are addressed to practitioners. They aim to aid them in developing and presenting evidence in a manner to enable adjudicators to determine its probative weight. They are also informative for decision-makers, aiding them in identifying and discarding baseless economic arguments, and dealing with seemingly inconsistent expert opinions.

As the experience with the *Merger Guidelines* and the *Commission Notice on market definition* shows, the validation of economic evidence is helped by a clear set of (non-binding) rules and standards. With the aim of providing guidance for an economic approach, the adoption by

[75] Federal Judicial Center, *Reference Manual on Scientific Evidence*, p. vi (2000), available at: www.fjc.gov/public/pdf.nsf/lookup/sciman00.pdf/$file/sciman00.pdf.

[76] Federal Judicial Center, *Reference Manual on Scientific Evidence*.

[77] FTC, *Best Practices for Data, and Economics and Financial Analyses in Antitrust Investigations* (n.d.), available at: www.ftc.gov/be/bestpractices.shtm#_ftn2; Autorité de la concurrence, *Lignes directrices relatives au contrôle des concentrations*, paras. 558–580 (2009), available at: www.autoritedelaconcurrence.fr/doc/ld_concentrations_dec09.pdf; Competition Commission, *Suggested Best Practice for Submissions of Technical Economic Analysis from Parties to the Competition Commission* (2009), available at: www.competition-commission.org.uk/rep_pub/corporate_documents/corporate_policies/best_practice.pdf; European Commission, *Best Practices for the Submission of Economic Evidence and Data Collection in Cases Concerning the Application of Article 101 and 102 TFEU and in Merger Cases* (2010), available at: http://ec.europa.eu/competition/consultations/2010_best_practices/best_practice_submissions.pdf (hereinafter *Commission Best Practices for Economic Evidence*); Office of Fair Trading and Competition Commission, *Good Practice in the Design and Presentation of Consumer Survey Evidence in Merger Inquiries* (2010), available at: www.oft.gov.uk/shared_oft/consultations/OFT1230con.pdf; Bundeskartellamt, *Best Practices for Expert Economic Opinions*, 20 October 2010, available at: www.bundeskartellamt.de/wEnglisch/download/pdf/Merkblaetter/Bekanntmachung_Standards_Englisch_final.pdf.

the DSB of a "consensus statement" has been suggested.[78] In the form of a decision by the DSB, it would offer non-binding recommendations on the use of economic and econometric evidence in dispute settlement proceedings. Similar to the *Border Tax Report*, it could specifically address the role and weight to be given to economics and identify acceptable quantitative methods in defining a trade market. If prepared by an *ad hoc* expert group for adoption by the DSB outside a specific dispute, this could avoid specific party interests shaping these matters.

D Panel-appointed independent economic experts

In antitrust scholarship, resort to court-appointed economic experts has widely been suggested as a means of mitigating the risks associated with using adversarial experts.[79] The possibility for the courts to appoint experts exists both in US federal law and in EU law.[80] However, this option has only rarely been used by courts to address economic issues.[81] Moreover, it has rarely been used by other international judicial institutions, for example under Article 50 of the International Court of Justice's (hereinafter ICJ) Statute.[82]

78 Malacrida, "Some Reflections on the Use of Economic Analysis in WTO Dispute Settlement Proceedings," in Bown and Pauwelyn (eds.), *The Law, Economics and Politics of Retaliation in WTO Dispute Settlement*, pp. 434, 442 (2010).

79 As a recent example, see Rubinfeld, "On the Pretrial Use of Economists," *Antitrust Bulletin*, 55 (2010), 679–697.

80 Rule 706 of the FRE; Article 25 of the ECJ Statute; Articles 45(2)(d) and 49 of the ECJ Rules; Articles 65(d) and 70 of the GC Rules. Agencies have no specific equivalent and are free to consult outside experts in addition to their economic staff. For the United States, see: Gavil, "Competition Policy, Economics, and Economists: Are We Expecting Too Much?" in Hawk (ed.), *Annual Proceedings of the Fordham Corporate Law Institute, International Antitrust Law & Policy*, pp. 575, 584 (2006). For the EU, see: Article 13(3) of the Commission Regulation No. 773/2004 relating to the conduct of proceedings by the Commission pursuant to Articles 81 and 82 of the EC Treaty [2004] OJ L123 18 (hereinafter Commission Regulation on Article 81 and 82 proceedings).

81 Most famously in US antitrust case law see *New York* v. *Kraft General Foods, Inc.*, 926 F.Supp. 321, 351–352 (SDNY 1995) (hereinafter *Kraft General Foods*). For EU case law, see *supra*, fn. 28. A prominent recent example from Germany is Düsseldorf's Regional Court of Appeals 2009 cement cartel ruling, OLG Düsseldorf, decision of June 26, 2009, VI-2a Kart 2–6/08 OWi, available at: www.nrwe.de.

82 The ICJ and its predecessor made use of this option in four cases only: *Case Concerning the Factory at Chorzów* (*Germany* v. *Poland*), Judgment on Claim for Indemnity, Merits of September 13, 1928, PCIJ Series A, No. 17, 3, at 99; *Corfu Channel* (*United Kingdom* v. *Albania*), Judgment on Merits of April 9, 1949, ICJ Report 1949, 4, at 142–169; *Corfu Channel* (*United Kingdom* v. *Albania*), Judgment on Assessment of Amount of Compensation of December 15, 1949, ICJ Report 1949, at 244; *Delimitation of the Maritime Boundary in the*

As outlined above, Panels have broad powers to appoint individual independent experts or expert review groups pursuant to Article 13 of the DSU. It is within their discretion to appoint experts *sua sponte* and to grant, or refuse, a party's request to do so.[83] Legally, Panels are entirely free to appoint whomsoever they choose as independent economic experts and whenever they so desire. Yet, as already alluded to, independent experts have been consulted in scientific trade disputes only in the context of the SPS Agreement. Panelists in these disputes did not content themselves with the factual and scientific submissions presented by the parties and engaged in thorough and searching enquiries.[84] By contrast, no Panel has so far found it either necessary or appropriate to call an independent expert for advice on economic issues. Most revealing is *EC – Asbestos*. In this case, the Panel appointed experts in order to obtain information on the circumstances surrounding the exposure to chrysotile asbestos and its associated risks, as well as the effectiveness of the controlled use of chrysotile.[85] At the same time, however, it did not consult experts in order to determine the issue of "like" products, which it explicitly held to be governed by economic principles.

Recourse to an expert review group pursuant to Article 13.2 of the DSU has not been made by any Panel, even when requested by the parties. Instead, the practice under Article 13 of the DSU has been to appoint experts individually, even where several were consulted at the same time.[86]

An independent economic expert has no stake in the material outcome of the case. The intention is that he will provide a more balanced, neutral,

Gulf of Maine Area (Canada/United States of America), Appointment of Expert, Order of March 30, 1984, ICJ Report 1984, at 165.

[83] Appellate Body Report, *Argentina – Measures Affecting Imports of Footwear, Textiles, Apparel and Other Items*, WT/DS56/R, adopted April 22, 1998, para. 84; Appellate Body Report, *United States – Import Prohibition of Certain Shrimp and Shrimp Products* (hereinafter *US – Shrimp*), WT/DS58/R, adopted November 6, 1998, para. 104.

[84] Cottier, who served as Panel chairman in one of the SPS cases (*EC – Hormones*), noted on the role of external scientific and technical experts in reviewing SPS measures that: "the panels strongly relied upon expert views, and could not have rendered their assessment and recommendation without such independent advice of individual experts." Cottier, "Risk Management Experience in WTO Dispute Settlement," in Robertson and Kellow (eds.), *Globalization and the Environment: Risk Assessment and the WTO*, pp. 41, 51 (2001).

[85] Panel Report, *EC – Asbestos, supra*, Ch. 3, fn. 106, paras. 5.1–5.659.

[86] Panel Report, *EC – Asbestos, supra*, Ch. 3, fn. 106, para. 8.10; Panel Report, *EC – Hormones (Canada), supra*, fn. 35, paras. 8.7–8.8; Panel Report, *EC – Hormones (US), supra*, fn. 35, paras. 8.7–8.8.

and therefore "objective" viewpoint in terms of independence and impartiality. He is there to help the adjudicator understand complex economic issues, to dissuade party experts from taking extreme positions, and to deter unprofessional testimony. But what exactly should be the role of a Panel-appointed expert in WTO dispute settlement? There are a range of possibilities depending on the scope of consultation. On the one side, he could have a limited neutral role clarifying and explaining economic evidence submitted by the parties to the adjudicator. For example, he could explain how the evidence is constructed, what it is intended to demonstrate, and why party experts disagree without opining himself on the actual results.[87] Consequently, if parties have not resorted to economic evidence, the panelists could not on their own initiative turn to economic analysis and the testimony of a Panel-appointed expert. On the other hand, his function could reach further to include evaluating party testimony as a neutral arbiter and providing his own views as to which party's expert testimony is more probative. He could even go as far as to perform his own economic analysis to produce independent economic evidence.[88] By inviting an independent expert to opine the Panel could then engage in a separate fact-finding mission of its own.

Under the wide inquisitorial authority of Article 13 of the DSU, Panels have the mandate to assume an activist stance in relation to the consultation of experts and the use of economic analysis. It is limited only by the principle that the provision must not be abused to "make the case" for a party. They may not find an infringement in the absence of a *prima facie* case being made by the complainant.[89] In addition, Panels have to remain within the ambit of the *legal claims* made by the parties and cannot use Article 13 of the DSU to alter or go beyond these claims, the *ne ultra petita* principle. Nevertheless, to make an objective assessment of the matter before it and the facts of the case as required by Article 11 of the DSU, they can, also by virtue of Article 13 of the DSU, form a view on these claims using *arguments* not advanced by the parties.[90] Thus, within the confines

[87] Baker and Bresnahan, *Economic Evidence in Antitrust: Defining Markets and Measuring Market Power*, p. 30, argue for a "clarifying expert" with such limited task.

[88] Critical of such broad role, see Gotts and Hemli, "Just the Facts: The Role of Customer and Economic Evidence in M&A Analysis," *George Mason Law Review*, 13 (2006), 1217, 1244.

[89] Appellate Body Report, *Japan – Agricultural Products*, *supra*, fn. 33, para. 129.

[90] For the distinction between legal *claims* and *arguments* see Appellate Body Report, *European Communities – Measures Concerning Meat and Meat Products (Hormones)* (hereinafter *EC – Hormones*), WT/DS26/AB/R, WT/DS48/AB/R, adopted February 13, 1998, para. 156.

of the legal claims presented by the parties, Panels are free to develop their own reasoning on the basis of evidence that goes beyond that which has been submitted by the parties. Panels can obtain expert advice in order to develop arguments the parties have not raised. Consequently, the scope of expert testimony under Article 13 of the DSU is not limited to explaining and evaluating (economic) evidence submitted by the parties, but extends to include economic analysis even if none has been attempted by the parties. For example, if the likeness of products is undisputed by the parties, or the complaining party has not established a *prima facie* case of likeness, the Panel cannot make the case for one party and consult an expert to undertake an economic analysis on this issue. The Panel can, however, turn to economic evidence developed on its own account (also by virtue of Article 13 of the DSU), if the market definition issue is contested but particular economic arguments have not been made, or no economic analysis was carried out by the parties at all.

E *Evidentiary and procedural solutions*

The substantive assessment of economic evidence can be broken down into two analytical steps: the issue of its admissibility and the subsequent issue of its sufficiency to meet the standard of proof. While EU and WTO law do not distinguish between these two steps, US law separates them out with each stage providing for a separate filter for economic evidence. The first, is a screening of the methodology. The second, on the motion of the defendant, tests the substantive (probative) value of the evidence to raise a *prima facie* case.[91] The following will focus on admissibility rules as a mechanism for quality control of party-appointed expert witnesses and the role of cross-examination as an instrument to ascertain the substantive weight of evidence. The second filter of expert economic evidence, namely, the analysis of the sufficiency of the evidence, will not be addressed because WTO Panel procedure does not contain any formal motion procedure akin to that of motions for summary judgment enabling the sufficiency of the claimant's evidence to be tested.[92]

[91] For the distinction between the separate analytical steps of admissibility (methodology) and sufficiency (conclusion) see Kaye, "The Dynamics of Daubert: Methodology, Conclusions and Fit in Statistical and Econometric Studies," *Virginia Law Review*, 87 (2001), 1933, 1972–1985.

[92] The US Supreme Court in *Matsushita Electric Industrial Corp.* v. *Zenith Radio Corp.*, 475 US 574, 585–587 (1986) developed the doctrine of an aggressive use of summary judgment pursuant to Rule 56(c) of the Federal Rules of Civil Procedure in order to

(i) Admissibility rules

Neither EU nor WTO law restrict the admissibility of party-sponsored expert evidence. Lacking specific statutory rules or case law regulating party expert witnesses, their status is "unclear" and "informal" in EU law.[93] Parties in administrative proceedings before the European Commission, as well as in judicial proceedings before the EU courts, have the broad freedom to submit the evidence and witnesses they consider pertinent.[94] This usually includes the freedom to resort to expert economic testimony as part of the party pleadings.[95]

Likewise, in WTO law, Article 13 of the DSU and its Annex only set out rudimentary rules for Panel-appointed experts, mainly on expert qualification and citizenship. No rules exist limiting the admissibility of evidence. In the absence of such rules, any type of evidence from any source is admissible before WTO adjudicators, including testimony by party-appointed experts.[96] It was explicitly recognized that Members have the right to compose their delegations for purposes of dispute settlement to include not only private counsel, but also any kind of expert.[97] This corresponds to the principle of free admissibility of evidence which generally governs international tribunals where sovereign states are parties to a dispute. In the absence of express rules to the contrary, international adjudicators must exercise their discretion against the backdrop of sovereignty and admit all evidence submitted by the parties.[98] Moreover, WTO

limit expert economic testimony specifically in antitrust litigation. On the motion of the defendant, it allows the court to pass judgment on the quality and weight of economic testimony submitted by the plaintiff by concluding that the testimony is insufficient to support a genuine issue of material fact. See Hovenkamp, "Economic Experts in Antitrust Cases," in Faigman *et al.*, (eds.), *Modern Scientific Evidence: The Law and Science of Expert Testimony*, vol. V, §§ 44:2, 44:9 (2008).

93 De la Serre and Sibony, "Expert Evidence before the EC Courts," p. 965. See also MacLennan, "Evidence, Standard and Burden of Proof and the Use of Experts in Procedure Before the Luxembourg Courts," pp. 269–270.

94 Article 10(3) of the Commission Regulation on Article 81 and 82 proceedings; Article 47(1) of the ECJ Rules; Article 68(1) of the GC Rules.

95 For examples of antitrust cases in which party expert witnesses figured see Case T-34/92, *Fiatagri UK Ltd and New Holland Ford Ltd* v. *Commission* [1994] ECR II-905, para. 82; Case T-25/99, *Roberts* v. *Commission* [2001] ECR II-1881, paras. 51, 69; *Airtours* v. *Commission*, para. 212.

96 Christoforou, "Settlement of Science-Based Trade Disputes in the WTO: A Critical Review of the Developing Case Law in the Face of Scientific Uncertainty," *NYU Environmental Law Journal*, 8 (2000), 622, 626–627.

97 Panel Report, *United States – Subsidies on Upland Cotton, supra*, Introduction, fn. 19, para. 7.1202 fn. 1323.

98 Kazazi, *Burden of Proof and Related Issues: A Study on Evidence before International Tribunals*, p. 212 (1996); e.g., International Court of Justice, *Case concerning Military and*

law does not contain any rules on relevance, reliability, weight, or sufficiency of (expert) evidence. It is therefore within the Panel's discretion in each case to freely appraise the weight and persuasiveness of the evidence before it and to base its decision on any piece of evidence that it finds relevant.[99]

The United States, by contrast, has prolific case law and statutory provisions that establish rules on the admissibility of party-appointed expert witnesses in federal courts.[100] In *Daubert* v. *Merrell Dow Pharmaceuticals, Inc.* and subsequent cases confirming and refining *Daubert*, the US Supreme Court adopted a strict standard for the admissibility of expert testimony.[101] It ruled that a trial judge has a "gatekeeping role" in reviewing expert testimony. He must decide whether proffered expert testimony is both "relevant" and "reliable."[102] Rule 702 of the FRE on the admissibility of expert testimony codified this precedent in 2000 and imposed "a trilogy of restrictions on expert testimony: qualification, reliability, and fit."[103] Applied to economics, precedent and Rule 702 taken together establish that expert testimony is inadmissible unless (1) the witness is an expert in the relevant aspects of economics (expert qualification), (2) the testimony's economic grounding is reliable (reliability), and (3) the method and tools used in determining the facts of the case are relevant

Paramilitary Activities in and against Nicaragua (*Nicaragua* v. *United States of America*), Judgment, June 27, 1986, ICJ Reports 1986, paras. 29–31.

99 Appellate Body Report, *US – Shrimp*, *supra*, fn. 83, para. 104: "It is particularly within the province and the authority of a panel to determine *the need for information and advice* in a specific case, to ascertain the *acceptability* and *relevancy* of information or advice received, and to decide *what weight to ascribe to that information or advice* or to conclude that no weight at all should be given to what has been received" (emphasis in original). See also Appellate Body Report, *European Communities – Selected Customs Matters*, WT/DS315/AB/R, adopted December 11, 2006, para. 258.

100 There are no equivalent rules for evidence presented to enforcement agencies.

101 *Daubert*, *supra*, fn. 54; *General Electric Co.* v. *Joiner*, 522 US 136 (1997); *Kumho Tire Co.* v. *Carmichael*, 526 US 137 (1999); see Berger, "The Supreme Court's Trilogy on the Admissibility of Expert Testimony," in Federal Judicial Center, *Reference Manual on Scientific Evidence*, pp. 10–38 (2000), available at: www.fjc.gov/public/pdf.nsf/lookup/sciman00.pdf/$file/sciman00.pdf.

102 *Daubert*, *supra*, fn. 54, at 589. Non-exclusive factors include whether the methodology has been tested and subjected to peer review and publication, whether it has a known or potential error rate, and whether it is generally accepted, *ibid.*, at 592–594.

103 *Schneider* v. *Fried*, 320 F.3d 396, 404 (3d Cir. 2003). In full, the provision provides that, apart from the requirement of sufficient expert qualification in terms of knowledge, skill, experience, training, or education, expert admissibility requires that (1) the testimony is based upon sufficient facts or data, (2) the testimony is the product of reliable principles and methods, and (3) the expert has applied the principles and methods reliably to the facts of the case.

(the "fit" requirement).[104] As already indicated, the task of the judge under the *Daubert* admissibility rules is not to assess and evaluate the correctness of the expert opinion. He is called upon to determine in a preliminary assessment the neutrality, reliability, and relevance of an expert's testimony. Therefore, the admissibility rules relate to the procedure (methodology) adopted, not the substance (conclusions) of economic evidence.[105] It is relevant for present purposes that the *Daubert* admissibility test also applies when parties rely on statistical methods such as multiple regression analysis.[106]

(ii) Cross-examination

In addition to admissibility rules, the US adversarial system is characterized by the confrontation between the parties and their witnesses in cross-examination. *Daubert* itself stressed that vigorous cross-examination is a useful instrument to control expert testimony of questionable admissibility.[107] In this way, the monitoring of party experts is not only practiced by the court, but also by the opposing party who has the opportunity to object to the testifying expert's opinions and qualifications. Cross-examination of party experts has the effect of mutual discipline, and produces well-grounded testimonies since any obvious lack of rigor would be revealed by the counterpart. It is therefore a useful tool enabling the adjudicator to distinguish "junk" from real science, especially in a system like the WTO where all evidence is admissible.[108]

In fact, although fully-fledged adversarial cross-examination is alien to WTO dispute settlement procedure, when Panels have consulted experts, they have usually adopted Working Procedures.[109] These procedures set

[104] Werden, "Making Economics More Useful in Competition Cases: Procedural Rules Governing Expert Opinions," in Hawk (ed.), *Annual Proceedings of the Fordham Corporate Law Institute, International Antitrust Law & Policy*, pp. 601–613 (2006).

[105] *Daubert, supra*, fn. 54, at 595: "The focus, of course, must be solely on principles and methodology, not on the conclusions that they generate."

[106] See, e.g., *State of Ohio ex rel. Montgomery* v. *Louis Trauth Dairy, Inc.*, 925 F.Supp. 1247, 1250–1254 (SD Ohio 1996); *In re Polypropylene Carpet Antitrust Litig.*, 996 F.Supp. 18, 26 (ND Ga. 1997) (hereinafter *In re Polypropylene Carpet Antitrust Litig.* (1997); *Estate of Hill* v. *ConAgra Poultry Co.*, No. 4:94-CV-0198-HLM, 1997, WL 538887 at 3–9 (ND Ga. 1997); *Conwood Co.* v. *United States Tobacco Co.*, 290 F.3d 768, 793 (6th Cir. 2002).

[107] *Daubert, supra*, fn. 54, at 596.

[108] On the issue of "junk science," see Bernstein, "Junk Science in the United States and the Commonwealth," *Yale Journal of International Law*, 21 (1996), 123, 124–125.

[109] Panel Report, *Japan – Apples, supra*, fn. 35, paras. 6.2 *et seq.*; Panel Report, *Japan – Apples (Article 21.5 of the DSU), supra*, fn. 35, paras. 6.3 *et seq.*; Panel Report, *EC – Biotech, supra*, fn. 35, paras. 7.20 *et seq.*; Panel Report, *US – Continued Suspension (Hormones)*,

out a two-stage consultation process, comprising both written and oral phases. Experts respond in writing to written questions of the Panel, parties may then comment on the experts' answers in writing, and a joint hearing may be held between the Panel, the experts, and the parties. This second, oral phase is particularly interesting. The meeting, lasting one to two days, affords to the Panel and parties the opportunity for explanation of the concepts, methods, and understanding of the science at play in a given case. However, there is not a direct dialogue of questions and answers between the parties and the expert. In the very limited time given, questions are usually posed by, or at the most through, the Panel. It can thus be noted that some rudimentary form of "cross-examination" already exists in Panel practice, yet only for Panel-appointed experts.[110] It has not, however, really been used by parties.[111] An effective instrument of cross-examination would therefore require, first, extending its application to party-appointed experts and, second, to extend its scope to a direct process of argument and rebuttal between the party experts on both sides.

4 Analysis of the remedial options

It has become apparent that the WTO system already provides for, or rather, with minor changes to already existing instruments, is open to, remedial options for the problems encountered with party-appointed expert testimony. The following will briefly discuss the pros and cons of the various solutions. The analysis gives strong support for the use of Panel-appointed independent experts. However, there is no single ideal way of mitigating the problems associated with partisan expert testimony. The remedial options are not mutually exclusive and to some extent reinforce each other. For example, where adjudicators have some economic background or guidance from the WTO Secretariat staff, they may be more comfortable in confronting economic evidence in cross-examination or consulting independent experts. Panel-appointed independent experts should be

supra, fn. 35, Annex A-5; Panel Report, *Canada – Continued Suspension (Hormones)*, *supra*, fn. 35, Annex A-5.

110 Christoforou, "WTO Panels in the Face of Scientific Uncertainty," p. 250 (the procedure being "a far cry from the cross-examination of a witness or expert by lawyers as this is practiced in common law jurisdictions").

111 Pauwelyn, "Expert Advice in WTO Dispute Settlement," in Bermann and Mavroidis (eds.), *Trade and Human Health and Safety*, pp. 235, 248 (2006).

a complementary instrument and not restrain a party's autonomy to rely on his own expert witnesses.

A *Evidentiary and procedural solutions*

Admissibility rules are not an adequate solution to the problems associated with partisan expert testimony generally and in the WTO context particularly. First, their introduction into WTO procedure would contradict the principle of free admissibility typical of international tribunals. In light of the sovereign right to freely present evidence, the introduction of admissibility rules would be feasible only if a consensus to amend the WTO rules can be reached by all its Members.

Second, admissibility rules would not relieve the panelists in most instances from still having recourse to other remedial options, in particular, internal or external economic expertise. An inquiry into the reliability and relevance of the methodology used will often go beyond the adjudicator's level of competence. That is why *Daubert*, on remand, provoked the criticism of a federal judge of the Court of Appeals of the Ninth Circuit, who stated that its application requires the judge to be a better expert than the expert himself.[112] Moreover, even if admissibility rules may be useful to exclude "unscientific" testimony, they do not solve the problem that adjudicators face when they are called to substantively resolve a conflict between sound, yet contradictory, expert testimony.

Third, WTO law does not share the same rationale for admissibility rules as the United States. The US judicial system assigns issues of fact to a jury composed of lay persons. In view of its adversarial nature, the judge acts as gatekeeper to prevent the jury from being unduly influenced by junk science, and confused or misled by an adversarial "battle of the experts." Concerns about their capacity to discern "good" from "bad" science have resulted in the creation of admissibility rules for scientific expert testimony. They "are designed to shield inexperienced fact-finders (the jurors) from evidence that might confuse, distract, or inflame them."[113]

[112] See *Daubert* v. *Merrell Dow Pharmaceuticals, Inc.*, 43 F.3d 1311, 1315–1316 (9th Cir. 1994).

[113] Posner, "The Law and Economics of the Economic Expert Witness," p. 92. As Lianos, "'Judging' Economists," pp. 281–282 explains, there is a further dimension. Since *Daubert* relieves the jury only from assessing the methodology, jurors, paradoxically, still have to make the harder finding on the merits (i.e., the substance and weight) of the expert evidence. Therefore, the rationale of *Daubert* is in fact to protect jurors from the typical propensity of lay people to focus on "peripheral" criteria, or proxies (such as the expert's credentials), and not on the quality and validity of the arguments.

In contrast to this common law model of adjudication, and comparable to inquisitorial civil law systems, panelists rule on both questions of fact and law. There is no jury of lay people to be protected, and (inquisitorial) panelists, by contrast, are themselves highly qualified experts in the fields relevant to the dispute or possess the means of informing themselves of the probative value of expert testimony. As there is no division of tasks between judge and jury, and panelists rule on all factual issues anyway, there is no reason to separate the issues of admissibility (focusing on the methodology) and sufficiency (focusing on the substantive conclusions) in the assessment of economic evidence. In fact, it is quite reasonable not to distinguish between these analytical steps. Technically, it is often impossible and artificial to draw the line between methodology and substance of economic evidence.[114] For example, US courts examine under the *Daubert* standard, among others, the data set, the selection and use of statistical methods, and whether a regression-based testimony comports with the established standards for the use of such models. In this process, however, the distinction between the separate inquiries into methodology and conclusions often becomes blurred. Courts in the United States have been increasingly observed to make an assessment of the testimony's substance in the course of applying the *Daubert* admissibility analysis.[115]

Moreover, in terms of cognitive process, admissibility rules involve an "all-or-nothing" determination and lead to an atomistic and exclusive approach to the appraisal of evidence. In contrast, an analysis of the evidence that collapses the issues of admissibility and sufficiency constitutes a holistic and inclusive approach. The latter has the advantage of accommodating the inclusion of all economic evidence in the judicial consideration of the facts and the law. The value of a particular piece of information and the truth of a particular proposition can be considered and evaluated in the context of all the evidence, not individually and in isolation.

Finally, challenging experts using admissibility rules can have an unintended chilling effect on the use of economic evidence, undermining the intention to promote economic analysis. In the United States, the

[114] For instance, is it enough for a court to note that an econometric regression analysis is "a methodology that is well-established as reliable" (*City of Tuscaloosa* v. *Harcros Chemicals, Inc.*, 158 F.3d 548, 566 (11th Cir. 1998)) or should it go into the details of the specific model, such as the consideration of alternative hypotheses or included and excluded independent variables? In the former case, the inquiry would be overly superficial and uninformative, in the latter case it would already go to the substantive heart (probative value) of the evidence.

[115] Lianos, "'Judging' Economists," pp. 273–275.

reliability and relevance criteria under the *Daubert* doctrine are disputed in (antitrust) litigation with increasing frequency.[116] A marked increase in the probability that proffered expert economic testimony, even in the case of renowned experts, will be successfully challenged and excluded on the basis of *Daubert* has been empirically shown.[117] It is against this background that *Daubert* motions, usually filed by the defense, are criticized as coming at the high cost of deterring and discouraging good economists from taking good cases and appearing as expert witnesses for parties.[118] The reason is that well-qualified experts of good standing may fear the risk of damage to their professional reputation that a successful *Daubert* attack may create. As a consequence, the best, most able economic experts may not participate as expert witnesses in proceedings where the risk of exclusion is high and only lower quality expert testimony may be available.[119]

Also, the adversarial instrument of cross-examination as an alternative procedural solution is not a panacea in itself. It may be true that the exposure of arguments to the adversarial dialectics can be instructive.[120] The confrontation through adversarial cross-examination is an effective instrument for weeding out unreliable expert testimony. But it can also be destructive, with attacks on the credibility of the opposing expert's expertise diverting attention from the merits of one's own evidence. The direct confrontation between the parties and their experts in fact brings the contradiction of expert testimonies to a climax. This can further mislead or confuse the non-expert adjudicator who is incapable of resolving these contradictions between the experts.

[116] See Blair and Herndon, "The Implications of Daubert for Economic Evidence in Antitrust Cases," *Washington & Lee Law Review*, 57 (2000), 801, 802; Lopatka and Page, "Economic Authority and the Limits of Expertise in Antitrust Cases," *Cornell Law Review*, 90 (2005), 617, 645–649.

[117] Langenfeld and Alexander, *Daubert Challenges of Antitrust Experts*, p. 3 (2008), available at: www.antitrustinstitute.org/files/AAI%20working%20paper%2008-06_120620082058.pdf, surveyed an exclusion rate of 70 percent of economic experts in antitrust cases between 2000 and 2008; see also Hockett and Hinman, "Admissibility of Expert Testimony in Antitrust Cases: Does Daubert Raise a New Barrier to Entry for Economists?" *Antitrust*, 10 (1996), 40–45.

[118] ABA Economic Evidence Task Force, at 8; Kanner and Casey, "Daubert and the Disappearing Jury Trial," *University of Pittsburgh Law Journal*, 69 (2007), 281, 316.

[119] This may create an "adverse selection problem," where adjudicators distrust experts for reason of asymmetric information and the risk of moral hazard, and thus readily exclude expert testimony.

[120] Neven, "Competition Economics and Antitrust in Europe," p. 776.

B Expert panelists, institutional support, and Panel-appointed experts

At the outset, it is clear that institutional support in the form of guidance to adjudicators through specific consultation material and publications or training programs can be helpful in increasing the economic literacy of adjudicators. They may then be able to ask probing questions and not be blown away by a blast of scientific jargon. But this approach appears insufficient on its own to handle expert testimony in all its complexity.[121]

When considering the remaining options of appointing expert panelists, enhancing the in-house economic secretarial support, and consulting Panel-appointed experts, they all alleviate the problems of information asymmetry and the principal–agent conflict of interests. In all of these instances, the interests of the adjudicator and the expert are aligned. The expert is not hired and remunerated by a party, and thus has no financial interest to tailor his testimony to a particular party's position. Since experts in all these three circumstances are untainted by partisanship, adjudicators can count on a neutral assessment of the facts of the case and a neutral resolution of conflicting party-appointed expert opinions.[122] In the literature on expert economic testimony, the use of court-appointed experts is favored, especially in antitrust law.[123] The recent judgment of the ICJ in *Case concerning Pulp Mills on the River Uruguay (Argentina v. Uruguay)* (hereinafter *Pulp Mills*) provides a different, but informative, context which ignited a discussion among the judges with respect to the role and methodological treatment of complex scientific and technical evidence. Several separate opinions considered the consultation of

[121] It has been suggested that training programs are ineffective when measured in terms of the number of successfully appealed economically complex cases, see Baye and Wright, *Is Antitrust Too Complicated for Generalist Judges? The Impact of Economic Complexity & Judicial Training on Appeals*, p. 5 (2009), available at: http://ssrn.com/abstract=1319888.

[122] For the concern that there is no such thing as a truly "neutral" economic expert free from conflicts and strong ideological presumptions, even if not influenced by compensation from one party, because economic experts are always either "hawks" or "doves," see Posner, "An Economic Approach to the Law of Evidence," p. 1540.

[123] Rubinfeld and Steiner, "Quantitative Methods in Antitrust Litigation," *Law and Contemporary Problems*, 46 (1983), 69, 140–141; Posner, "The Law and Economics of the Economic Expert Witness," p. 96; Botteman, "Mergers, Standard of Proof and Expert Economic Evidence," *Journal of Competition Law & Economics*, 2 (2006), 71, 87; ABA Economic Evidence Task Force, at 8–10; Bernstein, "Expert Witnesses, Adversarial Bias, and the (Partial) Failure of the Daubert Revolution," at 107. Critical, see Deason, "Court-Appointed Expert Witnesses: Scientific Positivism Meets Bias and Deference," *Oregon Law Review*, 77 (1998), 59, 62.

independent court-appointed experts the most compelling instrument of which the Court should have availed itself.[124] Indeed, there are strong reasons why independent Panel-appointed experts also appear as the best solution in the WTO context.[125]

First, independent experts can be consulted on an *ad hoc* basis, so allowing the expert in the "market" with the expertise and experience most relevant for the specific issue to be retained. Economic problems may not yet be manifest when a Panel is being composed, and an adequate expert panelist may not be appointed as a result. In addition, there will often be multiple economic and other scientific issues, each requiring very different expertise from a number of specialized experts who cannot all be appointed to serve on the Panel. Moreover, the non-legal specialization of panelists seems an unrealistic option given the currently dominant debate over the need for a permanent Panel body of full-time jurists. Put forward by some WTO Members and scholars, this proposed institutional reform is intended to alleviate the lack of judicial experience of panelists who, on average, serve on only two Panels.[126]

Likewise, it would appear too costly in comparison with a one-off hiring of external experts to maintain in the WTO Secretariat all this specialized knowledge that may only infrequently become relevant in international trade disputes. This is particularly true for the extremely specialized economic expertise in industrial organization and econometrics that is relevant for market definition purposes. Rather, the expansion of "in-house" economic expertise appears useful with regard to WTO-specific economic areas.

Second, as the ICJ judges Al-Khasawneh and Simma argued in their joint dissenting opinion in the *Pulp Mills* case, the use of independent court-appointed experts in an appropriate institutional framework in which the parties have the opportunity to comment upon or otherwise assist the Court in understanding the expert evidence before it (for example, by formal cross-examination) serves the important needs of transparency, openness, and procedural fairness.[127] Importantly, in the

[124] ICJ, *Case concerning Pulp Mills on the River Uruguay* (*Argentina* v. *Uruguay*), Judgment, April 20, 2010, ICJ Reports 2010, Joint Dissenting Opinion of Judges Al-Khasawneh and Simma, paras. 6–9; Declaration of Judge Yusuf, para. 1; Separate Opinion of Judge Cançado Trindade, para. 151; Dissenting Opinion of Judge *ad hoc* Vinuesa, para. 1.

[125] This view is shared by Malacrida, "Some Reflections on the Use of Economic Analysis in WTO Dispute Settlement Proceedings," pp. 438–439.

[126] See, e.g., Busch and Pelc, "Does the WTO Need a Permanent Body of Panelists?," *Journal of International Economic Law*, 12 (2009), 579, 582.

[127] *Pulp Mills*, *supra*, fn. 124, Joint Dissenting Opinion of Judge Al-Khasawneh and Judge Simma, paras. 13, 14.

case of quantitative evidence, parties should have the ability to critically scrutinize, review, and test opinions provided directly to adjudicators by internal or outside independent experts. This appears especially warranted where the function of the internal or court-appointed outside expert is not merely to educate the adjudicator regarding the parties' economic evidence, but, as suggested above for WTO law, to act as an arbiter between the views of the parties' experts and even to produce his own economic evidence.[128]

In WTO dispute settlement procedure mechanisms already exist that give parties such an opportunity to comment on Panel-appointed expert testimony. For the consultation of a Panel-appointed external expert group, paragraph 6 of Annex 4 of the DSU requires the submission of the draft and final expert reports to the parties and the opportunity for the parties to comment. With regard to the consultation of individual experts appointed by the Panel an expert report is not formally required. However, the practice under the Working Procedures has been the above outlined two-stage consultation process with a written and an oral phase.

This process for the consultation under the WTO Working Procedures has been characterized by Al-Khasawneh and Simma as "state-of-the-art" in the taking of expert evidence in international courts and tribunals.[129] Even though only a rudimentary form of cross-examination, this process allows for a proactive engagement of the adjudicators and parties with the experts. It puts the adjudicators and parties in a position to fully appreciate all dimensions of the mixed questions of law and fact that frequently characterize scientific or technical disputes. It has much in common with "witness conferencing" procedures. Witness conferencing is a novel evidentiary process used most frequently in international arbitrations.[130] Witnesses, in particular expert witnesses, testifying on a common issue sit together and give evidence in what involves a mix of traditional cross-examination and Panel discussion led by the tribunal. In a flexible procedure, it allows multiple witnesses to give testimony simultaneously, and party counsel and witnesses to pose questions to each other.

[128] See Gotts and Hemli, "Just the Facts: The Role of Customer and Economic Evidence in M&A Analysis," pp. 1243–1244.

[129] *Pulp Mills*, *supra*, fn. 124, Joint Dissenting Opinion of Judge Al-Khasawneh and Judge Simma, paras. 16, 28.

[130] See the seminal article by Peter, "Witness Conferencing," *Arbitration International*, 18 (2002), 47–58. Note that witness conferencing involves party- not tribunal-appointed witnesses.

In contrast, the possibility for parties to review and test expert opinions does not exist in the case of merely informal *in camera* advice by expert panelists or WTO Secretariat support. Consultation by adjudicators of such "internal 'experts fantômes,'" or "'invisible' experts," thus deprives the court and the parties of the advantages of transparent, open, and fair proceedings.[131]

Finally, an important concern with respect to the use of expert panelists and internal experts is the blurring of roles between expert advisors and judicial decision-makers. These two modes, through which expert knowledge can be supplied and acted upon by adjudicators, should be viewed critically. They may allow experts "on the inside" of the adjudicating process to become too closely involved in the interweaving of the legal process with expert knowledge and to exert uncontrolled power over, or be given too much deference by, the judicial adjudicators. In short, there is the risk that an expert "on the inside" may take away the role of the judge as the arbiter of fact and undermine the court's judicial function.

This risk seems less acute in case of independent Panel-appointed experts, who have no immediate access to the internal judicial decision-making process. For court-appointed outside experts, Judge Yusuf pointed out in *Pulp Mills* that: "[it would be] absurd to think that the judge has delegated his responsibility to the expert."[132] Consequently, "although experts may assist the Court to develop a finer grasp of the scientific and technical details of factual issues arising in the case, it always remains the ultimate responsibility of the judge to decide on the relevance and significance of those facts to the adjudication of the dispute."[133] Thus, even if the insights needed to make legal decisions may emanate from outside experts consulted by the court, it remains for the adjudicators themselves to discharge the exclusively judicial functions, such as the interpretation of legal terms, the legal categorization of factual issues, and the weighing of the probative value of the facts. After all, the best way to remedy the risk of the blurring of roles is transparency in the consultation with experts and in the reasoning of the adjudicators.[134] As explained, this is

[131] *Pulp Mills*, *supra*, fn. 124, Joint Dissenting Opinion of Judge Al-Khasawneh and Judge Simma, para. 13.

[132] *Pulp Mills*, *supra*, fn. 124, Declaration of Judge Yusuf, para. 11 citing the Arbitral Tribunal in *Application for Revision and Subsidiary Interpretation of the Award of 21 October 1994 submitted by Chile* (*Argentina* v. *Chile*), Judgment, October 13, 1995, XXII RIAA 162, para. 40.

[133] *Pulp Mills*, *supra*, fn. 124, Declaration of Judge Yusuf, para. 12.

[134] C. E. Foster, *Scientific Evidence and the Precautionary Principle in International Courts and Tribunals*, p. 12 (2010), available at: http://rmla.org.nz/upload/documents/Salmon_Lecture_2010.pdf.

best achieved under WTO dispute settlement procedures when using independent Panel-appointed experts.

5 Conclusion

"The disagreement [over an economic and quantitative approach to Article III market definition] had to do with ... the question of whether the WTO judge is appropriately equipped to incorporate such analysis in his or her reasoning."[135] This section has given an answer. It sketched the institutional and procedural arrangements in the WTO that affect the ability of adjudicators to undertake sound economic reasoning based on expert economic testimony. The result is that the WTO dispute settlement system is well situated to accommodate expert testimony in general and economic evidence in particular. The WTO combines the merits of the adversarial approach, namely, the benefits of party experts and cross-examination in terms of the quantity of economic evidence analyzed and mutual quality control, with the merits of the inquisitorial approach, characterized by the neutral expertise of external court-appointed experts or internal expertise. Thus, it already provides for instruments that facilitate the feeding of economic evidence into the legal findings and helps adjudicators to handle expert economic testimony. Slight improvements to the institutional structures already in place, such as increased reliance on Panel-appointed experts and improvements in the WTO internal economic support provided to adjudicators, would further enhance the use of economic evidence in WTO proceedings and mitigate some of the problems of party-appointed expert testimony.

Finally, it should be underscored that WTO Panels are exceptional in the judicial landscape for two reasons. First, they come closest to what has been described as "specialized tribunals," perceived as potential remedies to problems with expert witnesses. Panelists are somewhere between generalist judges and experts. They are highly qualified in their respective fields (mostly in international trade). Yet on specific non-trade expert issues, such as econometric evidence on market definition, they would still be in the position of "novices," unable to fully assess and evaluate an econometrician's testimony. What makes the difference in comparison with generalist judges is that as experts themselves they appear to feel more confident and comfortable dealing with other experts. They do not need to answer difficult scientific or economic questions themselves.

[135] Cottier and Mavroidis, "Concluding Remarks," in Cottier and Mavroidis (eds.), *The Role of the Judge in International Trade Regulation*, pp. 349, 351 (2003).

But in the best case they have some basic familiarity with scientific or economic methods, attitudes, usages, and vocabulary, as well as some knowledge of the economics that drive the legal issues. For example, this would mean that panelists know the basic economic reasoning behind the Article III market definition issues outlined in Chapter 4. On this basis they will then not hesitate to engage with experts when it comes to implementing the economic approach.

Second, with the explicit provision for expert review groups, WTO law has an exceptional, but unfortunately so far unused, potential in the judicial landscape. Although the process of an expert review group may be more costly and time-consuming than consulting only one expert, or several who work individually, it has an important advantage, in particular, in case of difficult scientific or economic issues.[136]

Fundamentally, in science, "truth" is sought through a pluralistic discourse incorporating, by way of assertion and refutation, various opposing views. In contrast to an individual expert, experts collaborating in an expert group can assess diverging expert views through a process of confrontation and dialogue. A Panel college of experts thus reduces the adversarial nature of expert testimony and emphasizes the pluralistic character of cooperative scientific discourse between a number of experts (in contrast to the "monologue" by a single Panel-appointed expert or the isolated work of several experts working individually).

Even if there is no formal requirement for consensus under the DSU, it is more likely that a group of experts called upon to produce a single expert report will achieve a more broadly acceptable and less confrontational result.[137] Because the individual contributions are subject to peer review, in an expert body the experts are likely to present a more balanced position for which there is broader agreement. In this way, the interaction in an expert group promises to come closer to scientific "objectivity" and legitimacy in terms of persuasiveness and epistemic competence. Importantly, the tendency of an expert group to reach a middle ground consensus position that best reflects scientific objectivity seems particularly appropriate in addressing two issues. First, it solves the problem of conflicting expert testimony, either between individual Panel-appointed

[136] For the idea of a "board of experts" see the famous Learned Hand, "Historical and Practical Considerations Regarding Expert Testimony," *Harvard Law Review*, 15 (1901), 40, 56.

[137] *Contra* Iynedjian, "The Case for Incorporating Scientists and Technicians into WTO Panels," pp. 287, 289.

experts or among party-retained experts.[138] Evaluation through several peers is most representative, and the need for the adjudicator to deal with the difficult task of making a choice between competing expert explanations is dispensed with. Second, it reduces the risk of intellectual bias of individual experts.[139] Even neutral experts, who are not necessarily susceptible to adversarial bias, are still likely to have an intellectual predisposition resulting from their particular background, adherence to a specific school of thought or network, or other involvement. This will certainly influence, and possibly bias (consciously or unconsciously), an expert's testimony. The promise is that these biases are neutralized in a diverse expert group.

III ANALYSIS OF PRICE ELASTICITIES OF DEMAND

After outlining that an economic approach to Article III market definition can be implemented institutionally and procedurally, this section analyzes its methodological implementation. The concept of price elasticities of demand is used in economics for the assessment of the sensitivity of consumer consumption to a price increase. It is an explicit measure of customers' willingness to switch and thus of buyer substitution between products. That is why it has the specific advantage of being directly linked to the pertinent market definition issue of demand substitutability.

This section draws on experience with the concept of elasticity in antitrust law, and describes the extent to which it can also be used under Article III of the GATT. For this purpose, the basics of price elasticities of demand and their theoretical role in antitrust law and under Article III of the GATT will be outlined in sections 1 and 2. Section 3 outlines a conceptual framework for the use of CPE of demand under Article III of the GATT, addressing certain complications that arise in the specific context of that provision. Section 4 describes how to econometrically estimate elasticities. As a very technical subject, this is usually left to economic experts. However, it will become clear that legal professionals cannot remain ignorant on this issue. Some basic knowledge is necessary

138 See Christoforou, "Settlement of Science-Based Trade Dispute in the WTO," p. 638; Pauwelyn, "The Use of Experts in WTO Dispute Settlement," p. 329.

139 Dwyer, *The Judicial Assessment of Expert Evidence*, p. 163 (2008); Lianos, "'Judging' Economists," p. 257.

to generally deal with econometric evidence and to knowledgeably discuss the merits and limits of an economics-based approach to market definition. The theoretical insights developed in Section 4 will be applied in sections 5 and 6. Section 5 describes the role non-econometric and econometric estimations of elasticities have played in antitrust and Article III analysis of market definition. It also critically assesses the use of econometrics in the specific context of Article III of the GATT. Finally, Section 6 addresses the merits and limits of econometrics in the context of legal analysis.

1 The foundations of the analysis of price elasticities of demand

One of the first concepts economics students learn is that of elasticities.[140] It measures the sensitivity of one variable to another. Specifically for market definition purposes, the price elasticity of demand is of importance. Price elasticities of demand are a measure of the relative responsiveness in quantity demanded as a result of a change in price. In other words, they measure the sensitivity of consumer reactions to price changes. Basic economic theory states that as the price of a product changes, demand for the product changes.[141] As the price of a product increases (or decreases) consumers will usually demand a lower (or higher) quantity of that good, as measured by the own-price elasticity of demand (hereinafter OPE), and may substitute it with another product, estimated by the CPE of demand.[142]

The OPE of demand is a summary indicator of the extent to which a product is subject to demand-side constraints. The OPE of demand is defined as the percentage change in quantity in response to a percentage change in price of the same product, all other things – in particular, the prices of other products – being equal.[143] It thus captures the responsiveness of its quantity demanded to a change in its price, and more precisely,

[140] See, e.g., Pindyck and Rubinfeld, *Microeconomics*, p. 34.

[141] According to the "law of demand," demand for a product and its price are inversely related.

[142] This refers to the elasticities of demand *of a product* or *of a firm* in contrast to the *aggregate* elasticities, which measure how total market demand, the combined demand for all products in a market, changes with a price increase.

[143] Elasticities of the traditional structural (Marshallian) demand curve are predicated on the *ceteris paribus* assumption: "other things being equal." They indicate the quantity purchased at each price, holding constant the prices of all other goods and other influences. They provide information about buyer preferences and thus account for demand-side substitution only. An alternative demand function without this assumption

the switching away in response to a price increase either by switching to competing products, or not purchasing the product at all. Formally, the OPE is calculated by dividing the percentage change in quantity by the percentage change in price. For example, as a SSNIP test typically looks at the impact of a 5 percent price increase, a value of 2 indicates a fall in sales by 10 percent for such a price rise.[144] When the price elasticity exceeds 1, demand is said to be elastic, that is, a 1 percent price increase leads to a reduction in quantity by at least 1 percent; it is said to be inelastic if its elasticity is less than 1.

In contrast, CPE of demand equals the percentage change in price for one product over the percentage change in demand for another product. It thus quantifies the responsiveness of the quantity demanded of a good to a change in the price of another good, *ceteris paribus*. It focuses on the rate at which buyers substitute one product for another and thus provides a measure for their substitutability. If two goods are demand-side substitutes, a rise in the price of one product should cause consumers to shift some of their purchases to the other product. The nominal value of CPE does not need to be high to signify demand substitution. If products are – at least to a very small degree – substitutes, then the CPE is positive. If they are perfect substitutes, the CPE is infinite; if the products are unrelated, the CPE value is zero; if they are complements, the CPE is negative. For instance, a CPE of 5 implies that a price increase of 10 percent for one product would cause a 50 percent increase in quantity demanded for the other product. On this basis, the CPE of demand is widely employed as a quantitative measure for a competitive relationship between two products.

2 The theoretical role of elasticity estimates in antitrust law and Article III of the GATT

Since CPE of demand relates to the proximity of substitutes, it is only natural to think that it can play a useful role in market definition purposes.[145]

is the "residual demand curve." The "residual demand elasticity" incorporates supply as well as demand responses. The *1992 Merger Guidelines* expressly introduced the *ceteris paribus* assumption (paras. 1.0, 1.11, 1.21) and thus endorsed the Marshallian OPE of demand. The *Commission Notice on market definition*, para. 38, also appears to have opted for it as it refers to "changes in the relative prices in the past (all else being equal)."

[144] The OPE is normally a negative number, but, conventionally, it is expressed in absolute terms.

[145] In economics, the use of CPE to characterize competitive relationships was suggested by Kaldor in the 1930s, and was then developed more fully by Triffin; see Bishop,

The first explicit proposal in jurisprudence to base antitrust market definition on CPE of demand was made by the US Supreme Court in the 1953 *Times-Picayune* case in a seemingly unimportant footnote.[146] Subsequently, it was taken up again in the notorious 1956 *Cellophane* case, in particular, by citing to Bain for this proposition.[147] Two decades after, the ECJ in its famous *United Brands* judgment applied the concept of CPE for the first time in EU antitrust law.[148] Later, the *Commission Notice on market definition* endorsed both OPE and CPE as quantitative evidence for market definition.[149]

Especially since the introduction of the SSNIP test, it is evident that price elasticities of demand play a useful role in antitrust market definition. A price increase is profitable only if the firm faces a relatively inelastic demand curve for its product. An elasticity estimate can give an indication of whether the demand for a product is inelastic enough for an SSNIP to be profitable. But the role of CPE has also been widely misunderstood by regulators, courts, and commentators as being suitable to draw market boundaries on its sole basis.[150] When turning to elasticity estimates, they often – exclusively and erroneously – rely on measures of CPE to determine whether two products form part of a relevant market, while usually paying no attention to the estimation of OPE.[151]

The CPE of demand for a pair of products does not delineate the relevant antitrust market on its own because it does not answer the SSNIP question directly. It is a popular misconception to conclude from a positive high CPE between two products that the relevant market is confined to those products; or to make the inverse inference from a low CPE that

"Elasticities, Cross-Elasticities, and Market Relationships," *American Economic Review*, 42 (1952), 779, 779.

146 *Times-Picayune Publishing Co.* v. *United States*, *supra*, Ch. 4, fn. 120, at 612 fn. 31: "For every product substitutes exist. But a relevant market cannot meaningfully encompass that infinite range. The circle must be drawn narrowly to exclude any other product to which, within reasonable variations in price, only a limited number of buyers will turn; in technical terms, products whose 'cross-elasticities of demand' are small."

147 *Cellophane*, *supra*, Ch. 2, fn. 26, at 394, 400 fn. 28.

148 *United Brands*, *supra*, Ch. 2, fn. 30, para. 28.

149 *Commission Notice on market definition*, para. 39.

150 Hovenkamp, *Federal Antitrust Policy*, para. 3.4a: "Judges have often misused the concept of cross-elasticity of demand because they have not understood its limitations." Recent examples in scholarship are: Schwalba, *Die wettbewerbsbezogene Abgrenzung des relevanten Marktes*, p. 52 (2000); Cárdenas, *Rolle, Kriterien und Methodik der kartellrechtlichen Marktabgrenzung*, p. 42; Müller, *Abschied vom Bedarfsmarktkonzept bei der Marktabgrenzung?* pp. 114–115, 126–128.

151 See, e.g., *Beatrice Foods Co.*, 101 FTC 733, 801 (1983): "Cross-elasticity of demand [is] the most important factor in product market definition"; *Hayden Publ'g Co.* v. *Cox Broad*

the relevant market is limited to the candidate product. The former is a misconception because the relevant market may still be broader. A SSNIP could still remain unprofitable if consumers also switch to a significant extent to other products. The latter is mistaken, since even if the CPEs for all possible substitutes are positive but very low the aggregate substitution by consumers may still suffice to make a SSNIP unprofitable. Importantly, even if the CPEs between all potential pairs of substitutes were to be calculated, it would remain unclear over which collection of products a price increase would be profitable and over which it would not.

In contrast, the estimation of the OPE of demand answers directly the SSNIP test question. Whether demand substitution is sufficient to render the SSNIP unprofitable depends on the extent to which consumers will decrease their demand for the relevant product in the event of a price increase. OPE provides this information.[152] It accounts for switching from a given product to all substitutes because it roughly corresponds to the sum of all the CPEs with respect to all possible substitutes.[153] This ensures that all products that impose a considerable competitive constraint on the product under investigation and thus determine whether an SSNIP would be profitable are considered.

Corp., 730 F.2d 64, 71 (2nd Cir. 1984): "We are persuaded that, as a general rule, the process of defining the relevant product market requires consideration of cross-elasticity of demand"; *Kraft General Foods*, *supra*, fn. 81, at 333: "Cross-price elasticity is a more useful tool than own-price elasticity in defining a relevant antitrust market. Cross-price elasticity estimates tell one where the lost sales will go when the price is raised, while own-price elasticity estimates simply tell one that a price increase would cause a decline in volume." See also Conseil de la concurrence, at Deuxième partie, Titre I: Le marché pertinent, para. 2: "L'étendue du marché dépend donc essentiellement de l'élasticité croisée de substitution des biens ou services."

152 More precisely, to answer directly the question of whether an SSNIP is profitable requires, beyond the mere calculation of OPE, comparing the extent of the reduction in sales volume due to the price increase to the extent of cost savings from the production of lower volumes and the higher margins earned on all of the remaining sales at the increased price. The SSNIP is profitable if the profit gains outweigh the negative effect of forgoing the entire margin on the lost sales. The so-called "critical loss analysis" compares the actual loss in sales that would result from a price rise against the amount of lost sales that would make such a price increase unprofitable. If, for a candidate market, the actual loss is greater than the critical loss, a price rise is unprofitable. Alternatively, using the same information in a different way, one can compare the OPE against the so-called "critical elasticity of demand" as the threshold elasticity at which a price increase becomes unprofitable.

153 Put differently, it captures the collective competitive effect of all substitutable products because it registers the falling demand in the particular product in response to a rise in its price as the result of the combined effect of switching to all competitive products; see Camesasca and van den Bergh, "Achilles Uncovered," p. 147.

CPE of demand is still a useful measure for the relative closeness of two products. The *Merger Guidelines* and the *Commission Notice on market definition* specify a process under the SSNIP framework that proceeds in discrete steps. It begins with a very narrow product group, which is successively expanded by the "next-best substitute" until a hypothetical price increase over the set of products would be profitable. To determine the next-best substitute, it is essential to rank substitutes in order of closeness. CPE estimates between different pairs of possible substitutes are a useful device for determining the appropriate ranking of substitutes.[154] For example, the CPE of products B, C, and D with respect to product A may amount to 2, 1.8, and 1.4, respectively.[155] These figures allow a ranking of substitutes, but do not allow for a decision as to whether A constitutes a market in itself or whether the market also includes product B and eventually also products C and D. Although CPE does not in itself indicate the boundaries of an antitrust market, it can more generally be useful for assessing whether or not a proposed market definition is reasonable.

The question of whether two products are each other's "next-best substitute" is irrelevant for purposes of Article III of the GATT, because products can be "like" or DCS even if they are not immediate next-best substitutes. Nevertheless, CPE of demand is the relevant measure of elasticity here.[156] The information on the competitive significance of individual substitutes on each other is the relevant one for Article III of the GATT.

[154] van den Bergh, "Modern Industrial Organisation versus Old-Fashioned European Competition Law," *European Competition Law Review*, 17 (1996), 75, 82; see *Kraft General Foods, supra*, fn. 81, at 356 for an example of such ranking in case law.

[155] Example taken from van den Bergh and Camesasca, *European Competition Law and Economics*, p. 133.

[156] For the use of CPE, yet without any theoretical explanations: Waelbroeck, "Comments on Damien Neven's Paper," in Cottier and Mavroidis (eds.), *Regulatory Barriers and the Principle of Non-discrimination in World Trade Law*, pp. 343–344 (2000); Verhoosel, *National Treatment and WTO Dispute Settlement*, p. 58; Quick and Lau, "Environmentally Motivated Tax Distinctions and WTO Law," p. 432; Choi, *"Like Products" in International Trade Law*, pp. 54–66; Horn and Mavroidis, "Still Hazy after all These Years," p. 62 (asserting that CPE is the sole criterion needed); Goco, "Non-Discrimination, 'Likeness,' and Market Definition in World Trade Organization Jurisprudence," p. 333 (suggesting a variation of the CPE test for GATT market definition taking the decrease in price of the candidate product as the benchmark.); Krajewski, *Wirtschaftsvölkerrecht*, p. 100 (2006); Mavroidis, *Trade in Goods*, p. 218. In contrast, and without justification, Hogg and Nawaz, "Japan – Alcoholic Beverages, Report of the Panel, 11 July 1996 and of the Appellate Body, 4 October 1996," pp. 351–352, assert OPE as the relevant measure. Against the use of elasticities, e.g., Fauchald, *Environmental Taxes and Trade Discrimination*, p. 150; Wille, "Recapturing a Lost Opportunity: Article III:2 GATT 1994 Japan – Alcoholic Beverages 1996," p. 16.

The reason is that the concepts of likeness and DCS revolve around the competitive significance of a particular pair of individual substitutes: one specific product subject to the trade measure under scrutiny and a specific domestic product. OPE does not provide the same information as it is a measure of the collective competitive significance of all substitutes.[157]

Conceptually, CPE of demand is also the appropriate economic measure, because it measures precisely what Article III of the GATT, when understood in terms of the proposed price increase test, seeks to prohibit. It captures products for which a price increase (for example, by a discriminatory fiscal measure) of the imported product benefits the domestic product in terms of increased sales. Or, as the Appellate Body said, it "attempt[s] to predict the change in demand that would result from a change in the price of a product following, *inter alia*, from a change in the relative tax burdens on domestic and imported products."[158]

In theory, the dispute settlement bodies did not distinguish between the different types of elasticities.[159] Yet the Panels and the Appellate Body in the five pertinent cases *Japan – Alcoholic Beverages II*, *Korea – Alcoholic Beverages*, *Chile – Alcoholic Beverages*, *Thailand – Cigarettes*, and *Philippines – Distilled Spirits* only endorsed CPE analyses as the relevant measure, despite party submissions also referring to the analysis of OPE.[160] In the first case, the Panel noted that: "under national antitrust and trade law regimes, the extent to which products directly compete is measured by the elasticity of substitution."[161] It further noted that: "independently of similarities with respect to physical characteristics or classification in tariff nomenclatures, greater emphasis should be placed on elasticity of substitution."[162] The recent *Philippines – Distilled Spirits* also appeared unusually open to CPE in Article III analysis, stating that:

157 It could prove informative only if it were so low as to indicate that there is little or no substitution to any other candidate substitute product.

158 Appellate Body Report, *Korea – Alcoholic Beverages*, *supra*, Ch. 2, fn. 71, para. 121.

159 Panel Report, *Chile – Alcoholic Beverages*, *supra*, Ch. 2, fn. 68, para. 7.73: "undue weight should not be placed on estimated price-elasticity, demand-elasticity or cross-price elasticity."

160 OPE analyses were submitted in Panel Report, *Japan – Alcoholic Beverages II*, *supra*, Ch. 3, fn. 73, paras. 4.85–4.89, 4.167–4.171, 6.31; Panel Report, *Chile – Alcoholic Beverages*, *supra*, Ch. 2, fn. 68, paras. 4.221, 4.225; Panel Report, *Philippines – Distilled Spirits*, *supra*, Introduction, fn. 23, para. 2.44.

161 Panel Report, *Japan – Alcoholic Beverages II*, *supra*, Ch. 3, fn. 73, para. 6.31, where the Panel also defined the elasticity of substitution as equivalent to CPE.

162 Panel Report, *Japan – Alcoholic Beverages II*, *supra*, Ch. 3, fn. 73, para. 6.28, confirmed by Appellate Body Report, *Japan – Alcoholic Beverages II*, *supra*, Introduction, fn. 15, at 25.

"the competitive relationship between relevant products may be assessed through cross-price elasticity studies, which can be a useful analytical tool to determine the degree of substitutability between two goods or if they are in a competitive relationship."[163] Yet the dispute settlement bodies underscored that although CPE of demand was "a strong indicator of substitutability,"[164] quantitative methods, and in particular CPE, would nevertheless neither be the exclusive, nor the decisive factor.[165]

Even though it is identical in methodology, from a litigation perspective CPE of demand may not play the same role in antitrust and international trade law. CPE can be a powerful argument for the defense side against a proposed narrow antitrust market definition.[166] By drawing up a ranking of substitutes, CPE can indicate that there is demand-side substitution between products inside and outside a suggested market. However, it cannot positively confirm that two products are in a market. In international trade law, CPE has a broader application in litigation because it is a device useful to both parties to the proceedings. A respondent in Article III proceedings will not argue for a larger market as a defendant in antitrust proceedings will do, whose market power depends on how broadly or narrowly market boundaries are drawn. Instead, the focus is on the comparison of two specific products. CPE can be invoked by both sides to prove or disprove that the particular two products are to some degree demand substitutes.

3 A conceptual framework for the use of cross-price elasticities under Article III of the GATT

The concept of CPE of demand seems intuitively appealing for Article III purposes, but its application reveals some significant complications. In fact, estimating CPE raises a number of complex issues. In section A below, some general observations about the use of CPE under Article III of the GATT will be made. Section B then addresses two important problems encountered in the estimation of CPE in Article III scenarios.

163 Panel Report, *Philippines – Distilled Spirits*, *supra*, Introduction, fn. 23, para. 7.108.

164 Panel Report, *Chile – Alcoholic Beverages*, *supra*, Ch. 2, fn. 68, para. 7.77.

165 Appellate Body Report, *Japan – Alcoholic Beverages II*, *supra*, Introduction, fn. 15, at 25; Appellate Body Report, *Korea – Alcoholic Beverages*, *supra*, Ch. 2, fn. 71, para. 134.

166 van den Bergh and Camesasca, *European Competition Law and Economics*, pp. 132–133. For an example where the merging parties successfully used a high CPE to attack a proposed narrow market definition see Rubinfeld, "Market Definition with Differentiated Products: The Post/Nabisco Cereal Merger," *Antitrust Law Journal*, 68 (2000), 163, 179.

A General observations

(i) The threshold issue

To define the boundaries of the relevant market precisely and to make CPE of demand operational on a coherent basis in trade law it is necessary to determine benchmarks: how high a level of CPE warrants the title of DCS? What level of CPE makes products even "like" each other? It comes back to the unresolved issue already alluded to that – under either qualitative or quantitative criteria – the necessary degree of substitution remains unclear. In both legal fields, courts and dispute settlement bodies have failed to provide meaningful guidance as to how much substitution is required in order to place two products in the same relevant market. In fact, as explained above, the Appellate Body appears to be hostile to the determination of any CPE threshold.[167] In what has been submitted here to be an erroneous reasoning, the Appellate Body rejected the showing of any degree of competition in quantitative terms, because it would result in a type of "trade effects" test being written into Article III cases. This reasoning has been shown to be incorrect, because the analytical step of the analysis of the conditions of competition must be distinguished from the examination of trade effects. Moreover, the Appellate Body seems to misunderstand what a particular CPE means. It is a measure of relative closeness and not of an intensity of substitution in absolute terms. The reason is that CPE provides only *relative* information with respect to the competitive influence exerted by different substitutes, as it is calculated from the *percentage* change in price of one product and the *percentage* change in quantity demanded of the other product.[168] Therefore, CPE of demand is not a measure of a certain (absolute) "amount" of competition or trade that is affected.

The fundamental problem is that there is no absolute value of CPE that would indicate that two products are effective substitutes. At the minimum, it is clear that products in a relevant market need not be perfect substitutes in terms of 100 percent substitutability and a CPE value approaching infinity.[169] Still, between very high and very low CPE values lies a grey area where it is unclear what conclusions to draw.

[167] See *supra*, fn. 13.

[168] Therefore, the CPE values can be identical for different product pairs even if the price or quantity changes are different in absolute magnitudes. For this reason, an identical CPE value for two product pairs cannot necessarily be equated with an identical (absolute) intensity of substitution between the two product pairs; see Ewald, "Paradigmenwechsel bei der Abgrenzung relevanter Märkte?" p. 531 and fn. 82.

[169] See *supra*, Ch. 4, fn. 87.

Somewhat vaguely, the Panel in *Chile – Alcoholic Beverages* stated that: "in general economic terms, a high estimated coefficient of elasticity would be important evidence that products are directly competitive or substitutable."[170] The Panel's finding that an elasticity of 0.26 is low provided only a little more assistance.[171] More generally, it even held that: "a high coefficient of cross-price elasticity would of course lend more credence to a claim of direct competitiveness or substitutability, although a low coefficient of cross-price elasticity is not necessarily fatal to a claim of direct competitiveness or substitutability."[172] This statement seems to largely deprive CPE estimates of their probative significance. Yet the Panel's reluctance to rule out substitutability in case of low CPE has to be seen in light of the concern that CPEs risk underestimation.[173] To what extent this is a valid concern will be discussed below.

Admittedly, the only rule of thumb might be that the CPE figure must be positive and of a value of 1 or greater. This would surely suggest that there is at least some competitive interaction between the products in question. However, a positive CPE is a necessary, but insufficient, condition for two products to form part of the same relevant market. For values above 1, it is difficult to objectively establish a threshold.

Where there is no underlying theory, it is actually true that "any choice of a particular level would necessarily be arbitrary."[174] In that case, choosing a particular elasticity level would be a pure policy decision, a value judgment at the discretion of the decision-maker.[175] In antitrust law, however, the SSNIP framework has provided an economically sound remedy to the threshold question. Substitution between two products is sufficient if an SSNIP is unprofitable. The threshold question is therefore answered by reference to the level of substitution at which a price increase becomes unprofitable.[176] For the application in GATT law, a similar framework

[170] Panel Report, *Chile – Alcoholic Beverages, supra*, Ch. 2, fn. 68, para. 7.71.

[171] Panel Report, *Chile – Alcoholic Beverages, supra*, Ch. 2, fn. 68, para. 7.71.

[172] Panel Report, *Chile – Alcoholic Beverages, supra*, Ch. 2, fn. 68, para. 7.70.

[173] Panel Report, *Chile – Alcoholic Beverages, supra*, Ch. 2, fn. 68, paras. 7.68–7.73.

[174] Appellate Submission by the United States to the Appellate Body in *Japan – Alcoholic Beverages II, supra*, Ch. 3, fn. 264, para. 102.

[175] This reflects the observations already made on the difference in degree of demand substitutability between Article III:2(1) and (2) of the GATT, see *supra*, Ch. 4, fn. 171.

[176] Under the measurement of OPE, the critical loss or critical elasticity of demand gives the benchmark against which to ascertain at which point an SSNIP is profitable, see *supra*, fn. 152. Although the level of substitution can thus be determined on a non-arbitrary basis, note that the initial price increase of 5–10 percent used for the SSNIP test remains an arbitrary number.

that provides a principled basis to delineate the market using CPEs is still missing. Above, a test has been proposed according to which the Article III market definition includes a set of products over which, in the absence of competition (that is, in the presence of the discriminatory measure), a domestic producer would be able to raise prices profitably above the competitive level that would prevail in the absence of the discriminatory measure. If this test is adopted, the question of how much substitution is necessary would also be answered by the profitability threshold. The level at which the gains from the price increase and the cost savings would offset and outweigh the loss in sales from the price increase would give an answer to the threshold question. However, to clarify, such an approach would still not provide an answer to the issue of where to draw the line between "like" and DCS products.

(ii) The relevant cross-price elasticity

The second issue is the question of which is the relevant CPE. For any given pair of products, there are two different CPEs. The price increase of the one product and the corresponding change in demand of the other product can be measured for each of the two products. Both CPEs can be significantly different in magnitude so that each may lead to a different market definition.[177] The symmetry condition, which is commonly imposed and which assumes the CPEs for a product pair to be identical, can therefore seriously mislead.[178]

The European Commission decision in *Procter & Gamble/VP Schickedanz* contains an example of confusing the two elasticities.[179] Which of the CPEs to correctly use is an issue as to which the dispute settlement bodies have so far apparently been unaware. Under the general definition of CPE given by the Appellate Body, it remained unclear as to which CPE would be the relevant one: CPE of the import with respect to the price of the domestic product, which measures the change in quantity of the import in response to a change in price of the domestic product

[177] For instance, a small price increase in the price of product A may induce only little substitution to product B, while a small rise in the price of B may generate substantial substitution to A.

[178] Werden, "Demand Elasticities in Antitrust Analysis," *Antitrust Law Journal*, 66 (1998), 363, 402.

[179] *Proctor & Gamble/VP Schickedanz*, *supra*, Ch. 3, fn. 240, para. 54. It was argued by the parties that demand for sanitary towels was influenced by the price of tampons, and that they therefore formed a common market. Yet the data reflected changes in the sales of tampons following changes in the price of sanitary towels. This is the opposite CPE, because it reflects the constraining effect of the sanitary towel on the tampon.

(hereinafter imported CPE); or the CPE of the domestic product with respect to the price of the import, which measures the change in quantity of the domestic product in response to the change in price of the import (hereinafter domestic CPE).[180] In fact, as will be explained below, Panel practice has been to take either one into account, depending on what was presented by the parties. In the majority of cases, this was in fact the imported CPE.[181]

Generally speaking, the relevant CPE when the question is whether the market for product A should include product B is the CPE of demand for A with respect to the price of B, measuring the change in price for B and the subsequent change in quantity for A.[182] However, the initial intuition in the trade law context is different. It would appear to be more correct to look at consumer switching from the domestic to the imported product. The reason is that Article III of the GATT protects competitive conditions for the foreign product, for which it seems crucial as to how many consumers substitute the domestic with the imported product.

However, such a categorical statement may over-simplify things. In fact, it appears that the relevant switching depends on the circumstances. Where an import is not yet in an established competitive relationship, for example, because it is new to the market, a protectionist measure will primarily try to prevent switching from the domestic to the imported product in order to afford protection to the domestic product. In this regard, the switching to the imported product does indeed appear determinative and the focus would consequently be on the imported CPE. In contrast, when a foreign and a domestic product are already competitors and the importing state now attempts to afford protection to the domestic product, the protectionist measure would aim at instigating switching from the imported to the domestic product by increasing the price of the import. Here, the inverse switching appears dispositive. This may explain why in the few instances in which an actual value of the CPE coefficient was calculated, it was that of domestic CPEs.

[180] Appellate Body Report, *Korea – Alcoholic Beverages*, *supra*, Ch. 2, fn. 71, para. 121: "Such studies [of CPE] attempt to predict the change in demand that would result from a change in the price of a product following, *inter alia*, from a change in the relative tax burdens on domestic and imported products."

[181] See *infra*, fnn. 327, 330, 331, 338, and 339. But see *infra*, fn. 347, where the Panel recently criticized a study that simultaneously changed the prices of the imported and the domestic products in order to measure the change in quantity of the imported product and held that the price of the imported product should have been held constant, thus advocating the measurement of the imported CPE.

[182] Carlton and Perloff, *Modern Industrial Organization*, 648 (2000).

After all, a simple alternative could be just to take the higher of the two CPEs as decisive for the estimation of substitutability between the two products. Where the CPE is highest, this indicates the more important direction of consumer switching and therefore the stronger competitive relationship. It also points to the switching relationship where the effect of a discriminatory measure would be the greatest and therefore would distort competition the most.[183] From the perspective of the underlying goal of protection of equal competitive conditions, this may be the more relevant of the two measures of substitutability.

(iii) Wholesale or retail level cross-price elasticity?

A further – usually overlooked – intricacy with elasticities is that those faced by upstream wholesalers or manufacturers ("wholesale price elasticity") need not be the same as those faced by retailers at downstream level ("retail price elasticity"). At first glance, it may come as a surprise to the untrained eye that price elasticities may differ at different levels in the production and distribution chain. Wholesale elasticities of what is termed the "derived demand" are heavily dependent on the retail elasticities of final demand. But they are not necessarily the same.[184] If a retailer, for example, partially absorbs a price increase at the wholesale level, retail elasticities will "overstate," that is, exceed, elasticities at wholesale level.[185] Price elasticities at retail level can also "understate," that is, be less than, the wholesale level price elasticities.

[183] Emch, "Fiscal Discrimination in WTO Law and EU Law," p. 386, suggests taking the average of the two elasticity measures. Also note that, in line with the SSNIP test in antitrust analysis, the price increase test suggested above does not predetermine a certain unidirectional analysis of consumer switching from the domestic to the imported product, as the question is to find a product set over which a price could be profitable.

[184] Hosken *et al.*, *Demand System Estimation and its Application to Horizontal Merger Analysis*, p. 22 (2002), available at: www.ftc.gov/be/workpapers/wp246.pdf; NERA (Dippon, Leonard, and Wu), *Application of Empirical Methods in Merger Analysis*, p. 129 fn. 161 (2005) (on file with author).

[185] For instance, a 10 percent rise in price by the manufacturer vis-à-vis a retailer could be passed on to consumers as a 5 percent price increase. The effect on the sales volume of the manufacturer would be smaller than predicted by measuring the retail elasticities for a 10 percent price rise (in this case the effect would only be half in magnitude). For this example see Nitsche, "Wettbewerbsökonomische Analyse der Auswirkungen von Fusionen," in Schwarze (ed.), *Recht und Ökonomie im Europäischen Wettbewerbsrecht*, pp. 53, 67 (2006). Another example where the retail price elasticity may surpass the wholesale price elasticity is where consumers display a more immediate reaction than retailers, e.g., when the latter are bound by long-term contractual obligations. For further illustrations see Bishop and Walker, *The Economics of EC Competition Law: Concepts, Application and Measurement*, 2nd edn., para. 10.21A (2002).

It is conceivable that retailers can, at times, respond to a price increase at wholesale level more effectively and more quickly than consumers, for example, by giving competing manufacturers more shelf space, supporting them with promotional activities, or strengthening own-label items.[186] Also, there is a further aspect that deserves attention. A certain percentage increase in price can have different effects on demand depending on what kind of volume buyer the customer is. For example, a 1 percent increase in price might be too small for small volume buyers to care about because the absolute price increases only by a negligible amount for the few items bought. However, when the same percentage increase in price is applied to a large volume buyer, this may generate substantial switching. This is due to the fact that the absolute price increase becomes significant for a large amount of items demanded. As in general buyers at wholesale level are large volume buyers in contrast to the small volume final consumers, the same percentage increase in price can trigger more substitution at the wholesale than at the retail level.

Therefore, the obvious question is at which level, wholesale or retail, to measure CPE. Usually, for antitrust law purposes it is the behavior of the manufacturer that is of actual concern. For that reason, the wholesale demand is considered more directly relevant to antitrust market definition than retail demand.[187]

For Article III of the GATT, it appears less obvious which demand should be decisive. The provision prohibits discrimination along the entire chain of distribution in the importing country, from wholesale to retail. Yet that "like" products must be treated in a non-discriminatory manner along the entire chain of distribution must be distinguished from the point that is decisive for determining the presence or absence of likeness. The assessment of likeness or DCS may be understood as a snapshot impression at the moment of entry into the domestic market. Products that were not "like" or DCS at this moment in time, but became "like" or DCS at a later stage in the distribution chain (for instance, because they underwent further treatment), would not fall under the ambit of Article

[186] Particularly, in case of delisting the product from shelf space in response to a wholesale price increase, wholesale elasticity is infinite regardless of what the retail elasticity is; see Hosken *et al.*, *Demand System Estimation and its Application to Horizontal Merger Analysis*, pp. 24, 26.

[187] Hosken *et al.*, *Demand System Estimation and its Application to Horizontal Merger Analysis*, 1 fn. 1; Bishop and Walker, *The Economics of EC Competition Law*, 2nd edn., para. 10.21A.

III protection.[188] Vice versa, products that were "like" or DCS at the point of entry, but later somehow turned "unlike" or not DCS would still be entitled to the protection of Article III of the GATT at the time of entry. This demonstrates that it is the instant of crossing the border that is relevant for the determination of substitutability. At this instant, products are usually at the wholesale distribution level. For this reason, and because retail demand may not even be ascertainable in certain instances at this stage, it stands to reason that the wholesale price elasticity is also the more immediate measure for Article III of the GATT purposes. In this vein, the Appellate Body in *EC – Asbestos* analyzed, under the CTH criterion, the perceptions of manufacturers in the importing country and also noted that wholesale demand will be influenced by the perceptions of the ultimate consumers.[189] The Appellate Body seemed to naturally assume the wholesalers as the relevant level in the production and distribution chain in order to assess the demand perceptions. However, it turns out that the dispute settlement bodies have not given any thought to this issue and its intricacies, since Panels have also incoherently analyzed ultimate and/or intermediate consumer behavior.[190]

(iv) Cross-price elasticity in tension with sovereignty?

There is an important policy dimension to the use of CPE in international trade law. One has to be clear that making CPE an important measure for demand-side perceptions has significant constraining consequences for the Members of the WTO. The main objection by the United States against the use of CPE by dispute settlement bodies was that: "making legal rights and obligations of governments depend on the level of cross-price elasticity of demand between two products makes governments legally responsible (and vulnerable to trade retaliations) for matters that are beyond their control."[191] Further, they claimed that: "the compliance of Members with GATT rules [would be] determined not by the actions these governments have done or not done, but by statistical surveys of the autonomous

[188] Note this is different from the issue of "potential competition," as it is not demand perceptions that change but the product itself – holding constant demand perceptions.

[189] Appellate Body Report, *EC – Asbestos*, *supra*, Ch. 2, fn. 70, para. 122. Yet *ibid.*, para. 130 left it expressly open whether the relevant customer is an intermediate commercial party or the final private buyer.

[190] In Panel Report, *Mexico – Soft Drinks*, *supra*, Ch. 2, fn. 80, paras. 8.32, 8.34, 8.71–8.74 the Panel analyzed the end-use criterion from the perspective of the intermediate consumer and the CTH criterion from the perspective of the final and intermediate consumer.

[191] Appellate Submission by the United States to the Appellate Body, *Japan – Taxes on Alcoholic Beverages*, *supra*, Ch. 3, fn. 264, para. 101.

reactions and perceptions of private consumers."[192] Using the same line of argument, Wille objects that CPE is difficult for governments to anticipate or prevent, and that it forces policy-makers to change governmental treatment in accordance with constant market changes or when new studies of CPE are issued.[193] Domestic fiscal and regulatory measures would be in danger of becoming illegal under GATT from one point in time to another without the government having done anything, and solely because of changing demand perceptions. All this amounts to saying that WTO law may not impose upon Members any obligation that relates to facts that are subject to change without the government's intervention. And, more fundamentally, it makes the point that CPE as a method of conducting product comparison is viewed as an assault on national sovereignty.

Yet these claims are of no merit. It may be true that the "stable" traditional criteria offer more legal certainty and predictability for a government in its fiscal or regulatory regime than dynamically changing consumer perceptions. However, ensuring equal competitive conditions is an ongoing obligation in an inherently dynamic market. The analysis must be flexible with regard to products that may become stronger or weaker competitors over time. If not, bindings under Article III of the GATT would move significantly out of line when the external environment changes. This type of flexible obligation is not exceptional in WTO law, and similarly applies, for example, with respect to the obligation to apply and maintain sanitary and phytosanitary measures only on the basis of scientific evidence.[194]

In fact, "matters," as the United States suggested, are not beyond government control. It is well within any government's control to decide whether or not to impose different taxes or regulatory measures on "like" or DCS products. In adopting Article III of the GATT, Members have consciously assumed the legal obligation to adapt their fiscal and regulatory regime if products become competitors over time. Ultimately, a government's legal responsibility under Article III of the GATT is not activated by a change in competitive conditions on the domestic market, but by the government's failure to adapt its laws and regulations to take account of the change. Thus, on a practical level, governments are not called upon to – unrealistically – constantly supervise changes in

[192] Appellate Submission by the United States to the Appellate Body, *Japan – Taxes on Alcoholic Beverages*, *supra*, Ch. 3, fn. 264, para. 99.

[193] Wille, "Recapturing a Lost Opportunity: Article III:2 GATT 1994 Japan – Alcoholic Beverages 1996," p. 16.

[194] Articles 2.2 and 5 of the SPS Agreement.

demand and to adapt their entire body of legislation accordingly on an ongoing basis. Rather, in practice, they are expected to adapt their legislation once they are specifically pointed to it by a complaint of another Member. A peculiarity of the dispute settlement system actually ensures that a *bona fide* government will not be prejudiced by the fact that it cannot constantly supervise the compliance of its legislation with market perceptions and that it can often bring into compliance its legislation only once it has been made aware of a violation. Under the DSU, remedies are always prospective. A losing respondent is under an obligation to bring into compliance its legislation, but there are no compensatory damages. Thus, a Member is not punished for past transgressions under WTO law.

B *Potential estimation problems under GATT*

(i) Misleading price elasticities of demand

Price elasticities of demand measure the substitutability of products *as perceived* by consumers under certain competitive conditions. Complications to the measurement in demand substitutability can arise when either the competitive conditions or the perceptions themselves are distorted. The estimated degree of price elasticity of demand may then be misleading.

(a) **Elasticities and distorted competitive conditions** In antitrust law, there can be two scenarios in which estimates of elasticities do not reflect the level of demand substitutability that would prevail under competitive conditions. Both issues are pervasive under Article 2 of the Sherman Act and Article 102 of the TFEU, where the inquiry focuses on the current competitiveness of the market. They relate to a distortion of the underlying competitive conditions on the basis of which consumer perceptions are measured. In those cases the underlying assumption does not hold that the prevailing prices constitute the appropriate benchmark for the analysis.

In the first case, demand elasticities are overestimated because the product from which switching would occur is priced *above* competitive level. CPE thus overstates substitutability resulting in the market being delineated too broadly. This misinterpretation is widely known in antitrust law as the "*Cellophane Fallacy*," after the *Cellophane* case, in which the US Supreme Court erroneously accepted as evidence distorted elasticity estimates.[195] The *Cellophane Fallacy* arises in monopolization or dominance cases. Here, the prevailing price is usually not at competitive level. A profit-maximizing monopolist or dominant firm will already have elevated prices to a supracompetitive level. This is a level in the high elasticity region of its demand curve, where consumers are just on the margin of switching to another product or dropping out of the market altogether. For this reason, a further price increase would be unprofitable. At this price level, demand is more elastic than at lower levels. The implication is that consumers will respond to any additional SSNIP with more switching than they would if the price had increased from a lower, competitive level. The price differential therefore artificially increases the shifting of consumers in case of a further price increase and lets even inferior substitutes appear attractive to consumers.

In the second case, rarely discussed in antitrust legal literature, demand elasticities are underestimated because the product from which switching occurs is *underpriced*. At this low price level, demand is more inelastic than at a competitive price level. CPE thus understates substitutability, resulting in the market being delineated too narrowly.[196] This situation, the mirror image of the *Cellophane Fallacy*, has been termed "*reverse Cellophane Fallacy*."[197] For instance, predatory pricing, that is, pricing below a competitive level to drive out competitors, can give rise to such a situation.[198]

The preceding paragraphs demonstrate that the degree of substitution between two products as measured by CPE depends in large part upon the current relative prices of the products concerned. Selection of the base price from which the price increase is taken is important in defining markets by way of CPE. The base price may be the prevailing price or the competitive price, if different. The *Cellophane Fallacy*, or its reverse, arises when consumer decisions are distorted because prevailing prices are not competitively set.

In international trade law, the estimation of price elasticities of demand can also be distorted as a consequence of the distortion of the competitive conditions, in particular the price levels. This draws on the insights

[195] *Cellophane, supra*, Ch. 2, fn. 26.

[196] See Crocioni, "The Hypothetical Monopolist Test: What it Can and What it Cannot Tell You," *European Competition Law Review*, (2002), 354, 361.

[197] Froeb and Werden, "The Reverse Cellophane Fallacy in Market Delineation," *Review of Industrial Organization*, 7 (1992), 241–247.

[198] See, e.g., UK Office of Fair Trading, *Predation by Aberdeen Journals Ltd*, CA98/14/2002, [2002] UKCLR 740, para. 94.

gained from antitrust law and relates to an artificially increased price differential between the domestic and the imported product. As a result of the discriminatory fiscal or regulatory burden, the import will often be overpriced in comparison with the domestic product.[199] In consequence, the CPE either under- or overstates demand substitutability. This has to do with the fact that, as explained, there are always two ways of measuring CPE.

The first possibility is what has been defined above as the imported CPE. The question, therefore, is how many consumers switch from the domestic to the imported product. Here, the situation of the *reverse Cellophane Fallacy* may arise in a slightly modified version, yet to the same effect. The CPE may be underestimated because the product *to which* switching occurs (the imported product) is overpriced. A small price increase for the domestic product, even if the price is at supra-competitive level provided it remains sufficiently lower than the one of the imported product, does not induce consumers to switch to the higher priced import. CPE thus understates the potential willingness of consumers to switch to other products resulting in the market being delineated too narrowly.

An alternative is to measure what has been termed the domestic CPE. The question here is how many consumers switch from the imported product to the domestic product. This case corresponds to the traditional *Cellophane Fallacy*, where the product *from which* switching occurs is overpriced. Any further price increase in addition to the already high price will generate more substitution than at a lower price level. Much like the situation in single firm antitrust cases, the market in NT non-discrimination cases is already distorted. Whether the focus is then on the imported or domestic CPE is the determining factor for whether the effect of a price increase on demand is potentially over- or underestimated.

In the two situations outlined, it is difficult to apply econometric analysis for market definition purposes. In the *Aberdeen Journals* case, the UK Competition Appeal Tribunal upheld the competition authority's reliance on non-econometric evidence in order to establish the relevant product market, stating that: "the fact that market conditions were already distorted, means that extreme caution must be exercised when dealing with the presence or absence of switching patterns. Such evidence is not a reliable guide to what would happen in normal competitive conditions."[200] In antitrust law, enforcers are aware of the *Cellophane Fallacy*.

[199] See *supra*, Ch. 4, "A price increase test for Article III of the GATT."
[200] *Aberdeen Journals Ltd* v. *OFT* [2003] CAT 11, CompAR 67, para. 262.

The *Commission Notice on market definition* alludes to the problem, but without suggesting any solution.[201] The *Cellophane Fallacy* is not a problem of merger cases, which – in a prospective manner – revolve around whether the merged entity will likely raise prices above the *prevailing* and not the competitive price level. Nevertheless, the *Merger Guidelines* point to the problem of the prevailing price not being at competitive level, in case of which "a price more reflective of the competitive price" shall be used.[202] Estimating the competitive price level that would prevail in the absence of the anticompetitive conduct of the firm or the discriminatory governmental measure is a solution to the problem of distorted elasticities. This has been suggested in antitrust law.[203] For instance, the *Article 82 Commission Discussion Paper* suggests reconstructing the competitive price; while at the same time indicating that determining a non-observable ideal competitive price will be impossible most of the time.[204] This solution has also been proposed in the context of Article III of the GATT.[205] The trade market definition exercise arguably should be performed by reference to the price that, in a forward-looking manner, will prevail in the future in the absence of the discriminatory governmental measure under investigation. Yet the concept of competitive prices, often equated to that of long-run marginal cost, is not very well defined, controversial, and extremely difficult to calculate. That is why the conceptually correct remedy of artificially constructing competitive prices is tantamount to nothing more than a mere theoretical nicety. While it is usually very difficult in antitrust practice to determine the price that would prevail under competitive conditions, it may be easier, however, to reconstruct the competitive price in international trade law practice. The price of the domestic product may serve as a benchmark and the price of the imported product may be reduced in the amount equivalent to the cost of the trade obstacle.[206] In any event, however, even if the "but for (the

201 *Commission Notice on market definition*, para. 19.

202 *1992 Merger Guidelines*, at 1.11. On benchmark prices under the new *2010 Merger Guidelines*, at 10.

203 O'Donoghue and Padilla, *The Law and Economics of Article 82 EC*, p. 82. Another suggested solution is to ask whether a small price reduction from the prevailing price level of the overpriced import would or would not lead to substitution away from the domestic to the imported product; Baker, "Market Definition: An Analytical Overview," *Antitrust Law Journal*, 74 (2007), 130, 154.

204 *Article 82 Commission Discussion Paper*, para. 16.

205 Fauchald, *Environmental Taxes and Trade Discrimination*, p. 151. In its effects, this approach also corresponds to the "but for" test suggested by Korea in Panel Report, *Korea – Alcoholic Beverages*, *supra*, Introduction, fn. 36, para. 10.47.

206 Note, however, that depending on the nature of the discriminatory measure assessing its value or the cost associated with it can also be impossible. Whereas it will be

discriminatory measure)" price could be identified, this "but for" test is not an effective solution in international trade law.

(b) Elasticities and distorted customer perceptions A "but for" test is unsuitable because of a second scenario under which demand elasticities may be distorted in international trade law. This relates to the distortion of consumer perceptions themselves. In fact, the effect of a discriminatory domestic measure may be twofold. It may not only create an artificial price differential that gives rise to distorted demand elasticities. To complicate things further, it may also lead consumers to internalize product distinctions over time.[207] The effect is that of shaping consumer perceptions, thus "creating and even freezing preferences for domestic goods."[208] This may be the result of the persisting price differential. It may also be due to, for example, discriminatory labeling, marketing, or distribution requirements. Thus, demand preferences can become significantly entrenched and only slowly change over time. Under those circumstances, even on the basis of "but for" prices, consumer responses to a price increase may not initially reflect any willingness to substitute.[209] Importantly, this applies to both CPEs of the domestic and of the imported product. No matter which product's change in quantity in response to the other's price increase is measured, consumers do not perceive the products as substitutes. Therefore, CPE would always remain underestimated, even if price levels are adjusted for.

straightforward in the case of fiscal treatment to reduce the price by the amount of the additional taxation, it will be more difficult to quantify the additional costs associated with a regulatory measure.

207 The ECJ recognized this problem in the context of Article 110 of the TFEU well before the GATT/WTO dispute settlement bodies became aware of it, see *Commission* v. *United Kingdom*, *supra*, Ch. 4, fn. 25, para. 8.

208 Panel Report, *Japan – Alcoholic Beverages II*, *supra*, Ch. 3, fn. 73, para. 6.28; see prior GATT Panel Report, *Japan – Alcoholic Beverages I*, *supra*, Ch. 2, fn. 65, para. 5.7. Note that in contrast to the Appellate Body's terminology of the *shaping of consumer preferences*, microeconomics understands consumer preferences as "fixed" and independent of the price level. Of course, consumers also consider prices. Therefore, consumer choice is determined by consumer preferences and budget constraints; Pindyck and Rubinfeld, *Microeconomics*, pp. 67–88. For this reason, it appears preferable to speak of the shaping of consumer *perceptions* instead of that of consumer *preferences*.

209 As a solution Emch, "Fiscal Discrimination in WTO Law and EU Law," p. 381 argues for a "but for" test that presumes that no differential treatment has *ever* existed. Yet, in practice, such an approach would not help with the technical problem of generating data reflective of undistorted demand with which the CPE could then be estimated. Surveying customers on the basis of adjusted price levels alone would not account for underlying skewed demand. Moreover, singling out the long-term effect of the discriminatory governmental measure to ascertain uninfluenced consumer patterns in a consumer survey seems practicably unfeasible.

It is true that the shaping of consumer perceptions is not peculiar to international trade law. Strong marketing and promotional activities by firms can also create the same effect. For antitrust law purposes it is only relevant whether or not an SSNIP induces sufficient substitution. If not, and regardless of entrenched consumer perceptions, products would not be deemed to be in the same relevant market.[210] In contrast to antitrust law, it quickly becomes clear why the concern for entrenched demand is justified in international trade law. If demand elasticities based on influenced demand perceptions were decisive, Members would be able to manipulate consumer perceptions to create product differentiations. On this basis, discriminatory measures would be permissible under Article III of the GATT. Ultimately, not accounting for underestimated substitutability would undermine the level playing field that GATT law aims to establish.

To deal with this problem of entrenched demand patterns econometrically is much more difficult. In the absence of any reliable data on undistorted current consumer substitution behavior, it can make sense to look at other comparable (geographic) markets for information on buyer substitution at the competitive price level. This has been the practice in antitrust law.[211] It has also been an accepted approach under Article III of the GATT, where the Appellate Body in *Korea – Alcoholic Beverages* approved the Panel's examination of (yet not quantitative) evidence from Japan to make inferences on the Korean market.[212] However, since "consumer habits are variable in time and space,"[213] and "consumer responsiveness to products may vary from country to country,"[214] referring to other markets can be appropriate only when both markets display sufficiently similar characteristics. Especially in international trade law, this can be problematic because disputes often revolve around "national" products to which a distinct national affinity in the domestic market exists. Consumer perceptions of such products may differ greatly from country to country, so that generalizations across borders can mislead. That is why it is a prerequisite to the use of information from other markets to verify the similarity and

[210] See *supra*, Ch. 4, fnn. 136 *et seq.* on "strategic" markets.

[211] *Proctor & Gamble/VP Schickedanz*, *supra*, Ch. 3, fn. 240, para. 60, where econometric elasticity estimations based on scanner data from the United States was used to determine substitutability in the German market. See also *Article 82 Commission Discussion Paper*, para. 19.

[212] Appellate Body Report, *Korea – Alcoholic Beverages, supra*, Ch. 2, fn. 71, paras. 135–138.

[213] GATT Panel Report, *Japan – Alcoholic Beverages I, supra*, Ch. 2, fn. 65, para. 5.7.

[214] Appellate Body Report, *Korea – Alcoholic Beverages, supra*, Ch. 2, fn. 71, para. 137.

comparability of the two markets in terms of demand patterns, income levels, tastes, etc. For example, in *Procter & Gamble/VP Schickedanz*, the European Commission explicitly ascertained the comparability of the US and the European market in terms of consumer switching behavior and key market characteristics.[215] The Appellate Body in *Korea – Alcoholic Beverages* had in theory insisted on the need for comparability of the markets as a condition for resorting to evidence from other markets. In practice, however, it did not ascertain the similarity of the Japanese and the Korean markets for alcoholic beverages.

Where no suitable evidence from other markets is available and the elasticity estimates are misleading, recourse must necessarily be had to qualitative evidence.[216] In that case, the conceptually correct approach is an assessment of the available qualitative evidence under the logic of the above outlined framework, in particular, demand-side substitution.

Evidently, one cannot ignore the complications presented by distorted competitive conditions or entrenched demand when engaging in the measurement of CPEs. Case law shows, however, that dispute settlement bodies have only been aware of one type of complication, namely, the possibility that the protectionist measure may underestimate demand elasticities in case of distorted demand. This concern has been voiced repeatedly.[217] By contrast, the possibility of the price differential being the cause of distorted elasticity estimates has not been discussed.[218] Strikingly, the dispute settlement bodies have, depending on what was submitted by the parties, incoherently looked at the imported and/or domestic CPE. They did not distinguish between the two types of CPE. One may deduce from this fact that they have been unaware that the two types of CPEs can produce very different results under normal

215 The Commission, e.g., noted that the relative usage patterns in the United States and Germany were very similar, for tampon/towels it was a ratio of 40:60 in the United States and 39:61 in Germany, *Proctor & Gamble/VP Schickedanz*, *supra*, Ch. 3, fn. 240, para. 60.

216 See, e.g., Horn and Mavroidis, "Still Hazy after all These Years," p. 66; *Article 82 Commission Discussion Paper*, para. 18; O'Donoghue and Padilla, *The Law and Economics of Article 82 EC*, p. 82.

217 Panel Report, *Japan – Alcoholic Beverages II*, *supra*, Ch. 3, fn. 73, para. 6.28; Panel Report, *Korea – Alcoholic Beverages*, *supra*, Introduction, fn. 36, para. 10.44; Panel Report, *Chile – Alcoholic Beverages*, *supra*, Ch. 2, fn. 68, paras. 7.70–7.72; Panel Report, *Philippines – Distilled Spirits*, *supra*, Introduction, fn. 23, para. 7.105.

218 Horn and Mavroidis, "Still Hazy after all These Years," fn. 64, allude to the problem of overestimation. Emch, "Fiscal Discrimination in WTO Law and EU Law," p. 385 sees the problem of the reverse *Cellophane* fallacy, but not that the traditional *Cellophane* fallacy can also occur.

conditions and lead to under- or overstated results in case of distorted pricing conditions.

For example, *Japan – Alcoholic Beverages II* and *Chile – Alcoholic Beverages* were two cases in which Panels appraised the significance of concrete CPE values.[219] Those were indeed instances of the use of domestic CPE. Against this background, it is even more surprising that the only issue of concern was the underestimation of CPE. In fact, this is only half the truth in the case of this particular CPE. Apart from an underestimation because of entrenched demand perceptions, it is precisely this CPE which is also prone to an overestimation of substitutability, because a further increase in price of the already overpriced import may trigger consumers to switch more readily to the domestic product.[220]

A closer look at the reasoning in *Chile – Alcoholic Beverages* highlights the Panel's limited awareness of the inherent pitfalls of CPE where uncritically applied. Here, the estimation of CPE measuring the switching from the imported whisky to the domestic pisco in case of a price increase of whisky was calculated on historical sales and price data in the period of 1985–92.[221] In order to explain why the Panel considered the low CPE coefficient (0.26) as sufficient evidence of substitutability, it made the following comment:

> We also think that the estimated elasticity would have been higher, had whisky been less expensive ... Factors, which include the very measures at issue here, can have a noticeable impact on the price of the imports, both directly and indirectly. For instance, the tax and tariff structure can change product offerings towards more expensive items and partly as a result, increase other costs such as distribution. If the retail price of whisky were lower than what it is now ... it is not unreasonable to expect based on the information before the panel that ... the actual cross-price elasticity would be higher than the current estimates. [Footnote]: The Panel in *Japan – Taxes on Alcoholic Beverages II* specifically noted that calculated cross-price elasticities in cases such as these will generally underestimate the actual degree of substitutability.[222]

To recall, in this passage, the Panel elaborated on the CPE measuring the switching from the imported product to the domestic product in case of a

[219] See *infra*, fnn. 325, 330, and 331.

[220] As a further complication, both distorting effects of under- and overestimation of CPE may even coincide where one consumer segment has internalized the product distinction, while another is more sensitive to the price increase of the import and thus more willing to switch.

[221] Panel Report, *Chile – Alcoholic Beverages*, *supra*, Ch. 2, fn. 68, para. 7.65.

[222] Panel Report, *Chile – Alcoholic Beverages*, *supra*, Ch. 2, fn. 68, para. 7.72.

price increase of the imported product.[223] It considered the magnitude of CPE estimates under current, distorted market conditions. The Panel was clearly aware of the fact that the discriminatory measure had the effect of overpricing the imported product to a level above normal prices. Yet its analysis of the ensuing hypothetical complications in the estimation of CPE was incomplete. As the footnote shows, it took note of the risk of underestimation of demand substitutability. But it did not realize that a price increase for an already overpriced import also bears the risk of underestimation.

(ii) New products problem

Another – at least theoretically relevant[224] – complication to CPE is the situation in which a new product is introduced to a marketplace.[225] This is not a problem of distorted elasticities. In fact, elasticity estimates would correctly depict current consumer perceptions regarding substitutability. Still, they would be misleading for a trade-specific reason that has already been explained. WTO law is also concerned with opening markets by introducing products which are new to the marketplace. In a market where consumers are not yet familiar with a new product, there may be a lag in time after the market entry until consumers learn about the product and perceive it as substitutable with a domestic product. This is especially true "in the case of 'experience goods', such as food and beverages, which consumers tend to purchase because they are familiar with them and with which consumers experiment only reluctantly."[226] During this learning process, an estimation of CPE correctly registers low demand substitutability. On this basis, the importing Member could argue that econometric evidence suggests that the products are not in a competitive relationship because consumers do not perceive them as substitutes. Consequently, the government may discriminate against the import and effectively undermine GATT law's aim of opening the market to international trade.

It has already been argued that this situation requires a prospective focus of the analysis of demand-side substitutability taking account of

[223] *Infra*, fn. 330.

[224] Whether today there really still exist products that are entirely "new" to consumers of a certain market can actually be doubted.

[225] This limitation to CPE has not been raised in case law (but see in this direction Panel Report, *Korea – Alcoholic Beverages*, *supra*, Introduction, fn. 36, para. 10.92) and has only been addressed by Horn and Weiler, "EC – Asbestos European Communities: Measures Affecting Asbestos and Asbestos-Containing Products," p. 5 fn. 5.

[226] Appellate Body Report, *Korea – Alcoholic Beverages*, *supra*, Ch. 2, fn. 71, para. 123.

"potential competition." In addition to the instance of distorted demand, this poses a further limitation on the use of CPE in the international trade law context. This can be explained by the conceptual difference between "potential competition" and CPE. CPE is a static concept; specifically it captures a static picture of demand patterns. It is based on the notion of examining one distinct event: the change in price. The CPE inquiry has a very limited temporal horizon with a focus on the change in price and the reactions to price changes. It is an inherent restriction upon CPE estimation that it does not take into account the dynamics of markets. Multiple regression analysis, as will be explained below, can take account of a variety of different competing influences when estimating CPEs. But CPE is a static measure in so far as it focuses upon price, quantity, and other influences within the existing competitive environment (that is, given the existing price, technology, and cost structure). Other dynamic factors are hard to grasp in a model, such as evolving consumer perception, innovations, newly evolving competitors. In this respect CPE is capable of conveying only a partial presentation of the ongoing and evolving competitive process, which is particularly problematic in dynamic innovation markets.

This, in contrast, is very different from the presumption that underlies the "potential competition" concept – on the basis of which the dispute settlement bodies explicitly "decline to take a static view … where consumers *already* regard products as alternatives."[227] Here, the analysis tries to grasp the future evolution of consumer perceptions. Potential competition is, however, difficult to ascertain and quantify – and therefore difficult to render operational. The need to account for the future evolution in demand in order to draw the current market boundaries highlights an inherent limitation to the measurement of current demand responses to price increases.[228] A solution could be to look at other similar markets for information on future demand substitutability. If this is not possible, it may be necessary to use qualitative evidence to the extent that it allows inferences about future consumer perceptions. A first step could be to look for functional similarity. If products have the same purpose, consumers may then, through a learning process, come to perceive and internalize the products as being substitutable.

[227] Appellate Body Report, *Korea – Alcoholic Beverages, supra*, Ch. 2, fn. 71, para. 120 (emphasis in original).

[228] A similar problem arises where market definition has to account for the rapid and dynamic changes of "innovation markets" in new economies. This can be relevant to international trade law in markets such as electronics.

C What can be learned from cross-price elasticities of demand for Article III purposes?

It has become clear that international trade law cannot endorse an approach wherein "there would be no need to bring in any additional indicators, the econometric estimate would say all we need to know about the CPE, and the CPE says all we need to know about the relationship between the two products."[229] The other extreme, that the legal problem of textual interpretation of the "like" and DCS terminology cannot be expressed by aid of a numerical comparison of elasticity estimates, is equally unconvincing.

The discriminatory measure's distortion of the prevailing price conditions, as well as the distortion of the current demand perceptions, may appear to represent a fatal blow to any market definition methodology based on the identification of substitutes by the measurement of CPE.[230] The risk of over-enforcement in case of high CPE and under-enforcement in case of low CPE seems to completely undermine the probative value of CPE estimates. However, despite these complications, it is argued here that CPE still has a role to play in the market definition exercise under Article III of the GATT. This is confirmed by the Panels in *Thailand – Cigarettes* and *Philippines – Distilled Spirits*, where they engaged in the evaluation of quantitative evidence and CPE estimations presented to them.

For the appraisal of CPEs under Article III of the GATT, certain general rules can be formulated from the fact that products claimed to be part of the same market are substitutable or not under prevailing prices. According to antitrust literature, CPE at prevailing prices remains useful in the sense that it is indicative of substitution patterns at those given prices. It is proposed as a general rule that a high CPE at current price level is not evidence of substitutability because of the potential overestimation of substitution under the rubric of the *Cellophane Fallacy*.[231] In contrast, a low CPE at current price levels is considered probative evidence of the absence of substitutability. The reason being that products which can be excluded from forming a common relevant market at prevailing

[229] Horn and Mavroidis, "Still Hazy after all These Years," p. 64.

[230] See, e.g., Slotboom, "Do Different Treaty Purposes Matter?" p. 570.

[231] Office of Fair Trading, *The Role of Market Definition in Monopoly and Dominance Inquiries*, para. 3.32; *Article 82 Commission Discussion Paper*, para. 16; Bishop and Baldauf, *Theoretische Grundlagen und praktische Anwendung wettbewerbsökonomischer Methoden*, p. 25.

prices, even in case of a *Cellophane Fallacy* scenario, would, *a fortiori*, be excluded at any lower competitive price level.

The dispute settlement bodies seem to have espoused a rule of thumb as well. Whereas a high CPE estimate may have high probative value as evidence for a high degree of substitutability, a low CPE is, for reason of potentially distorted demand understating the CPE, not necessarily probative of the absence of a competitive relationship.[232] The Panel in *Chile – Alcoholic Beverages* may be interpreted so this general rule arguably translates into a presumption of likeness and direct competitiveness or substitutability if a high CPE is demonstrated.[233]

For Article III purposes, neither the antitrust presumption nor the rule articulated by the Panel seems to be correct. In particular, the latter might even be misleading, because it is based on an incomplete legal analysis of the intricacies of CPE in international trade law. It disregards the possibility of overstated demand substitutability under the *Cellophane Fallacy* situation. From the above analysis, a more complete set of rules can be deduced for the handling of CPEs under Article III of the GATT. To this end, one has to distinguish between the two possible scenarios that can cause problems for the estimation of CPEs.

First is the case of price distortions, causing the imported product to be overpriced in comparison with the domestic product. Depending on which CPE is measured, the following general rules can be made. If substitution from the imported product to the domestic product is measured (the domestic CPE), a high CPE has little or no probative value. Here, the CPE estimate might overstate substitution (the *Cellophane Fallacy*). By contrast, a low CPE has probative value for the lack of substitutability. While CPE overstates substitution at current prices, the CPE estimate would be even lower at competitive prices. This corresponds to the above

[232] Panel Report, *Korea – Alcoholic Beverages, supra*, Introduction, fn. 36, para. 10.44: "While a high degree of cross-price elasticity of demand would tend to support the argument that there is a direct competitive relationship … the lack of such evidence may be due to the governmental measures in question."

[233] Panel Report, *Chile – Alcoholic Beverages, supra*, Ch. 2, fn. 68, paras. 7.70, 7.71: "A high coefficient of cross-price elasticity would of course lend more credence to a claim of direct competitiveness or substitutability, although a low coefficient of cross-price elasticity is not necessarily fatal to a claim of direct competitiveness or substitutability. Indeed, a low coefficient of cross-price elasticity may be due to the very measures in question in the dispute. … It is our view that in general economic terms, a high estimated coefficient of elasticity would be important evidence to demonstrate that products are DCS provided that the quality of the statistical analysis is high" and para. 7.77: "As we noted, earlier cases have stated that the *concept* of cross-price elasticity is a **strong indicator** of substitutability" (emphasis in bold added).

rule formulated under antitrust law and may be termed Rule 1. Although there is no empirical evidence at hand, it may be assumed that this rule applies in the majority of cases. This is because it is the typical result of a protectionist measure to distort price competition.[234] If substitution is measured from the domestic product to the import (the imported CPE), a high CPE has probative value. The rationale is that even if the CPE estimate understates substitution at the prevailing prices, it would register an even higher value in case of competitive pricing. This may be termed Rule 2, and will apply most of the time for the same reason given for Rule 1. In contrast, a low CPE when measuring the imported CPE does not have much probative value. The CPE estimate may understate substitution, since there is less switching to the overpriced import (the *reverse Cellophane Fallacy*).

Second is the scenario of distorted demand patterns. Regardless of the direction of the CPE measurement, a high CPE always yields probative value. Even if CPE understates substitution, it would be higher in cases of undistorted demand patterns. This may be termed Rule 3, and it may not be as prevalent in the real world as Rules 1 and 2 because demand perceptions will not always be distorted. By contrast, a low CPE, as suggested by the Panel, has no probative value in view of the possibility that CPE understates substitution. The Panels in the alcoholic beverages cases simply assumed – without any evidentiary foundation – that all taxes imposed in a discriminatory fashion resulted in the crystallization of consumer preferences and hence considered CPE values to be misleading. However, precisely because there is no default rule that demand perceptions are always entrenched, there cannot be a presumption that low CPE is *per se* underestimated. In fact, the assertion of the mere possibility of entrenched demand is in itself insufficient to reject giving probative value to CPE estimates. There is no empirical verification that discriminatory treatment has as a consequence the distortion of consumer perceptions or preferences. Therefore, whether this is actually the case should be positively ascertained in each case. This will depend on the specific circumstances of the case: the nature of the products; the length in time of the application of the discriminatory measure; its effectiveness and severity; among others. Moreover, nowadays consumer decisions are made in an environment of multiple channels of information and of multiple competing influences. Among the many influences exerted on consumers by firms, trade and consumer associations, or other non-governmental

[234] See *supra*, Ch. 4, "A price increase test for Article III of the GATT" and notes therein.

organizations, governmental influence is only one among many competing and partially conflicting influences. Thus, distortion of consumer perceptions through discriminatory governmental treatment does not put into question the usefulness of CPE as a criterion generally, but may do so only if specifically ascertained in the individual case.

As a further complication to the application of the above-described rules, the first and the second scenarios may coincide where a discriminatory governmental measure has as its effect the shaping of consumer perceptions, as well as the creation of an artificial price differential. This could occur, for example, in case of a discriminatory labeling and distribution requirement from which consumers "learn" that certain imported and domestic products are not substitutable, while it also imposes additional costs on the imported product.

It should not be assumed without more evidence that this is the standard situation under Article III of the GATT, because there is no general rule that demand will always be entrenched in case of a governmental discrimination. If concurrence of both situations has been ascertained, however, CPE estimates have no probative value as evidence of a lack of substitutability when measuring the substitution from the import to the domestic product. When measuring the opposite pattern of substitution from the domestic to the imported product, a high CPE has probative value as evidence of substitutability. This follows from the application of Rules 2 and 3.

This collection of different scenarios, in addition to the different CPEs that can be measured between any pair of products, underscores that it cannot seriously be claimed that CPEs never have any significant role to play in market definition under Article III of the GATT. Rather, the preceding paragraphs show that one has to be very clear under which circumstances one calculates CPEs and exactly which one is measured. Thus, although CPE can be an empirically flawed measure of substitutability at times, a fact-finder can in many instances infer valuable information on the degree of substitutability from CPEs. The economic indicator of CPE should therefore be the starting point, which can be corrected through recourse to other traditional criteria applied in a way that sheds light on demand substitutability. Even in an instance where CPE does not yield reliable results, this limitation does not question the conceptual premise that the marketplace test as devised above determines the definition of likeness and DCS.

4 The foundations of the econometric estimation of price elasticities of demand

A Introduction

In econometrics, statistical methods have been developed that can be employed to estimate price elasticities of demand. A common technique, based on actual historical data, is to "regress" sales volumes against the prices of the product in question and its assumed substitutes. Regression analysis is a standard quantitative tool for understanding the relationships between variables.[235] There are three uses of regression analysis. The first is to ascertain whether or not a particular variable has *any* effect on some other variable. In its second application, there is not so much doubt that one variable affects another; the interest lies in measuring the magnitude of a particular effect. This is termed "parameter estimation." The third use is forecasting what a particular effect will be. For the present purpose of market definition, regression analysis aims at parameter estimation from which the values of elasticity estimates can be inferred.

The practical use of regression analysis in a legal context has grown substantially over the last decades, in particular in the United States.[236] For instance, regression analysis has been used most frequently in the context of racial, sex, and employment discrimination cases in order to establish statistical proof as to whether or not discrimination takes place against a certain group of people.[237] Other applications include census undercounts, voting rights, or the study of the deterrent effect of the death penalty. Beyond market definition, it is also used in antitrust litigation for

[235] For more complete descriptions of regression analysis and its role in litigation, see Fisher, "Multiple Regression in Legal Proceedings," *Columbia Law Review*, 80 (1980), 702–736; Sykes, *An Introduction to Regression Analysis* (1992), available at: www.law.uchicago.edu/files/files/20.Sykes_.Regression_0.pdf; Rubinfeld, "Reference Guide on Multiple Regression," in Federal Judicial Center, *Reference Manual on Scientific Evidence*, pp. 179–227 (2000), available at: www.fjc.gov/public/pdf.nsf/lookup/sciman00.pdf/$file/sciman00.pdf. For more technical introductions, see Hogg and Craig, *Introduction to Mathematical Statistics* (1995); Wooldridge, *Introductory Econometrics: A Modern Approach*, pp. 21–424 (2003).

[236] A watershed was created in 1977, when the US Supreme Court calculated statistics in footnotes to two opinions in *Castaneda* v. *Partida*, 430 US 482 (1977) and *Hazelwood School District* v. *United States*, 433 US 299 (1977).

[237] See, e.g., Tyson, "Presumed Guilty Until Proven Innocent: Using Results of Statistical or Econometric Studies as Evidence," *St. Thomas Law Review*, 10 (1997), 387–406.

a variety of purposes.[238] For example, it can be employed to provide evidence of the existence of a conspiracy, the presence of market power, the likelihood of anticompetitive effects, or the fact of injury.

Regression analysis involves a variable to be explained – called the "dependent" variable – and at least one other "independent" or "explanatory" variable which is thought to produce changes in the dependent variable. The dependent variable "depends" on the independent variables, while the independent variables are (1) assumed to be independent of other variables in the model and (2) can themselves be altered. Regression analysis thus allows an examination not only of the relationship between two variables, such as price and quantity of a product, but even more complicated relationships that involve more variables, such as the prices of rival firms' products. A regression model makes it possible to isolate the impact of each of the independent variables on the dependent variable. It thus enables the investigator to ascertain the causal effect of one (independent) variable upon another (dependent) variable, for instance, the effect of a price increase of product A on demand for product B. Using observed historical data on the dependent and independent variables, regression analysis provides the quantitative tool to find the relationships between the dependent variable and the independent variables that best "explain" the dependent variable and thereby determine the causal link that flows from a number of independent variables to the dependent variable. Statistical significance tests can then be carried out to ascertain how robust these relationships are. This allows a court to isolate a key relationship or critical influence between a number of influences.

Lawyers are profoundly uncomfortable deciphering econometric models. But due to their legal training they are also accustomed to weaving a complex set of facts into a theory of cause and effect. It is interesting to point out that, in a strikingly similar way, this is what the econometric

[238] For an introduction to regression analysis in the context of antitrust law, see, e.g., Rosenfield, "The Use of Economics in Antitrust Litigation and Counseling," *Columbia Business Law Review*, (1986), 49–82; Hausman and Leonard, "Economic Analysis of Differentiated Products Mergers Using Real World Data," *George Mason Law Review*, 5 (1997), 321–346; Baker, "Contemporary Empirical Merger Analysis," *George Mason Law Review*, 5 (1997), 347–361; Baker and Rubinfeld, "Empirical Methods in Antitrust Litigation: Review and Critique," *American Law and Economics Review*, 1 (1999), 386–435; ABA Section of Antitrust Law, *Econometrics: Legal, Practical, and Technical Issues* (2005); Bishop and Baldauf, *Theoretische Grundlagen und praktische Anwendung wettbewerbsökonomischer Methoden*, pp. 88–110; Fegatilli and Petit, *Économétrie du droit de la concurrence: un essai de conceptualisation* (2008), available at: www.coleurope.eu/content/gclc/documents/GCLC%20WP%2003-08.pdf.

model in a regression analysis does, "albeit in economic shorthand."[239] Because regression analysis can aid lawyers in their structurally similar legal reasoning, it is important for them to understand what regression analysis is, how it works, and what its probative value is. Of equal importance, however, is to fathom how, when used inappropriately, it can confuse – or even be abused.

The purpose of this section is not to provide a guide to "doing" regression analysis. Instead, regression analysis is presented with the aim of illustrating its potential and its limitations for an economics-based Article III market definition approach – and for legal decision making in general as this method becomes increasingly used in other legal contexts. For this purpose, regression analysis in its simplest form and its basic properties will be outlined. In addition, the tools for appraising the quality of a regression, that is, the accuracy and reliability of its estimates, will be discussed. This is crucial for any adjudicator confronted with evidence based on regression analysis, because it determines whether the model and its results are worth crediting with evidentiary weight. Finally, its specific use for market definition purposes in WTO/GATT case law will be explored and assessed. The discussion takes place at the most basic, intuitive, and non-technical level.

B The basics of regression analysis

(i) Simple regression

For simplicity of exposition, the relationship to be examined shall preliminarily be restricted to two variables only: the dependent variable and one independent variable. In such a "simple regression," a dependent variable can be measured by a single attribute. For present purposes, the relationship of interest shall be the influence of the price of product Y on the quantity sold of product X. The dependent variable shall then be the demand for product X, denoted by Q_x, and the independent variable the price for product Y, denoted by P_y. A hypothesis about the relationship between these variables is formulated at the outset of a regression analysis. Such a hypothesis could be to expect a positive correlation between the two variables, that is, the higher the price for product Y, the higher the demand for product X. Ordinarily, regression analysis is predicated on

239 Scheffman and Coleman, *FTC Perspectives on the Use of Econometric Analyses in Antitrust Cases*, p. 2 (undated), available at: www.ftc.gov/be/ftcperspectivesoneconometrics.pdf.

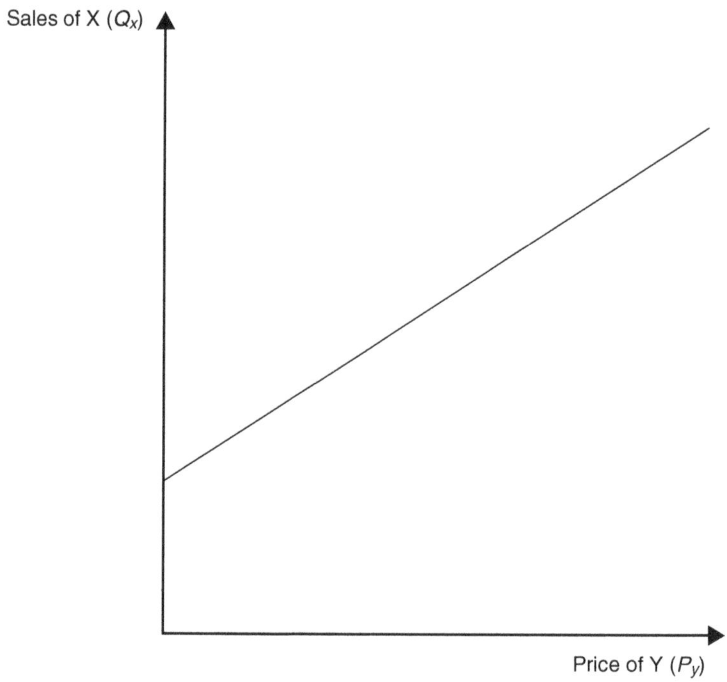

Figure 5.1 Linear relationship price and demand

a linearity assumption. Linear regression analysis presupposes that each unit increment in the independent variable adds the same amount in the dependent variable. Here, this would assume that the price of Y affects the demand of X in a linear manner. This relationship can be plotted in a simplified two-dimensional diagram as shown in Figure 5.1.[240]

Supposing that the relationship between these variables is linear, the hypothesized relationship can be expressed using the mathematical notation for a straight line:

$$Q_x = \alpha + \beta P_y \qquad \text{Equation (1)}$$

[240] In regression analysis, it is customary to display the dependent variable on the vertical axis (y-axis) and the independent variable on the horizontal axis (x-axis). Note, however, that in economics, it is conventional to plot price on the y-axis and quantity on the x-axis, even though quantity is thought to be a function of price. For the use of the inverse demand function in the estimation of demand elasticities which expresses the price as a function of quantity see Rubinfeld, "Quantitative Methods in Antitrust," in ABA Section of Antitrust Law, *Issues in Competition Law and Policy*, vol. 1, pp. 723, 728 (2008).

In a regression equation, the dependent variable is on the left-hand and all independent variables are on the right-hand. In this two-variable equation, α is the "constant term" which designates the intercept of the straight line with the y-axis. It does not vary with different values of the independent variable and designates the value of Q_x when P_y takes on the value zero. β represents the slope of the line. It is termed the "coefficient" of the particular independent variable and states how much the dependent variable changes with a one unit change in the independent variable. What this means is that for each additional increment of an independent variable, one would expect the dependent variable to increase by the value of the coefficient. If the relationship between Q_x and P_y is a positive one, that is, if Q_x increases as P_y increases, the slope will be positive. On the other hand, if Q_x falls when P_y increases, the slope will be negative.

The problem for an investigator is to discover the values of the parameters α and β, that is, the intercept and the slope of the line. If the relationship were truly and precisely linear, this would be an easy task. One would only need two observations of P_y and Q_x as two points determine a line. In reality, however, the relationships are not linear. From actual observations at different moments in time, a sample of data points on the demand of X at different prices of Y may be gathered. This information, the scatter of points, can be plotted in a "scatter diagram" as in Figure 5.2.[241]

The graphical representation seems to confirm the underlying hypothesis of a positive relationship, because higher values of P_y yield higher values of Q_x. Yet, due to other influences on the dependent variable, the correlation is not perfect and information on P_y only is not enough to precisely predict the values of Q_x. Hence, the correct relationship is not equation (1), but rather:

$$Q_x = \alpha + \beta P_y + \varepsilon \qquad \text{Equation (2)}$$

Where ε is the random error term and represents random influences. It picks up the effects of omitted – and thus unobservable, or at least unobserved – influences such as omitted variables. Here, it reflects factors other than the price of product Y that influence demand for product X.

The task of regression analysis is to produce an *estimate* of the two parameters α and β, based upon the available information on observations for Q_x and P_y contained in the data set (and upon some assumptions about the characteristics of ε). More precisely, the investigator will seek to identify the

[241] The scatter of points in this diagram has been chosen for demonstration purposes only. It does not represent actual observations.

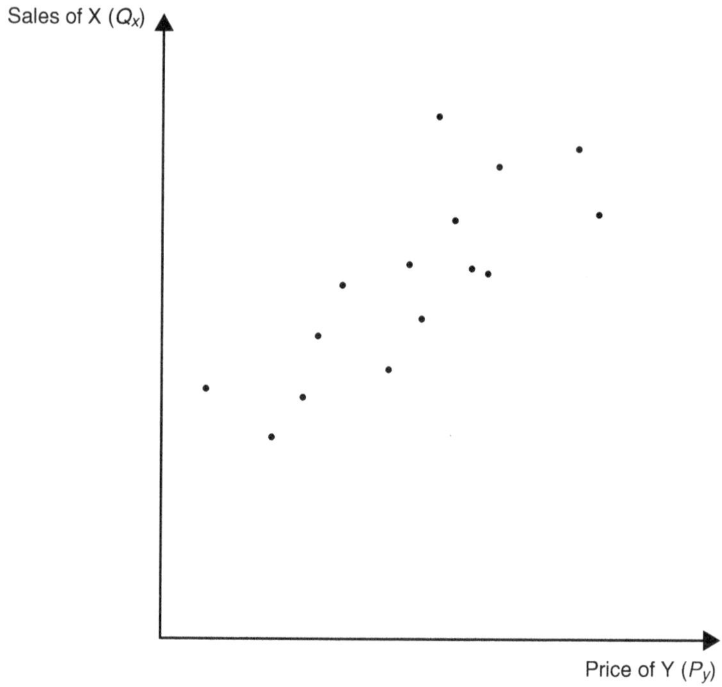

Figure 5.2 Scatter diagram price and demand

line around which the points are scattered, the "regression line." Regression analysis assumes the error term to be on average equal to zero, which suggests an estimate of the line that lies roughly in the midst of the data points.[242] This means that the regression line will not lie on all the actual data points in the scatter diagram, but will leave some observations below and some above. Regression is thus a generalized form of "averaging."

For the choice of the regression line it is important to distinguish for each data point between the actual values of the dependent variable in the data (where the point "is," or its "true" value) and the predicted or "fitted" values (where the point "should be"). Ignoring the error term as described, each possible set of coefficients for a given equation produces a set of "fitted" values for the dependent variable (generated by using the actual value of P in equation (2)). All predicted values lie on the regression

[242] The scatter of actual data points around the regression mean due to omitted influences is represented by the error term in the regression model. The distribution of the data points around the regression mean is approximately normal. This means that the error term can be thought of as a random variable with normal distribution.

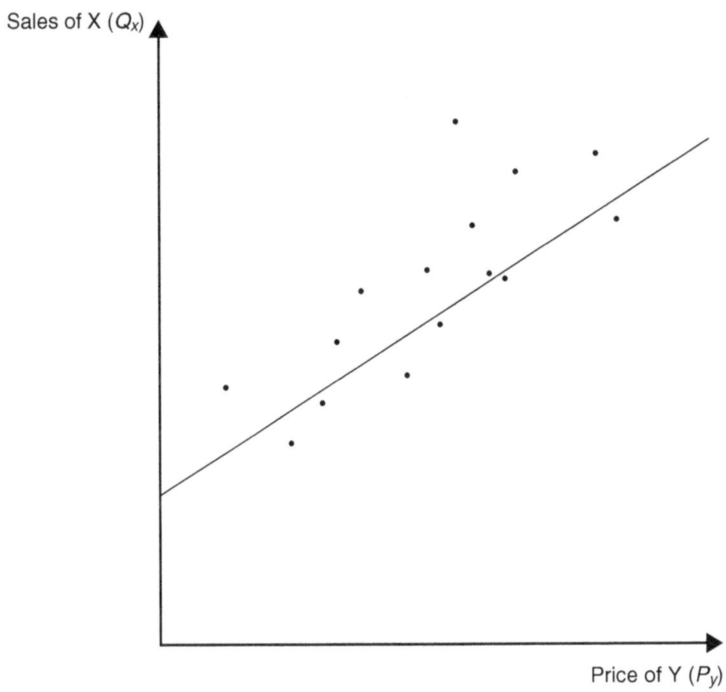

Figure 5.3 Regression line price and demand

line, which by definition connects those points, and is thus said to be "fitted." When the predicted values do not lie on the straight line, the mistake, or vertical deviation of the predicted value from the actual value of the dependent variable, is the prediction error for each observation, known as "residual." When the actual value of the variable lies above the regression estimate the residual is positive; when below, the residual is negative. A candidate regression line may be depicted as in Figure 5.3.[243]

Broadly speaking, regression analysis aims at identifying a "line of best fit" through the data points, which minimizes the differences between the actual observations and the plotted line, the residuals.[244] The intercept of

[243] Note that the plotted line in this figure is not the result of an actual regression. It only serves the purpose to give an intuitive idea of the underlying concept.

[244] The most popular regression procedure is termed "ordinary least squares" ("OLS") regression. It chooses the regression line by selecting the one for which the sum of the squares of the deviations (the residuals) between predicted and actual values of Q_x is at a minimum. The reason for minimizing the squared sum and not the sum of errors in absolute values lies in the fact that negative and positive errors would cancel out, so that the sum could be at a minimum even though the line selected fits the data very poorly.

the chosen line provides the estimate of α, and its slope provides the estimate of β. In conclusion, regression analysis is a statistical technique that allows an estimation of the individual effect of an independent variable on a dependent variable by calculating a line that best fits the observed values of the dependent and independent variables. Translated to the market definition inquiry, this means that the effect of the price of Y on sales of X is unknown, but data on sales of X and the prices of Y is available. By drawing the regression line through the scatter diagram, one can approximate the relationship between price and demand from actual data on these variables. From the slope of the line, one can derive an estimate of the price elasticity.[245]

(ii) Multiple regression

With only one independent variable, the regression line is the best-fitting straight line through a set of data points in a scatter plot. When expanding the simple regression equation above to include additional independent variables, the technical estimation becomes more complex, but the general explanations above still apply.

In the above example of a simple regression model, Q_x was affected by a multitude of other factors in addition to P_y. Those other influences were aggregated into the error term. "Multiple regression analysis," in contrast, allows additional factors to enter the analysis separately so that the effect of each can be estimated individually. To this end, it takes advantage of the fact that the independent variables seldom move in perfect step together, but rather move – as the name suggests – independently. By determining how the dependent variable changes when the independent variables move in a variety of ways, the effect of each of the independent variables is extracted.[246] Therefore, multiple regression is valuable for quantifying the impact of various simultaneous influences upon a single dependent variable.

For the purpose of illustration in the market definition context, the price of a close substitute product Z (P_z) is introduced as a second independent variable. As with P_y it is assumed that it has a linear effect upon the demand of X. This means that holding P_y constant, one would expect Q_x to increase when P_z rises. The regression equation now reads:

$$Q_x = \alpha + \beta P_y + \gamma P_z + \varepsilon \qquad \text{Equation (3)}$$

245 Note that when estimating the OPE, the elasticity is simply a way of describing the slope of the demand curve facing the firm.

246 Fisher, "Multiple Regression in Legal Proceedings," p. 712.

The conceptual principles remain identical to simple regressions when estimating the parameters of α, β, and γ. The difference is that the regression can no longer be thought of as choosing a line in a two-dimensional diagram. When there are two independent variables, one is fitting a plane to a scatter of points in a three-dimensional space. Multiple regression analysis will select a plane that best fits the data.[247] In the interpretation of the coefficient estimates, it is important to note that β is an estimate of the effect of the changes in price of Y on the quantity of X, holding the price of Z constant. Likewise, γ is the estimated effect of the change in price of Z on the quantity of X, holding the price of Y constant.

Multiple regression analysis is in fact capable of dealing with an arbitrarily large number of independent variables, for example, by extending the above equation:

$$Q_x = \alpha + \beta P_y + \gamma P_z + \delta I + \ldots + \varepsilon \qquad \text{Equation (4)}$$

Nevertheless, the principles are still the same, although the visualization is no longer easy. With multiple independent variables one is fitting a line of best fit through multidimensional space, a hyperplane (the generalization of a plane to more than three dimensions) with the respective number of dimensions. Its intercept implies the constant term, and its slope in each dimension implies one of the regression coefficients.

In a multiple regression model, it is important to explicitly include all major independent variables that are believed to influence the dependent variable. This means specifying the important or systematic factors that are hypothesized to be causally related to the dependent variable. Yet statisticians recognize that it is impossible to include all possible independent variables which might have some (minor) influence. There usually remains a myriad of minor influences, each perhaps small individually but with a non-negligible effect in the aggregate. This means that the group of independent variables will not completely explain the dependent variable. The summary effect of these excluded influences is included in the random error term ε, the "chance" component in the observations (which produces the "scatter" in the graph).[248] Thus, it can be concluded that multiple regression is a procedure that separates the systematic effects (associ-

[247] The intercept of that plane with the *y*-axis designates where P_y and P_z are 0. It gives the constant term a, its slope in the price of Y dimension implies the coefficient β, and its slope in the price of Z dimension implies the coefficient γ.

[248] The assumption is that the joint effect of the excluded influences is not systematically related to the effects of the independent variables being investigated, but due to chance.

ated with the independent variables) from the random effects (associated with the error term).[249]

The fact that a regression model does not expressly account for all possible explanations is quite alien to legal thinking.[250] The scientifically sound "imperfection" of regression models can – wrongfully and in a misleading manner – provide ammunition to the opponent in legal proceedings. The reason is that legal reasoning is quite sensitive to the objection that an explicative model does not take every conceivable and plausible argument into account. For example, in *Procter & Gamble/VP Schickedanz* the European Commission criticized a party's two-variable regression model:

> A better way to estimate elasticities is to estimate a model including *as many relevant variables as possible*, i.e. to use a multivariate rather than a univariate approach. In this way it is possible to distinguish the various effects of the explanatory variables from each other. Therefore, a model based on a multivariate approach explains market behavior in a more comprehensive way than would just price variations, and therefore reduces the risk of confusing one type of variation with another.[251]

Although it is correct to include the effects with non-negligible consequences as independent variables, this should not be misunderstood to mean that any possibly relevant influence should be included. This would result in inaccurate coefficients.[252] GATT case law will illustrate below how parties have attempted to compromise regression evidence by offering *ad hoc* explanations based on excluded influences. In the context of omitted variables, US Supreme Court precedent will provide a solution to the dilemma that arises from the clash between scientific and legal thinking.

[249] Rubinfeld, "Reference Guide on Multiple Regression," p. 205.

[250] Fisher, "Statisticians, Econometricians, and Adversary Proceedings," *Journal of the American Statistical Association*, 81 (1986), 277, 278.

[251] *Proctor & Gamble/VP Schickedanz*, *supra*, Ch. 3, fn. 240, para. 56 (emphasis added).

[252] This is partly due to the difficulty of distinguishing between the different effects of each variable (the multicollinearity problem). To illustrate the complexity of a growing number of variables, the estimation of demand relationships among five different products requires estimation of twenty-five OPE and CPEs. In the case of ten products, the number of elasticities that must be estimated increases to 100. But there is a variety of ways to restrict the number of parameters included in each equation in order to generate trustworthy estimations. Thus, the complexity of a high number of different independent variables in a demand equation can be dealt with, e.g., in a multistage approach by breaking consumer purchasing decisions down into a number of stages for which elasticities can be estimated separately, or by estimating segment equations which split products and other influences up into segments.

(iii) The estimation of demand elasticities using multiple regression

When seeking to identify and quantify the effect of potential substitute products for market definition purposes, the sizes of the coefficients of the independent variables are of interest. By way of multiple regression, one can thus estimate the values of OPE and CPE of demand, while taking account of other possible influences on demand. A very simple regression equation for market definition could take the following form:[253]

$$Q_x = \alpha + \beta P_x + \gamma P_y + \delta P_z + \varepsilon \qquad \text{Equation (5)}$$

Here, the dependent variable Q_x is the demand for the product X in question. The independent variables P_x, P_y and P_z represent the own price of X and the prices of products Y and Z that are believed to be close substitutes. Other factors assumed to influence the demand (further hypothesized substitute products, expenditure for marketing, advertising campaigns, time of the year, income, state of the economy, etc.) may be included in the model as additional independent variables. After estimating the fitted values, the coefficients of the price variables would provide (under a certain model specification explained below) a direct estimate of the elasticity of demand for each product. Thus, they give the values for OPE and CPE of demand, in each case holding constant all the other factors that might affect demand.

To provide a concrete example, if whisky, gin, and vodka are substituted into an equation of the same type as equation (5) for X, Y, and Z, the following combination of regression equations would be necessary to estimate the possible elasticities between the products:[254]

$$Q_{Whisky} = \alpha_1 + \beta_1 P_{Whisky} + \gamma_1 P_{Gin} + \delta_1 P_{Vodka} + \varepsilon_1 \qquad \text{Equation (6)}$$
$$Q_{Gin} = \alpha_2 + \beta_2 P_{Whisky} + \gamma_2 P_{Gin} + \delta_2 P_{Vodka} + \varepsilon_2 \qquad \text{Equation (7)}$$
$$Q_{Vodka} = \alpha_3 + \beta_3 P_{Whisky} + \gamma_3 P_{Gin} + \delta_3 P_{Vodka} + \varepsilon_3 \qquad \text{Equation (8)}$$

This system would explain the sales of each spirit in terms of the prices of all spirits.

[253] For simplified hypothetical regression equations for market definition purposes see, e.g., NERA Economic Consulting, *The Role of Quantitative Analysis in Competition Assessments*, p. 13 (2005), available at: www.nera.com/67_5009.htm. An actual example of regression analysis being employed for market definition is *Kraft General Foods*, see Rubinfeld, "Market Definition with Differentiated Products."

[254] For this example see Bishop and Walker, *The Economics of EC Competition Law*, 2nd edn., para. 10.04.

When demand elasticities are econometrically estimated, the important methodological issue of the proper "functional form" arises. The functional form describes the shape of the regression "line," or "plane." As the following will describe, the most common functional form for the estimation of elasticities is that of a log–linear specification, the linearity assumption being addressed first and then turning to the conversion into logarithms.

It is common to start with the linear functional form in litigation. It describes the relationship between the quantity of the product demanded and the independent variables that affect its sales, in particular, the prices charged for the good and close substitutes – a straight line in a two variable regression model. As already outlined, linear regression models presume that the magnitude of the change in the dependent variable associated with the change in any of the independent variables is the same no matter what the level of the independent variables. Here, changes in the quantity sold of product X would be presumed to be proportional to changes in the prices of products X, Y, and Z.

This linear form is not entirely accurate for the estimation of price elasticities. Demand elasticity is usually measured at a particular point on the demand curve (point elasticity).[255] This means that it measures the percentage change in quantity at a specific point (or percentage change in price) along the demand curve. Demand elasticities will generally change when moving along the demand curve, as they will vary from one price–quantity point to another. Usually, the elasticity of demand increases as the own price increases. Economically speaking, demand becomes more elastic at higher own prices (or at lower prices of a substitute). Thus, the effect of a price increase on demand is usually non-linear. By contrast, linear functional form with its constant elasticity assumption presumes that demand does not become more elastic as one moves upwards on the demand curve, that is, that elasticity is the same whatever the price. It therefore constrains the way demand elasticities can be estimated correctly.[256] Yet it is an appropriate and commonplace assumption to reduce the number of parameters so that only one elasticity value (at one point

[255] Pindyck and Rubinfeld, *Microeconomics*, p. 35.

[256] Especially in merger analysis, alternative and more flexible demand systems are employed in order to investigate statistically the extent to which demand elasticities change with price; see Hosken *et al.*, *Demand System Estimation and its Application to Horizontal Merger Analysis*, p. 15; Nevo-Ilan, "Definition of the Relevant Market," pp. 122–125.

on the demand curve) has to be estimated. This is particularly pertinent when the number of data points available is relatively low.[257]

Insights on the properties of point elasticities have already become relevant in the discussion on the *Cellophane Fallacy*, where consumer switching is overstated if measured from a supracompetitive price level. They are also behind objections made by the United States against the use of CPE for the definition of product likeness.[258] For the moment, however, it is sufficient to point to the potential shortcomings of linear demand function as the standard demand system employed in regression analysis.

In addition, the methodological question arises of how the variables should enter the model for the coefficients to be read as elasticities. This issue will also become pertinent later, when critically reviewing the application of the regression approach under Article III of the GATT.

As has been explained, the elasticity estimates can be derived from the slope of the regression line. However, the numerical value for the slope does not, without further computation, represent elasticity estimates. The slope relates quantity changes (in units) with price changes (for example, in Euros), and thus changes in absolute values. In contrast, elasticities relate percentage changes in quantity and in price.[259] In order to identify and estimate elasticities, the variables have to be mathematically transformed by taking the logarithms (denoted by log, or ln) and then using these in the regression equation giving an equation in a log–linear functional form.[260] A logarithmic scale measures equal units of percentage changes, rather than equal absolute units. Such transformation consequently allows the coefficients on each price variable to be read directly as elasticities. Thus, the coefficients give the values of elasticity estimates only if specified in the appropriate functional form.

[257] Another simplification is to assume that the two CPEs of a product pair satisfy a symmetry condition assuming that both CPEs equal each other.

[258] Appellate Submission by the United States to the Appellate Body, *Japan – Taxes on Alcoholic Beverages*, *supra*, Ch. 3, fn. 264, Annex A.

[259] Consider the following regression equation: $Q_x = 1{,}000 - (5 \times P_x) + (1 \text{ x } P_y) + \varepsilon$. Every time the price of X and Y rise by one unit, sales of X fall by five units and those of Y rise by one unit. In this example, the coefficients give a numerical expression in absolute terms for the effect of the respective independent variable on the demand of X. If, however, the variables were specified appropriately to read the coefficients as elasticities, the model would be interpreted differently: a price rise for X and Y by 1 percent would then mean a decrease in sales of X by 5 percent, and an increase in quantity by 1 percent, respectively.

[260] Taking the logarithm is essentially expressing prices and quantities in terms of growth rates starting from a certain base level, e.g., the lowest level observed in the sample.

C *Appraising multiple regression analysis*

Multiple regression analysis does not only provide estimates of coefficients, it also gives measures of how precise and reliable the results are and how well the model fits the data as a whole. The evaluation of econometric evidence has obvious applications in the courtroom because, as will be demonstrated below, the lack of unachievable perfection of a regression analysis should not be a bar to it being given evidentiary weight. The appraisal of its evidentiary weight depends instead on these measures of precision and reliability. These diagnostic tests allow adjudicators to distinguish good from bad econometric analyses. Much of the back and forth over empirical work between expert economists can also be understood this way.

(i) Standard errors, confidence intervals, statistical significance, and *t*-statistics

For each coefficient estimate, there is a "true" value and there is the estimate found by drawing the line of best fit through the available data. The "standard errors" (SE) of the estimated coefficients provide a measure of the reliability of the coefficient estimates by measuring the variability of each of the estimated regression coefficients. The concern is whether the coefficient provides an accurate measure of the effect of one variable on another, as one must expect that the measured coefficient may deviate from the true coefficient. To explain how the standard error of the coefficient is obtained, some basic statistical concepts need to be outlined.

The "normal distribution" (also known as "Gaussian" distribution) is the probability law of a continuous random variable with the familiar "bell curve" shape, where the values are distributed symmetrically with a single peak. It indicates, among other things, that if a sample is drawn from the distribution, the most likely values for the observations in the sample are those close to the mean, or the arithmetic average value. The least likely values are those farthest from the mean. The supposition of normal distribution is based on probability theory's central limit theorems, which hold that the average of a large number of independent random variables tends toward a normal distribution.

This also applies to the coefficient estimates. Each can be viewed as a random sample drawn from some probability distribution. This is to say, that if the regression were calculated over and over again with different samples, the estimates of each parameter would follow a normal probability distribution.[261]

[261] Rubinfeld, "Reference Guide on Multiple Regression," pp. 212–213. Note that the normal distribution of the coefficients is premised on the assumption that the error term

What this means is that estimates of the true, but unknown, coefficients are numbers that depend on the particular sample of observations. If a different sample were used, a different estimate would be calculated.[262] Therefore, if one varied the sample a large number of times, for each sample one would obtain a new estimate of the coefficient. The coefficient estimates would not necessarily be equal each time, but vary around the true value of the parameter in the form of a normal distribution. The average of the many estimates for each coefficient, or, more technically, the mean of the probability distribution, would be equal to the true value of the parameter. The standard error of the coefficients measures the variation of these parameter estimates around the true parameter.[263] The result of a greater variation in parameter estimates from sample to sample will be a larger standard error of the coefficient, and less reliable regression results. Small standard errors imply results that are likely to be similar from sample to sample and which, consequently, are more likely to be reliable.[264] Against this background, the probability that the parameter estimate differs from the true value by any given amount depends directly on the number of standard errors.

To be more specific about how reliable the coefficient estimates are, the statistical concept of "confidence levels" is useful. The normal distribution is symmetrical around its mean, so that deviations above the mean are as likely as deviations below the mean. For relatively large samples (often thirty or more data points will be sufficient for regressions with a small number of explanatory variables[265]), the probability that a normally distributed random variable lies within an interval of approximately ± 2 SE, or "standard deviations" (SD), around the true parameter will be

ε follows a normal distribution, which is to say that there is no systematic trend in the unobserved factors.

262 The OLS method generates the parameter estimates, also called the least-squares estimators, whose values vary from sample to sample.

263 Technically, the standard error of the coefficient is equal to the square root of the variance of the estimated coefficient about its true value. Variance is, as a measure of the dispersion of the probability distribution of a random variable, the average square deviation around its mean. Consider two random variables with the same mean. If one of them has a distribution with greater variance, then, roughly speaking, the probability that the variable will take on a value far from the mean is greater.

264 One can understand the concept by imagining four scales each measuring a person, who actually weighs 100 kg, as 97 kg, 99 kg, 101 kg, and 103 kg. The errors in these measurements are –3, –1, 1, and 3. The standard error of these measuring errors is assumed to be 2. Comparing the actual deviations of 3, 3, 1, and 1 to the standard error of 2, a deviation of 2 seems to be a fairly typical deviation in the sense that the actual errors cluster around it.

265 ABA Section of Antitrust Law, *Econometrics*, p. 405; Giannelli and Imwinkelried, *Scientific Evidence*, vol. I, para. 15.04(a) (2007).

about 0.95, or 95 percent.[266] The reason is that a normal distribution of a sufficiently large sample has the property that the area within 1.96 SE of the mean is equal to 95 percent of the total area under the (bell-shaped) curve. Approximately 2.5 percent of the distribution lies at the end of each tail under the curve.[267] What is termed the "confidence interval" depicts the range of values around the obtained coefficient estimate for which there is relative certainty – for example, at the conventional 95 percent level of certainty – that it will contain the true value of the coefficient.[268]

It is important to note the size of the confidence interval when dealing with coefficient estimates. This is likely to be particularly true in the case of elasticity estimates, because it is the size rather than the sign of the coefficient that matters. To say that the chances are 95 percent that the true coefficient lies in the confidence interval does not mean that the true coefficient is equally likely to be in any part of that range. It is most probably identical or close to the estimate and the probability decreases as one moves away from the estimate in either direction within the confidence interval.[269]

A concept that is closely related to the standard error is that of "statistical significance." It is a measure to ascertain that the value of the coefficient estimate is not a result of pure chance, or random error.[270] Hypothesis testing is the technique for determining statistical significance.[271] In the context of multiple regression, it is testing the hypothesis, termed the "null hypothesis," that an independent variable of interest has no association

[266] The exact number of standard errors that make up the 95 percent confidence interval depends on the exact number of data points available. As the number of available data points becomes larger, the figure approaches 1.96. At the 90 percent confidence level the standard errors amount to approximately 1.64.

[267] The uppermost tail of the distribution (above 1.96 SD) contains 2.5 percent of the draws representing the largest positive values, and the lowermost tail (below –1.96 SD) contains 2.5 percent of the draws representing the largest negative values; Rubinfeld, "Reference Guide on Multiple Regression," p. 213.

[268] For instance, if the elasticity estimate has been estimated as being 5.0, the question is how close this estimate is to the true coefficient. If the standard error is 0.5, then there can be 95 percent certainty that the true estimate lies within approximately 2 SE from the estimate, i.e., in the 95 percent confidence interval between approximately 4.0 (= 5.0 – (0.5 × 2)) and 6.0 (= 5.0 + (0.5 × 2)). For this example see Bishop and Walker, *The Economics of EC Competition Law*, 3rd edn., para. AN-019.

[269] If, for instance, a coefficient estimate is 5.0, then it is more likely that the true estimate is 5.0 than that it is 4.99, or 5.01. There is about a 70 percent chance that the true coefficient is within 1 SE of the estimate, and about a 50 percent chance that the true coefficient is within 2 or 3 of 1 SE of the estimate.

[270] Rubinfeld, "Reference Guide on Multiple Regression," pp. 191 *et seq.*

[271] See in more detail Rubinfeld, "Econometrics in the Courtroom," *Columbia Law Review*, 85 (1985), 1048, 1054–1065; Freund and Perles, *Modern Elementary Statistics*, paras. 12.1, 12.2 (2007).

with a dependent variable against the alternative hypothesis that there is an association.[272] More precisely, for a single independent variable, the null hypothesis is stated in terms of the true value of a particular regression coefficient being equal to zero. This is to say that there is no effect of the independent variable on the dependent variable.[273] A coefficient that is significantly different from zero justifies the *rejection* of the null hypothesis and is termed to be "statistically significant." Essentially, the statistical test is constructed by asking how likely it is that the confidence interval includes zero. The null hypothesis of a parameter being equal to zero is tested by looking at the *t*-statistic.[274] If the *t*-statistic is above 1.96 (or below –1.96) in magnitude, the 95 percent confidence interval around the parameter does not include zero. In that case, the null hypothesis that the coefficient equals zero can be rejected. In other words, one can be almost (95 percent) certain that the true coefficient is not zero. The coefficient is said to be significantly different from zero at the 95 percent confidence level or to be statistically significant at the 5 percent level (when above 1.64 or below –1.64, it is statistically significant at the 10 percent level).[275]

The computation of the standard errors of the coefficients and the corresponding *t*-statistics is a matter of considerable importance. It is routinely done by computerized regression packages, with the 5 percent significance level generally accepted to test the null hypothesis.

A coefficient of an independent variable that is statistically significant usually justifies rejection of the null hypothesis associated with a zero coefficient, for example, rejection of the assertion that the price for product Y plays no role for the demand for product X. Yet it is important to understand that the converse situation of not rejecting (non-technically

[272] A null hypothesis is set up to be *nullified* or *refuted* in order to support an alternative hypothesis. The former is presumed to be true until statistical evidence in the form of a hypothesis test indicates otherwise.

[273] Fisher, "Multiple Regression in Legal Proceedings," p. 716.

[274] The *t*-statistic is the coefficient estimate divided by the standard error of the coefficient. The *t*-statistic is then compared with tables of the *t*-distribution to assess its significance; Finkelstein and Levin, *Statistics for Lawyers*, para. 13.4 (2007).

[275] Suppose, for instance, that the estimate of a coefficient is 1 and the standard error is 2. This implies that the 95 percent confidence interval for the coefficient runs from –3 to +5. In this case, the *t*-statistic is 0.5 (i.e., 1 ÷ 2). As the confidence interval is such that it includes zero, one cannot be sure (with 95 percent confidence) that the true coefficient is not zero (i.e., that the relevant independent variable has no effect on the dependent variable). On the other hand, if the standard error is 0.25, then the 95 percent confidence interval ranges from 0.5 to 1.5. The *t*-statistic in this case is 4 (i.e., 1 ÷ 0.25). Here, one can be almost certain that the true coefficient is not zero and that therefore the relevant variable is a determinant of the dependent variable. For these examples see Bishop and Walker, *The Economics of EC Competition Law*, 3rd edn., para. AN-019.

"accepting") the null hypothesis is more open to interpretation. Not rejecting the null hypothesis (that there is *no* relationship) does not necessarily exclude the alternative hypothesis that there *is* a relationship! The reason is that not rejecting a null hypothesis cannot be interpreted as proof that the true parameter is in fact zero. All it means is that the possibility that it is actually zero cannot be rejected. For this reason, the *lack* of a statistically significant elasticity estimate does *not* prove the *absence* of substitutability. This is why failure to reject the null hypothesis must not, as it will be shown to have been the case in WTO law, enable jumping to conclusions regarding the validity of the alternative hypothesis.[276] Overall, there is tension between any attempt to reach conclusions with near certainty and the inherently probabilistic nature of multiple regression analysis.

(ii) "Goodness of fit"

The error term can be thought of as the sum of all those factors that affect the dependent variable, but which have not been explicitly included in the model. In general, all the important independent variables should have been included in the model, and so the error term ought to be relatively small. When regression results are reported, a measure of the "goodness of fit" of the multiple regression model is usually also reported. This is an indication of how well the overall model, which is the totality of the independent variables, explains the variation in the dependent variable.

The most commonly reported measure of the overall "goodness of fit" is the R^2 statistic, or, as a better measure, the *adjusted* R^2.[277] It measures the percentage of variation in the dependent variable that is accounted for by all the independent variables.[278] Its value ranges from 0 to 1. An R^2 figure of 1 means that the independent variables explain 100 percent of the variation in the dependent variable; an R^2 of 0 means that the independent variables explain none of the variation.

In general, it is usually assumed that the higher the R^2, the better the model. Associated with the tendency of lawyers to believe that an

[276] See *infra*, fn. 335.

[277] The extent to which a regression model fits the data is also appraised by the standard error of regression as distinguished from the standard error of the coefficient. See Fisher, "Multiple Regression in Legal Proceedings," p. 718; Finkelstein and Levin, *Statistics for Lawyers*, para. 13.3.

[278] R^2 can be shown to equal 1 minus the ratio of the sum of squared estimated errors (the deviations of the actual value of the dependent variable from the regression line) to the sum of squared deviations about the mean of the dependent variable. Intuitively, the sum of squared deviations about its mean is a measure of the total variation of the dependent variable. The sum of squared deviations about the regression line is a measure of the extent to which the regression fails to explain the dependent variable.

explicative model must fit all cases, is the tendency to judge models purely on how well they fit the data. Therefore, lawyers tend to turn to the R^2 in order to ascertain whether a model must be believed. However, contrary to a lawyer's intuition, one must not equate a high R^2 with the model being good, or vice versa. For a variety of technical reasons, these conclusions would be a serious, and are frequently, misuse of econometric analysis.[279] Especially in the context of elasticity estimation, adjudicators should be reluctant to rely on R^2, because the insight of how well the collection of independent variables explain the dependent variable is considerably less important if one is interested in particular parameter estimates, as is the case in the estimation of elasticities.

D Statistical and economic significance

The notion of "statistical significance" in the context of multiple regression is complex. It has already been addressed in relation to testing the null hypothesis of the true value of a particular regression coefficient being equal to zero. In general, a result is called statistically significant if it is unlikely to have occurred by chance. More precisely here, statistical significance of the estimated relationship is the degree of confidence that the estimated relationship is close to the true relationship. The amount of certainty required to accept that an event is unlikely to have arisen by chance has been presented as the significance level. In a typical case, economic theory might predict that an independent variable of interest will have a particular causal effect on a dependent variable. Using multiple regression analysis, one can calculate the probability that the estimated coefficients would have been obtained had there been *no* relationship between the independent variable and the dependent variable (the null hypothesis). Statistical significance means that the probability of such an occurrence is less than or equal to a pre-established significance level. Put differently, the significance level when testing a hypothesis is such that the probability of mistakenly rejecting the null hypothesis is no more than the stated probability. In most scientific study, this level of statistical significance required is set conventionally at 0.05, or 5 percent.[280] This is often inversely referred to as the 95 percent confidence level – and associated with a *t*-statistic having an absolute value of approximately 2 or higher. From a statistician's vantage point, there is good reason to require

[279] For these reasons see Finkelstein and Levin, *Statistics for Lawyers*, para. 13.3.

[280] Kaye, "Is Proof of Statistical Significance Relevant?" *Washington Law Review*, 61 (1986), 1333, 1343–1344.

such a stringent significance level. Since, even with a large sample, it is quite possible to obtain results differing from a coefficient's true value, it is conventionally thought that there must be a very high probability that the coefficient is not zero before it can be claimed conclusively that the variable associated with the coefficient has a definite effect on the dependent variable. But there are also less stringent significance levels. A level of 10 percent is often, but less frequently, used. Levels below 10 percent are rarely accepted in legal practice.[281] Overall, formally, statistical significance provides information that helps one to *reject* the view that the independent variable of interest and the dependent variable are directly related. Informally, a statistically significant coefficient is one that tends to *support* the view that this independent variable is correlated with (and perhaps causally related to) the dependent variable.[282]

The meaning of the term "significance" in statistics is different from that used in everyday language, which suggests that something is important or meaningful. What the latter alludes to is often referred to as "practical" or "economic" significance.[283] What is statistically significant need not be economically significant. Moreover, legal adjudicators do not follow the scientific tenet of scientific certainty, but the legal tenet of legal sufficiency in rendering a decision.

Although it is crucial to distinguish between them, statistical significance is often wrongly equated with practical significance.[284] While statistical significance characterizes the precision with which a parameter is measured, practical significance is the magnitude that matters economically. The latter means that the magnitude of the effect being studied is not *de minimis*.[285] It is sufficiently important in substantive terms for the court to be concerned, for which reason it is legally significant.

Often, a coefficient that is statistically significant is also economically significant. However, it is possible to find statistically significant coefficients that are so small that they are not of economic importance and vice versa. For example, a CPE estimate may be statistically distinguishable from zero, but low in economic terms (for example, 0.15). By contrast, a CPE may not be statistically different from zero, but still quite

[281] The court in *FTC* v. *Swedish Match North America*, 131 F.Supp. 2d 151, 161 fn. 10 (DDC 2000), for example, rejected an econometric estimation of demand where the observed level of significance was 15 percent.

[282] ABA Section of Antitrust Law, *Econometrics*, p. 15.

[283] See, e.g., Rubinfeld, "Quantitative Methods in Antitrust," p. 738.

[284] See the reference in Bishop and Walker, *The Economics of EC Competition Law*, 2nd edn., para. AN-024.

[285] Rubinfeld, "Reference Guide on Multiple Regression," p. 192.

high and important (for example, 3.0). Importantly, the absolute value of the elasticity estimates depends crucially on the magnitude of the parameter estimates, that is, the economic significance. Even if one can be extremely confident of the relationship between price and demand (statistical significance), the change in sales volume may not be enough for sufficient substitution between the products to count them as substitutes in the same relevant market.

The practice of antitrust market definition in fact provides an example of the risk of confusion of statistical and economic significance. Under the SSNIP test, results are economically significant once a 5–10 percent price increase is profitable. Even if a highly statistically significant study indicates the presence of substitution, the products may not belong to the same relevant antitrust market if a 5–10 percent price rise is unprofitable. To draw the parallel under GATT, the results must be practically significant if substitutability reaches a magnitude at which it would make sense to implement a protectionist measure, or, according to the test proposed above, if the domestic producer can profitably increase the price.

5 Econometrics in market definition case law

Although CPE has a mathematically precise meaning in economics that can be estimated by virtue of regression analysis, it comes as a surprise that adjudicators in legal proceedings often use the term differently. As it will be outlined in a first step, it is an observation common to both antitrust as well as WTO/GATT case law that CPE of demand as a concept for market definition has been employed by adjudicators in two ways. Either it has been employed as a specific quantitative measure of substitutability, or it has been used in a non-quantitative and descriptive manner as an approximation of substitutability based on circumstantial and anecdotal evidence. Based on the theoretical insights gained on multiple regression analysis, the econometric estimations of CPE in Article III case law will be critically assessed in a second step.

A *The non-econometric and econometric estimation of price elasticities of demand*

(i) Descriptive approximations of elasticities

First, the non-technical approach to the use of CPE of demand shall be addressed. This approach can be thought of as determining CPE on the basis of inferences which are themselves based on rudimentary information. The approach relies on qualitative evidence or, at best, on customer testimony solicited by way of customer survey methods which hypothetically ask about the switching under certain circumstances, for example, in the event of a price increase.

Although CPE of demand has been referred to routinely for several decades in the process of delineating antitrust markets, courts have rarely employed the concept using precise elasticity estimates.[286] In a non-quantitative manner, they usually refer to the tendency of a rise in the price for one product to generate a corresponding increase in the demand for another product. In effect, courts often use the term as a synonym for reasonable or functional interchangeability, rather than as a specific mathematical measure that may help estimate the degree of substitutability.[287] It is regular practice in the courts to infer non-technical conclusions on the presence or absence of CPE of demand on the basis of descriptive and qualitative evidence, such as on sales, marketing activities, and other material describing the nature, cost, usage, or other comparative features of competing products. Correspondingly, the SSNIP test is mentioned in virtually all market definition cases, though it is almost always summarily applied in a descriptive and approximative, rather than in a mathematically exact, manner.[288]

Similarly, non-quantitative approximations of CPE in descriptive studies have been common in WTO dispute settlement proceedings where the concept of CPE has been used. For example, in several submissions, the parties presented various studies (on market share changes, consumer surveys, etc.) which purported to give evidence for or against demand elasticity. Such studies were either historic analyses of the correlation between price and consumption trends (looking at changes in market shares) or analyses of contemporary reactions of consumers to survey questions. Yet it is rare that such studies actually calculated elasticity coefficients. These instances are addressed in greater detail below. They demonstrate that the main WTO cases that are widely understood to represent an economic

[286] See *supra*, Ch. 3, fnn. 26–27.

[287] See, e.g., *US Anchor Mfg., Inc.* v. *Rule Indus., Inc.*, 7 F.3d 986, 995 (11th Cir. 1993); *Olin Corp.* v. *FTC*; *Allen-Myland, Inc.* v. *IBM Corp.*, 33 F.3d 194, 201 fn. 8 (3d Cir. 1994); *United Farmers Agents Ass'n* v. *Farmers Ins. Exch.*, 89 F.3d 233, 236 fn. 3 (5th Cir. 1996); *HDC Med.* v. *Minntech Corp.*, 411 F.Supp. 2d 1096, 1103–1104 (D Minn. 2006); *Tetra Pak/Alfa-Laval*, at IV.B.2.1.

[288] Schwalbe and Zimmer, *Kartellrecht und Ökonomie*, p. 183; Klein, "SSNIP-Test oder Bedarfsmarktkonzept?" *Wirtschaft und Wettbewerb*, (2010), 169, 176.

approach, in fact, relied mostly on non-econometric estimations of elasticities.

The complainants in *Japan – Alcoholic Beverages II* submitted a consumer survey (the "ASI study") that analyzed different hypothetical scenarios in which the prices for the eight Western-style spirits were lowered and the price for shochu remained either fixed or was increased.[289] In all scenarios the demand for shochu would fall by approximately 25 percent. Although actual elasticity estimates were not calculated, the Panel endorsed the study to suggest there was a high degree of CPE between shochu and Western-style spirits.

The respondent, Japan, introduced a different consumer survey conducted by the Japanese Institute for Social Science. Consumers had been questioned as to which other alcoholic beverages they would choose if a particular one was unavailable.[290] According to the survey, 10 percent of the consumers would switch to other spirits if shochu was unavailable. Japan submitted that this was proof of the absence of substitution between whisky and shochu. The Panel, however, instead interpreted this result as constituting sufficient evidence to establish demand elasticity.

Analogous to the descriptive method of "shock analysis" referred to above, observations of reactions to sudden changes in the markets were also deemed to establish a competitive relationship between the products at issue.[291] In the case of *Japan – Alcoholic Beverages II*, this was a change in the tax reform in 1989.[292] As a result, the tax rate for certain kinds of whisky increased and their retail prices almost doubled. At the same time, sales of shochu started to grow. Its market share increased from 61.6 percent in 1989 to 74.2 percent in 1994. This was interpreted as evidence that the demand for shochu was largely influenced by the fluctuations in the prices of other distilled spirits. Thus, it was accepted as proof of the existence of demand elasticity between whisky and shochu.

Complainants in *Korea – Alcoholic Beverages* presented a study of Korean consumer behavior (the "Dodwell study") in response to a hypothetical price increase of soju and price decrease of Western-style alcoholic beverages.[293] Even though the complainants did not actually calculate the CPE ratios, they submitted that the data evidenced a trend of

[289] Panel Report, *Japan – Alcoholic Beverages II, supra*, Ch. 3, fn. 73, paras. 4.172, 6.29, 6.32.
[290] Panel Report, *Japan – Alcoholic Beverages II, supra*, Ch. 3, fn. 73, paras. 4.83–4.85, 6.31.
[291] *Supra*, fn. 19.
[292] Panel Report, *Japan – Alcoholic Beverages II, supra*, Ch. 3, fn. 73, paras. 4.1, 4.82, 6.30.
[293] Panel Report, *Korea – Alcoholic Beverages, supra*, Introduction, fn. 36, paras. 10.87–10.92.

substitutability.[294] The Panel found the study to be supportive of a finding of a competitive relationship.[295]

Interestingly, even the complainants, who submitted the Dodwell study, did not make the examination of CPEs a central point of the arguments. Instead, the complainants conceded obstacles to a calculation of CPEs. The "difficulties inherent in the situation" were: (1) the insufficient availability of imports that prevented adequate consumer familiarity with the imported products; (2) the Korean discriminatory measures at issue that skewed the pricing; and (3) the nature of alcoholic beverages as "experience goods" that prevented consumers from switching easily.[296] These are three different issues. The first and second issues, the lack of familiarity with the import and the distortion of competitive conditions due to the discriminatory measure, are valid complications to the use of CPE as has been shown above. Yet they also do not exclude the usefulness of demand elasticities *per se* as the complainants seemed to imply. The third issue, the fact that a good is an "experience good" is not in itself an argument against using CPEs, but only a reason that can render demand inelastic.

In *Korea – Alcoholic Beverages*, a descriptive mode of quantitative evidence similar to "shock analysis" was also employed.[297] Tax and customs reforms between 1990 and 1996 led to lower prices on whisky. Concurrently, a transfer of market shares from soju to whisky was observed. An inverse trend was observed in response to later market developments, in particular, the depreciation of the Korean currency, a campaign of boycotts against imported products, and a financial crisis. This evidence was taken to indicate that consumers' demand for soju had been responsive to changes in the price of whisky, which would prove that

[294] Strong evidence of substitutability was seen in the results of the study, according to which survey respondents would choose imported brown spirits rather than soju 15.22 percent of the time under current price conditions, but 28.4 percent of the time when the price of diluted soju was raised 20 percent and the price of brown spirits was lowered to its lowest point in the survey. Similarly, with respect to white spirits the choice went from 13.8 percent for imports at current levels to 23.8 percent when soju was again increased 20 percent in price and imports were at their lowest survey levels.

[295] The Panel made clear its reservation toward empirical and econometrical studies: "Indeed, it must be recalled that the Appellate Body confirmed that such surveys are not the decisive factor in decision-making under Article III:2, second sentence. We do not find the Dodwell study decisive, but it is consistent with other information and is therefore helpful evidence" (*Korea – Alcoholic Beverages, supra*, Introduction, fn. 36, para. 10.92).

[296] Panel Report, *Korea – Alcoholic Beverages, supra*, Introduction, fn. 36, para. 10.87.

[297] Panel Report, *Korea – Alcoholic Beverages, supra*, Introduction, fn. 36, paras. 5.139–5.142.

both are in competition with each other. In other words, this was accepted as descriptive evidence of CPE.[298]

In *Chile – Alcoholic Beverages*, the EC's main piece of evidence was the 1998 Search Marketing SA Survey (SM Survey). It asked a representative sample of consumers two questions about their willingness to substitute pisco with other spirits.[299] In particular, the second survey question inquired into the respondents' preferences in the event that prices of pisco and imported spirits were to change in response to a hypothetical uniform tax applicable to all domestic and imported spirits.[300] According to the EC, the answers to this question accounted for the existence of a significant degree of CPE between pisco and imported spirits.

The EC also referred to the 1996 Gemines study, commissioned by the Chilean pisco industry, the results of which were widely published, although the full content was withheld by Chile despite the Panel's request for it.[301] Therefore, the only information available was that a reduction in the tax on whisky by 50 percent would lead to a 47 percent drop in the price of whisky, which would in turn lead to a 17 percent decrease in the demand for pisco. From this, the EC inferred a significant degree of CPE.

In *Philippines – Distilled Spirits*, the EU and the United States submitted a consumer survey produced by Euromonitor International "suggesting that consumers in the Philippines would be more willing to purchase imported distilled spirits if the price of those spirits decreases and the price of domestic Philippine spirits increases, even if the prices of imported spirits remains higher than those of domestic spirits."[302] The Panel clearly described the anecdotal and descriptive nature of the study, which was "not an attempt to estimate and provide figures for the cross-price elasticity."[303] In a section on "price elasticity" the study

298 For an implicit endorsement of this evidence see Panel Report, *Korea – Alcoholic Beverages*, *supra*, Introduction, fn. 36, para. 10.94.

299 Panel Report, *Chile – Alcoholic Beverages*, *supra*, Ch. 2, fn. 68, paras. 4.186 *et seq*. The first question was aimed at measuring the substitutability of pisco and other distilled spirits under current taxation and pricing conditions, and asked which of a list of proposed alcoholic or non-alcoholic beverages a consumer would buy if pisco was unavailable and vice versa. In response, a large majority of consumers (70 percent) regarded other distilled spirits as the closest substitute for pisco.

300 It was estimated that the envisaged tax change would bring about an increase of 1.7 percent in the prices of pisco and a simultaneous reduction in the prices of whisky and of "other spirits" of 25.3 percent and 2.3 percent, respectively. The share of respondents choosing whisky and other spirits instead of pisco would increase from 17.7 percent to 30.5 percent.

301 Panel Report, *Chile – Alcoholic Beverages*, *supra*, Ch. 2, fn. 68, para. 4.240.

302 Panel Report, *Philippines – Distilled Spirits*, *supra*, Introduction, fn. 23, paras. 7.52, 7.109.

303 Panel Report, *Philippines – Distilled Spirits*, *supra*, Introduction, fn. 23, paras. 7.56, 7.112.

concluded that: "overall, the closer the price between imported and domestic spirits, the more likely consumers are to increase their consumption of imports while decreasing their consumption of domestics."[304] Despite certain shortcomings addressed below, the Panel credited the survey as conclusive evidence for the substitutability between the spirits at issue.

In all these instances, rather vague inferences to CPE were made. This approach contains far less information than the more precise elasticity estimates derived from regression analysis. Instead of CPE as a numerical expression for substitution, it has been reduced to a merely descriptive shorthand of substitution – arguably a lawyer's way of superficially combining law and economics. In most cases, such crude inferences about demand elasticities are useful only to rule out the possibilities of patently inelastic or highly elastic demand. However, such an approach leaves out the range of uncertainty that, as a practical matter, will usually give rise to legal disputes.

Surveying customer and competitor opinions is, admittedly, a recognized method in empirical economics, and is in fact the most common method for employing the concept of CPE.[305] When properly designed, executed, and described, surveys upon a population or sample thereof are widely accepted in order to form inferences in legal proceedings.[306] Still, Chile criticized the EC's use of the 1998 SM Survey, for example, "as a kind of substitute for econometric analysis" that, as a survey, is by nature "inherently much less reliable than an econometric analysis."[307] Even though such distinction between the survey method and econometric

[304] Panel Report, *Philippines – Distilled Spirits, supra*, Introduction, fn. 23, para. 7.54 (internal footnote omitted). The Panel continued: "In the same section, the report adds that: 'On average, at an import price decrease of 25% and domestic increase of 50%, consumers were 4.9% more willing to purchase imports and 4.0% less likely to purchase domestics'; 'On average, at an import price decrease of 40% to 60% and domestic increase of 100% to 200%, consumers were 10.1% more willing to purchase imports and 6.5% less likely to purchase domestics'; and, 'If price were no issue, on average, consumers were 43% more likely [to] purchase local brands and 86% more likely to purchase imported ones'" (internal footnotes omitted).

[305] See, e.g., Case COMP/M.3848, *Sea-Invest/EMO-EKOM* [2007] OJ L282 47, paras. 17, 18, 53; Case COMP/M.4734, *Ineos/Kerling* [2008] OJ C219 18, paras. 34, 38, 39. See especially on the use of conjoint survey analysis, Hildebrand, "Using Conjoint Analysis for Market Definition: Application of Modern Market Research Tools to Implement the Hypothetical Monopolist Test," *World Competition*, 29 (2006), 315–336.

[306] Diamond, "Reference Guide on Survey Research," in Federal Judicial Center, *Reference Manual on Scientific Evidence*, pp. 229–276 (2000), available at: www.fjc.gov/public/pdf.nsf/lookup/sciman00.pdf/$file/sciman00.pdf.

[307] Panel Report, *Chile – Alcoholic Beverages, supra*, Ch. 2, fn. 68, para. 4.196. Chile seems to wrongly equate the survey method with less meaningful "qualitative analysis" as opposed to quantitative econometric analysis, *ibid.*, para. 4.201.

analysis does not necessarily exist, as the latter, for example, regression analysis, may be conducted on the basis of historic data as well as on data generated through surveys, there are indeed many weaknesses to the survey method. Such include whether the responses gained from hypothetical questions to consumers reveal actual purchase intentions, whether the information is subject to bias (survey responses are highly sensitive to the particular question asked; also customers or competitors surveyed may have a self-interest to influence the results of the market definition inquiry), and whether the sample is of sufficient and representative size and elicited a sufficient response rate. Beyond these general complications associated with the survey method, there are also more specific problems in the case of elasticity estimation.

From a methodological point of view, there is considerable doubt about the validity of CPE approximations. As noted above, CPE is properly estimated on the basis that all factors other than one quantity variable and one price variable are held constant. Yet the surveys outlined above (for example, the 1998 SM Survey or the Euromonitor International survey) simultaneously changed the prices of all goods. This does not allow for the accurate estimation of elasticities, because the *ceteris paribus* requirement was not observed and the effect of a price increase in one product on the quantity demanded of the other could not be isolated.[308]

Another shortcoming of the survey method is that survey questions, as the above examples show, do not establish what consumers would actually do, but only what they say they would do in a hypothetical situation. Actual and hypothetical choices may significantly diverge, as there can be a considerable difference between stated preferences (established through customer surveys) and revealed preferences (established on the basis of historic price and quantity data). For this reason, the Panel in *Philippines – Distilled Spirits* was very cautious regarding the probative value of the Euromonitor International survey.[309]

While the Panel in *Philippines – Distilled Spirits* has now underscored its preference for revealed preferences as the basis for the determination of product "likeness," prior case law was not so clear about it. The Panel in *Chile – Alcoholic Beverages* even appeared to hold that revealed preferences, and thus a purely factual determination of actual consumer preferences, are irrelevant for the assessment of substitution in GATT.[310] The Panel manifestly distinguished between the "economic concept of

308 Panel Report, *Chile – Alcoholic Beverages*, *supra*, Ch. 2, fn. 68, para. 7.67; Panel Report, *Philippines – Distilled Spirits*, *supra*, Introduction, fn. 23, paras. 7.56, 7.112.

309 Panel Report, *Philippines – Distilled Spirits*, Introduction, fn. 23, para. 7.111.

310 Panel Report, *Chile – Alcoholic Beverages*, *supra*, Ch. 2, fn. 68, paras. 7.68, 7.69.

substitution," which can be specified precisely by the coefficient of CPE, and the "concept of substitution in markets" as "the fundamental issue in light of the treaty text and in terms of the analytical approach."[311] The Panel stated that the latter "should not be confused or equated with a numerical measurement of the extent of substitution as found in the coefficient of cross-elasticity."[312] Thus, the Panel appears to suggest a distinction between the economic conception of substitution and the somewhat different and peculiar notion of substitution under GATT. By giving economic labels to their analyses, in particular, the term CPE or the concept of substitution, lawyers and adjudicators give their analyses an air of scientific rigor, which in fact lacks a systematic and methodical economic basis. In actuality, a qualitative litmus test masquerades as a quantitative economic concept – ostensibly to avoid a jurist's practical difficulties in understanding and correctly interpreting econometric models. More fundamentally, this reflects the observation that when there are competing, ambiguous, or complex facts, legal systems and tribunals tend to make legal rather than factual determinations in their decisions.[313]

(ii) Econometric estimations of elasticities

By contrast, the econometric estimation of elasticities can be thought of as more "tangible" evidence of customer perceptions. Ideally, it is based on instances of actual prior purchasing decisions and past switching behavior. Looking at historic market sales and price data it is then possible to distill price elasticities of demand by way of regression analysis.

Courts in the United States have often welcomed econometrics. They usually recognize that: "as a general rule, a properly constructed regression analysis 'can play a vital role in legal proceedings … and can be a valuable tool for resolving factual disputes.'"[314] Specifically for the purpose of market definition, it has been concluded that an econometric model is "the most sophisticated and reliable analytical technique available today."[315] In a number of cases, econometric evidence on price elasticities of demand played a role in market definition as the evidentiary centerpiece,[316] or

[311] Panel Report, *Chile – Alcoholic Beverages*, *supra*, Ch. 2, fn. 68, paras. 7.68, 7.69.

[312] Panel Report, *Chile – Alcoholic Beverages*, *supra*, Ch. 2, fn. 68, para. 7.69.

[313] Waincymer, *WTO Litigation*, pp. 535–536.

[314] *In re Polypropylene Carpet Antitrust Litig.* (1997), *supra*, fn. 106, at 26, quoting Fisher, "Multiple Regression in Legal Proceedings," p. 735.

[315] *United States* v. *United Technologies Corp.*, 1977–2 Trade Cas. (CCH) ¶ 61,647 at 18,137 (ND Ohio 1977).

[316] For example, *Kraft General Foods*, *supra*, fn. 81, at 333, 357.

credited as being consistent with other qualitative evidence,[317] or rejected as flawed giving weight to qualitative evidence instead.[318]

Most strikingly, on the importance of econometric evidence for market definition, some, though not the majority of courts, suggest that market definition cannot be established in the absence of expert testimony.[319] They rejected plaintiffs' proffered submissions on relevant markets for failure to introduce any econometric evidence on the definition of the relevant market, and held that plaintiffs had thus failed to meet the burden of proof on this issue.[320] The courts stated that merely anecdotal, descriptive, or even survey evidence was insufficient to draw a technical conclusion of CPE from.[321] This contrasts with the earlier case of *United States* v. *Mrs. Smith's Pie Co.*, in which the court found that use of an econometric model as proof of elasticities was "completely useless primarily because we have no basis for evaluating what a particular elasticity coefficient means."[322]

Econometric analysis in EU antitrust law has a short history. The earliest instances of econometric evidence being employed in relation to the market definition issue appear to be in the late 1980s and early 1990s.[323] Since then, a number of cases have followed in which the European Commission either commissioned econometric studies, or in which it appraised positively or negatively econometric evidence adduced by the parties.[324]

317 For example, *FTC* v. *Staples, Inc.*, 970 F.Supp. 1066, 1073–1081 (DDC 1997).

318 For example, *FTC* v. *Swedish Match North America*, *supra*, fn. 281, at 158–162.

319 See, e.g., *Colsa Corp.* v. *Martin Marietta Servs.*, 133 F.3d 853, 855 fn. 4 (11th Cir. 1998); *Virginia Vermiculite Ltd* v. *W. R. Grace & Co.*, 108 F.Supp. 2d 549, 576 fn. 16 (WD Va. 2000); *Bailey* v. *Allgas, Inc.*, 284 F.3d 1237, 1246 (11th Cir. 2002).

320 *H.J., Inc.* v. *International Tel. & Tel. Corp.*, 867 F.2d 1531, 1538 (8th Cir. 1989); *Menasha Corp.* v. *News America In-Store Marketing, Inc.*, 354 F.3d 661, 664 (7th Cir. 2004) (hereinafter *Menasha Corp.*); *Worldwide Basketball & Sport Tours* v. *NCAA*, 388 F.3d 955, 962 (6th Cir. 2004).

321 *H.J., Inc.* v. *International Tel. & Tel. Corp.*, *supra*, fn. 320, at 1540: "This court has been insistent upon market data or similar hard evidence in identifying the relevant market. In the absence of such proof courts are incapable of determining the extent of cross-elasticity of demand in the market"; *Menasha Corp.*, *supra*, fn. 320, at 664 (Judge Easterbrook was critical of the plaintiff, noting that: "instead of econometric analysis, [the plaintiff] offered a potpourri of survey research and armchair economics").

322 440 F.Supp. 220, 228 (ED Penn. 1976).

323 Case IV/30.787, *Eurofix-Bauco/Hilti* [1988] OJ L65 19, para. 73; *Proctor & Gamble/VP Schickedanz*, *supra*, Ch. 3, fn. 240, paras. 53–60.

324 *Kimberly-Clark/Scott Paper*, *supra*, Ch. 3, fn. 240, paras. 172–177 (albeit featured only in the discussion of the parties' position on the markets already defined, the econometric analysis was already referenced at the market definition stage); Case IV/M.619, *Gencor/Lonrho* [1997] OJ L11 30, paras. 42, 43, 56–59; *Guinness/Grand Metropolitan*, *supra*, Ch. 4, fn. 154, paras. 23, 82; Case IV/M.1313, *Danish Crown/Vestjyske Slagterier* [2000] OJ L20 1, paras. 28, 29; Case IV/M.2187, *CVC/Lenzing* [2004] OJ L82 20, paras. 75–76; Case COMP/M.3796, *Omya/Huber* [2007] OJ L72 24, paras. 18, 22, 23.

In WTO dispute settlement proceedings, econometrics has been used in four cases to consider the issues of whether products are DCS or, as the Panels most recently extended the use of quantitative methods to Article III:2(1) of the GATT, whether they are "like." Although there is a paucity of case law, these cases are quite illuminating on how legal adjudicators treat econometrics. However, only the Panel Reports in *Japan – Alcoholic Beverages II* and *Chile – Alcoholic Beverages* provided a more detailed but still rudimentary account of the econometrics, in particular, the underlying regressions. While the part on quantitative analyses in *Thailand – Cigarettes* and *Philippines – Distilled Spirits* will therefore remain brief and descriptive in nature, it is worth presenting in greater detail the regressions in the two earlier cases in a first step in order to critically assess in a second step how the Panels dealt with them. Overall, given the limited extent of information about the econometric models in all Panel Reports, only a cautious assessment and commentary can be given on the results of the studies.

Econometrics were first used in Article III market definition in *Japan – Alcoholic Beverages II*, in which Japan submitted an econometric analysis of national household survey statistics.[325] The study accounted for seven independent variables: the prices of shochu, whisky, beer, wine, and sake; the household consumption expenditures; and a trend factor (that is, a simple temporal indicator, capturing all sorts of evolutions in time, such as inflation, technological progress, and growth) using annual data from the last twenty years. Sixteen regression equations were developed in order to explain the dependent variables of shochu and whisky consumption, respectively.[326] The results of the regression model were striking and curious. Using the volume of shochu consumed as the dependent variable, it found that shochu's OPE was positive and the CPE with respect to whisky was negative: the higher the price for shochu, the larger the shochu consumption and the higher the price for whisky, the lower the demand for shochu.[327] The finding is peculiar as it runs contrary to basic economic theory, which suggests an increase in price will lead to a decrease in demand. Moreover, it is surprising because it suggests whisky and shochu

[325] Panel Report, *Japan – Alcoholic Beverages II, supra*, Ch. 3, fn. 73, paras. 4.85–4.89, 4.167–4.171, 6.31.

[326] The Panel Report did not reproduce the regressions and regression results, for which reason this discussion relies entirely on the arguments by the parties which were reproduced in the Report.

[327] From the Panel Report it does not appear that Japan used log-linear transformation, which forms the coefficients of the price variables representing the actual OPE and CPE, *Japan – Alcoholic Beverages II, supra*, Ch. 3, fn. 73, para. 4.87.

are complements instead of substitutes. The t-statistics corresponding to the model's estimated coefficients were greater than 2 or less than –2, meaning that the model attached a high degree of statistical significance to these results.[328] Therefore, neither the impact of the whisky price on the shochu consumption, nor the impact of the shochu price on the whisky consumption was proven significant. Japan thus rejected the hypothesis that "the consumption of shochu is affected by the shochu price and the whisky price," and concluded that shochu and whisky were not competing with each other in the Japanese market.[329]

The second instance in which econometrics featured to ascertain whether products were DCS was in *Chile – Alcoholic Beverages*. Here, the EC presented the results of its study, the "1995 Gemines study," of a time series estimation using quarterly sales and price data for the period 1985–1992. This study was commissioned by the Chilean pisco industry and calculated a CPE coefficient for pisco and whisky of 0.26, which the Panel found low, but – as it could potentially be understated – sufficient as evidence of substitutability.[330] Yet no record is given of the model employed to calculate the elasticity.

However, the same Panel Report also contains the results of a regression analysis submitted by the respondent Chile. This study was conducted for the Chilean industry. Using a time series estimation based on data for fifteen years, it reported that shochu and whisky were in a competitive relationship. Table 1 printed in the Panel Report shows the output of the regression as a typical example of the output of a computer regression program:[331]

[328] Panel Report, *Japan – Alcoholic Beverages II*, *supra*, Ch. 3, fn. 73, para. 4.86.

[329] Panel Report, *Japan – Alcoholic Beverages II*, *supra*, Ch. 3, fn. 73, para. 4.87.

[330] The elasticity rate between pisco and whisky was 0.26 percent, indicating that if the price of whisky went up by 10 percent, the demand and sales volume of pisco would increase by 2.6 percent, Panel Report, *Chile – Alcoholic Beverages*, *supra*, Ch. 2, fn. 68, para. 7.65. Gemines did not find sufficient CPE with regard to wine and beer, *ibid.*, para. 4.219. In addition, the changes in consumption of pisco and whisky were calculated to take place under two scenarios of equal taxation, the first in which pisco and whisky would be taxed at 35 percent, and the second in which they would be taxed at 30 percent. Gemines concluded that sales of pisco would drop by 10.2 percent in the first scenario and by 8.6 percent in the second scenario, whereas sales of whisky would increase by 5.8 percent and 6.5 percent, respectively. It was highly contentious whether this accurately reflected or underestimated the increase in whisky consumption and what role that CPE and OPE should play in this estimation, *ibid.*, para. 4.221. From the record it is unclear whether only the results of the study or the study and its methodology were available to the Panel.

[331] Panel Report, *Chile – Alcoholic Beverages*, *supra*, Ch. 2, fn. 68, para. 4.223.

Cross-price elasticity of pisco with other spirits, wine, and beer

Results of the regression

Statistics of the regression

Multiple coefficient correlation	0.9878
Coefficient of determination R^2	0.9758
Adjusted R^2	0.9624
Typical error	0.0640
Observations	15

Analysis of the variable

		Sum of the squares	Average of the squares	*F*	Critical value of *F*
Regression	5	1.4895	0.2979	72.6767	5.32677E-07
Residual	9	0.0369	0.0041		
Total	14	1.5264			

Analysis of coefficients

	Coefficients	Typical error	*t*-Statistics	Probability	Inferior 95%	Superior 95%
Interception	3.5771	3.6554	0.9786	0.3534	-4.6920	11.8461
Variable X1 (income)	-0.0072	1.2109	-0.0059	0.9954	-2.7465	2.7321
Variable X2 (pisco price)	-1.3109	0.4574	-2.8661	0.0186	-2.3456	-0.2762
Variable X3 (whisky price)	0.1248	0.5158	0.2419	0.8143	-1.0421	1.2917
Variable X4 (wine price)	0.5963	0.4030	1.4796	0.1731	-0.3154	1.5079
Variable X5 (beer price)	0.3622	1.2132	0.2985	0.7721	-2.3823	3.1067

At the top, the table gives the values of the multiple correlation coefficient, the R^2, the adjusted R^2, the standard error of the regression ("typical error"), and the number of data points ("observations"). The table displays a time series regression, where the observations over time cover fifteen annual data points. Listed at the bottom are the constant term ("Interception"), the independent variables, the estimated regression coefficients, the standard errors of the regression coefficient ("Typical error"), the respective *t*-statistics, and the 95 percent confidence interval. In a simplified equation, the regression would be specified as follows:[332]

$$\text{Demand-pisco} = \alpha \text{ income} + \beta \text{ price pisco} + \gamma \text{ price whisky} + \delta \text{ price wine} + \delta \text{ price beer} + \varepsilon$$

Information on the CPE between whisky and pisco is reflected in the parameter γ for whisky price in a regression explaining the demand for pisco. The parameter – which should be positive if the products are DCS – has the estimated value of 0.1248. If the regression model were in a log–linear specification, the value of 0.1248 would indicate that a 1 percent price increase in whisky would lead to a 0.1248 percent increase in demand for pisco. Yet according to the specification of the regression, this value is not equal to the CPE and requires further computation.[333]

With the column on *t*-statistics, the above output also provides information on the significance of the relevant parameters, that is, whether the estimated parameters represent a statistically significant or purely coincidental relationship. As a common measure, a coefficient estimate is statistically significant at the 95 percent level, if the absolute value of the *t*-statistic is greater than 1.96 or smaller than –1.96. Here, for the estimated parameter of 0.1248, the *t*-statistic (0.2419) is even considerably lower than 1.65 in magnitude, the threshold of (only) a 90 percent confidence level, or 10 percent level of significance. To explain, the standard error is 0.5158 and the range of 2 SD about the coefficient in this case is the range from –0.9068 (= (0.1248 × 2) – 0.5158) to 1.564 (= (0.1248 × 2) + 0.5158). This range includes the value zero. The effect of the particular independent variable is therefore not significantly different from zero. For this reason, one cannot be confident that this variable does not have zero effect on the dependent variable. Hence, the estimated coefficient parameter cannot be considered significant at the 10 percent level. That is why the null hypothesis assertion that the price of whisky did not play a role in pisco quantity could not be rejected.[334] From this, it was inferred that the price of whisky was not statistically significant for the demand

[332] WTO World Trade Report, *Quantitative Economics in WTO Dispute Settlement*, p. 194.

[333] The Chilean regression analysis did not have a log functional form, Panel Report, *Chile – Alcoholic Beverages*, *supra*, Ch. 2, fn. 68, para. 4.230.

[334] The 1995 Gemines also found a positive but – according to a statement by Chile – non-significant elasticity coefficient at the 5 percent level, Panel Report, *Chile – Alcoholic Beverages*, *supra*, Ch. 2, fn. 68, para. 4.236. The Panel Report does not contain information on the actual *t*-statistics, for which reason it cannot be ascertained whether the estimated parameter may have been significant at the 5 percent or 10 percent level.

for pisco.[335] This interpretation was consistent with Chile's assertion that whisky was not a substitute for pisco. In fact, the only coefficient estimate that is statistically significant at the 90 percent level, that is, whose absolute value of the *t*-statistic is greater than 1.65 or less than –1.65, is the price of pisco, numbering –2,8661.

The regression statistics shows that the model passes an adjusted R^2 test. It indicates the percentage of the variation on the sales of pisco that can be explained by the variation in the variables included in the regression. As already explained, this "goodness of fit" is a measure of how well the regression results portray the real relationship. Here the adjusted R^2 value is 0.9624, and therefore close to unity. This means that the model, that is, the price of pisco, whisky, wine, and beer, together with the consumer income, explain 96 percent of the observed variation in the demand for pisco.

For reasons that will be explained below, the Panels, correctly, did not give credence to any of the above regression analyses. Instead, they relied on consumer surveys and thus gave preference to non-technical approximations over flawed econometrical estimations of CPE.

The Panels in *Thailand – Cigarettes* and *Philippines – Distilled Spirits* also considered econometric evidence in order to estimate substitutability, in particular, through the measurement of CPE. However, a critical review of the studies or of the Panels' assessment of this kind of evidence is nearly impossible as the Panel Reports did not lay out details of the studies. The following will therefore be limited to a description of the studies as provided by the Panel Reports.

In *Thailand – Cigarettes* the Panel addressed three econometric studies submitted by the Philippines in order to prove substitutability. The first, the "TNS Market Study," was on switching rates between certain imported and domestic cigarette brands, as well as CPE of demand. Regarding the estimation of elasticities, the Panel Report only described that the study had found that: "when the price of an imported brand increases by 10 per cent, purchases of that brand decreases by 27.6 per cent, whereas when the prices of two domestic brands also increase by 8.7 per cent at the same time, purchases of the same imported brand decreases by 19.5 per cent."[336]

[335] Note that this is a dangerous inference to be made since *not* rejecting the null hypothesis does not necessarily exclude the alternative hypothesis that there is a relationship, *supra*, fn. 276.

[336] Panel Report, *Thailand – Cigarettes*, *supra*, Introduction, fn. 23, para. 7.443.

The second study presented by the Philippines was submitted as evidence of "elasticity of substitution between domestic and imported cigarettes: if prices for imported cigarettes increase, purchases of domestic cigarettes would also increase."[337] The Panel did not reproduce the elasticity figures estimated by this study, although it considered them to be potentially spurious.[338]

Finally, the Philippines submitted an econometric study by an economics professor, Jamie de Melo, on CPE of demand between imported and domestic cigarettes in Thailand between 2007 and 2009. It measured an increase in demand for the domestic products in response to a rise in price for the imported products and, on the basis of a sufficient degree of CPE, came to the result that the products at issue were substitutable.[339] Although it was this last study that the Panel credited as conclusive on product "likeness" (apparently because it was the only one based on a multivariant model and, therefore, less likely to be corrupted by spurious correlation[340]), the Panel Report remained silent on the precise results, in particular, the precise estimation model and the CPE figures.

Philippines – Distilled Spirits also contained an econometric estimation of CPE submitted by the Philippines as evidence of the lack of substitution between the contested spirits. The study was a survey by Abrenica and Ducanes from the University of Philippines School of Economics. As the Panel explained, the survey "is based on a 'conjoint choice experiment,' 'using stated preferences of consumers in response to hypothetical adjustments in prices.'"[341] The Panel continued:

> According to this survey, a narrowing of price differentials between imported distilled spirits and domestic Philippine distilled spirits results in a small change in their respective market shares. The same survey also concludes that, if the excise tax is imposed at a uniform rate on all distilled spirits in the Philippines, the share of imported spirits would increase between 16 and 17 per cent (from a current level of 9.4 per cent to between 10.9 to 11 per cent). Likewise, if the excise tax is imposed at similar *ad valorem* rates on all distilled spirits in the Philippines, the share of imported spirits would increase to between 13 and 19 per cent (from a current level of 9.4 per cent to between 10.6 to 11.2 per cent). Finally, the survey concludes

[337] Panel Report, *Thailand – Cigarettes*, *supra*, Introduction, fn. 23, para. 7.445 (footnote omitted).

[338] Panel Report, *Thailand – Cigarettes*, *supra*, Introduction, fn. 23, para. 7.449.

[339] Panel Report, *Thailand – Cigarettes*, *supra*, Introduction, fn. 23, para. 7.446.

[340] See Panel Report, *Thailand – Cigarettes*, *supra*, Introduction, fn. 23, para. 7.450.

[341] Panel Report, *Philippines – Distilled Spirits*, *supra*, Introduction, fn. 23, para. 7.55 (internal footnote omitted).

> that if the excise tax is completely removed on all distilled spirits, the market share of imported spirits would increase by about 24.5 per cent (from a current level of 9.4 per cent to around 11.7 per cent).[342]

On this basis, the survey concluded that: "distilled spirits have low own- and cross-price elasticity in the Philippine market and that [therefore] 'local and imported brands [of spirits are] non-substitutable.'"[343] More precisely, the Panel reported that: "the Abrenica & Ducanes survey estimates cross-price elasticities for imported and domestic distilled spirits in the Philippines market to range between −0.01 and 0.07, which it considers 'low.'"[344]

As with the Euromonitor International survey, the Panel criticized this econometric survey on two counts. First, it relied on survey instead of historic data (and thus actual revealed preferences).[345] Second, it did not, as it is typical for a regression analysis, hold all influences constant except for one independent price variable and the dependent quantity variable. Instead, the study's estimation was "based on scenarios where the prices of imported and domestic distilled spirits [were] both said to change at the same time."[346] For this reason the Panel found that the study did not permit the isolation of the effect of an increase in the price of domestic spirits on the quantities of imported spirits consumed. It suggested that the price of the imported product should have been held constant, thus advocating the measurement of the imported CPE.[347]

Contrary to the intention of the Philippines as the proponent of the study, the Panel in the end even credited the study as evidencing substitutability between the products. This was based on the study's above outlined observations, which suggested that: "a simultaneous increase in the price of domestic spirits and decrease in the price of imported spirits, such as that which would result from an equalization in the respective level of the excise tax, could result in the substitution of the consumption of imported spirits in lieu of domestic spirits."[348] Why this proposition in the study was more convincing than the low CPE remained obscure

[342] Panel Report, *Philippines – Distilled Spirits* (internal footnotes omitted); see also *ibid.*, paras. 2.44, 7.52.

[343] Panel Report, *Philippines – Distilled Spirits*, Introduction, fn. 23, para. 2.44 (internal footnote omitted).

[344] Panel Report, *Philippines – Distilled Spirits*, Introduction, fn. 23, para. 7.55.

[345] Panel Report, *Philippines – Distilled Spirits*, Introduction, fn. 23, paras. 7.111–7.112.

[346] Panel Report, *Philippines – Distilled Spirits*, Introduction, fn. 23, para. 7.112.

[347] Panel Report, *Philippines – Distilled Spirits*, Introduction, fn. 23, para. 7.112.

[348] Panel Report, *Philippines – Distilled Spirits*, Introduction, fn. 23, para. 2.45 (internal footnote omitted); see *ibid.*, paras. 7.57, 7.115.

considering that the shortcomings noted by the Panel, in particular, the impossibility of attributing the increase in consumption of the imported product to the increase in price of the domestic product, apparently applied to the entire study.

On appeal by the Philippines, the Appellate Body held that the Panel was partially incorrect in its assessment that the study did not meet the *ceteris paribus* standard. Moreover, it considered that "the Panel could have better explained" why it credited the study's conclusion of low substitutability as evidence of a significant degree of substitutability.[349] Despite these shortcomings, the Appellate Body "consider[ed] that the weight and significance to be attributed to [the] estimated cross-price elasticity coefficient is a matter falling within the Panel's discretion as initial trier of facts."[350] In addition, it stated: "that not every error in the appreciation of a particular piece of evidence [would] rise to the level of failure by the Panel to comply with its duties under Article 11 of the DSU," that is, its obligation to make an objective assessment of the matter and the facts of the case.[351] Manifestly, the Appellate Body avoided going into the substantive evaluation of the quantitative evidence and its treatment by the Panel. It is evident that the Appellate Body ultimately granted *de facto* unrestricted discretion to the Panel when it came to the assessment and appraisal of quantitative evidence. Without the need for much of an explanation, the Panel is even free to turn the results of a quantitative study upside down. Contrary to the Panel and the Appellate Body, it is extremely doubtful that a low CPE coefficient should be taken as evidence of a significant degree of substitutability based on the pure speculative risk of understated demand elasticity. Even if one had ascertained the risk of the presence of understated CPE values, one may only disregard a low CPE coefficient as devoid of probative value. But reinterpreting shaky evidence of low substitutability into hard evidence of high substitutability appears somewhat of a (bad) magic trick.

B *Critical assessment of the econometric estimation of elasticities in Article III case law*

The method of multiple regression analysis has been outlined above as instrumental in econometrically estimating elasticities. Understanding

349 Appellate Body Report, *Philippines – Distilled Spirits*, *supra*, Ch. 2, fn. 44, para. 236.
350 Appellate Body Report, *Philippines – Distilled Spirits*, *supra*, Ch. 2, fn. 44, para. 236.
351 Appellate Body Report, *Philippines – Distilled Spirits*, *supra*, Ch. 2, fn. 44, para. 240 (internal citation omitted).

this technical process and the complications associated with it allows for discussion beyond the superficial of the role that econometrically estimated price elasticities have played under Article III market definition.

In *Japan – Alcoholic Beverages II* and *Chile – Alcoholic Beverages*, the respondents submitted regression models to disprove the existence of competitive relationships between imported spirits, especially imported whisky, and domestic shochu and pisco, respectively. The EC submitted the econometric computation of CPE in the 1995 Gemines study. Yet the Panels did not endorse any of this evidence. The interpretation of regression results and questions concerning the specification of regressions for the purpose of measuring CPE were subject to considerable controversy. Moreover, only Chile's regression was fully reproduced in the Panel Report. A critical assessment of Japan's regression is much harder. However, on the basis of what has been recounted in the arguments of the parties, one can cast substantial doubt as to the validity of the regression procedure.[352]

Moreover, *Thailand – Cigarettes* and *Philippines – Distilled Spirits* also invoked econometric evidence, although they did not disclose much on the underlying econometrics employed to come to the reported results. The following will therefore be almost entirely concerned with the first two Panel Reports.

(i) Variables included in the regressions

One problem with the regression analyses used in the two WTO cases relates to the models being specified incorrectly following the omission of an independent variable in a regression model – the omitted variable bias. If a relevant variable is omitted, this can lead to bias in the included coefficients and an incorrect elasticity estimate.[353] Failure to include an important independent variable that is positively correlated with the variable of interest may cause an included variable to be partially credited with an effect that is actually caused by the excluded variable. Therefore, the bias is to overstate the coefficient of included variables, as they in part "pick up" the correlated explanation that "belongs" to the omitted variable.[354]

[352] Panel Report, *Japan – Alcoholic Beverages II*, *supra*, Ch. 3, fn. 73, paras. 4.85 *et seq*.

[353] For an illustration of how an econometric model can lead to biased results in case of omitted variables see Bishop and Walker, *The Economics of EC Competition Law*, 3rd edn., paras. AN-015, AN-016.

[354] For illustration purposes, the sale of ice cream A may depend on its own price and those of substitutes B, C, and D, and on seasonality, that is, whether it is summer or not. The prices of all products are assumed to increase in summer and are therefore positively

As noted previously, completeness of the explicative model is a common concern for lawyers. For this reason, the issue of omitted variables is frequently raised in courtroom situations.[355] The US Supreme Court in *Bazemore* v. *Friday* declared that failure to include all potential and measurable independent variables is not *per se* detrimental. It goes to the regression's probative value, but not its admissibility.[356] It may be excluded as inadmissible (under the *Daubert* standard) only in cases where a patently influential variable has been omitted. This is a sensible approach, and is consistent with the scientific thinking referenced above, namely, that a regression analysis is not capable of including every conceivable relevant variable. In consequence, adjudicators should not reject suspect regression analysis for failure to include all potential variables. Rather, they should resolve the issue substantively and make a finding on its probative value.

The Panel in *Thailand – Cigarettes* rejected two econometric studies submitted by the Philippines, the "TNS Market Study" and the study on elasticity of substitution, as inconclusive. In contrast to the study by de Melo, it considered them not to control for all relevant variables, such as changes in consumers' income levels or in the conditions of distribution of a certain brand.[357] The Panel was concerned that the results may have been spurious, because such potentially influential factors may also have driven the switching patterns and elasticity estimates. Whether this concern was warranted cannot be ascertained, as the Panel Report did not provide information on the underlying econometric models.

A more detailed review can be undertaken with regard to the regression models in *Japan – Alcoholic Beverages* and *Chile – Alcoholic Beverages*. Here, the inclusion of certain independent variables provides information about which factors were presumed to influence the dependent variables. Japan's regression included seven independent variables, whereas the Chilean model took five independent variables into account. The inclusion of wine and beer in both regressions implies that these products

correlated with seasonality. On the right-hand side, the correctly specified regression equation would include, in addition to the price variables, a "dummy variable." It takes on a value of either 1 in the case of high season and 0 for off-peak season. If the model were to be estimated omitting the seasonal variable, the remaining independent variables would capture the omitted effect and their estimates would be biased.

355 For a prominent example, see *Proctor & Gamble/VP Schickedanz*, *supra*, Ch. 3, fn. 240, para. 55.

356 *Bazemore* v. *Friday*, 478 US 385, 399–400 (1986).

357 Panel Report, *Thailand – Cigarettes*, *supra*, Introduction, fn. 23, paras. 7.448–7.449, 7.451.

were expected to have some kind of relationship with pisco and shochu and were considered by the respondents as substitutes. Evidently, the good's own price is first and foremost determinative of the demand. The prices of pisco and shochu were therefore accounted for in the regressions. Consumers' income, however, is also an important factor, but was not included in Japan's regression, which was based only on the prices for different products and household consumption expenditures in explaining demand for shochu.

For WTO purposes, inspiration can be drawn from the US approach, whereby a regression is not expected to include all relevant variables, although the omission of variables that are considered influential may seriously compromise a regression's probative value. With regard to the regressions at hand, one can, in fact, think of a number of important omitted independent variables. The consumption of alcoholic beverages when considered over a long period of fifteen to twenty years may conceivably be influenced, among other things, by economic growth, population growth, fashion, or advertising campaigns. The market "shocks" due to tax and customs reforms could also be expected to have affected demand as well as the prices of the products.[358] Moreover, possible seasonal variations – such as hot summers – in the demand, are unaccounted for.[359] The omission of such seemingly important competing influences legitimately discredits the probative force of the regressions. At the same time, the contention that not all possible (even minor and remotely related) influences have been accounted for is too far reaching. Korea, for example, contended that whisky was consumed primarily in high-class hotel bars, night clubs, room saloons, and karaoke bars.[360] In contrast, diluted soju was drunk mainly in Korean restaurants, mobile street vendors, and inexpensive restaurants. Following this line of argument, it would go too far to demand inclusion, for example, of the prices of meals in different types of restaurant and entry prices at various premises in a regression explaining the relationship between the price of whisky and the sales of soju.[361]

Finally, an instance where elasticities were not estimated econometrically may still be informative on how the Panel fails to properly appraise evidence where important variables have been omitted. In *Japan – Alcoholic Beverages II*, the Panel considered as probative the ASI Study,

[358] *Supra*, fnn. 292 and 297.

[359] See Panel Report, *Japan – Alcoholic Beverages II*, *supra*, Ch. 3, fn. 73, para. 4.88.

[360] Panel Report, *Korea – Alcoholic Beverages*, *supra*, Introduction, fn. 36, paras. 5.247 *et seq*.

[361] WTO World Trade Report, *Quantitative Economics in WTO Dispute Settlement*, p. 195.

which evidenced a high degree of CPE between shochu and a number of other spirits. However, the Panel acknowledged Japan's argument that beer, sake, and wine were not accounted for.[362] The Panel assumed that the omission of these three influences did not alter the CPE estimates of the included products, and that, at best and irrelevant to the dispute, the CPE of the three omitted products would yield higher CPEs with shochu than the included ones. The Panel's reasoning is problematic, because if the elasticities had been properly estimated by way of regression analysis, the included variables would probably have picked up the effect of (correlated) omitted variables and the elasticity estimates of the included potential substitutes would have been inflated. Thus, the Panel's conclusion that such omitted variables were irrelevant would have been incorrect.

(ii) Data issues

It is important to realize that there are certain issues with data observations that have important repercussions on the value of the elasticity estimates. First, there is the number of observations. There is also the question of the appropriate time interval for measuring elasticities.

If there are too few observations, this is insufficient for statistical analysis. Only a higher number of observations ensures the precision of elasticity estimates. As a rule of thumb, a sample size of thirty or more observations provides stable statistics in a linear regression model with a rather small number of independent variables.[363] By contrast, the calculations in Japan's model contained twenty annual observations, while Chile's model contained fifteen. Such insufficient numbers of observations undermines the reliability of the regression results. This is what the Panel concluded in relation to Chile's study, for which reason it treated the study with caution.[364]

In terms of time intervals for the measurement of elasticities, one may distinguish the extremes of short-run versus long-run elasticity intervals.[365] The reason why the distinction is important is that the immediate

[362] Panel Report, *Japan – Alcoholic Beverages II*, *supra*, Ch. 3, fn. 73, para. 6.29.

[363] *Supra*, fn. 265.

[364] Panel Report, *Chile – Alcoholic Beverages*, *supra*, Ch. 2, fn. 68, para. 7.64.

[365] Whereas the time interval is an economic issue, there is the related but distinct statistical issue of the frequency of the observations. Short-run demand elasticities based on a high frequency of observations (e.g., weekly supermarket scanner data) risk overestimating elasticities in the longer run, in particular, in the case of short-term price promotions of consumer goods and the subsequent stocking-up effect; see Baker, "Contemporary Empirical Merger Analysis," pp. 352–355; Hosken *et al.*, *Demand System Estimation and its Application to Horizontal Merger Analysis*, p. 7.

response of customers to a price increase is likely to differ from the long-term response. This may be due, for example, to a significant stocking-up effect if further price increases are expected, or to the contractual preclusion of immediate switching. In the two regressions, the models were based on annual (that is, long-run) intervals. However, there was no reflection on the appropriateness of this particular time interval. The choice of the elasticity interval should be such that it relates best to the time period of concern. In antitrust law, it is accepted that the relevant time frame for a small but significant increase in price to be considered non-transitory is approximately one to two years. Since particularly in merger cases this is the time period with which enforcement authorities tend to be concerned regarding potential price increases, it is also generally recommended for measuring demand responses over a period of one to two years in order to measure price elasticities.[366] In relation to Article III of the GATT, the time period of concern is a long-run interval. The reason is that one may expect short-term elasticities to be lower than longer-run elasticities, and only the latter to reflect the true competitive relationship. The following reasons point to the conclusion that short-run elasticity estimates may underestimate the elasticity in the longer term. First, (ultimate) consumers may take some time to adjust their purchasing habits, in particular, if the discriminatory regime has entrenched consumer perceptions or if a new product is introduced to the domestic market. Second, on the premise that it is the wholesale level that is the most appropriate for measuring demand elasticities in the Article III context, short-term demand reactions may be impossible. Long-term contractual obligations are common at the wholesale level – this particularly being the case in international trade. Such long-term contractual obligations may prevent customers at the wholesale level from switching on short notice. Although it was most probably not an informed decision to use long-run intervals in Japan's and Chile's regressions covering periods of twenty and fifteen years, this approach is better than using short-run elasticity intervals.

(iii) Interpretation of the relevant parameters

At the most basic level, for coefficient estimates to provide evidence of a competitive relationship, it is necessary that they read as elasticities. As described above, this requires the correct specification with respect to the functional form. What appears to be a seemingly simple task has stirred much confusion in WTO cases. The Chilean regression analysis was a

[366] Nevo-Ilan, "Definition of the Relevant Market," p. 136.

simple linear regression not in log form, meaning that the parameters estimated did not represent elasticities.[367] Nonetheless, Chile interpreted those parameters as elasticities.[368] This raises doubts as to the level of proficiency with which statistical evidence is treated.

Once specified correctly, the interpretation of the coefficients as elasticities raises another interpretative issue which is often overlooked. As the parties and the Panels apparently failed to do in WTO disputes, it is important not only to look at the magnitude of the coefficients to make inferences on demand elasticities. Instead, one must also take note of the size of the confidence interval when dealing with coefficient estimates, particularly when dealing with elasticity estimates.[369] For instance, in Chile's regression, the confidence interval at the 95 percent level (that is, the interval within which there is a relative certainty that the true value of the coefficient lies) for the effect of whisky was rather large (–1.0421 to 1.2917). Thus, one could not be sure that the estimated coefficient was close to the true value of the coefficient, and therefore, the true value of the CPE. Theoretically, though unlikely,[370] the true value could even have assumed a value of –1.0421 or 1.2917, thus having the highest magnitude apart from the coefficient of the price of pisco. This confidence interval alone could have been, but was not in fact, reason for the Panel to conclude that a low elasticity of 0.26 would not be sufficient to exclude substitutability. A low demand elasticity for a product might not be sufficient to infer a distinct relevant market if the confidence band surrounding the elasticity estimate is sufficiently wide that, even assuming a correctly specified model, one could not rule out a higher true value of the parameter.

(iv) Reliability of regression results

The estimation of CPEs by multiple regression analysis is typically – and the regressions performed in *Japan – Alcoholic Beverages II* and *Chile – Alcoholic Beverages* actually were – based on the analysis of time series. In the analysis of time series, observations are taken from different moments in time, for instance, data on sales and prices over time. Hence, it is a type

[367] Panel Report, *Chile – Alcoholic Beverages, supra*, Ch. 2, fn. 68, para. 4.230.

[368] See *Chile – Alcoholic Beverages, supra*, Ch. 2, fn. 68, para. 4.225: "An elasticity of 0.125 means that a 10% increase in the price of whisky (for whatever reason), will increase pisco consumption by 1.25%. But this elasticity, being so low that these products cannot be considered close substitutes to each other."

[369] This is because it is the size, rather than the sign, of the coefficient that matters.

[370] Still, the coefficient estimate will have a central tendency within the confidence interval. So, it is more likely that the true coefficient is close to the estimated coefficient than that it is far away, even within the confidence interval.

of data important for market definition purposes. Yet it has certain characteristics which make it particularly susceptible to certain complications with regard to the interpretation and reliability of regression results.[371] These characteristics render regression analysis vulnerable to attack and provide a frequent legal "battle ground" in cases of econometric evidence, such as the regressions in the Japan and Chile cases.

A first issue in time series are outside influences (disturbances) not included in the regression that persist over several observations. The persistence in a sequence of such effects that are not included as independent variables, but that have an influence on the dependent variable, leads to so-called autocorrelation.[372] It may occur when omitted independent variables are correlated, such as the level of inflation from one year to the next. One can see why autocorrelation matters. Regression is a generalized form of averaging. Averaging is an excellent way to take care of random errors, provided that one is averaging over independent events. If the random disturbances from different observations are not mutually independent, however, then the averaging will not defuse the random effects.[373] The effect of autocorrelation is to overstate the precision of the regression result (a high R^2 may overestimate the "goodness of fit") and the results may lack sufficient confidence (the *t*-statistics may not accurately reflect the statistical significance of the estimated relationship). Although the coefficient estimate is correct, autocorrelation makes the regression results unreliable.

Another issue that raises concern for the validity of the regression models in time series is multicollinearity. This characterizes an approximate linear relationship between two or more of the independent variables.[374]

[371] More precisely, these problems relate to the violation of certain fundamental statistical "assumptions" on which OLS regression analysis is premised; see P. Kennedy, *A Guide to Econometrics*, pp. 41–42 (2008). The accuracy and reliability of the coefficient estimates and the validity of the measures for appraisal of the estimates, such as the standard errors, the *t*-statistics, and the confidence intervals, depend on these assumptions. They are all expressed as requirements on the error term. If these assumptions hold true, the regression model will provide the "best" estimations of the true parameters. The model will then generate the same results over different samples for reasons other than chance. Parameter estimates will be stable and robust ("parameter constancy"), as they have a certain set of "desirable properties" which all relate to the relationship between the probability distribution of the parameter estimates and their true values. They are then said to be "unbiased," "consistent," and "efficient."

[372] More precisely, it is the violation of the assumption that the error terms are independent of each other, i.e., that the error terms in different observations are not correlated.

[373] Fisher, "Multiple Regression in Legal Proceedings," p. 710.

[374] This is a violation of the statistical assumption that the independent variables are not (highly) correlated with each other.

It occurs when independent variables are highly correlated. In such situations, the assessment of their separate effects, crucial for parameter estimation, is difficult because they move in tandem and the estimation depends on the few instances in which they do not. One source for multicollinearity may be in instances when the correlated independent variables share a common time trend, for example, when prices are affected in a similar way by the rate of inflation. The parameter estimates are not precise, because their individual effects cannot be disentangled (individual coefficients will have large standard errors indicating that they are not statistically significant), while the R^2 may be high (as together the coefficients will be highly significant).

Autocorrelation and multicollinearity were superficially discussed in *Japan – Alcoholic Beverages II* and *Chile – Alcoholic Beverages*, and were among the grounds on which the Panels rejected the regression analyses.[375] In *Japan – Alcoholic Beverages II*, the Panel's justification was a brief – and solely theoretical – reference to the problems of autocorrelation and multicollinearity in time series analysis.[376] On neither issue did the Panel or the opponent to the regression substantiate their concerns. Rather, the Panel found it sufficient that: "in statistical studies of related markets involving time series data (as in the present study), one could normally expect to encounter all of [the above mentioned] problems."[377] The Panel's statement suggests that regression analysis is, by its very nature, inherently flawed and unreliable, for which reason it must be ignored. In *Chile – Alcoholic Beverages*, the analysis was attacked on grounds of multicollinearity. But again, the Panel Report remained vague and gave only unsubstantiated allegations of the analysis being flawed in this way. The only comment on the issue of multicollinearity was the vague statement by the EC that a hot summer may increase the consumption of all beverages.[378]

The Panels made no concrete finding on the presence of autocorrelation or multicollinearity. Indicative of the generic analysis, the Panel in

[375] For the former, see Panel Report, *Japan – Alcoholic Beverages II, supra*, Ch. 3, fn. 73, paras. 4.87 *et seq.*, 4.168 *et seq.*, 6.31. For the latter, see *ibid.*, paras. 4.88, 4.169, 6.31, and in Panel Report, *Chile – Alcoholic Beverages, supra*, Ch. 2, fn. 68, paras. 4.70, 4.231, 4.235.

[376] Panel Report, *Japan – Alcoholic Beverages II, supra*, Ch. 3, fn. 73, para. 6.31.

[377] Panel Report, *Japan – Alcoholic Beverages II, supra*, Ch. 3, fn. 73, para. 6.31.

[378] Panel Report, *Chile – Alcoholic Beverages, supra*, Ch. 2, fn. 68, para. 4.88. The only indication in the Panel Report of the actual presence of such problems was that: "according to the Community expert, the data set used for the Japanese statistical analysis is fraught with all three problems, which would make it difficult to prove any statistical connection between shochu and whisky consumption."

Japan – Alcoholic Beverages II considered in purely abstract terms the possibility that underlying trends in time series data might affect the apparent relationship between the variables examined, causing the regression model to be mis-specified.[379] It is true that, theoretically, demand for a product may, for example, change due to fashion, economic growth, population growth, etc. If influential enough on demand, these influences would make it difficult to statistically separate the influence of price movements from that of trends.[380] With regard to the problem of multicollinearity, it was therefore argued that, where different variables follow a common trend, a naive statistical analysis could "prove" that the developments of the different variables are due to a causal relationship.[381]

In fact, beyond mere conjecture, the Japanese model actually appeared to exhibit signs of mis-specification. Japan's regression model concluded with a high degree of statistical robustness: that consumers react to an increase in the price of shochu by increased demand for shochu and decreased demand for whisky. It thus displayed a positive OPE for shochu and a negative CPE for shochu with respect to whisky. As already stated, this is a strikingly counterintuitive result contrary to the fundamental tenets of microeconomic theory. It is also a strong indication that the regression methodology is flawed, by not taking into account a common underlying trend. Incorrectly linking an increase in the consumption of shochu to its concurrent price rise (perhaps due to inflation), the regression suggests that an increase in the price of shochu leads to an increase in its demand. The reason for the mis-specification could be that Japan's regression was based on real instead of nominal prices. Over the long period of twenty years covered by the study, the effect of inflation on prices is significant. That is why nominal prices should be revalued to real (deflated) terms by taking into account the effect of inflation.[382] And, as an opponent submitted, the real prices of shochu in fact fell during

[379] Panel Report, *Japan – Alcoholic Beverages II*, *supra*, Ch. 3, fn. 73, paras. 4.168 *et seq.*, 6.31.

[380] Either there is a persistent trend in an omitted influence, which would cause autocorrelation, or there is a common trend among included independent variables causing multicollinearity.

[381] See *Japan – Alcoholic Beverages II*, *supra*, Ch. 3, fn. 73, para. 4.168. The EC argued that one could basically show anything with a falsely interpreted time series analysis, including, e.g., that the cucumber production in France is causally related to shochu consumption in Japan, which only requires that both variables follow the same common trend by coincidence.

[382] This may not be necessary if prices are homogeneous, i.e., if all prices rise by the same factor so that using nominal or real prices will give the same elasticity estimates.

this period after taking into account the average inflation rate – which would explain the increase in consumption more effectively.[383] However, the Panel did not actually make any such findings.

In *Chile – Alcoholic Beverages*, Chile itself "agreed that the data contains some insolvable problems (namely multicollinearity)."[384] Again, for lack of substantiation, it can only be speculated that the three independent price variables may have been correlated due to a common time trend, such as inflation. An indication for multicollinearity may be found in the regression's high adjusted R^2 value. As discussed, it is usually – and sometimes erroneously – assumed that the higher the R^2, the better the model, because a model which explains more of the variation in the dependent variable is generally preferred to one that explains less. In this case, at first glance, the high adjusted R^2 ratio, indicating that the variables together account for 96 percent of observed variations in the demand for pisco, implies that the regression is properly specified. However, the high R^2 coupled with the low *t*-statistics may point to multicollinearity in the regression (rather than autocorrelation, where *t*-statistics tend to be high). Thus, the Panel not only "treated [the regression study] with caution,"[385] but actually found – contrary to the regression results – the existence of a competitive relationship between pisco and whisky.

(v) Transparency and accountability

As observed in antitrust law, it is common to make available econometric evidence to the opposing party and to the adjudicators in a piecemeal fashion, and to a substantial degree through second-hand accounts only.[386] There is also ample proof to this effect in *Japan – Alcoholic Beverages* and *Chile – Alcoholic Beverages*. Therefore, an important problem in the use of econometric evidence is the lack of transparency. It is primarily a deficiency on the part of the proponent of the regression results. But it is also an issue on the part of the decision makers when appraising econometric evidence. The issue of transparency cannot be overestimated. It determines the degree of accountability of the proponent or the decision maker when using quantitative analysis. In particular, complete submission of the requisite information permits the assessment of the probative value of the evidence by the adjudicator and the opponent. Moreover, publication

383 *Japan – Alcoholic Beverages II*, *supra*, Ch. 3, fn. 73, para. 4.168.

384 Panel Report, *Chile – Alcoholic Beverages*, *supra*, Ch. 2, fn. 68, para. 4.235.

385 Panel Report, *Chile – Alcoholic Beverages*, *supra*, Ch. 2, fn. 68, para. 7.64.

386 Werden, "A Perspective on the Use of Econometrics in Merger Investigations and Litigation," *Antitrust*, 16 (2002), 55, 56.

of the economic evidence and testimony ensures peer review and may deter experts from giving biased testimony.

As a matter of process, only the results of a regression analysis are usually communicated to the adjudicator and the opposing party, while the underlying data, the methodological choices, and specifications often remain undisclosed. Without this information, the adjudicator and the opposing side are unable to fully understand, test, and critically assess the model and its workings. This may lead adjudicators to reject valid econometric evidence or, alternatively, to rely on econometric evidence that is flawed. For this reason, there is widespread consensus that econometric evidence must be laid bare.[387] The legal process must ensure that the data and its sources, the methods for collecting and analyzing the data, and the model set-up and reasoning on which the conclusions rely are fully disclosed. Where, as argued above, the opposing party bears the burden of demonstrating the impact of an alleged flaw in the proponent's model, disclosure is imperative in order for a proper analysis capable of supporting the opponent's claim.

With regard to the regressions at issue in the WTO proceedings discussed above, there were no measures reported to have been taken by the parties who presented the regressions to ensure transparency and accountability. On the contrary, the results of the 1996 Gemines study were introduced as evidence in *Chile – Alcoholic Beverages*, but the study itself was not made available by Chile even upon request by the Panel. By restricting access to the data and the study, the probative value of the elasticity estimates could not be ascertained. Withholding this relevant evidence seriously undermined procedural fairness and the efficiency of the dispute settlement procedure.[388]

Recent WTO case law further confirms the persistence of the transparency issue. In the different context of the SCM Agreement, Brazil in *United States – Subsidies on Upland Cotton* relied on an econometric simulation model which was not made available in its submission.[389]

[387] See, e.g., Scheffman, *Best Practices for Data, and Economics and Financial Analyses in Antitrust Investigations*, pp. 3–4 (2002), available at: www.ftc.gov/speeches/scheffman.shtm; Werden, "The Admissibility of Expert Economic Testimony in Antitrust Cases," in ABA Section of Antitrust Law, *Issues in Competition Law and Policy*, pp. 802, 807–808 (2007). For procedures to enhance statistical testimony see Kaye and Freedman, "Reference Guide on Statistics," in Federal Judicial Center, *Reference Manual on Scientific Evidence*, pp. 83, 88 *et seq.* (2000), available at: www.fjc.gov/public/pdf.nsf/lookup/sciman00.pdf/$file/sciman00.pdf.

[388] Panel Report, *Chile – Alcoholic Beverages*, *supra*, Ch. 2, fn. 68, fn. 390.

[389] Panel Report, *United States – Subsidies on Upland Cotton*, *supra*, Introduction, fn. 19, para. 7.1206.

Consequently, neither the Panel nor the opponent were able to fully understand and evaluate the model. As the Panel explicitly noted, this impaired procedural fairness and the weight of the evidence. In *US – Upland Cotton (Article 21.5 of the DSU)*, Brazil relied on an econometric simulation model again.[390] Yet this time Brazil fully disclosed the model, prompting the Panel to expressly "note the transparency of the model."[391] This permitted the parties to take the opportunity to discuss the model in their submissions and rebuttal submissions, and allowed the Panel to provide a detailed discussion of the model in its Report.

Mandatory disclosure rules could solve the transparency problem. In the case of the United States, Rule 26(a)(2) of the Federal Rules of Civil Procedure (hereinafter FRCP) mandates broad discovery of data and the entire model in cases where econometrics is introduced by a testifying expert.[392] In contrast, WTO procedure does not provide for any transparency or discovery rules. Therefore, in the absence of mandatory disclosure rules in the WTO, other solutions would need to be considered to increase transparency. In scholarship and in the *Commission Best Practices for Economic Evidence*, it has been recommended that econometric evidence should not be permitted unless disclosure has been made.[393] It is in fact using this line of thinking that a US District Court declared that the initial burden of production on the proponent of econometric evidence requires the provision of sufficient details to enable the court to perform an initial review of the study's methodology.[394] However, this does not seem to be the approach used by WTO adjudicators. Although the Panel in *United*

[390] Panel Report, *United States – Subsidies on Upland Cotton – Recourse to Article 21.5 of the DSU by Brazil*, WT/DS267/R, adopted June 20, 2008, paras. 10.197–10.222.

[391] Panel Report, *United States – Subsidies on Upland Cotton – Recourse to Article 21.5 of the DSU by Brazil*, para. 10.198 fn. 491: "The full set of equations is explicitly written out and an electronic version of the simulation model, in the form of an Excel spreadsheet, has been provided to the United States and to the Panel. This gives all parties to the dispute and the Panel full access to the model, its assumptions and the results. In fact, the United States has used the Excel spreadsheet provided by Brazil to conduct alternative simulations using a different set of parameter assumptions."

[392] For case law references, see ABA Section of Antitrust Law, *Antitrust Evidence Handbook*, p. 184 (2002). By contrast, a non-testifying expert is afforded substantial protection from discovery: Rule 26(b)(4)(B) of the FRCP.

[393] Harkrider, *The Use of Econometrics in Antitrust Analysis*, p. 11 (u.d.), available at: www.avhlaw.com/assets/attachments.29.pdf; *Commission Best Practices for Economic Evidence*, para. 44.

[394] *In re Polypropylene Carpet Antitrust Litig.* (1997), *supra*, fn. 106, at 26. See also *FTC v. Swedish Match North America*, *supra*, fn. 281, at 169–170 as an example of a court unwilling to accept as credible evidence the econometric estimation of demand elasticities based on undisclosed (and therefore untested) modeling.

States – Subsidies on Upland Cotton did "not [rely] upon the quantitative results" of the undisclosed econometric study, it nevertheless took "the analyses in question into account where relevant" and "attributed to them the evidentiary weight [it] deemed appropriate."[395] The undisclosed evidence does not appear to have been considered in terms of its primary quantitative results, although it appeared to play a role in the decision-making process despite its probative weight being left open. This does not represent a strong signal to compel full and timely disclosure by parties in future WTO cases.

On the side of the decision-makers, transparency should also be ensured by including a detailed report on the econometric model and the technical review in the decision. For example, in EU merger decisions by the European Commission there has been an evolution from no information on the underlying econometrics, to a limited description thereof.[396] Most recently, there has even been a growing practice of providing a detailed and extensive description and discussion of the data and models submitted, and their appraisal by the parties and the European Commission.[397]

Panel Reports give a mixed impression of how transparency has been handled by the adjudicators. In cases including Panel-appointed expert testimony, the Reports commonly include summaries of the Panel's questions to the experts, the experts' written responses thereto, a transcript of the joint meeting of the Panel with the experts and parties, and, at times, extend to the reproduction of the comments by the parties on the replies by the experts and a description of the expert selection process.[398] In terms of party-proffered expert testimony, as was the case for Article III market

[395] Panel Report, *United States – Subsidies on Upland Cotton*, *supra*, Introduction, fn. 19, paras. 7.1205, 7.1209.

[396] See, e.g., *Kimberly-Clark/Scott Paper*, *supra*, Ch. 3, fn. 240, paras. 172–177; *Guinness/Grand Metropolitan*, *supra*, Ch. 4, fn. 154, paras. 23, 82, 126.

[397] See the Annexes to the decisions in *Arjowiggins/M-real Zanders Reflex*, *supra*, Ch. 4, fn. 128, and *Arsenal/DSP*, *supra*, Ch. 4, fn. 128. Other recent instances of exemplary transparency in the appraisal of regression analysis, though not in the context of market definition, are Case COMP/M.2416, *Tetra Laval/Sidel* [2004] OJ L43 13, paras. 351–358 and *Ryanair/Aer Lingus*, *supra*, Ch. 4, fn. 128, Annex IV.

[398] See Panel Report, *EC – Hormones (Canada)*, *supra*, fn. 35, paras. VI.11–VI.241, VI.10–VI.240 and the Annex; Panel Report, *EC – Hormones (US)*, *supra*, fn. 35, paras. VI.11–VI.241, VI.10–VI.240 and the Annex; Panel Report, *Japan – Apples*, *supra*, fn. 35, paras. 6.5–6.194 and Annex 3; Panel Report, *Japan – Apples (Article 21.5 of the DSU)*, *supra*, fn. 35, paras. 6.6–6.163 and Annex 3; Panel Report, *EC – Biotech*, *supra*, fn. 35, Annexes H, I, J; Panel Report, *US – Continued Suspension (Hormones)*, *supra*, fn. 35, paras. 7.76–7.99 and Annexes D, F, and G; Panel Report, *Canada – Continued Suspension (Hormones)*, *supra*, fn. 35, paras. 7.74–7.96 and Annexes D, F, and G.

definition, the Panel Reports were less transparent. With the exception of Chile's regression, the Panel Reports failed to fully report and explain the model specifications, the variables included, the standard errors, and significance levels. The underlying data was not explained at all. On the basis of such information, the results of the models cannot be fully evaluated, nor can their robustness and validity be verified. Even worse, the most recent Panel Reports in *Thailand – Cigarettes* and *Philippines – Distilled Spirits* provided so little information on the econometric evidence submitted by the parties, and partly relied upon by the Panels, that an informed review and discussion is rendered practically impossible. It is open to question whether the Panels attempted to prevent any critical review of their treatment of quantitative evidence. Of concern for future cases, parties may be discouraged from employing (costly) quantitative evidence due to an inability to divine from the case law what Panels expect from a well-specified econometric model and what evidentiary weight they attribute to it. The Appellate Body's holding in *Philippines – Distilled Spirits* may even exacerbate the situation. The Panel has been granted so much discretion in dealing with quantitative evidence that it is impossible to predict what kind of conclusions the Panel may draw from this kind of evidence.[399]

6 Advantages and disadvantages of quantitative evidence

The foregoing discussion of the practical experience with econometrics in WTO case law provides the basis to discuss the advantages and disadvantages of econometric evidence.

A Advantages of quantitative evidence

Econometric analysis, in particular, multiple regression analysis, has been shown to be a useful tool for the direct estimation of CPEs of demand. First, it allows for quantification where the precise value of a CPE estimate is important. It not only yields information on the presence of substitution in general, it also makes it possible to assign a number and thus to give a measure of the size of substitution between products.

Second, multiple regression analysis provides a comprehensive view of the totality of important influences, while accounting for confounding factors. For the purposes of estimating CPE in the market definition context, this is a valuable tool because it is unlikely that the demand for

[399] See *supra*, fn. 350.

one product is solely dependent on the price of any other particular good. Multiple regression analysis allows for the filtering out of other influences that affect demand of the product of interest. Thus, multiple linkages can be accounted for and more robust inferences can be made.

Third, multiple regression analysis has the advantage of providing measures to test the accuracy and reliability of its results. It thus gives some degree of certainty that the measured relationship exists. Specifically, it is possible to determine whether an observed relationship between two variables, such as demand for one product and the price for another, is a (statistically) significant relationship as opposed to a coincidental one. This is especially valuable in litigation where the adjudicator has to appraise the probative value of evidence. The indication that a relationship is not due to pure chance, however, does not permit one to make an inference on the economic significance of this relationship.

Against the background of these advantages associated with the econometric estimation of CPE, one can also better assess the merits of several objections to the use of CPE. Three shall be presented briefly. They have been put forward in the context of antitrust law, but can be generalized to apply to the use of CPE under Article III of the GATT as well.

First, a recurring criticism, especially in European antitrust literature, against the use of CPE is that it concentrates solely on price competition and entirely neglects non-price competition.[400] It is argued by scholars that competition driven by non-price factors, for instance, advertisement campaigns, marketing, quality, service, etc., would be excluded from the analysis when relying on CPE. This criticism views CPE as limited to price as the sole comparator, while disregarding all other means by which firms may influence demand.

A second strand of criticism correctly observes that the determination of CPE requires that the change in sales volume be traceable directly and unambiguously to the change in price. However, according to some legal commentators, it is impossible to identify and separate out all competitive influences on demand.[401] Thus, they assert that it is impossible to appraise separately the influence of interest and the change in price.

[400] Cárdenas, *Rolle, Kriterien und Methodik der kartellrechtlichen Marktabgrenzung*, p. 42; Brinker, "Praktische Probleme der Marktabgrenzung aus rechtlicher Sicht," p. 44; Müller, *Abschied vom Bedarfsmarktkonzept bei der Marktabgrenzung?* p. 126; Füller, "Market Definition," in Hirsch *et al.* (eds.), *Competition Law: European Community Practice and Procedure*, para. 1-11-017 (2008).

[401] Schmidt, "Relevanter Markt, Marktbeherrschung und Missbrauch in § 22 GWB und Art. 86 EWGV," *Wirtschaft und Wettbewerb*, (1965), 451, 456; Leberl, *Zur Zeitkomponente im*

As a third point, some commentators argue against the use of CPE, because its measurement requires an arbitrary pre-selection of products for which CPEs are then calculated.[402] This is seen as a problem in antitrust market definition, because there may be a multitude of products that need to be compared in the assessment of an antitrust market. Although there are only the two specific products in the trade dispute that need to be compared, this criticism also seems to apply to Article III market definition. Any arbitrary pre-selection among the broader array of potential substitutes may cause an omitted variable bias in the econometric estimation of CPE (and the associated risk of crediting included variables with the effect of correlated omitted variables).

The first criticism would be true if price were the sole comparator for the estimation of CPE, which is the case when comparing absolute prices. However, such criticism misunderstands CPE. CPE looks at the response to a price increase and does not take price in itself as the *tertium comparationis*. As already noted with regard to the same erroneous objection to the SSNIP test, the decision of a consumer to switch to a different product in the event of a price increase, as measured by the CPE, incorporates all price and non-price considerations relevant to the consumer.[403] In his decision, the consumer weighs and balances all relevant factors. For example, in some instances a price increase may have a negligible impact on a consumer's purchasing decision if he values the perceived additional quality of a branded product more than a cheaper non-branded product. In this way, CPE can actually be thought of not as a new distinct criterion separate from the *Border Tax* list, but as a quantitative measure that incorporates physical characteristics, end-uses, and CTH judged from the consumer perspective.[404]

More importantly with regard to the role of econometrics, the three criticisms highlight the fundamental lack of knowledge by most legal professionals of how CPE estimates are arrived at when calculated properly using econometrics. They exemplify why it is essential for lawyers who deal with issues of market definition to grasp – at least at a basic

Marktbegriff des GWB, pp. 35–36 (1988); Müller, *Abschied vom Bedarfsmarktkonzept bei der Marktabgrenzung?* pp. 129–130.

402 Möschel, "Missbrauch einer Marktbeherrschenden Stellung," in Immenga and Mestmäcker (eds.), *Wettbewerbsrecht GWB: Kommentar zum Deutschen Kartellrecht*, § 19, para. 33 (2007); Füller, "Market Definition," para. 1-11-016.

403 *Supra*, fn. 356.

404 Bhala, *Modern GATT Law*, para. 1-049; Goco, "Non-Discrimination, 'Likeness,' and Market Definition in World Trade Organization Jurisprudence," p. 332; Mavroidis, *Trade in Goods*, p. 220.

level – the econometric methods underlying CPE estimation. The above treatment of regression analysis underscores that the measurement of CPE does not only account for the price element as a competitive influence. As has been noted to the contrary, a multitude of independent (also non-price) variables may be included in the model as competing influences on the dependent variable. Moreover, their individual competitive significance can be inferred from the specific parameter estimates. Thus, multiple regression analysis allows for not only the assessment of simultaneous influences, but also the separating out of their individual effects on demand.

The criticism that there is an arbitrary pre-selection of potential substitutes in the estimation of CPE also reflects the criticism alluded to earlier that it is impossible to account for all potentially relevant influences in an explicative model. However, it also reveals the lack of understanding for how elasticities are in fact econometrically estimated. As discussed, a regression analysis cannot include all remotely influential independent variables in order to ensure that the coefficients of the included variables are of probative value. Thus, there is a pre-selection of independent variables, which is conducted in an informed, non-arbitrary manner. A properly conducted regression analysis actually avoids omitting a key independent variable and chooses the most relevant independent variables. There are common procedures and tests in order to find the relevant independent variables.[405] Furthermore, full disclosure should normally be made on the selection process, rendering the estimation process accountable and transparent.

To conclude, it is also noteworthy that the criticism of CPE is prevalent only in Europe, where econometrics still plays a less prominent role in legal proceedings and analysis, and where knowledge of econometrics is not widespread in legal circles. The concerns among the legal profession regarding the use of CPE are to a large extent founded on a lack of knowledge of the underlying econometrics. It is only with a sufficient understanding of econometrics that one can intelligibly discuss the merits and limitations of the use of CPE for market definition purposes in either antitrust or GATT law.

[405] See Finkelstein and Levin, *Statistics for Lawyers*, para. 13.5 for techniques in the selection of independent variables. One approach to identify the omission of a relevant variable is to inquire whether the inclusion of an independent variable improves the explanatory power of the model (e.g., whether the adjusted R^2 remains the same), and whether the coefficient on this variable is statistically and/or economically significant.

B Disadvantages of quantitative evidence

Nevertheless, there are legitimate concerns about the use of quantitative methods. The following will cast light on several important complications and limitations that play a role in legal decision making.

(i) Difficulties in the appraisal of quantitative evidence

To legally trained adjudicators, complex econometric evidence can all too often seem like a "black box." They may react to such evidence either with fascination or skepticism. As a result, they may fail to assign the appropriate weight to the quantitative evidence.

On the one hand, adjudicators may place too much weight on quantitative analysis. Statistical software may be perceived by non-statisticians as an example of *deus ex machina*. Such software is fed with lengthy columns of numbers, and once the button is pressed, it produces computer-generated, numerical answers seemingly invested with scientific and mathematical accuracy. The appearance of objectivity and precision that this imparts on the process can give a spurious and misleading sense of certainty.[406]

But it should not hide the fact that precision is an illusion, because uncertainty as to the model's explanatory and predictive power may persist. Moreover, the numerical values may not be as "objective" as they purport to be. The general expectation is that the analysis of quantitative evidence is more "objective" than what has been described as subjective and arbitrary conclusions drawn from traditional, qualitative models of analysis. In fact, a review of the same set of qualitative evidence can easily lead to opposite conclusions, while quantitative measures are more easily comparable and the results of which are reproducible by other analysts. At the same time, although "scientifically objective," quantitative evidence may not be perceived to be "legally objective."[407] While quantitative evidence may be the result of a proper (that is, independent, impartial, and neutral) scientific truth-seeking process, it may not reach the ultimate truth. Even in the absence of malpractice, quantitative evidence is influenced by normative choices and assumptions. Subjectivity factors into the making of statistical inferences, because the quantitative model requires the expert to make (ideally informed and scientifically sound) choices on issues such as the selection of the data set and the included variables, the

406 Tribe, "Trial by Mathematics: Precision and Ritual in the Legal Process," *Harvard Law Review*, 84 (1971), 1329–1393.

407 See on this difference, *supra*, fn. 54.

model specification to be used, and the methodology to be applied. A specific quantitative model is only one among a number of alternatives to address a certain problem. The results of a specific model may be sensitive to changes in any of the choices and assumptions. Therefore, more than one econometrically "true" or "objective" answer may exist.

Even if there is not a single clear-cut answer provided by econometrics, the results are not *per se* arbitrary as long as the procedure is scientifically sound (that is, "scientifically objective"). But the scope for presenting misleading results, whether by neglect or by design, is considerable. There is room for abuse and what has been termed "data mining," that is, when an unscrupulous expert tries numerous models with different specifications until the desired results appear.[408] This is highly unscientific because one is almost always able to find an unrepresentative sample that is capable of buttressing the desired position. An advocate will naturally be inclined to present only those results that support the client's position and leave numerous less impressive results hidden. Econometric evidence can become specifically engineered evidence. Thus, quantitative evidence may also be subject to the risk of gerrymandering, already identified for qualitative evidence.[409]

On the other hand, when faced with complex economic evidence, adjudicators can be too quick to dismiss or diminish the weight of evidence in the face of criticism. It is often very easy to criticize complex economic work, as one can almost always point to some flaw that shows that the analysis falls short of "perfection." In the face of this, decision-makers may be tempted to dismiss an imperfect analysis altogether. The observations above on the robustness of the regression analyses employed in *Japan – Alcoholic Beverages II* and *Chile – Alcoholic Beverages* provide appropriate examples.

If the Panels in those cases had made a substantive assessment of the regression models (as was attempted above with considerations as to why autocorrelation and multicollinearity could in fact have been present in the given models), they likely would have revealed that the regression results were tainted by mis-specification, in particular, due to autocorrelation and/or multicollinearity. For this reason, it seems correct that the Panels treated the regressions with caution and ultimately did not rely on

408 Office of Fair Trading, *Quantitative Techniques in Competition Analysis*, para. 18.11 (1999), available at: www.oft.gov.uk/shared_oft/reports/comp_policy/oft266.pdf.

409 The requirement proposed above to make available more underlying data on the models submitted as evidence may attenuate the risk of experts only exploiting data that is supportive of their clients' position.

their results. In the end, the Panels in those instances ascribed the correct weight to the evidence.

However, the concern is that the presence of these (potentially fatal) complications was not positively ascertained. As described, the mere existence of potential complications, here the general textbook problems of autocorrelation and multicollinearity encountered in regression analysis of time series data, appeared sufficient for the Panels to reject econometric evidence altogether. No effort was made to ascertain whether these potential flaws would in fact render obsolete the probative value of the evidence at hand.

Moreover, the econometric models may have been discarded not only for their lack of perfection (in fact, they were far from perfection), but also for another reason. Certain routine statistical robustness tests that can diagnose the violation of the underlying statistical assumptions which cause autocorrelation and multicollinearity had apparently not been conducted – or remained insufficient.[410] In the United States, several District Courts have suggested that the proponents bear the burden of demonstrating "that the assumptions necessary for the [regression] model's use [have] been satisfied."[411] Under the modern doctrine, failure to test whether the assumptions hold may be enough to fail the *Daubert* admissibility test.[412] Similarly, the *Commission Best Practices for Economic Evidence* also require that economic submissions be accompanied by a thorough robustness analysis.[413]

But the presence of (potential) complications, and therefore the lack of perfection, as well as the absence of robustness tests should not *per se* be fatal to econometric evidence.[414] There is no such thing as a perfect and flawless econometric model. This goes back to the general and pervasive

410 Apparently, Japan had applied certain well-established techniques to make the appropriate adjustments for autocorrelation, Panel Report, *Japan – Alcoholic Beverages II*, *supra*, Ch. 3, fn. 73, para. 4.87. Yet the Panel was convinced by the opponent's assertion that autocorrelation remained unaccounted for, *ibid.*, para. 6.31.

411 *Sobel* v. *Yeshiva University*, 566 F.Supp. 1166, 1182 (SDNY 1983). See also *Carroll* v *Sears, Roebuck & Co.*, 514 F.Supp. 788, 801 (WD La. 1981): "The burden is upon plaintiffs to establish a *prima facie* case by competent proof; this they cannot do by making a self-serving assumption which underlies their statistical presentation and for which no competent proof was adduced"; *Penk* v. *Oregon State Bd of Higher Educ.*, 1985 US Dist. LEXIS 22624, at § 170 (D Or. 1985): "As the party offering regression models as proof and as the party with the ultimate burden or persuasion, plaintiffs bear the burden … of demonstrating that the assumptions necessary for the model's use have been satisfied."

412 See Harkrider, *The Use of Econometrics in Antitrust Analysis*, p. 8.

413 *Commission Best Practices for Economic Evidence*, para. 37.

414 Neven and de la Mano, *Economics at DG Competition, 2009–2010*, para. 24 (2010), available at: http://antitrustlair.files.wordpress.com/2010/11/neven-de-la-mano-20101.pdf.

theme that the legal concern for completeness clashes with the statistical/scientific necessity for imperfection. All econometric models involve simplifying assumptions and/or are based on imperfect data.[415] However, in most circumstances, those simplifications and imperfections do not have a material impact on the results of the analysis. Imperfect evidence may still provide some valuable information and its probative value can still be assessed. For instance, it may be that a particular analysis can be criticized in terms of its accuracy.[416] However, it is often possible to evaluate that inaccuracy, for example, by providing confidence intervals around an estimate. It may also be that an inaccurate answer is sufficient for the analysis to provide valuable evidence. For example, a particular coefficient estimate may be imprecise. However, it may be known that the estimate is over- or underestimated. This can be enough to give probative force to the result. If, for example, a CPE estimate is too large, though it is insufficient in size to reach a critical value to make a finding of substitution, the bias does not invalidate the conclusion that substitution does not exist.

This is also why robustness testing should be encouraged, but too strict an application of this requirement may lead to the incorrect dismissal of imperfect, yet otherwise meaningful and helpful, econometric submissions. At least, the parties must be allowed to discard robustness tests when they are practically impossible, for example, in situations where alternative modeling approaches are not feasible given the data or the time available.

Consequently, "lack of unachievable perfection should not prevent an economic study from being given weight."[417] As the US Court of Appeals for the Sixth Circuit declared: "the conclusion that flaws in the data deprived it of any probative value is itself flawed."[418] Similarly, the *Commission Best Practices for Economic Evidence* recognize that while an economic analysis may contain imperfections, this does not necessarily mean that it should be accorded no evidentiary value. They state that "failure to observe and validate all key assumptions or deficiencies in the data should not prevent an economic analysis to be given weight, though caution must be exercised before relying on its conclusions."[419]

[415] Neven and de la Mano, *Economics at DG Competition*, para. 22.

[416] Accuracy describes the potential of a methodology to deliver *unbiased* (estimates which are correct on average) and *precise* (estimates which are close to the truth) results.

[417] Scheffman and Coleman, *FTC Perspectives on the Use of Econometric Analyses in Antitrust Cases*, p. 3.

[418] *Detroit Police Officers Ass'n v. Young*, 608 F.2d 671, 687 (6th Cir. 1979).

[419] *Commission Best Practices for Economic Evidence*, para. 23.

A comparison with non-econometric evidence justifies the point that perfection is too exigent a standard for econometric evidence. Dismissal of econometric evidence for failure to attain this level of quality would significantly and unjustifiably limit the role of econometric evidence compared with other types of evidence. It would result in an asymmetry between the standards that are set for sophisticated econometric evidence and the standards (or lack thereof) that apply to other types of (qualitative) evidence. It seems unjustified to demand standards of excellence from econometric analysis, and discard a serious, though less than "perfect" econometric study, while accepting dubious or non-robust, non-economic, qualitative evidence. In consequence, the asymmetrical standards for different types of evidence may discourage the submission of serious econometric evidence in favor of looser economic arguments and non-economic evidence.

As with "imperfect" non-econometric evidence, which is normally admissible and appraised as to its probative value, adjudicators should not blindly and categorically reject econometric evidence as a result of imperfections. Econometric evidence should not be excluded from substantive assessment, except in exceptional circumstances when such evidence is seriously and facially flawed to the extent that it offers no evidentiary value at all.[420] The Appellate Body recently emphasized that: "like other categories of evidence, a panel should reach conclusions with respect to the probative value it accords to economic simulations or models" and that "this kind of assessment falls within the panel's authority as the initial trier of facts."[421] From this excerpt, one can infer that adjudicators cannot simply rely on inferences and speculation to reject proposed econometric evidence. Instead, one must solve the substantive question of the validity of econometric evidence and consider the appropriate weight to place on its results. In order to exercise this independent judgment in assessing the probative value of econometric evidence, it is imperative that adjudicators be comfortable evaluating statistical testimony. Nevertheless, this is still the exception rather than the rule. Quite to the contrary, the two above WTO cases highlight that adjudicators unfamiliar with quantitative evidence will likely not choose to resolve conflicting econometric testimony

[420] It is plausible that an econometric study which produces manifest economical nonsense, such as Japan's study which suggested that the higher the price of shochu, the higher its consumption, may in fact be so seriously and facially flawed that it warrants outright rejection for lack of any probative value.

[421] Appellate Body Report, *US – Subsidies on Upland Cotton (Article 21.5 of the DSU)*, para. 357.

by substantively assessing the models and deciding how much weight to assign to each testimony.

To conclude, adjudicators will not be misled to give too much or too little weight to quantitative evidence if they are aware of precisely what "evidence" an econometric analysis can reliably present and what conclusions that analysis can sustain. This, however, requires that they have a basic familiarity with the characteristics and potential shortcomings of this type of evidence. One of the objectives of this book is to raise more awareness in this regard.

(ii) Data requirements and the consequences

The second issue relates to the data requirements of quantitative methods. A large amount of good quality data is usually required in order to ensure that quantitative methods produce robust results. The short history of regression models in the WTO context demonstrates that the presence of sufficient and reliable empirical data is not a given. The introduction of modern information technology in the form of computerized billing techniques at retail outlets and stock-keeping systems has provided a rich set of scanner data on the price and quantity of products sold. This information is commercialized by market research companies, such as AC Nielsen, IRI, and GfK. This is why there is already an ample supply of data readily available on the relationship between the price and quantity of products sold, at least at the retail level for bar-coded mass consumer goods.[422] Yet important data limitations still persist.[423]

Market research companies have the best scanner data coverage for supermarket retail sales. Conversely, there is less retail information on products that have substantial sales through other channels of distribution (for example, mass merchandisers or convenience stores). In addition, market research companies solely collect scanner data regarding store purchases. This concerns demand at retail level and does not necessarily reflect the wholesale level elasticities, a measure that, as outlined above, is more informative for GATT purposes. Moreover, for sound econometric estimation of price elasticities of demand, supermarket scanner data on price and

[422] Monti, "Market Definition as a Cornerstone of EU Competition Policy." For more on the data issue, see Donath, "The Use of Pricing Analysis for Market Definition Purposes: The Arjowiggins/M-real Zanders Reflex and Arsenal/DSP Mergers," *Competition Policy Newsletter*, 1 (2009), 41, 44–45.

[423] See Jacobson, "Problems in the Use of Econometrics in Antitrust Matters," Presentation to the Conference Board's 2003 Antitrust Conference, March 13, 2003, available at: www.akingump.com/docs/publication/548.PPT.

quantity changes of the disputed products is only a minimum requirement. Information on other competing influences, such as on the prices of potential substitutes, consumer income, and advertising expenditures, need to be included in order to isolate the true competitive relationship between the products at issue.[424] Data on these additional influences may be difficult to obtain. The availability of appropriate data frequently poses a problem in the econometric estimation of elasticities. As a result, antitrust enforcers rely on non-econometric evidence in the majority of cases.[425]

These limitations are likely to be compounded in the context of WTO disputes. These disputes involve industries and distribution levels where price and sales data is not commercialized or otherwise available. Frequently, they also involve less developed WTO Members, countries where gathering such data is more difficult and costly. Moreover, if such data exists, it is often only collected by the relevant industry, which may be reluctant to make it available if it could be used against its interests.[426] Without broad discovery and subpoena powers in WTO law it is impossible to obtain the requisite data from another party or non-party. Finally, there is the risk of what has been termed "data rich distortion."[427] Where a legal system establishes a rule (or at least a preference) requiring the use of quantitative evidence to prove a claim, for example, on product likeness, the data quality and availability can lead to bias. Sectors or countries that are data rich, because electronically captured point-of-sale data is widely available, could get disproportionately more judicial attention than those that are not. Such a tendency would put industrially advanced WTO Members, and within those countries, those sectors with a lot of data, under increased Article III scrutiny.

[424] Moreover, in such analysis, it is important to keep factors other than price and quantity constant. Real market conditions generally make this difficult, if not impossible, so that there may not be much appropriate data, ABA Section of Antitrust Law, *Market Power Handbook*, p. 59.

[425] Bundeskartellamt, *Diskussionspapier: Wettbewerbsschutz und Verbraucherinteressen im Lichte neuerer ökonomischer Methoden*, pp. 4–7, 29 (2004), available at: www.bundeskartellamt.de/wDeutsch/download/pdf/Diskussionsbeitraege/04_AKK.pdf; US Department of Justice and Federal Trade Commission, *Commentary on the 1992 Horizontal Merger Guidelines*, p. 9 (2006), available at: www.ftc.gov/os/2006/03/CommentaryontheHorizontalMergerGuidelinesMarch2006.pdf; Conseil de la concurrence, Deuxième partie, Titre I, Le marché pertinent.

[426] This was the case with the "1996 Gemines" study in Panel Report, *Chile – Alcoholic Beverages*, *supra*, Ch. 2, fn. 68, para. 7.66 fn. 390.

[427] Freeman, Chairman of the Competition Commission, *The Significance of Economic Evidence in Competition Cases*, p. 12 (2009), available at: www.competition-commission.org.uk/our_role/speeches/pdf/freeman_151009.pdf.

However, data scarcity is not a reason to categorically exclude quantitative methods. It may just relegate econometrics to the level of secondary support to be used to corroborate other non-econometric evidence. Alternatively, it may dictate a preference for a less sophisticated technique, for example, price correlation analysis. Regardless, where no historic data is available survey methods offer a potential solution to generate data.[428]

(iii) Weight and cost of the proceedings

Connected to the preceding issue is the criticism that quantitative analysis engenders a considerable administrative burden. As it is data intensive, it requires complex procedures of generating, organizing, and assessing data.[429] The combination of enhanced information technology, applied to ever more data offers new possibilities of going down paths of increasing complexity, in the interests of thoroughness and completeness. Slow, long, and costly proceedings are the consequence.[430] This is worrisome, as the enforcement system risks collapsing under its own weight.[431] This is especially the case where there are no limits placed on the amount of evidence and arguments that can be considered. Although time limits exist under the DSU, most cases at the Panel stage fail to observe such limits.[432] There appears to be little room for additional sophisticated empirical tests

[428] Rubinfeld, Economics Roundtable, Testimony before the Antitrust Modernization Commission, January 19, 2006, available at: http://govinfo.library.unt.edu/amc/commission_hearings/pdf/rubinfeld_statement_final.pdf.

[429] For instance, it is necessary to incorporate discounts and rebates, often not reflected in the price data, to "clean" the data from outliers and to put the data into the proper format for statistical analysis.

[430] A complete econometric analysis done simply in an effort to convince that the government should not be sued can reportedly cost "hundreds of thousands of dollars," Lande and Langenfeld, "From Surrogates to Stories: The Evolution of Federal Merger Policy," *Antitrust*, 11 (1997), 5, 7.

[431] Recent submissions in the consultation process on the *Commission Best Practices on Economic Evidence* indicate the concern that parties will become increasingly overwhelmed by burdensome quantitative assessments and data requests by the European Commission; see, e.g., WilmerHale to DG Competition, *Memorandum: Consultation concerning DG Competition: Best Practices on Article 101 and 102 TFEU proceedings; Submission of Economic Evidence and Data Collection in Article 101 and 102 TFEU and merger cases; Guidance on Procedures of the Hearing Officers in relation to Article 101 and 102 TFEU*, para. 61, March 3, 2010, available at: http://ec.europa.eu/competition/consultations/2010_best_practices/wilmerhale_en.pdf.

[432] In principle, cases in Panel proceedings should not exceed nine months, Article 12.9 of the DSU. In practice, however, they last on average twelve months, van den Bossche, *The Law and Policy of the World Trade Organization*, pp. 200, 288 (2010). Note that there are no time limits for the submission of evidence by a party during the proceedings. But most *ad hoc* working procedures of the Panels set out such deadlines, *ibid.*, p. 281.

without further undermining the existing time limits. Moreover, the cost of econometric studies remains considerable and may bar less wealthy parties from producing or effectively attacking this type of evidence.[433]

(iv) Eroding the ability to prove while increasing the ability to disprove

Finally, there is what has been observed by Freeman as the "more subtle risk of eroding the ability to prove" while increasing the ability to disprove by the opposing party.[434] The technical burden that must be met in order to make a claim based on econometrics is by its very nature higher than in case of non-econometric evidence. This will be outlined in a first step. At the same time, as will be described subsequently, the treatment of econometric evidence by legal professionals leads to an additional hurdle for econometric evidence. Several factors give rise to an increased burden of proof on the proponent, while lowering the opponent's burden to successfully rebut econometric evidence.

(a) The high technical burden for establishing econometric evidence The following passage will describe the tension that exists between the concept of statistical significance and the concept of the burden of proof. It will become clear that it is harder for a proponent to prove an allegation to the requisite legal standard when relying on econometric evidence.

As discussed, statistical analysis involves the formal expression of uncertainty in terms of probabilities. The fact that statistical analysis merely generates probabilities that a relationship exists should not be seen in itself as an argument against the use of statistical evidence in legal decision making. In fact, statistical analysis and legal adjudication both share the common pursuit of finding the correct result and seeking the "truth" in the face of conflicting propositions.[435] Absolute certainty, however, is unattainable in either case. Statisticians as well as judges therefore have to make the best decision on the basis of incomplete information and a balancing of probabilities. In this endeavor, as Posner observed, "the deepest gulf between the legal and scientific cultures" lies in how they deal with uncertainties.[436] Econometrics provides statistical tests to assure the

433 Such concern was also raised in Panel Report, *Korea – Alcoholic Beverages*, *supra*, Introduction, fn. 36, para. 10.92 fn. 405.

434 Freeman, *The Significance of Economic Evidence in Competition Cases*, p. 13.

435 On this issue see, *supra*, fn. 54.

436 Posner, *Catastrophe: Risk and Response*, p. 200.

correct outcome. Legal systems provide rules as to the burden and standard of proof.

When introducing regression analysis as evidence into legal proceedings, the issue arises as to what level of certainty must be attained to meet the requisite legal standard of proof. This raises the question of the relationship between the standard of proof and statistical significance, and whether to associate a particular level of legal persuasion with a certain level of statistical certainty.

(1) *General principles of the standard of proof* The concepts of the burden of proof and the standard of proof address the related problems of uncertainty and risk of error in adjudication. The burden of proof is the procedural rule that determines who has to establish a disputed point, that is, who must discharge the evidentiary threshold. It is the burden of production of evidence that, as a general rule, is incumbent on the party asserting a claim.[437] In contrast, the standard of proof refers to the necessary probative value of the evidence required to discharge the burden of proof. It is commonly understood as the necessary evidentiary threshold that must be met before an adjudicator decides that an assertion of fact is proven in law. In other words, it is the degree of persuasion or probability that a disputed, and therefore uncertain, fact is held to be true.

The concept of the standard of proof is interpreted differently across different legal systems.[438] Nevertheless, across different jurisdictions certain similar measurements of probative value, and thus similar standards of proof, are traditionally distinguished. Depending on the type of matter at hand, civil or criminal, the burden of persuasion will be more or less intensive. At one end, the burden is set at a relatively low level. It requires proof on "the preponderance of the evidence" or on "the balance of probabilities." This standard is usually employed in common law civil matters. The party bearing the burden of proof must show that it is "more probable than not" – which often is numerically expressed as more than

[437] In common law, the concept of the burden of proof is divided into two distinct ideas: the (initial) "burden of going forward" or "burden of adducing evidence" (to convince the court that there is in fact a triable case, that is, a *prima facie* case); and the (ultimate) "burden of persuasion" to prove the merits of the case. Pauwelyn, "Evidence, Proof and Persuasion in WTO Dispute Settlement: Who Bears the Burden?" *Journal of International Economic Law*, 1 (1998), 227, 229; Grando, *Evidence, Proof, and Fact-finding in WTO Dispute Settlement*, p. 74 (2010).

[438] For a comparison of common law and civil law approaches to standards of proof see Clermont and Sherwin, "A Comparative View of Standards of Proof," *American Journal of Comparative Law*, 50 (2002), 243–275.

50 percent probable – that an asserted claim or fact is true.[439] In civil law jurisdictions, the standard of proof is less clear.[440] The standard of proof in civilian jurisdictions is more difficult to define generally, but is often described as the judge's personal inner conviction.[441] However, it is not clear what degree of proof is required to satisfy this apparently subjective standard.[442]

At the other end of the spectrum, the standard is set at a very stringent threshold, namely, the proof "beyond reasonable doubt" standard used in both common law and civil law criminal matters. This threshold is the most exigent of standards and demands the highest degree of probative value of the evidence. Between the two extremes, the standard of proof can move across the spectrum. For example, in the United States an intermediate standard by "clear and convincing evidence" applies to certain issues in civil cases, which requires more persuasion than the former but less than the latter discussed standards.

A standard that is somewhat lower than preponderance of the evidence is *prima facie* evidence. In common law, it applies at the initial stage of civil proceedings.[443] This burden requires production of sufficient evidence to justify the judge putting an issue to the jury, or in the absence of a jury trial, to allow the hearing to continue – and thus to withstand a motion to dismiss the claim. Importantly for the question of standard of proof, this burden corresponds to the duty resting on the proponent of a claim to present a *prima facie* case, that is, "to adduce enough evidence in order to convince the court that there is a case to answer."[444] This usually means

[439] See Clermont, "Procedure's Magical Number Three: Psychological Bases for Standards of Decision," *Cornell Law Review*, 72 (1987), 1115, 1119. For criticism of expressing this standard in numeric terms, see: Walker, "Preponderance, Probability and Warranted Factfinding," *Brooklyn Law Review*, 62 (1996), 1075, 1080.

[440] See Kazazi, *Burden of Proof and Related Issues*, p. 324; Clermont and Sherwin, "A Comparative View of Standards of Proof," pp. 253–254.

[441] Waincymer, *WTO Litigation*, p. 538; Clermont and Sherwin, "A Comparative View of Standards of Proof," p. 243.

[442] This standard is variously interpreted as "more probable than not," the conviction of the court "beyond a reasonable doubt," or a proposition that is highly probable or almost certain. For references see Grando, *Evidence, Proof, and Fact-finding in WTO Dispute Settlement*, n. 88.

[443] In the absence of jury trials, there is no similar concept of *prima facie* evidence, and therefore no "duty of passing the judge," in civil law systems. In these jurisdictions, *prima facie* terminology refers to different concepts, e.g., "Anscheinsbeweis," or "*prima facie*-Beweis," which in German civil law corresponds to the common law doctrine of *res ipsa loquitur*; Barceló III, "Burden of Proof, Prima Facie Case, and Presumption in WTO Dispute Settlement," *Cornell International Law Journal*, 42 (2009), 23, 27, 31.

[444] Pauwelyn, "Evidence, Proof and Persuasion in WTO Dispute Settlement," p. 229.

evidence on the basis of which reasonable people can disagree about how to decide on the claim.[445]

(2) *Standard of proof in antitrust and WTO law* Multiple enforcers, multiple laws, and multistage procedures result in a complex tangle of different standards of proof in US antitrust law.[446] The preponderance of the evidence standard constitutes, however, the default standard of proof at the trial stage of an antitrust case in civil litigation.[447] Most importantly for present purposes, and notwithstanding the multitude of standards of proof, an antitrust party offering scientific or technical evidence has the initial burden of establishing by a preponderance of the evidence the admissibility under the admissibility standard set by *Daubert*/Rule 702 of the FRE.[448]

In EU antitrust law, the relevant standard of proof has been under debate for some time.[449] While a definite and precise standard of proof has yet to be articulated for EU antitrust law, and EU law more generally, the EU courts seem to have a "balance of the probabilities" standard in mind.[450] Yet the EU courts appear, by way of more measured expressions, to describe the required standard both in infringement as well as in merger cases to be a heightened standard. It falls somewhere between the

[445] Barceló III, "Burden of Proof, Prima Facie Case, and Presumption in WTO Dispute Settlement," p. 30; Grando, *Evidence, Proof, and Fact-finding in WTO Dispute Settlement*, p. 88.

[446] For a complete overview of the different standards of proof in each instance, see Steuer, "Standards of Proof and Judicial Review: A US Perspective," in Hawk (ed.), *Annual Proceedings of the Fordham Corporate Law Institute, International Antitrust Law & Policy*, pp. 143–156 (2006).

[447] See *Park* v. *El Paso Board of Realtors*, 764 F.2d 1053 (5th Cir. 1985).

[448] *Daubert*, *supra*, fn. 54, at 587 fn. 10. Quantitative methods, such as regression analysis, have been declared in principle admissible by US courts, e.g., *State of Ohio ex rel. Montgomery* v. *Louis Trauth Dairy, Inc.*, at 1252; *City of Tuscaloosa* v. *Harcros Chemicals, Inc.*, *supra*, fn. 114, at 566.

[449] See, e.g., Legal, "Standards of Proof and Standards of Judicial Review in EU Competition Law," in Hawk (ed.), *Annual Proceedings of the Fordham Corporate Law Institute, International Antitrust Law & Policy*, pp. 107–116 (2006); Reeves and Dodoo, "Standards of Proof and Standards of Judicial Review in EC Merger Law," in Hawk (ed.), *Annual Proceedings of the Fordham Corporate Law Institute, International Antitrust Law & Policy*, pp. 117–142 (2006).

[450] MacLennan, "Evidence, Standard and Burden of Proof and the Use of Experts in Procedure Before the Luxembourg Courts," p. 268; van Rompuy, "The Standard of Proof in EC Merger Control," IES Working Paper (2008), available at: www.ies.be/files/repo/IES%20Working%20Paper%204_Ben%20Van%20Rompuy.pdf.

preponderance of the evidence and the proof beyond reasonable doubt, although closer to the former than to the latter.[451]

However, the EU courts have not revealed specific guidelines against which econometrics can be weighed to determine their evidentiary value. The Courts have recognized that the European Commission enjoys a certain "margin of discretion" in economic or technical matters, particularly when complex assessments are involved.[452] This deference extends to the European Commission's treatment and handling of econometric evidence and is understood to be a permissive standard.[453] Still, there is virtually no guidance on the level of confidence or probability that the European Commission must arrive at in relation to the results generated by econometric models. The ECJ indicated only that the economic effects predicted by the econometric theories and models should be "plausible."[454] It is likely that the preponderance of the evidence standard comes closest to this plausibility standard.

Similar to most international treaties and statutes, as well as the jurisprudence of international courts and tribunals, the WTO agreements, including the DSU, do not contain general rules on the standard of proof. Moreover, the dispute settlement bodies have failed to develop a consistent approach. In a rare pronouncement, the Panel rejected the application of the beyond reasonable doubt standard.[455] Beyond that, the topic remains much debated, but still unresolved.

Many argue that dispute settlement bodies have applied a *prima facie* standard.[456] Thus, the complainant would need to make a *prima facie*

[451] Vesterdorf, "Standard of Proof in Merger Cases: Reflections in the Light of Recent Case Law of the Community Courts," *European Competition Journal*, 1 (2005), 3–33; Faull and Nikpay, *The EC Law of Competition*, para. 8.508.

[452] Joined Cases C-68/94, *French Republic* v. *Commission* and C-30/95 *Société Commerciale des Potasses et de l'Azote (SCPA) and Entreprise Minière et Chimique (EMC)* v. *Commission* [1998] ECR I-1375, paras. 223–224; Case C-12/03 P, *Commission* v. *Tetra Laval* [2005] ECR I-987, para. 38; Case T-201/04, *Microsoft* v. *Commission* [2007] ECR II-3601, paras. 87–89.

[453] Botteman, "Mergers, Standard of Proof and Expert Economic Evidence," p. 71.

[454] Case C-12/03 P, *Commission* v. *Tetra Laval*, *supra*, fn. 452, para. 44.

[455] Panel Report, *Canada – Measures Affecting the Importation of Milk and the Exportation of Dairy Products – Second Recourse to Article 21.5 of the DSU by New Zealand and the United States*, WT/DS103/RW2, WT/DS113/RW2, adopted January 17, 2003, para. 5.67.

[456] See, e.g., Mavroidis, "Development of WTO Dispute Settlement Procedures Through Case-Law (We Will Fix It)," in Ortino and Petersmann (eds.), *The WTO Dispute Settlement System 1995–2003*, pp. 153, 168 (2004).

case of likeness or DCS.[457] The *prima facie* standard has been frequently referred to in case law.[458] Yet it has remained elusive, because "precisely how much and precisely what kind of evidence will be required to establish … a presumption [of a *prima facie* case] will vary from measure to measure, provision to provision, and case to case."[459] Scholars have thus struggled to decipher this standard.[460] Commentators seem to agree that the degree of certainty needed to establish a *prima facie* case is relatively low – at least somewhat lower than the preponderance of the evidence standard.[461] It appears that the mere possibility – and not the conviction – that the claimant's proposition is true is enough to satisfy that standard. Among the reasons for this approach is the term's literal meaning, "at first appearance," the commonly used definition by international tribunals as evidence "which, unexplained or uncontradicted is sufficient to maintain the proposition affirmed,"[462] and the above outlined common law understanding of the term.

Others argue that, although not spelled out explicitly, in practice the Panels apply a preponderance of the evidence standard.[463] At times, the dispute settlement bodies have implicitly referred to such a standard.[464]

[457] Fauchald, "Flexibility and Predictability Under the World Trade Organization's Non-Discrimination Clauses," p. 454; Trebilcock and Howse, *The Regulation of International Trade*, p. 106.

[458] The implicit starting point is Appellate Body Report, *United States – Measure Affecting Imports of Woven Wool Shirts and Blouses from India*, WT/DS33/AB/R, adopted May 23, 1997 (hereinafter *US – Shirts and Blouses*), at 14. The *prima facie* standard then explicitly entered jurisprudence in Appellate Body Report, *EC – Hormones*, *supra*, fn. 90, paras. 98, 104.

[459] Appellate Body Report, *US – Shirts and Blouses*, *supra*, fn. 458, at 14.

[460] See, e.g., Pauwelyn, "Evidence, Proof and Persuasion in WTO Dispute Settlement," p. 227; Tanigichi, "Understanding the Concept of Prima Facie Proof in WTO Dispute Settlement," in Janow *et al.* (eds.), *The WTO: Governance, Dispute Settlement, and Developing Countries*, pp. 553–572 (2008).

[461] Cameron and Orava, "GATT/WTO Panels between Recording and Finding Facts: Issues of Due Process, Evidence, Burden of Proof, and Standard of Review in GATT/WTO Dispute Settlement," in Weiss (ed), *Improving WTO Dispute Settlement Procedures: Issues and Lessons from the Practice of Other International Courts and Tribunals*, pp. 195, 236 (2000).

[462] Kazazi, *Burden of Proof and Related Issues*, p. 328.

[463] Unterhalter, "The Burden of Proof in WTO Dispute Settlement," in Janow *et al.* (eds.), *The WTO: Governance, Dispute Settlement & Developing Countries*, pp. 543, 552 (2008); Pfitzer and Sabune, "Burden of Proof in Dispute Settlement: Contemplating Preponderance of the Evidence," International Centre for Trade and Sustainable Development, Issue Paper No. 9, 2009, available at: http://ictsd.org/downloads/2009/04/burden_of_proof.pdf; McGovern, *International Trade Regulation*, paras. 2.23–2.85 (2010).

[464] Panel Report, *India – Measures Affecting the Automotive Sector*, WT/DS146/R, WT/DS175/R, adopted April 5, 2002, para. 7.233 ("not proven on balance"); Appellate Body

More explicitly, and despite the fact that case law also adopts the *prima facie* language, there appears to be an established practice of the *weighing and balancing* of the evidence.[465] The Appellate Body has in fact not objected when Panels have preferred to speak in terms of weighing the evidence.[466]

In conclusion, a standard of proof similar to, or to a certain extent even less stringent than, the preponderance of the evidence standard seems to apply in WTO law. For both antitrust and WTO law it may be summarized as some form of proof by the preponderance of the evidence seems to be the unifying concept.

(3) *Relationship between statistical significance and standard of proof* In the next step, the relationship between statistical significance and the burden of proof is in question. This relationship is not a simple one.

The conventional 5 percent significance level (or 95 percent confidence level) might be regarded as the statistical equivalent, in probabilistic formulation, of "beyond reasonable doubt."[467] At the 5 percent level, a coefficient is labeled significant even though it is not significant one time in twenty. Whether such a test is appropriate in legal proceedings where, as in antitrust and WTO law, a preponderance of the evidence is the legal standard, is problematic.[468] In its purest form, a preponderance of the evidence may be translated as requiring a mere 51 percent likelihood of something occurring.[469] Therefore, when this standard of proof applies, lawyers might question the 5 percent significance level applicable to statistical evidence as imposing too strict a standard, since the plaintiff must prove his allegations by a preponderance of the evidence, not by scientific certainty. Why reject the hypothesis that a certain coefficient is zero only

Report, *US – Subsidies on Upland Cotton (Article 21.5 of the DSU)*, para. 321 ("sufficient evidentiary basis for the conclusion that it is more likely than not").

465 See Panel Report, *Korea – Definitive Safeguard Measure on Imports of Certain Dairy Products*, WT/DS98/R, adopted January 12, 2000, para. 7.24; Panel Report, *United States – Sections 301–310 of the Trade Act of 1974*, WT/DS152/R, adopted January 27, 2000, para. 7.14.

466 Appellate Body Report, *European Communities – Anti-Dumping Duties on Imports of Cotton-Type Bed Linen From India – Recourse to Article 21.5 of the DSU by India*, WT/DS141/AB/RW, adopted April 24, 2003, para. 174.

467 Gastwirth, "Statistical Reasoning in the Legal Setting," *The American Statistician*, 46 (1992), 55, 57.

468 For the following see Fisher, "Multiple Regression in Legal Proceedings," p. 717; Rubinfeld and Steiner, "Quantitative Methods in Antitrust Litigation," pp. 99–100.

469 The famous British lawyer, Tom Denning (later Lord Denning), in *Miller* v. *Minister of Pensions* [1947] 2 All ER 372 once described it simply as "more probable than not."

if the probability that the results obtained are due to chance is 5 percent or less? Where the hypothesis involved is of legal importance, in particular, when an exact parameter estimate is needed for some purpose, would it not make more sense to use a preponderance of the evidence standard and require significance at 51 percent only (or even lower where the standard of proof is even more relaxed)?

Such an approach, though reasonable to untrained eyes, would reflect a flawed understanding of what significance levels really mean. In fact, a statistical significance level of 51 percent does not correspond to a legal preponderance of the evidence standard. The significance level only dictates the probability of obtaining the measured coefficient value *if* the true value is zero; it does *not* give the probability that the coefficient's true value *is* zero,[470] nor does subtracting the significance level from 100 percent give the probability that the hypothesis is not true. Thus, to say that the probability is 51 percent that a variable's true coefficient is zero would be an incorrect statement. The fact that the coefficient is statistically significant simply means that by conventional tests one can reject the hypothesis that its true value is zero.

For this reason, the concepts of statistical significance and legal burden of proof are distinct from each other. That is why it would be improper to argue that the statistical significance level should be relaxed in order to reflect the requisite legal burden of proof. The following will demonstrate why it is justified to have different levels of certainty in statistics and the law, with the conclusion that a proponent of quantitative evidence should in fact meet a standard of statistical certainty that is far higher than the legal burden that a proposition is more likely than not.

(4) *A law and economics perspective on the level of statistical significance and standard of proof* The preponderance of the evidence standard and the conventional 5 percent significance level are instruments to manage the risk of uncertainty as well as the risk and costs of errors. In fact, the choice of the level of standard of proof and of the level of significance influence the relative frequency of fact-finding errors.

What are conventionally referred to as "Type I" errors, or "false positives," denote the error of mistakenly rejecting a null hypothesis when it is in fact true. In legal terms, the equivalent would be finding a violation

[470] This means it is incorrect to interpret the significance level as the probability that the null hypothesis is true, see Fienberg *et al.*, "Understanding and Evaluating Statistical Evidence in Litigation," *Jurimetrics Journal*, 36 (1995), 1, 23.

or liability where none exists. Thus, it is an error in favor of the claimant – a case of overenforcement. In contrast, "Type II" errors, or "false negatives," describe the error of failing to reject a null hypothesis when it is in fact not true. In the legal context, the equivalent would be finding no violation or liability where such violation or liability actually exists. This case represents an error in favor of the respondent – an instance of underenforcement.

Statistics and the law of evidence determine the allocation of risk by choosing between avoiding Type I or II errors. This choice involves a value judgment over the weight to be given to each risk of error, which implies evaluating the costs associated with each type of error. The aim is to minimize two types of social costs, error costs, and direct or process costs.[471] The former consists of the social costs associated with an erroneous decision (false positives and false negatives). The latter consists of those costs incurred in the decision-making process, for example, costs of gathering, preparing, and presenting evidence, or the resources devoted by the decision-maker to deliver a decision that reduces the rate of error costs.[472] An optimal standard would balance the error costs of Type I and II errors, which would need to be further weighed against the direct costs.

As the US Supreme Court held, "the preponderance of the evidence standard results in a roughly equal allocation of the risk of error between litigants" and applies in civil actions "unless particularly important individual interests or rights are at stake."[473] Further, it is suggested that this standard minimizes the total number of errors made in fact-finding.[474] The allocation of the risk of error by way of a mid-range standard of proof is premised on the assumption that the interests of the parties are valued equally. This is the case when an error in favor of the claimant costs the same as an error in favor of the respondent. Thus, the assumption of equal

[471] Posner, "An Economic Approach to Legal Procedure and Judicial Administration," *Journal of Legal Studies*, 2 (1973), 399, 400; B. L. Hay, "Allocating the Burden of Proof," *Indiana Law Journal*, 72 (1997), 651, 654. For a discussion regarding the allocation of evidentiary burdens of production and persuasion in accordance with the broader social costs associated with false positives, see Rubinfeld, "Econometrics in the Courtroom," pp. 1050–1054. For an application to WTO law, see Grando, "Allocating the Burden of Proof in WTO Disputes: A Critical Analysis," *Journal of International Economic Law*, 9 (2006), 615, 643–646.

[472] T. R. Lee, "Pleading and Proof: The Economics of Legal Burdens," *Brigham Young University Law Review*, (1997), 1, 5.

[473] *Grogan* v. *Garner*, 498 US 279, 286 (1991) (internal quotations and citations omitted).

[474] Kaye, "Naked Statistical Evidence," pp. 603–605; T. R. Lee, "Pleading and Proof," pp. 25–26. *Contra* Walker, "Preponderance, Probability and Warranted Factfinding," pp. 1101–1104.

error costs is the basic rationale behind the preponderance of the evidence or balance of probabilities standard.[475]

A standard of proof higher than preponderance of the evidence, for example, that of "clear and convincing evidence" or even "beyond a reasonable doubt," may be appropriate in cases in which the error costs of a Type I error are judged to be unusually high. These are situations in which the interests of the disputing parties are not valued similarly because an error against the respondent (the Type I error) would be more costly than an error against the claimant (the Type II error). An example of potentially greater costs of an error on the respondent's side includes cases involving fundamental individual rights.

As it has been observed: "as a general rule, in WTO dispute settlement, false positives and false negatives [under Article III of the GATT: erroneously permitting a discriminatory measure and erroneously enjoining a non-discriminatory measure] are valued similarly."[476] For this reason, a preponderance of the evidence standard seems to be the most appropriate to apply in the context of WTO dispute settlement. Nonetheless, a greater weight may conceivably be put on the respondent's interests, that is, the target government, in cases where important societal values of that WTO Member need to be protected from easy litigious attacks and the associated risk of Type I errors. These may be cases where the respondent has more than trade interests at stake, for example, where human, animal, or plant life or health in the territory of the respondent are affected.[477]

As explained, the law usually assumes the interests of the parties to be of equal value. Thus, the risks of false positives and false negatives are valued similarly under the preponderance of the evidence standard. By contrast, the conventional significance level in statistics confers by default more weight to the avoidance of Type I errors, and less to the avoidance of Type II errors. This is due to the fact that a high degree of confidence in the falsity of the null hypothesis is required before rejecting it.[478] When employing a regression, the proponent (of the alternative hypothesis and thus of the regression) must prove its claim to a level of near absolute certainty. In other words, the proponent bears a heavy burden before it is accepted that the model establishes a causal relation – a weight that clashes with

[475] Kaplan, "Decision Theory and the Factfinding Process," *Stanford Law Review*, 20 (1968), 1065, 1072; Posner, *Economic Analysis of Law*, p. 647 (2007).

[476] Grando, *Evidence, Proof, and Fact-finding in WTO Dispute Settlement*, p. 140.

[477] This would be especially relevant for cases under the SPS Agreement, Article 141.

[478] Where there is a 5 percent significance level, Type I errors occur in less than 5 percent of cases.

the standard of proof of preponderance of the evidence. The high degree of confidence required makes it more difficult for the plaintiff to provide statistical evidence on product likeness that rejects the null hypothesis that products are not competitive. When technical evidence of a very high degree of certainty is required, proof to the requisite legal standard becomes harder to adduce, resulting in an inability to make valid findings. Put differently, the task of proving that an assertion is "more likely than not," purely on the basis of econometric evidence can be difficult and usually requires additional supporting evidence.

This is the result of a trade-off. When the individual interests at stake are valued similarly, and the risk of error (which is assumed to have equal magnitude) is equally distributed, then the direct costs will tip the balance. On the one hand, the cost of producing statistical evidence yielding results with near absolute certainty may be higher for the proponent than in the case of a model with results of lesser conclusiveness or when producing non-statistical evidence. On the other hand, without emphasis on avoiding Type I errors, additional high (process) costs would be incurred in the process of testing and attacking (potentially unreliable) statistical evidence. For sophisticated econometric evidence, process costs are especially high for the court and the opponent, who are faced with having to retain an expert, evaluate the proponent's model, and possibly collect additional data and/or set up an alternative model. Thus, according to an analysis under the error costs theory, due to the high process costs and the equally distributed risk of error, placing a higher hurdle on the party seeking to rely on statistical evidence is justified. The conventional default rule requiring a high confidence level ensures an efficient allocation of party and adjudicatory resources. It avoids spending resources in litigation that do not warrant the expenditure when the proponent is as likely, or slightly more likely, as the opponent to be correct.[479]

(b) The imperfection of econometric evidence and its implications for the standard of proof It has been shown that proving a claim with econometric evidence brings a heavy burden on the proponent under statistical standards compared with a less stringent legal burden of proof. It has also been established that the high degree of scientific certainty required for statistical evidence has a proper and legitimate justification. However, there is another reason why the burden on the proponent to

[479] The issue of whether costs savings from the heightened standard are not outweighed by the costs associated with the risk of underenforcement is not explored here.

establish a claim with econometric evidence is higher, while the burden for the opponent to rebut this type of evidence appears to be lower than in cases using only non-econometric evidence.

This is due mainly to the erroneous expectation of perfection of econometric evidence by legal professionals and the ensuing risk of quick dismissal of such evidence by adjudicators. As already indicated, it is generally easier to discredit an econometric analysis for its imperfection than it is to produce a positive alternative. Further, it is very difficult for a non-expert to assess how reliable a given piece of econometric evidence is. Where econometric evidence contains apparent imperfections, an adjudicator may not be convinced that the requisite standard of proof has been met. As an unintended consequence, this may lead to the standard of proof for the proponent being raised, while lowering the standard of rebuttal for the opponent.

An illustration of this point can be found again in *Japan – Alcoholic Beverages II* and *Chile – Alcoholic Beverages*. As presented earlier, actual proof of the presence of the alleged flaws of autocorrelation and multicollinearity was not adduced by the opponents. It was merely sufficient to raise concerns over potential complications and imperfections in order to rebut the econometric evidence. The manner in which potential complications to the regression analysis have been dealt with by the Panels has an important consequence on the evidentiary burden of the proponent of econometric evidence in dispute settlement proceedings. It appears that, as in Japan's case, the standard of proof in cases involving economic evidence is on the proponent to completely rule out any possibility of potential (but not actually ascertained) flaws in the quantitative evidence.[480] This would require a standard of near perfection for econometric evidence. This confirms the above prediction that adjudicators overwhelmed by economic evidence will avail themselves of the rules on the standard of proof to overcome this predicament.[481]

Since perfection is in fact unachievable and scientifically not required, it is an unbalanced result to allow opponents to give econometric evidence a fatal blow solely on the ground that the proponent's evidence is not perfect. To do so would be to confer an advantage on the opponents, who would only have to raise general doubts as to the validity and reliability of the evidence without the need to show that such potential problems actually exist and have a causal effect on the inferences drawn from

[480] See Panel Report, *Japan – Alcoholic Beverages II*, *supra*, Ch. 3, fn. 73, para. 6.31.
[481] *Supra*, fn. 59.

the evidence. The result may well be underenforcement (Type II errors). Moreover, setting such a high bar on the quality of the proponent's econometric evidence would, by default, privilege the opponent in the event of conflicting expert testimony. Even with inferior and less reliable economic evidence, the opponent could cast sufficient doubt on the "perfection" of the proponent's economic evidence.[482]

(c) Establishing a level playing field in the case of econometric evidence If it is up to the adjudicator to assess and weigh the evidence even in case of imperfection, what must an opponent do to refute econometric evidence? If flaws are not *per se* detrimental to the probative value of econometric evidence, it cannot be enough for the opposing side to solely assert generalizations and potential complications. In legal terms the question is which standard of proof the opponent must meet in order to rebut econometric evidence. Case law in the United States is particularly developed in this regard and can shed light on how courts have generally dealt with this issue.

It is common knowledge that the opponent must do more than merely bring flaws to a court's attention in order to compromise the evidentiary value. Reliability must be "called sufficiently into question."[483] Several US courts have held that the opponents have "a burden to produce tangible evidence, beyond mere speculation and inference, to support their claims that [the proponents'] analysis reflects flawed econometric techniques."[484] The *Commission Best Practices for Economic Evidence* also explain that it is "normally not sufficient to disprove a particular argument or model, to point out that it is 'based on seemingly unrealistic assumptions.'"[485]

[482] Compare the excerpt from *Chile – Alcoholic Beverages*, where it was stated that: "neither [parties'] regression analysis is sufficiently reliable, but the EC's is less reliable than that of Chile, and it is the European Communities, not Chile, that has the burden of the proof," Panel Report, *Chile – Alcoholic Beverages*, *supra*, Ch. 2, fn. 68, para. 4.237.

[483] *In re Polypropylene Carpet Antitrust Litig.*, 93 F.Supp. 2d 1348, 1352 (ND Ga. 2000).

[484] *In re Polypropylene Carpet Antitrust Litig.* (1997), *supra*, fn. 106, at 26–27. See also *Palmer* v. *Shultz*, 815 F.2d 84, 101 (DC Cir. 1987) (a party cannot rebut a regression analysis without introducing evidence to support the contention that an alleged flaw creates fatal bias in the analysis); *Sobel* v. *Yeshiva University*, 839 F.2d 18, 34 (2nd Cir. 1988) (requiring a party "challenging the validity of a multiple regression analysis to make a showing that the factors it contends ought to have been included would weaken the showing … made by the analysis"); *Estate of Hill* v. *ConAgra Poultry Co.*, *supra*, fn. 106, at 5: "The burden of explaining how [the plaintiff's] failure to satisfy the constant variance assumption impacts the regression analysis belongs to Defendants, as they are the parties raising the issue."

[485] *Commission Best Practices for Economic Evidence*, para. 12.

Instead, opponents must affirmatively present some evidence to challenge the econometric study.

Controversy revolves around the ensuing question of whether an opponent has to present an alternative statistical model in order to sufficiently call into question the proponent's study. This would be by contrasting the allegedly flawed model with the results of an allegedly correct model and thereby proving the error in the model to causally affect its outcome. Certain US courts have rejected the notion that flaws in a regression model must be ignored unless the opposing party comes forward with a regression model in which the flaws are corrected.[486] According to the opposite line of thinking among US courts: "where the defendant adduces no evidence of alternative methodologies or statistics, but merely criticizes those employed by the plaintiff's expert, acceptance of the projections of plaintiff's expert is appropriate, since they do have a rational basis."[487] The US Supreme Court in its *Bazemore* v. *Friday* decision also indicated in a footnote that it is not enough merely to object to a regression on the ground that some factor has been omitted, and suggested that the party challenging a regression must demonstrate that the omitted factors would have a causal effect on the outcome.[488] Consistent with this precedent, courts have required that the party challenging a regression analysis for omission of a relevant variable make a showing (beyond mere conjecture) of the relevance of the particular variable.[489] Similarly, the *Commission Best Practices for Economic Evidence* consider it "necessary to explicitly identify which aspects of reality should be better reflected in the model or argumentation, and to indicate why this would alter the conclusions."[490] Baker concurs that: "criticism of an econometric or simulation methodology should be treated with skepticism absent a demonstration that a reasonable alternative leads to a substantially different result, where such an analysis is possible."[491]

[486] See, e.g., *Penk* v. *Oregon State Bd. of Higher Educ.*, *supra*, fn. 411, at 169–170.

[487] *Int.'l Wood Processors* v. *Power Dry, Inc.*, 593 F.Supp. 710 (DSC 1984); see also *Taxi Weekly, Inc.* v. *Metro Taxicab Bd. of Trade, Inc.*, 539 F.2d 907, 914–915 (2nd Cir. 1976); *Palmer* v. *Shultz*, at 101; *Law* v. *NCAA*, No. 94-2053, 1998 US Dist. LEXIS 6640, § 14 fn. 9 (D Kan. 1998).

[488] *Bazemore* v. *Friday*, *supra*, fn. 356, at 404 fn. 14.

[489] See, e.g., *Catlett* v. *Missouri Highway and Transportation Commission*, 828 F.2d 1260, 1266 (8th Cir. 1987); *Sobel* v. *Yeshiva University*, *supra*, fn. 484, at 33–34; *EEOC* v. *General Telephone Co.*, 885 F.2d 575, 579–583 (9th Cir. 1989).

[490] *Commission Best Practices for Economic Evidence*, para. 12.

[491] Baker, "Econometric Analysis in *FTC* v. *Staples*," Prepared Remarks before the Economics Committee of the American Bar Association Section of Antitrust Law, July 18, 1997, available at: www.ftc.gov/speeches/other/stspch.shtm.

Thus, the dominant view is that the opponent bears the burden of demonstrating the causal impact of an alleged flaw on the outcome and of specifying the (numerical) implications on the overall conclusions of the model. Intuitively, this is correct since an error that does not affect the outcome cannot be a legitimate ground on which to deny giving probative value to evidence.

In the two WTO disputes, the allegations of mis-specification remained mostly unsubstantiated.[492] More importantly, the opponents did not causally link the regression results to the alleged flaws. One noteworthy exception in which an opponent showed that the flaws were, in fact, fatal was the attempt by the EC to show that using inflation-adjusted real prices instead of nominal prices may have caused the mis-specification of Japan's regression.[493]

Against this backdrop, it appears that WTO law is in need of a practical approach in connection with the use of econometric evidence in dispute settlement proceedings. As a general rule, the adjudicator should not prematurely dismiss, but rather substantively appraise the econometric evidence. Additionally, the opponent should not be able to insist on evidentiary perfection, but should be required to specify errors and their causal impact on the outcome.

To take this approach one step further, a suggestion would be to adjust the standard of proof. Under what has been proposed as a "two-sided standard of proof" specifically designed for economic evidence, it would not be enough for the opposing side to raise doubts on the other party's economic evidence.[494] The opponent would be obliged to present a reasonable and at least equally plausible alternative. In the two-sided (symmetrical) standard of proof model, whatever the standard of proof is for the plaintiff (claimant) in order to prove an allegation, it should be equally easy or difficult for the defendant (respondent) to disprove the allegation.[495] For instance, if the plaintiff relies on circumstantial qualitative evidence for market definition purposes, such as physical characteristics or end-uses, the defendant should also be able to adduce qualitative

[492] In *Philippines – Distilled Spirits*, the parties were also reported to have criticized each other's methodology and conclusions, although the precise arguments were not reproduced, see Panel Report, *Philippines – Distilled Spirits*, *supra*, Introduction, fn. 23, para. 7.110.

[493] See *supra*, fn. 383. Yet Japan contended that using real (deflated) prices yielded similar results, at paras. 4.87, 4.171.

[494] Budzinski and Christiansen, *Simulating the (Unilateral) Effects of Mergers: Implications of the Oracle/PeopleSoft Case*, p. 26 (2006), available at: http://ssrn.com/abstract=924375.

[495] Lianos, "'Judging' Economists," p. 306.

evidence to rebut the proposed market definition. If the plaintiff professes direct quantitative evidence of buyer substitution for market definition purposes, for example, an econometric estimation of CPE, the defendant should also be able (or required) to rely on direct quantitative evidence to refute the allegation. If the standard of proof for the plaintiff is to make a *prima facie* case by a "preponderance of the evidence," then the standard of proof for the defendant to disprove the allegation should be the same.

In terms of economic evidence, this "would allow for a level playing field ... between the affected parties on the merits of their models with the prospect of increasing the economic quality of the outcome."[496] And, importantly, it would achieve the objective of economizing overall social costs. Where the risk of error is equally distributed, the symmetrical standard of proof seeks to minimize error costs, because no party is favored when making or disproving a claim. Also, this standard ensures that the costs of decision making (process costs) remain at a minimum. On the one hand, it guarantees that the process costs for economic evidence borne by the plaintiff are not futile as a result of a defendant undermining its probative value by merely casting doubt on it. On the other hand, it ensures that the process costs incurred by the adjudicator or the defendant are minimized to the level necessary to disprove the plaintiff's evidence.[497]

7 Conclusion

This chapter has shown that econometrically estimated CPEs are a useful tool with which to (directly) analyze demand-side substitutability. But it has also shown that CPEs can be misleading for reasons which lie in the concept of CPE itself or in the process of its econometric estimation. Rubinfeld notes that "expanded use of multiple regression techniques is accompanied by the possibility of their misuse" and that "substantial normative questions about their use remain unanswered."[498] The United States in *Japan – Alcoholic Beverages II* emphasized some of the problems

[496] Budzinski and Christiansen, *Simulating the (Unilateral) Effects of Mergers*, p. 26.

[497] Under this model, the process costs of the plaintiff would determine the necessary process costs incurred by the adjudicator and/or defendant. If the plaintiff chooses to incur greater process costs to make his claim on the basis of sophisticated economic evidence (indicating that his interests at stake are high), it is legitimate to demand that the adjudicator and/or defendant invest greater process costs. Admittedly, the danger is that a plaintiff with deep-pockets may quickly out-spend a less financially potent defendant solely because he can invest in expensive economic evidence that the defendant is unable to finance.

[498] Rubinfeld, "Econometrics in the Courtroom," pp. 1094–1095.

encountered in the use of CPE and in its econometric estimation. In that case, it found that econometrics make the use of CPE neither accurate nor robust, and is therefore meaningless for assessing legal consequences in GATT.[499] This chapter does not support this conclusion. The problems are all well known and can for the most part be dealt with, as the foregoing discussion on CPE and the use of regression models has shown. Thus, as the EC convincingly argued in the same case, these complications call for circumspection, but are not a sufficient reason to exclude *a priori* the relevance of CPE.[500] One fails to see why these problems should deter adjudicators from even considering evidence on CPE. As the growing experience in antitrust law confirms, WTO adjudicators are adequately equipped, under the appropriate institutional and procedural framework discussed above, to evaluate and appraise econometric models and economic evidence on market definition.

[499] Appellate Submission by the United States to the Appellate Body, *Japan – Taxes on Alcoholic Beverages*, *supra*, Ch. 3, fn. 264, Annex A.

[500] Appellate Submission by the European Community to the Appellate Body, *Japan – Taxes on Alcoholic Beverages*, at 30–31 (u.d.) (on file with author).

Conclusion

This book started with the observation that the market definition inquiries in antitrust law and under Article III of the GATT have traditionally (and usually exclusively) relied on qualitative evidence (Chapter 3). They have also lacked any underlying theory on which this exercise could have been based. The study then traced the evolution of an economics-based approach in the two disciplines. Starting from the *1982 US Merger Guidelines*, market definition in antitrust law was given an economically sound framework from which the appropriate criteria of demand- (and supply-) side substitutability follow. Since then, the trend has been for increasingly complex quantitative analyses. WTO dispute settlement bodies, by contrast, have employed economic terminology, but offered little in terms of operational tests to determine when products are in a competitive relationship in the marketplace. Quantitative evidence surfaced originally in three cases, where it was – correctly, due to methodological flaws – not given probative weight. This alone was likely sufficient to discourage litigants from making the effort and incurring the costs of compiling quantitative evidence in subsequent cases. The Philippines broke the spell and were the main proponent of econometric evidence in two very recent cases. It remains to be seen whether other Members will follow suit or whether economic analysis and quantitative evidence will disappear again from litigation on the issues of likeness and DCS. At least for the moment the Panels seem to have adopted a pragmatic approach adhering to the traditional *Border Tax* criteria, while also engaging in economic and quantitative analysis where prompted to do so by the parties. *Sub silencio* this may be taken to bring the dispute settlement bodies one step closer to an overall conceptual framework based on sound economics.

In view of the still uncertain role of economics in the definition of "like" and DCS products under Article III of the GATT, this book proposed a conceptual basis for an economics-based approach (Chapter 4). It shaped a clear framework in law, informed by economic insights and analysis, from which can be defined the relevant criteria for Article III product comparison.

At a conceptual level, the economic approach provides a coherent framework of analysis. A comparative analysis of the antitrust and the Article III approaches to market definition demonstrated that market definition under Article III of the GATT cannot merely replicate the antitrust approach. Instead, the study devised a trade-specific economic approach based on the "competitive relationship in the marketplace" paradigm. It did, however, adopt the central insight from antitrust law that market definition is not an aim in itself. The legal interpretation of likeness and DCS has been connected to the underlying policy objectives of Article III of the GATT. At the core of this framework are the concept of demand-side substitutability and a test that focuses on the typical effect of protectionism: the creation of price differentials. This test considers products to be at least DCS (or even "like"), if the domestic producer can profitably raise prices above the competitive level in the presence of the trade barrier. Two important points need to be made in this context.

First, in theory, one can distinguish between DCS and likeness according to a higher degree in demand-side substitutability for likeness than for DCS. In practice, however, the distinction remains unresolved, because there is no objective threshold where the line between the two concepts can be drawn.

Second, the proposed test should not be misunderstood as doing away with the separation of the legal elements in the analysis of *de facto* discrimination: the first step of product comparison and the subsequent step of the analysis of differential treatment. In antitrust law, the SSNIP test links the definition of the relevant antitrust market to the market power inquiry. However, it is only a hypothetical assessment, which does not anticipate the findings of market power in the concrete case. Similarly, the determination of likeness or DCS according to a price increase test links the trade relevant market to the examination of protectionism (understood as an actual or potential adverse modification of the conditions of competition). As a hypothetical assessment, it does not predetermine the findings on disparate treatment and therefore on protectionism.

This leads to an interesting observation of possible convergence in the most recent discussion on market definition in antitrust and international trade law. As noted, the direct measurement of market power continues to gain increasing approval in antitrust circles. Direct measurement makes a separate market definition unnecessary, because the quantitative methods used to directly estimate market power integrate the definition of a relevant market into the analysis. Similarly, some international trade scholars have recently proposed the integration of the analysis of differential treatment ("less favorable treatment") and the likeness/DCS requirement for WTO law.[1] This has been justified on the ground that the definition of "less favorable treatment" in itself requires the assessment of the effect of a measure on the relevant market. The present study provides a further reason why an overall assessment that does not distinguish between the separate legal elements could be a future avenue within an economic approach to Article III market definition. The economic market power concept (ability to price above the competitive level) was used as a proxy for the concept of protectionism in order to conceptualize a test for the determination of likeness and DCS. If, as the recent discussion in the antitrust community shows, the ability to price above the competitive level can be measured directly, then it can be argued that protectionism could also be measured directly. The assessment of protectionism would then become a matter of sophisticated econometric analysis. Critics might be expected to object on the basis that, under established case law, Article III of the GATT does not require actual trade effects for finding an infringement.[2] For this reason, quantitative analysis of differential treatment would be considered unsuitable. However, this view is incorrect. A parallel can be drawn with the quantitative antitrust analysis of the *likelihood* that a merger creates, for example, unilateral effects (in particular, a post-merger price increase). Similarly, the quantitative analysis of protectionism would in fact examine the *ability* to price above competitive level that the governmental measure confers on the domestic producer. The quantitative analysis would not necessarily explore actual trade effects. Still, the quantitative measurement of protectionism is a very unlikely prospect for WTO law. This is because there is a strong suspicion among many international trade scholars and adjudicators of an economic approach as such. They would be even more critical of importing the market power concept into WTO law.[3]

Chapter 5 has shown that the WTO dispute settlement system has the institutional and procedural capabilities to deal effectively with sophisticated economic evidence and to ensure sufficient economic literacy of the panelists – ideally through external Panel-appointed expert advice.

[1] See *supra*, Ch. 2, fn. 94. [2] See *supra*, Ch. 4, fn. 49.

[3] This, however, is only a matter of terminology. Behind it is the idea that the ability to increase prices above a competitive level is relevant for the situation of antitrust market power, as well as for the Article III question of whether protection is afforded to domestic producers.

This chapter has also shown that quantitative methods have an important substantive role to play in the determination of likeness and DCS. CPE of demand provides a direct measure for determining the degree of demand-side substitutability. Multiple regression analysis is instrumental in giving precise numerical estimates of CPE. Quantitative methods are therefore helpful tools for market definition purposes.

Nevertheless, these are imperfect tools; and surely they are not "magic bullets."[4] One reason is that CPE itself is a theoretical ideal, but in practice a potentially flawed measure of substitutability; for example, due to the distortion of competition conditions or consumer perceptions. A second reason is more technical and relates to the econometric estimation of CPE. As shown, quantitative methods, even when undertaken diligently and appropriately, have restrictions on the data or on the methods that raise the need for caution.[5] But it is important to note that the complications that give rise to concern relate to quantitative methods and thus to the methodological level. They do not call into question the overall economic framework and therefore an economic approach altogether.

The conclusion of this study is that there cannot be a categorical distinction between a quantitative and a qualitative approach. Both interact in a more complex way. Either one will rarely be individually dispositive. Each has its own shortcomings and may not provide clear and authoritative answers in each and every case. Depending on the circumstances of the case and the nature of the information available, one type of evidence or the other may be more appropriate. The knowledge of its usefulness, coupled with awareness about its potential shortcomings, lead to the conclusion that quantitative analysis will most likely not substitute, but complement the traditional criteria. The *Commission Notice on the definition of the relevant market* contemplates the combination of qualitative and quantitative evidence by stating that: "the Commission does not follow a rigid hierarchy of different sources of information or types of evidence."[6] In fact, a market definition becomes plausible because of a mix of

[4] Office of Fair Trading, *Quantitative Techniques in Competition Analysis*, para. 18.12.

[5] See Malacrida, "Some Reflections on the Use of Economic Analysis in WTO Dispute Settlement Proceedings," p. 441 insisting on a "healthy degree of caution" in view of its inherent limitations when dealing with econometric analysis in the WTO context. For the same reason, the European Commission generally applies a "strict cautionary principle," which is why it "can only attach limited weight to econometric results," *Ryanair/Aer Lingus, supra*, Ch. 4, fn. 128, Annex IV, para. 9.

[6] *Commission Notice on market definition*, para. 25. This is in contrast to the more assertive point of view of Horn and Mavroidis, "Still Hazy after all These Years," p. 62 "that

qualitative and quantitative evidence – the combination of which makes a convincing case. In addition to being complementary, quantitative and qualitative evidence should be appraised in an integrated evaluation.[7] Both propositions are in fact in line with the Appellate Body's holding that "*all* of the pertinent evidence" should be taken into account on the basis of an "overall determination."[8] Adjudicators should thus consider all the evidence, weigh it depending on its source, relevance, and reliability and then combine it into an overall assessment of quantitative and qualitative evidence in order to come to a fully informed decision. The most recent case law may indicate that the Panels have chosen to follow this path.[9]

This actually gives proper content to the general notion of an economics-based approach. When endorsing an overall assessment of all the evidence, an economic approach does not designate an exclusive or predominant consideration of quantitative methods in the definition of relevant markets. In particular, it cannot be reduced to the econometric estimation of CPE as the sole or primary evidentiary element. Thus, it is not a "more quantitative approach." Instead, it is rather a "more but not exclusively economic approach," which is based on an overall economic framework that takes account of qualitative and quantitative evidence.

Under an economic approach to market definition, it is only logical that the selection of the type of evidence should also be determined economically. Thus, the role of quantitative evidence ideally depends on a cost–benefit analysis.[10] The choice between quantitative or qualitative evidence relates to a trade-off between the goal of minimizing the risk of erroneous decisions (over- or underenforcement) and the aim of minimizing direct or process costs. Parties and adjudicators must expend substantial

econometrics is the primary tool to use, whatever the particular choice for the concept of likeness."

[7] Rubinfeld, "Quantitative Methods in Antitrust," p. 742.

[8] Appellate Body Report, *EC – Asbestos*, *supra*, Ch. 2, fn. 70, paras. 102, 109 (emphasis in original).

[9] The Panel in *Thailand – Cigarettes* found part of the econometric evidence on CPE conclusive on the "likeness" issue and then continued: "*Considered together* with our conclusion above on the likeness between the imported and domestic cigarettes at issue related to their physical characteristics, end-uses and tariff classification, the Philippines has established a prima facie case [on product "likeness"]," Panel Report, *Thailand – Cigarettes*, *supra*, Introduction, fn. 23, para. 7.451 (emphasis added).

[10] Christiansen, "Die 'Ökonomisierung' der EU-Fusionskontrolle: Mehr Kosten als Nutzen?" *Wirtschaft und Wettbewerb*, (2005), 285–293; Friederiszick and Röller, "Quantification of Harm in Damages Actions for Antitrust Infringements: Insights from German Cartel Cases," *Journal of Competition Law & Economics*, 6 (2010), 595, 608–618.

resources in time, effort, and money when producing and dealing with quantitative evidence. Under a cost–benefit analysis, quantitative analysis should be undertaken only if the increase in process costs is outweighed by a significant reduction in the risk of error. This assessment poses somewhat of a dilemma, because it is hard to quantify ("how much in the way of increased processing costs is a reduction in error costs worth?"[11]) and, as has been shown, economic evidence, in particular, the estimation of CPE, is not free from the risk of erroneous decisions itself. However, all things considered, quantitative analysis will usually be beneficial when an issue is complex and difficult, and where the correct result is not obvious.

In practice, the choice of the type of evidence is made differently. Antitrust practice gives the impression that quantitative evidence is usually used as a supportive tool to confirm what qualitative evidence seems to indicate.[12] That is why the European Commission emphasized that it "has never exclusively relied on ... cross-price elasticities but has used these analyses as a supplementary element to support the results of its market investigation."[13] In fact, antitrust practice gives the impression that econometric evidence is most useful as a corrective to minimize the risk of error and to weigh correctly the qualitative information. It is quite understandable for quantitative evidence to have this confirmatory role, because adjudicators will naturally and intuitively start with qualitative evidence.

When used independently, quantitative evidence is usually used to reject a proposed candidate market definition based on qualitative criteria, rather than to positively prove an alternative market definition.[14] The role of quantitative methods will often be limited to rebuttal evidence for a reason that lies in statistics itself. It is a well-known statistical proposition that it is possible to prove that a hypothesis is not true, but it is logically more difficult to prove that it is true. Whereas insignificant statistical relationships can fairly exclude the existence of substantial competitive interaction between products, a positive test result does not necessarily prove that the products belong to the same market. That is why it is much more difficult to establish the validity of a market definition with statistical methods than to cast doubt on it.

[11] Gavil, "The Challenges of Economic Proof in a Decentralized and Privatized European Competition Policy System: Lessons From the American Experience," *Journal of Competition Law & Economics*, 4 (2007), 177, 182.

[12] Kauper, "The Problem of Market Definition under EC Competition Law," p. 251.

[13] *CVC/Lenzing*, para. 112.

[14] See references to case law in Conseil de la concurrence, Deuxième partie, Titre I, Le marché pertinent, para. 1.3.

It has become manifestly obvious that "market definition is not quite a science and not quite an art."[15] For the rational study of the law, including that of WTO law, legal professionals need not become men of statistics and masters of economics, as the US Supreme Court Justice Holmes, cited at the beginning of this book, predicted in 1897. But as market definition calls for the interaction of law with economics, it is not enough for them to remain black lettermen. Legal professionals practicing WTO law must have a basic background in the economic concepts that underpin market definition in order to apply the law. This book has sought to bring the law one step toward economics.

[15] Glassman, "Market Definition as a Practical Matter," p. 1165.

BIBLIOGRAPHY

Alese, F., *Federal Antitrust and EC Competition Law Analysis*, Aldershot: Ashgate, 2008.

American Bar Association (ABA), *Antitrust Evidence Handbook*, 2nd edn., Chicago, IL: ABA Book Publishing, 2002.

Antitrust Law Developments, 6th edn., Chicago, IL: ABA Book Publishing, 2007.

Econometrics: Legal, Practical, and Technical Issues, eds. J. Harkrider and D. L. Rubinfeld, Chicago, IL: ABA Book Publishing, 2005.

Economic Evidence Task Force, *Final Report of Economic Evidence Task Force* (2006), available at: www.abanet.org/antitrust/at-reports/01-c-ii.pdf.

Market Power Handbook: Competition Law and Economic Foundations, Chicago, IL: ABA Book Publishing, 2005.

Areeda, P. and Turner, D. F., *Antitrust Law: An Analysis of Antitrust Principles and Their Application*, vol. II, Boston, MA: Little, Brown, 1978.

Bain, J. S., *Price Theory*, New York: Henry Holt, 1952.

"Relation of Profit Rate to Industry Concentration: American Manufacturing, 1936–1940," *Quarterly Journal of Economics*, 65 (1951), 293–324.

Baker, J. B., "Contemporary Empirical Merger Analysis," *George Mason Law Review*, 5 (1997), 347–361.

"Econometric Analysis in *FTC* v. *Staples*," Prepared Remarks before the Economics Committee of the American Bar Association Section of Antitrust Law, July 18, 1997, available at: www.ftc.gov/speeches/other/stspch.shtm.

"Market Definition: An Analytical Overview," *Antitrust Law Journal*, 74 (2007), 130–173.

Baker, J. B. and Bresnahan, T. F., *Economic Evidence in Antitrust: Defining Markets and Measuring Market Power* (2006), available at: http://ssrn.com/abstract=931225.

"Empirical Methods of Identifying and Measuring Market Power," *Antitrust Law Journal*, 61 (1992), 3–16.

Baker, J. B. and Rubinfeld, D. L., "Empirical Methods in Antitrust Litigation: Review and Critique," *American Law and Economics Review*, 1 (1999), 386–435.

Barceló III, J. J., "Burden of Proof, Prima Facie Case, and Presumption in WTO Dispute Settlement," *Cornell International Law Journal*, 42 (2009), 23–43.

Barnett, T. O., "Competition Law and Policy Modernization: Lessons from the US Common-law Experience," Presentation to the Lisbon Conference on Competition Law and Economics, Lisbon, November 16, 2007, available at: www.justice.gov/atr/public/speeches/227755.htm.

Baron, M., "Artikel 2 FKVO," in H-J. Bunte (ed.), *Langen & Bunte: Kommentar zum deutschen und europäischen Kartellrecht, Band 2: Europäisches Kartellrecht*, 10th edn., Munich: Luchterhand, 2006, pp. 876–970.

Baye, M. R. and Wright, J. D., *Is Antitrust Too Complicated for Generalist Judges? The Impact of Economic Complexity & Judicial Training on Appeals* (2009), available at: http://ssrn.com/abstract=1319888.

Behrens, P., "Der Marktbeherrschungsbegriff in Artikel 82 EG," in B. Ahrens, P. Behrens, and P. von Dietze (eds.), *Marktmacht und Missbrauch*, Baden-Baden: Nomos, 2007, pp. 37–42.

Die ökonomischen Grundlagen des Rechts, Tübingen: Mohr Siebeck, 1986.

"Economic Law between Harmonization and Competition: The Law and Economics Approach," in K. M. Meessen (ed.), *Economic Law as an Economic Good: Its Rule Function and its Tool Function in the Competition of Systems*, Munich: Sellier, 2009, pp. 45–60.

"Markets," in D. S. Clark (ed.), *Encyclopedia of Law & Society*, vol. II, Thousand Oaks, CA: Sage, 2007, pp. 985–990.

Bellamy, C., "An EU Competition Court: The Continuing Debate," in I. Lianos and I. Kokkoris (eds.), *The Reform of EC Competition Law: New Challenges*, Alphen aan den Rijn: Kluwer Law International, 2010, pp. 33–52.

Bender, T., "GATT 1994," in M. Hilf and S. Oeter (eds.), *WTO-Recht: Rechtsordnung des Welthandels*, Baden-Baden: Nomos, 2005, § 9.

Bercero, I. G. and Amarasinha, S. D., "Moving the Trade and Competition Debate Forward," *Journal of International Economic Law*, 4 (2001), 481–506.

Berg, G. C., "An Economic Interpretation of 'Like Product,'" *Journal of World Trade*, 30 (1996), 195–209.

Berger, M. A., "The Supreme Court's Trilogy on the Admissibility of Expert Testimony," in Federal Judicial Center, *Reference Manual on Scientific Evidence*, 2nd edn. (2000), pp. 10–38 available at: www.fjc.gov/public/pdf.nsf/lookup/sciman00.pdf/$file/sciman00.pdf.

Bergh, R. J. van den, "Modern Industrial Organisation versus Old-Fashioned European Competition Law," *European Competition Law Review*, 17 (1996), 75–87.

Bergh, R. J. van den and Camesasca, P., *European Competition Law and Economics: A Comparative Perspective*, London: Sweet & Maxwell, 2006.

Bernhardt, R., "Interpretation of International Law," in R. Bernhardt (ed.), *Encyclopedia of Public International Law*, vol. II, Amsterdam: Elsevier, 1999, pp. 1416–1426.

Bernstein, D. E., "Expert Witnesses, Adversarial Bias, and the (Partial) Failure of the Daubert Revolution," *Iowa Law Review*, 93 (2008), 451–489.

"Junk Science in the United States and the Commonwealth," *Yale Journal of International Law*, 21 (1996), 123–182.

Berrisch, G. M., "Das Allgemeine Zoll- und Handelsabkommen (GATT 1994)," in H-J. Prie ß, G. M. Berrisch, and C. Pitschas (eds.), *WTO-Handbuch*, Munich: Beck, 2003, pp. 71–167.

Bhala, R., *International Trade Law: Interdisciplinary Theory and Practice*, 3rd edn., Newark, NY: LexisNexis, 2008.

Modern GATT Law, London: Sweet & Maxwell, 2005.

Bishop, R. L., "Elasticities, Cross-Elasticities, and Market Relationships," *American Economic Review*, 42 (1952), 779–803.

Bishop, S. and Baldauf, M., *Theoretische Grundlagen und praktische Anwendung wettbewerbsökonomischer Methoden in Bezug auf die Abgrenzung des relevanten Marktes und Fragen zur praktischen Anwendbarkeit des Herfindahl-Hirschman Indexes zur Ermittlung des Konzentrationsgrades* (2006), available at: www.bwb.gv.at/NR/rdonlyres/312D10EA-6476-4932-AFED-6280A0563C3C/28106/MarktabgrenzungrbbStudiefinal.pdf.

Bishop, S. and Walker, M., *The Economics of EC Competition Law: Concepts, Application and Measurement*, 2nd edn., London: Sweet & Maxwell, 2002.

The Economics of EC Competition Law: Concepts, Application and Measurement, 3rd edn., London: Sweet & Maxwell, 2010.

Bishop, W., "Editorial: The Modernisation of DGIV," *European Competition Law Review*, 8 (1997), 481.

Blair, R. D. and Herndon, J. B., "The Implications of Daubert for Economic Evidence in Antitrust Cases," *Washington & Lee Law Review*, 57 (2000), 801–830.

Bogdandy, A. von, "Verfassungsrechtliche Dimensionen der Welthandelsorganisation – 2. Teil: Neue Wege globaler Demokratie?" *Kritische Justiz*, (2001), 425–441.

Bork, R., *The Antitrust Paradox: A Policy at War with Itself*, New York: Basic Books, 1978.

Bossche, P. van den, *The Law and Policy of the World Trade Organization: Text, Cases, Materials*, 2nd edn., Cambridge University Press, 2010.

Botteman, Y., "Mergers, Standard of Proof and Expert Economic Evidence," *Journal of Competition Law & Economics*, 2 (2006), 71–100.

Bown, C. P., "The WTO Secretariat and the Role of Economics in Panels and Arbitrations," in C.P. Bown and J. Pauwelyn (eds.), *The Law, Economics and Politics of Retaliation in WTO Dispute Settlement*, Cambridge University Press, 2010, pp. 391–433.

Brandeis, L., "The Living Law," *Illinois Law Review*, 10 (1916), 461–471.

Brinker, I., "Praktische Probleme der Marktabgrenzung aus rechtlicher Sicht: Von der Bedeutung ökonometrischer Modelle für die Fusionskontrolle," in

J. Schwarze (ed.), *Recht und Ökonomie im Europäischen Wettbewerbsrecht*, Baden-Baden: Nomos, 2006, pp. 41–52.

Bronkers, M. and McNelis, N., "Rethinking the 'Like Product' Definition in WTO Antidumping Law," *Journal of World Trade*, 33 (1991), 73–91.

Budzinski, O. and Christiansen, A., *Simulating the (Unilateral) Effects of Mergers: Implications of the Oracle/PeopleSoft Case* (2006), available at: http://ssrn.com/abstract=924375.

Busch, M. L. and Pelc, K. J., "Does the WTO Need a Permanent Body of Panelists?" *Journal of International Economic Law*, 12 (2009), 579–594.

Cameron, J. and Orava, S. J., "GATT/WTO Panels between Recording and Finding Facts: Issues of Due Process, Evidence, Burden of Proof, and Standard of Review in GATT/WTO Dispute Settlement," in F. Weiss (ed), *Improving WTO Dispute Settlement Procedures: Issues and Lessons from the Practice of Other International Courts and Tribunals*, London: Cameron May, 2000, pp. 195–242.

Camesasca, P. D. and van den Bergh, R. J., "Achilles Uncovered: Revisiting the European Commission's 1997 Market Definition Notice," *Antitrust Bulletin*, 47 (2002), 143–186.

Cárdenas, J. L., *Rolle, Kriterien und Methodik der kartellrechtlichen Marktabgrenzung: eine juristische und ökonomische Analyse* (2005), available at: http://digbib.ubka.uni-karlsruhe.de/volltexte/documents/2973.

Carlton, D. W., "Market Definition: Use and Abuse," *Competition Policy International*, 3 (2007), available at: http://ssrn.com/abstract=987061.

Carlton, D. W. and Perloff, J. M., *Modern Industrial Organization*, 3rd edn., Reading: Addison-Wesley Longman, 2000.

Cass, D. Z., "The 'Constitutionalization' of International Trade Law: Judicial Norm-Generation as the Engine of Constitutional Development in International Trade," *European Journal of International Law*, 12 (2001), 39–75.

Chang, S. W., "Interaction between Trade and Competition: Why a Multilateral Approach for the United States?," *Duke Journal of Comparative & International Law*, 14 (2004), 1–37.

Charnovitz, S., "Book Review: 'Like Products' in International Trade Law: Towards a Consistent GATT/WTO Jurisprudence," *American Journal of International Law*, 98 (2004), 610–614.

Choi, W-M., *"Like Products" in International Trade Law: Towards a Consistent GATT/WTO Jurisprudence*, Oxford University Press, 2003.

"Overcoming the 'Aim and Effect' Theory: Interpretation of the 'Like Product' in GATT Article III," *UC Davis Journal of International Law & Policy*, 8 (2002), 107–131.

Christiansen, A., "Die 'Ökonomisierung' der EU-Fusionskontrolle: Mehr Kosten als Nutzen?" *Wirtschaft und Wettbewerb*, (2005), 285–293.

Christiansen, A. and Locher, L., "Die neuen Standards des Bundeskartellamts für ökonomische Gutachten in der Kartellrechtsanwendung," *Wirtschaft und Wettbewerb*, (2011), 444–453.

Christoforou, T., "Settlement of Science-Based Trade Disputes in the WTO: A Critical Review of the Developing Case Law in the Face of Scientific Uncertainty," *NYU Environmental Law Journal*, 8 (2000), 622–648.

"WTO Panels in the Face of Scientific Uncertainty," in F. Weiss (ed.), *Improving WTO Dispute Settlement Procedures: Issues and Lessons from the Practice of Other International Courts and Tribunals*, London: Cameron May, 2000, pp. 243–263.

Church, J. and Ware, R., *Industrial Organization: A Strategic Approach* (2000), available at: http://works.bepress.com/cgi/viewcontent.cgi?article=1022&context=jeffrey_church.

Clermont, K. M., "Procedure's Magical Number Three: Psychological Bases for Standards of Decision," *Cornell Law Review*, 72 (1987), 1115–1156.

Clermont, K. M. and Sherwin, E., "A Comparative View of Standards of Proof," *American Journal of Comparative Law*, 50 (2002), 243–275.

Coate, M. B. and Fischer, J. H., "A Practical Guide to the Hypothetical Monopolist Test for Market Definition," *Journal of Competition Law & Economics*, 4 (2008), 1031–1063.

Coppi, L. and Walker, M., "Substantial Convergence or Parallel Paths? Similarities and Differences in the Economic Analysis of Horizontal Mergers in US and EU Competition Law," *Antitrust Bulletin*, 49 (2004), 101–152.

Cottier, T., "Risk Management Experience in WTO Dispute Settlement," in D. Robertson and A. Kellow (eds.), *Globalization and the Environment: Risk Assessment and the WTO*, Cheltenham: Edward Elgar, 2001, pp. 41–62.

Cottier, T. and Mavroidis, P. C., "Concluding Remarks," in T. Cottier and P. C. Mavroidis (eds.), *The Role of the Judge in International Trade Regulation*, Ann Arbor, MI: University of Michigan Press, 2003, pp. 349–358.

Cottier, T. and Oesch, M., *International Trade Regulation*, Berne: Staempfli, 2005.

Cottier, T., Pauwelyn, J., and Bürgi, E., *Human Rights and International Trade*, Oxford University Press, 2005.

Crocioni, P., "The Hypothetical Monopolist Test: What it Can and What it Cannot Tell You," *European Competition Law Review*, (2002), 354–362.

Davey, W. J. and Pauwelyn, J., "MFN Unconditionality: A Legal Analysis of the Concept in View of its Evolution in the GATT/WTO Jurisprudence with Particular Reference to the Issue of 'Like Product,'" in T. Cottier and P. C. Mavroidis (eds.), *Regulatory Barriers and the Principle of Non-discrimination in World Trade Law*, Ann Arbor, MI: University of Michigan Press, 2000, pp. 13–50.

De la Serre, E. B. and Sibony, A-L., "Expert Evidence before the EC Courts," *Common Market Law Review*, 45 (2008), 941–985.

Deason, E. E., "Court-Appointed Expert Witnesses: Scientific Positivism Meets Bias and Deference," *Oregon Law Review*, 77 (1998), 59–156.

Demaret, P., "The Non-Discrimination Principle and the Removal of Fiscal Barriers to Intra-Community Trade," in T. Cottier and P. C. Mavroidis (eds.), *Regulatory Barriers and the Principle of Non-discrimination in World Trade Law*, Ann Arbor, MI: University of Michigan Press, 2000, pp. 171–189.

Desai, K., "The European Commission's Draft Notice on Market Definition: A Brief Guide to the Economics," *European Competition Law Review*, (1997), 473–477.

Diamond, S. S., "Reference Guide on Survey Research," in Federal Judicial Center, *Reference Manual on Scientific Evidence*, 2nd edn., 2000, pp. 229–276, available at: www.fjc.gov/public/pdf.nsf/lookup/sciman00.pdf/$file/sciman00.pdf.

Diebold, N. F., "Assessing Competition in International Economic Law: A Comparison of 'Market Definition' and 'Comparability,'" *Legal Issues of Economic Integration*, 38 (2011), 115–141.

Non-Discrimination and the Pillars of International Economic Law: Comparative Analysis and Building Coherency, 2010, available at: http://ssrn.com/abstract=1632927.

Non-Discrimination in International Trade in Services: A Contextual and Comparative Analysis of "Likeness" in WTO/GATS, Cambridge University Press, 2010.

DiMascio, N. and Pauwelyn, J., "Nondiscrimination and Investment Treaties: Worlds Apart or Two Sides of the Same Coin?" *American Journal of International Trade*, 102 (2008), 48–89.

Donath, D., "The Use of Pricing Analysis for Market Definition Purposes: The Arjowiggins/M-real Zanders Reflex and Arsenal/DSP Mergers," *Competition Policy Newsletter*, 1 (2009), 41–50.

Dwyer, D., *The Judicial Assessment of Expert Evidence*, Cambridge University Press, 2008.

Edmond, G., "After Objectivity: Expert Evidence and Procedural Reform," *Sydney Law Review*, 25 (2003), 131–163.

Edmond, G. and Mercer, D., "Trashing 'Junk Science,'" *Stanford Technology Law Review*, 3 (1998), available at: http://stlr.stanford.edu/STLR/Articles/98_STLR_3.

Ehring, L., "De facto Discrimination in World Trade Law," *Journal of World Trade*, 36 (2002), 921–977.

Elsig, M., "Agency Theory and the WTO: Complex Agency and 'Missing Delegation'?" *European Journal of International Relations*, 17 (2011), 495–517.

Elsig, M. and Pollack, M. A., *Agents, Trustees, and International Courts: The Politics of Judicial Appointment at the World Trade Organization*, (2011), available at: http://ssrn.com/abstract=1861443.

Emch, A., "Fiscal Discrimination in WTO Law and EU Law," *Legal Issues of Economic Integration*, 32 (2005), 369–415.

Englisch, J., *Wettbewerbsgleichheit im grenzüberschreitenden Handel*, Tübingen: Mohr Siebeck, 2008.

Ewald, C., "Ökonomie im Kartellrecht: Vom more economic approach zu sachgerechten Standards forensischer Ökonomie," *Wirtschaft und Wettbewerb*, (2011), 15–47.

"Paradigmenwechsel bei der Abgrenzung relevanter Märkte?" *Zeitschrift für Wettbewerbsrecht*, (2004), 512–544.

Farrell, J. and Shapiro, C., "Antitrust Evaluation of Horizontal Mergers: An Economic Alternative to Market Definition," *B.E. Journal of Theoretical Economics*, 10 (2010), available at: www.bepress.com/bejte/vol10/iss1/art9.

Fauchald, O. K., *Environmental Taxes and Trade Discrimination*, London: Kluwer Law, 1998.

"Flexibility and Predictability Under the World Trade Organization's Non-Discrimination Clauses," *Journal of World Trade*, 37 (2003), 443–482.

Faull, J. and Nikpay, A., *The EC Law of Competition*, 2nd edn., Oxford University Press, 2007.

Federal Judicial Center, *Reference Manual on Scientific Evidence*, 2nd ed. (2000), available at: www.fjc.gov/public/pdf.nsf/lookup/sciman00.pdf/$file/sciman00.pdf.

Fegatilli, E. and Petit, N., *Économétrie du droit de la concurrence: un essai de conceptualisation* (2008), available at: www.coleurope.eu/content/gclc/documents/GCLC%20WP%2003-08.pdf.

Fienberg, S. E., Krislov, S. H., and Straf, M. L., "Understanding and Evaluating Statistical Evidence in Litigation," *Jurimetrics Journal*, 36 (1995), 1–32.

Finkelstein, M. O. and Levin, B., *Statistics for Lawyers*, 2nd edn., New York: Springer, 2007.

Fisher, F. M., "Economic Analysis and 'Bright-line' Tests," *Journal of Competition Law & Economics*, 4 (2007),129–153.

Market Definition: A User's Guide (u.d.), available at: http://econ-www.mit.edu/files/2630.

"Multiple Regression in Legal Proceedings," *Columbia Law Review*, 80 (1980), 702–736.

"Statisticians, Econometricians, and Adversary Proceedings," *Journal of the American Statistical Association*, 81 (1986), 277–286.

Foster, C. E., *Scientific Evidence and the Precautionary Principle in International Courts and Tribunals* (2010), available at: http://rmla.org.nz/upload/documents/Salmon_Lecture_2010.pdf.

Foster, W. L., "Expert Testimony: Prevalent Complaints and Proposed Remedies," *Harvard Law Review*, 11 (1897), 169–186.

Freeman, P., Chairman of the Competition Commission, *The Significance of Economic Evidence in Competition Cases* (2009), available at: www.

competition-commission.org.uk/our_role/speeches/pdf/freeman_151009.pdf.

Freund, J. E. and Perles, B. M., *Modern Elementary Statistics*, 12th edn., Upper Saddle River, NJ: Pearson Prentice Hall, 2007.

Friederiszick, H. W., "Economic Analysis in EU Competition Cases," in J. Drexel, L. Idot, and J. Monéger (eds.), *Economic Theory and Competition Law*, Cheltenham: Edward Elgar, 2009, pp. 3–19.

"Marktabgrenzung und Marktmacht," in J. Schwarze (ed.), *Recht und Ökonomie im Europäischen Wettbewerbsrecht*, Baden-Baden: Nomos, 2006, pp. 29–40.

Friederiszick, H. W. and Röller, L-H., "Quantification of Harm in Damages Actions for Antitrust Infringements: Insights from German Cartel Cases," *Journal of Competition Law & Economics*, 6 (2010), 595–618.

Froeb, L. M. and Kobayashi, B. H., "Evidence Production in Adversarial vs. Inquisitorial Regimes," *Economic Letters*, 70 (2001), 267–722.

Froeb, L. M. and Werden, G. J., "The Reverse Cellophane Fallacy in Market Delineation," *Review of Industrial Organization*, 7 (1992), 241–247.

Froeb, L. M., Pautler, P. A., and Röller, L-H., "The Economics of Organizing Economists," *Antitrust Law Journal*, 76 (2009), 569–584.

Füller, J., "Market Definition," in G. Hirsch, F. Montag, and F. J. Säcker (eds.), *Competition Law: European Community Practice and Procedure*, London: Sweet & Maxwell, 2008, pp. 434–468.

Gastwirth, J. L., "Statistical Reasoning in the Legal Setting," *The American Statistician*, 46 (1992), 55–69.

Gavil, A. I., "After Daubert: Discerning the Increasingly Fine Line Between the Admissibility and Sufficiency of Expert Testimony in Antitrust Litigation," *Antitrust Law Journal*, 65 (1997), 663–711.

"Competition Policy, Economics, and Economists: Are We Expecting Too Much?" in B. E. Hawk (ed.), *Annual Proceedings of the Fordham Corporate Law Institute, International Antitrust Law & Policy*, New York: Juris Publishing, 2006, pp. 575–601.

"The Challenges of Economic Proof in a Decentralized and Privatized European Competition Policy System: Lessons From the American Experience," *Journal of Competition Law and Economics*, 4 (2007), 177–206.

Gerber, D. J., "The European Competition Law Story: Some German Roles," in B. Großfeld, R. Sack, T. M. J. Möllers, J. Drexl, and A. Heinemann (eds.), *Festschrift für Wolfgang Fikentscher*, Tübingen: Mohr Siebeck, 1998, pp. 654–670.

Geroski, P., "Thinking Creatively About Markets," *International Journal of Industrial Organization*, 16 (1998), 677–695.

Geroski, P. and Griffith, R., "Identifying Antitrust Markets," in M. Neumann and J. Weigand (eds.), *The International Handbook of Competition*, Cheltenham: Edward Elgar, 2004, pp. 290–305.

Giannelli, P. C. and Imwinkelried, E. L., *Scientific Evidence*, 4th edn., vol. I, Newark, NJ: LexisNexis, 2007.

Glassman, M. L., "Market Definition as a Practical Matter," *Antitrust Law Journal*, 49 (1980), 1155–1166.

Goco, J. B., "Non-Discrimination, 'Likeness,' and Market Definition in World Trade Organization Jurisprudence," *Journal of World Trade*, 40 (2006), 315–340.

Gotts, I. K. and Hemli, D. E., "Just the Facts: The Role of Customer and Economic Evidence in M&A Analysis," *George Mason Law Review*, 13 (2006), 1217–1245.

Grando, M. T., "Allocating the Burden of Proof in WTO Disputes: A Critical Analysis," *Journal of International Economic Law*, 9 (2006), 615–656.

Evidence, Proof, and Fact-finding in WTO Dispute Settlement, Oxford University Press, 2010.

Gross, S. R., "Expert Evidence," *Wisconsin Law Review*, (1991), 1113–1232.

Gupta, R. R., "Appellate Body Interpretation of the WTO Agreement: A Critique in Light of *Japan – Taxes on Alcoholic Beverages*," *Pacific Rim Law & Policy Journal*, (1997), 683–715.

Gutiérrez-Rodríguez, J. D., *Expert Economic Testimony, Economic Evidence and Asymmetry of Information in Antitrust Cases* (2007), available at: http://ssrn.com/abstract=1023494.

"Expert Economic Testimony in Antitrust Cases: A Comparative Law and Economics Study," *International Law, Revista Colombiana de Derecho Internacional*, 14 (2009), 221–251.

Hale, G. E. and Hale, R. D., "A Line of Commerce: Market Definition in Anti-Merger Cases," *Iowa Law Review*, 52 (1966), 406–431.

Market Power: Size and Shape Under the Sherman Act, Boston, MA: Little, Brown, 1958.

Hall, G. R. and Phillips, C. F., "Antimerger Criteria: Power, Concentration, Foreclosure and Size," *Villanova Law Review*, 9 (1964), 211–232.

Harkrider, J. D., *The Use of Econometrics in Antitrust Analysis* (u.d.), available at: www.avhlaw.com/assets/attachments/29.pdf.

Hausman, J. A. and Leonard, G. K., "Economic Analysis of Differentiated Products Mergers Using Real World Data," *George Mason Law Review*, 5 (1997), 321–346.

Hay, B. L., "Allocating the Burden of Proof," *Indiana Law Journal*, 72 (1997), 651–680.

Hay, G. A., "Market Power in Antitrust," *Antitrust Law Journal*, 60 (1992), 807–828.

Heitzer, B., *Economic Assessment in Competition Enforcement: Developments in France and Germany – Statement for the Panel*, CRA International, Annual Conference "Economic Developments in European Competition Policy,"

December 3, 2008, available at: www.bundeskartellamt.de/wDeutsch/download/pdf/Diskussionsbeitraege/081203_CRA.pdf.

Hildebrand, D., *The Role of Economic Analysis in the EC Competition Rules*, 2nd edn., The Hague: Kluwer Law International, 2002.

The Role of Economic Analysis in the EC Competition Rules, 3rd edn., Alphen aan den Rijn: Kluwer Law International, 2009.

"Using Conjoint Analysis for Market Definition: Application of Modern Market Research Tools to Implement the Hypothetical Monopolist Test," *World Competition*, 29 (2006), 315–336.

Hockett, C. B. and Hinman, F. M., "Admissibility of Expert Testimony in Antitrust Cases: Does Daubert Raise a New Barrier to Entry for Economists?" *Antitrust*, 10 (1996), 40–45.

Hogg, R. V. and Craig, A. T., *Introduction to Mathematical Statistics*, 5th edn., New Jersey: Prentice Hall, 1995.

Hogg, S. and Nawaz, M., "Japan – Alcoholic Beverages, Report of the Panel, 11 July 1996 and of the Appellate Body, 4 October 1996," in J. Cameron and K. Campbell (eds.), *Dispute Resolution in the World Trade Organisation*, London: Cameron May, 1998, pp. 343–360.

Holmes, O. W., "The Path of the Law," *Harvard Law Review*, 10 (1897), 457–478.

Hoppmann, E., *Fusionskontrolle*, Tübingen: Mohr Siebeck, 1972.

Horn, H. and Mavroidis, P. C., "Still Hazy After All These Years: The Interpretation of National Treatment in the GATT/WTO Case Law on Tax Discrimination," *European Journal of International Law*, 15 (2001), 39–69.

Horn, H. and Weiler, J. H. H., "EC – Asbestos European Communities: Measures Affecting Asbestos and Asbestos-Containing Products," *World Trade Review*, 3 (2004), 129–151.

Horowitz, I., "Market Definition in Antitrust Analysis: A Regression-based Approach," *Southern Economics Journal*, 48 (1981), 1–16.

Hosken, D., O'Brien, D., Scheffman, D. and Vita, M., *Demand System Estimation and its Application to Horizontal Merger Analysis* (2002), available at: www.ftc.gov/be/workpapers/wp246.pdf.

Hovenkamp, H., "Economic Experts in Antitrust Cases," in D. L. Faigman, M. J. Saks, J. Sanders, and E. K. Cheng (eds.), *Modern Scientific Evidence: The Law and Science of Expert Testimony*, vol. V, Eagan, MN: Thompson West, 2008, ch. 44.

Federal Antitrust Policy: The Law of Competition and its Practice, 3rd edn., St. Paul, MN: Thompson West, 2005.

The Antitrust Enterprise: Principle and Execution, Cambridge, MA: Harvard University Press, 2005.

Howse, R. L., "Adjudicative Legitimacy and Treaty Interpretation in International Trade Law: The Early Years of WTO Jurisprudence," in J. H. H. Weiler (ed.),

The EU, the WTO, and the NAFTA: Towards a Common Law of International Trade? Oxford University Press, 2000, pp. 33–69.

"Democracy, Science, and Free Trade: Risk Regulation on Trial at the World Trade Organization," *Michigan Law Review*, 98 (2000), 2329–2357.

"The Appellate Body Rulings in the Shrimp/Turtle Case: A New Legal Baseline for the Trade and Environment Debate," *Columbia Journal of Environmental Law*, 27 (2002), 491–521.

Howse, R. L. and Regan, D., "The Product/Process Distinction: An Illusory Basis for Disciplining 'Unilateralism' in Trade Policy," *European Journal of International Law*, 11 (2000), 249–289.

Howse, R. L. and Tuerk, E., "The WTO Impact on Internal Regulations: A Case Study of the *Canada – EC Asbestos* Dispute," in G. de Búrca and J. Scott (eds.), *The EU and the WTO: Legal and Constitutional Issues*, Oxford: Hart, 2001, pp. 283–328.

Hudec, R. E., *Essays on the Nature of International Trade Law*, London: Cameron May, 1999.

"GATT/WTO Constraints on National Regulation: Requiem for an 'Aim and Effects' Test," *International Lawyer*, 32 (1998), 619–648.

"'Like Product': The Differences in Meaning in GATT Articles I and III," in T. Cottier and P. C. Mavroidis (eds.), *Regulatory Barriers and the Principle of Non-discrimination in World Trade Law*, Ann Arbor, MI: University of Michigan Press, 2000, pp. 101–123.

Immenga, U. and Körber, T., "Artikel 2 Beurteilung von Zusammenschlüssen," in U. Immenga and E-J. Mestmäcker (eds.), *Wettbewerbsrecht Band 1 EG/Teil 2*, 4th edn., Munich: C. H. Beck, 2007.

Irwin, D. A., Mavroidis, P. C., and Sykes, A. O., *The Genesis of the GATT*, Cambridge University Press, 2008.

Iynedjian, M., "The Case for Incorporating Scientists and Technicians into WTO Panels," *Journal of World Trade*, 42 (2008), 279–297.

Jackson, J. H., "Comments on Shrimp/Turtle and the Product/Process Distinction," *European Journal of International Law*, 11 (2000), 291–307.

Sovereignty, the WTO and Changing Fundamentals of International Law, Cambridge University Press, 2006.

World Trade and the Law of GATT, Indianapolis, IN: Bobbs-Merrill Co., 1969.

Jacobson, J. M., "Problems in the Use of Econometrics in Antitrust Matters," presentation to the Conference Board's 2003 Antitrust Conference, March 13, 2003, available at: www.akingump.com/docs/publication/548.PPT.

Jones, A. and Sufrin, B., *EC Competition Law*, 3rd edn., Oxford University Press, 2008.

Kanner, A. and Casey, M. R., "Daubert and the Disappearing Jury Trial," *University of Pittsburgh Law Journal*, 69 (2007), 281–329.

Kalinowski, J. O. von, Sullivan, P., and McGuirl, M., *Antitrust Laws and Trade Regulation*, 2nd edn., vol. II, San Francisco, CA: Matthew Bender, 2007.

Kaplan, J., "Decision Theory and the Factfinding Process," *Stanford Law Review*, 20 (1968), 1065–1092.

Karp, D. C., "A Consumer Oriented Approach to Market Definition Under the Antitrust Laws," *University of San Francisco Law Review*, 18 (1983), 221–251.

Kauper, T. E., "The Problem of Market Definition under EC Competition Law," in B. E. Hawk (ed.), *Annual Proceedings of the Fordham Corporate Law Institute, International Antitrust Law & Policy*, New York: Juris Publishing, 1997, pp. 239–306.

Kaye, D. H., "Is Proof of Statistical Significance Relevant?" *Washington Law Review*, 61 (1986), 1333–1365.

"Naked Statistical Evidence," *Yale Law Journal*, 89 (1980), 601–611.

"The Dynamics of Daubert: Methodology, Conclusions and Fit in Statistical and Econometric Studies," *Virginia Law Review*, 86 (2001), 1933–2018.

"The Limits of the Preponderance of the Evidence Standard: Justifiably Naked Statistical Evidence and Multiple Causation," *American Bar Foundation Research Journal*, 7 (1982), 487–516.

Kaye, D. H. and Freedman, D. A., "Reference Guide on Statistics," in Federal Judicial Center, *Reference Manual on Scientific Evidence*, 2nd edn., 2000, pp. 83–178, available at: www.fjc.gov/public/pdf.nsf/lookup/sciman00.pdf/$file/sciman00.pdf.

Kazazi, M., *Burden of Proof and Related Issues: A Study on Evidence before International Tribunals*, The Hague: Kluwer Law International, 1996.

Keck, A., "WTO Dispute Settlement: What Role for Economic Analysis? A Commentary on Fritz Beuss," *Journal of Industry, Competition and Trade*, 4 (2004), 365–371.

Keck, A., Malashevich, B., and Gray, I., "A 'Probabilistic' Approach to the Use of Econometric Models in Sunset Reviews," *World Trade Review*, 6 (2007), 371–396.

Kenen, P. B., *The International Economy*, 4th edn., Cambridge University Press, 2000.

Kennedy, K. C., *Competition Law and the World Trade Organisation: The Limits of Multilateralism*, London: Sweet & Maxwell, 2001.

Kennedy, P., *A Guide to Econometrics*, 6th edn., Malden, MA: Blackwell, 2008.

Keyte, J. A., "Market Definition and Differentiated Products: The Need for a Workable Standard," *Antitrust Law Journal*, 63 (1995), 697–748.

Klein, T., "SSNIP-Test oder Bedarfsmarktkonzept?" *Wirtschaft und Wettbewerb*, (2010), 169–177.

Kotler, P., Keller, K. L., Brady, M., Goodman, M., and Hansen, T., *Marketing Management*, Harlow: Pearson Prentice Hall, 2009.

Kovacic, W. E. and Shapiro, C., "Antitrust Policy: Century of Economic and Legal Thinking," *Journal of Economic Perspectives*, 14 (2000), 43–60.

Krafka, C., Dunn, M. A., Johnson, M. T., Cecil, J. S., and Miletich, D., "Judge and Attorney Experiences, Practices, and Concerns Regarding Expert Testimony in Federal Civil Trials," *Psychology, Public Policy, and Law*, 8 (2002), 309–332.

Krajewski, M., *Wirtschaftsvölkerrecht*, Heidelberg: C. F. Müller, 2006.

Krattenmaker, T. and Salop, S., "Anticompetitive Exclusion: Raising Rivals' Costs to Achieve Power over Price," *Yale Law Journal*, 96 (1986), 209–293.

Kroes, N., *European Competition Policy: Delivering Better Markets and Better Choices*, European Consumer and Competition Day, London, September 15, 2005, available at: http://europa.eu/rapid/pressReleasesAction.do?reference=SPEECH/05/512&format=HTML&aged=1&language=EN&guiLanguage=en.

"Exclusionary Abuses of Dominance: The European Commission's Enforcement Priorities," Fordham University Symposium, New York, September 25, 2008, available at: http://europa.eu/rapid/pressReleasesAction.do?reference=SPEECH/08/457&format=HTML&aged=0&language=EN&guiLanguage=en.

"Preliminary Thoughts on Policy Review of Article 82," Fordham University Symposium, New York City, September 23, 2005, available at: http://europa.eu/rapid/pressReleasesAction.do?reference=SPEECH/05/537.

Krugman, P. R. and Obstfeld, M., *International Economics: Theory & Practice*, 8th edn., Boston, MA: Pearson Addison Wesley, 2009.

Kuyper, P. J., "Booze and Fast Cars: Tax Discrimination under GATT and the EC," *Legal Issues of European Integration*, (1996), 129–144.

Lamy, P., Director-General of the WTO, "China hält sich an die Regeln," *Handelsblatt-Gespräch*, July 16/17, 2010, p. 6.

Lande, R. H. and Langenfeld, J., "From Surrogates to Stories: The Evolution of Federal Merger Policy," *Antitrust*, 11 (1997), 5–10.

Landes, W. M. and Posner, R. A., "Market Power in Antitrust Cases," *Harvard Law Review*, 94 (1981), 937–996.

Langenfeld, J. and Alexander, C., *Daubert Challenges of Antitrust Experts* (2008), available at: www.antitrustinstitute.org/files/AAI%20working%20paper%2008-06_120620082058.pdf.

Learned Hand, "Historical and Practical Considerations Regarding Expert Testimony," *Harvard Law Review*, 15 (1901), 40–58.

Leberl, D., *Zur Zeitkomponente im Marktbegriff des GWB*, Pfaffenweiler: Centaurus, 1988.

Lee, T. R., "Pleading and Proof: The Economics of Legal Burdens," *Brigham Young University Law Review*, (1997), 1–34.

Lee, T. V., "Court-Appointed Experts and Judicial Reluctance: A Proposal to Amend Rule 706 of the Federal Rules of Evidence," *Yale Law and Policy Review*, 6 (1988), 480–504.

Legal, H., "Standards of Proof and Standards of Judicial Review in EU Competition Law," in B. E. Hawk (ed.), *Annual Proceedings of the Fordham Corporate Law Institute, International Antitrust Law & Policy*, New York: Juris Publishing, 2006, pp. 107–116.

Lerner, A. P., "The Concept of Monopoly and the Measurement of Monopoly Power," *Review of Economic Studies*, 1 (1934), 157–175.

Lester, S. and Mercurio, B., *World Trade Law: Text, Materials and Commentary*, Oxford: Hart, 2008.

Lexecon, *An Introduction to Quantitative Techniques in Competition Analysis* (u.d.), available at: www.crai.com/ecp/assets/quantitative_techniques.pdf.

Lianos, I., "'Judging' Economists: Economic Expertise in Competition Law Litigation: A European View," in I. Lianos and I. Kokkoris (eds.), *The Reform of EC Competition Law: New Challenges*, Alphen aan den Rijn: Kluwer Law International, 2010, pp. 185–321.

Lipsky, A. B., "Antitrust Economics: Making Progress, Avoiding Regression," *George Mason Law Review*, 12 (2003), 163–177.

Lopatka, J. E. and Page, W. H., "Economic Authority and the Limits of Expertise in Antitrust Cases," *Cornell Law Review*, 90 (2005), 617–703.

Lord Woolf, *Access to Justice*, Interim Report to the Lord Chancellor on the Civil Justice System in England and Wales (1995), available at: www.dca.gov.uk/civil/interim/woolf.htm.

Lowenfeld, A. F., "Remedies Along with Rights: Institutional Reform in the new GATT," *American Journal of International Law*, 88 (1994), 477–488.

Lubkin, G. P., "Is Europe's Glass Half Empty or Half Full? Alcoholic Beverage Taxation and the Development of a European Identity," *Columbia Journal of European Law*, 3 (1997), 357–411.

Lücking, J. and Simon, S., "Definition of the Relevant Market," in G. Drauz and C. Jones (eds.), *EC Competition Law, vol. II: Mergers and Acquisitions*, Leuven: Claeys & Casteels, 2006.

MacLennan, J., "Evidence, Standard and Burden of Proof and the Use of Experts in Procedure Before the Luxembourg Courts," in F. Weiss (ed.), *Improving WTO Dispute Settlement Procedures: Issues and Lessons from the Practice of Other International Courts and Tribunals*, London: Cameron May, 2000, pp. 265–288.

Malacrida, R., "Some Reflections on the Use of Economic Analysis in WTO Dispute Settlement Proceedings," in C. P. Bown and J. Pauwelyn (eds.), *The Law, Economics and Politics of Retaliation in WTO Dispute Settlement*, Cambridge University Press, 2010, pp. 434–445.

Mason, E. S., "Price and Production Policies of Large-Scale Enterprise," 29 *American Economic Review*, Supplement Papers and Proceedings of the Fifty-first Annual Meeting of the American Economic Association, 29 (1939), 61–74.

Matsushita, M., Schoenbaum, T. J., and Mavroidis, P. C., *The World Trade Organization*, Oxford University Press, 2003.

Mattoo, A. and Subramanian, A., "Regulatory Autonomy and Multilateral Disciplines: The Dilemma and a Possible Resolution," *Journal of International Economic Law*, 1 (1998), 303–322.

Mavroidis, P. C., "Development of WTO Dispute Settlement Procedures Through Case-Law (We Will Fix It)," in F. Ortino and E-U. Petersmann (eds.), *The WTO Dispute Settlement System 1995–2003*, The Hague: Kluwer Law International, 2004, pp. 153–176.

The General Agreement on Tariffs and Trade: A Commentary, Oxford University Press, 2005.

Trade in Goods: The GATT and the Other Agreements Regulating Trade in Goods, Oxford University Press, 2007.

McGovern, E., *International Trade Regulation*, Issue 27, Exeter: Globefield Press, 2010.

Melloni, M., *The Principle of National Treatment in the GATT: A Survey of the Jurisprudence, Practice and Policy*, Brussels: Bruylant, 2005.

Monti, M., "Market Definition as a Cornerstone of EU Competition Policy," Workshop on Market Definition, Helsinki, October 5, 2001, available at: http://europa.eu/rapid/pressReleasesAction.do?reference=SPEECH/01/439 &format=HTML&aged=0&language=EN&guiLanguage=en.

Mora, M. M., "A GATT with Teeth: Law Wins Over Politics in the Resolution of International Trade Disputes," *Columbia Journal of Transnational Law*, 31 (1993), 103–180.

Möschel, W., "Missbrauch einer Marktbeherrschenden Stellung," in U. Immenga and E-J. Mestmäcker (eds.), *Wettbewerbsrecht GWB: Kommentar zum Deutschen Kartellrecht*, 4th edn., Munich: C. H. Beck, 2007, § 19.

Motta, M., *Competition Policy: Theory and Practice*, Cambridge University Press, 2004.

Müller, C., *Abschied vom Bedarfsmarktkonzept bei der Marktabgrenzung?* Baden-Baden: Nomos, 2007.

NERA Economic Consulting (C. Dippon, G. Leonard, and L. Wu), *Application of Empirical Methods in Merger Analysis* (2005) (on file with author).

The Role of Quantitative Analysis in Competition Assessments (2005), available at: www.nera.com/67_5009.htm.

Neven, D., "Competition Economics and Antitrust in Europe," *Economic Policy*, (2006), 743–791.

Economic Analysis in European Competition Policy: The First 2000 (or so) Years (2008), available at: http://ec.europa.eu/dgs/competition/economist/oxera.pdf.

"How Should 'Protection' be Evaluated in Article III GATT Disputes?" *European Journal of Political Economy*, 17 (2001), 421–444.

"The Economic Evaluation of Protection under Art III: Some Principles and Suggestions for the Definition of a Trade Relevant Market," in T. Cottier and P. C. Mavroidis (eds.), *Regulatory Barriers and the Principle of Non-discrimination in World Trade Law*, Ann Arbor, MI: University of Michigan Press, 2000, pp. 331–342.

Neven, D. and Coninck, R. de, *Best Practices on the Submission of Economic Evidence and Data Collection* (2010), available at: http://ec.europa.eu/dgs/competition/economist/neven_deconinck_best_practices.pdf.

Neven, D. and de la Mano, M., *Economics at DG Competition, 2009–2010* (2010), available at: http://antitrustlair.files.wordpress.com/2010/11/neven-de-la-mano-20101.pdf.

Nevo-Ilan, H., "Definition of the Relevant Market: (Lack of) Harmony between Industrial Economics and Competition Law" (2007) (on file with author).

Nitsche, R., "Wettbewerbsökonomische Analyse der Auswirkungen von Fusionen," in J. Schwarze (ed.), *Recht und Ökonomie im Europäischen Wettbewerbsrecht*, Baden-Baden: Nomos, 2006, pp. 53–70.

Nordström, H., "The World Trade Organization Secretariat in a Changing World," *Journal of World Trade*, 39 (2005), 819–853.

O'Donoghue, R. and Padilla, A. J., *The Law and Economics of Article 82 EC*, Oxford: Hart, 2006.

OECD, *Presenting Complex Economic Theories to Judges* (2008), available at: www.oecd.org/dataoecd/39/59/41776770.pdf.

Oesch, M., *Standards of Review in WTO Dispute Resolution*, Oxford University Press, 2003.

Ortino, F., *Basic Legal Instruments for the Liberalisation of Trade: A Comparative Analysis of EC and WTO Law*, Oxford: Hart, 2004.

Palmeter, D. and Mavroidis, P. C., *Dispute Settlement in the World Trade Organization: Practice and Procedure*, 2nd edn., Cambridge University Press, 2004.

Pauwelyn, J., "Evidence, Proof and Persuasion in WTO Dispute Settlement: Who Bears the Burden?" *Journal of International Economic Law*, 1 (1998), 227–258.

"Expert Advice in WTO Dispute Settlement," in G. A. Bermann and P. C. Mavroidis (eds.), *Trade and Human Health and Safety*, Cambridge University Press, 2006, pp. 235–256.

"Recent Books on Trade and Environment: GATT Phantoms Still Haunt the WTO," *European Journal of International Law*, 15 (2004), 575–592.

"The Use of Experts in WTO Dispute Settlement," *International & Comparative Law Quarterly*, 51 (2002), 325–364.

Peter, W., "Witness Conferencing," *Arbitration International*, 18 (2002), 47–58.

Pfitzer, J. H. and Sabune, S., "Burden of Proof in Dispute Settlement: Contemplating Preponderance of the Evidence,"(International Centre for Trade and

Sustainable Development, Issue Paper No. 9, 2009, available at: http://ictsd.org/downloads/2009/04/burden_of_proof.pdf.

Pindyck, R. S. and Rubinfeld, D. L., *Microeconomics*, 7th edn., Upper Saddle River, NJ: Pearson, 2009.

Pitofsky, R., "New Definitions of Relevant Market and the Assault on Antitrust," *Columbia Law Review*, 90 (1990), 1805–1864.

The Effect of Global Trade on United States Competition Law and Enforcement Policies, New York City, October 15, 1999, available at: www.ftc.gov/speeches/pitofsky/fobebf1.shtm.

Popper, K., *Logik der Forschung*, 11th edn., Tübingen: Mohr Siebeck, 2005.

Porges, A. and Trachtman, J., "Robert Hudec and Domestic Regulation: The Resurrection of Aim and Effects," *Journal of World Trade*, 37 (2003), 783–799.

Posner, R. A., "A Program for the Antitrust Division," *University of Chicago Law Review*, 38 (1971), 500–536.

"An Economic Approach to Legal Procedure and Judicial Administration," *Journal of Legal Studies*, 2 (1973), 399–458.

"An Economic Approach to the Law of Evidence," *Stanford Law Review*, 51 (1999), 1477–1546.

Antitrust Law: An Economic Perspective, Chicago University Press, 1976.

Catastrophe: Risk and Response, Oxford University Press, 2004.

Economic Analysis of Law, 7th edn., New York: Aspen, 2007.

"The Law and Economics of the Economic Expert Witness," *Journal of Economic Perspectives*, 13 (1999), 91–99.

The Problematics of Moral and Legal Theory, Cambridge, MA: Harvard University Press, 1999.

Puth, S., *WTO und Umwelt: Die Produkt-Prozess-Doktrin*, Berlin: Duncker & Humblot, 2003.

"Zölle und allgemeine Fragen des Marktzugangs," in M. Hilf and S. Oeter (eds.), *WTO-Recht: Rechtsordnung des Welthandels*, Baden-Baden: Nomos, 2005, § 10.

Quick, R. and Lau, C., "Environmentally Motivated Tax Distinctions and WTO Law: The European Commission's Green Paper on Integrated Product Policy in Light of the 'Like Product-' and 'PPM-' Debates," *Journal of International Economic Law*, 6 (2003), 419–458.

Raible, M., *Protektionismusverbote im Recht der Wirtschaftsintegration: Eine vergleichende Untersuchung der Regelung des Freihandels der USA, der EU und der WTO*, Baden-Baden: Nomos, 2005.

Reeves, T. and Dodoo, N., "Standards of Proof and Standards of Judicial Review in EC Merger Law," in B. E. Hawk (ed.), *Annual Proceedings of the Fordham Corporate Law Institute, International Antitrust Law & Policy*, New York: Juris Publishing, 2006, pp. 117–142.

Regan, D. H., "Further Thoughts on the Role of Regulatory Purpose Under Article III of the GATT: A Tribute to Bob Hudec," *Journal of World Trade*, 37 (2003), 737–760.

"Regulatory Purpose and 'Like Products' in Article III:4 of the GATT (With Additional Remarks on Article III:2)," *Journal of World Trade*, 36 (2002), 443–478.

"Report of the Task Force on Productivity and Competition," reprinted in *Journal for Reprints for Antitrust Law and Economics*, 1 (1969), 827–881.

Roessler, F., "Beyond the Ostensible: A Tribute to Professor Robert Hudec's Insights on the Determination of the Likeness of Products Under the National Treatment Provisions of the General Agreement on Tariffs and Trade," *Journal of World Trade*, 37 (2003), 771–781.

Röller, L-H., "Economic Analysis and Competition Policy Enforcement in Europe," in P. A. G. van Bergeijk and E. Kloosterhuis (eds.), *Modelling European Mergers*, Cheltenham: Edward Elgar, 2005, pp. 13–26.

Rompuy, B. van, "The Standard of Proof in EC Merger Control," IES Working Paper (2008), available at: www.ies.be/files/repo/IES%20Working%20Paper%204_Ben%20Van%20Rompuy.pdf.

Rosenfield, A. M., "The Use of Economics in Antitrust Litigation and Counseling," *Columbia Business Law Review*, (1986), 49–82.

Rösler, P., "Der relevante Markt in der Europäischen Fusionskontrolle," *Neue Zeitschrift für Gesellschaftsrecht*, (2000), 761–770.

Roth, W-H. and Ackermann, T., "Grundfragen Art. 81 Abs. 1," in W. Jaeger, P. Pohlmann, H. Rieger, and D. Schroeder (eds.), *Frankfurter Kommentar zum Kartellrecht*, Band II, Cologne: Verlag Dr. Otto Schmidt, 2009.

Rubinfeld, D. L., Econometric Issues in Antitrust Analysis, *Journal of Institutional and Theoretical Economics*, 166 (2010), 62–77.

"Econometrics in the Courtroom," *Columbia Law Review*, 85 (1985), 1048–1097.

Economics Roundtable, Testimony before the Antitrust Modernization Commission, January 19, 2006, available at: http://govinfo.library.unt.edu/amc/commission_hearings/pdf/rubinfeld_statement_final.pdf.

"Market Definition with Differentiated Products: The Post/Nabisco Cereal Merger," *Antitrust Law Journal*, 68 (2000), 163–182.

"On the Foundations of Antitrust Law and Economics," in R. Pitofsky (ed.), *How the Chicago School Overshot the Market: The Effect of Conservative Economic Analysis on US Antitrust*, Oxford University Press, 2008, pp. 51–73.

"On the Pretrial Use of Economists," *Antitrust Bulletin*, 55 (2010), 679–697.

"Quantitative Methods in Antitrust," in ABA Section of Antitrust Law, *Issues in Competition Law and Policy*, vol. I, Chicago, IL: ABA Publishing, 2008, pp. 723–742.

"Reference Guide on Multiple Regression," in Federal Judicial Center, *Reference Manual on Scientific Evidence*, 2nd edn., 2000, pp. 179–227, available at: www.fjc.gov/public/pdf.nsf/lookup/sciman00.pdf/$file/sciman00.pdf.

Rubinfeld, D. L. and Steiner, P. O., "Quantitative Methods in Antitrust Litigation," *Law and Contemporary Problems*, 46 (1983), 69–141.

Säcker, F. J., *The Concept of the Relevant Product Market: Between Demand-side Substitutability and Supply-side Substitutability in Competition Law*, Frankfurt a. M.: Peter Lang, 2008.

Sanders, J., "The Merits of the Paternalistic Justifications of Restrictions on the Admissibility of Expert Evidence," *Seton Hall Law Review*, 33 (2003), 881–941.

Sandrock, O., "Grundprobleme der sachlichen Marktabgrenzung," in H. Merz and W. R. Schluep (eds.), *Recht und Wirtschaft heute: Festgabe zum 65. Geburtstag von Max Kummer*, Berne: Stämpfli, 1980, pp. 449–486.

Scheffman, D., *Best Practices for Data, and Economics and Financial Analyses in Antitrust Investigations* (2002), available at: www.ftc.gov/speeches/scheffman.shtm.

Scheffman, D. and Coleman, M., *FTC Perspectives on the Use of Econometric Analyses in Antitrust Cases* (u.d.), available at: www.ftc.gov/be/ftcperspectivesoneconometrics.pdf.

Scheffman, D. and Spiller, P. T., "Geographic Market Definition Under the US Department of Justice Merger Guidelines," *Journal of Law & Economics*, 30 (1987), 123–147.

Schmidt, I., "Relevanter Markt, Marktbeherrschung und Missbrauch in § 22 GWB und Art 86 EWGV," *Wirtschaft und Wettbewerb*, (1965), 451–494.

Schropp, S. A. B., *Trade Policy Flexibility and Enforcement in the WTO: A Law and Economics Analysis*, Cambridge University Press, 2009.

Schumpeter, J. A., *Capitalism, Socialism, and Democracy*, London: George Allen & Unwin, 1942.

Schwalba, M., *Die wettbewerbsbezogene Abgrenzung des relevanten Marktes*, Frankfurt a. M.: Peter Lang, 2000.

Schwalbe, U. and Zimmer, D., *Kartellrecht und Ökonomie: Moderne ökonomische Ansätze in der europäischen und deutschen Zusammenschlusskontrolle*, Frankfurt a. M.: Verlag Recht und Wirtschaft, 2006.

Senti, R., *WTO: System und Funktionsweise der Welthandelsordnung*, Zurich: Schluthess, 2000.

Shadikhodjaev, S., "National Treatment under GATT Article III:2 and its Applicability in the Context of Korea's FTAs," *Journal of International Economic Studies*, 12 (2008), 65–111.

Shin, H. S., "Adversarial and Inquisitorial Procedures in Arbitration," *RAND Journal of Economics*, 29 (1998), 378–405.

Shrives, R. E., "Geographic Market Areas and Market Structure in the Bituminous Coal Industry," *Antitrust Bulletin*, 23 (1978), 589–625.

Sievers, F., *Wettbewerbsgutachten: Ökonomen als Dienstleister,* Handelsblatt, November 2, 2009, p. 7.

Simons, J. J. and Williams, M. A., "The Renaissance of Market Definition," *Antitrust Bulletin*, 38 (1993), 799–857.

Slotboom, M. M., *A Comparison of WTO and EC Law: Do Different Objects and Purposes Matter For Treaty Interpretation?* London: Cameron May, 2007.

"Do Different Treaty Purposes Matter? The Elimination of Discriminatory Internal Taxes in EC and WTO Law," *Journal of International Economic Law*, 4 (2001), 557–579.

Solow, J. L. and Fletcher, D., "Doing Good Economics in the Courtroom: Thoughts on Daubert and Expert Testimony in Antitrust," *Journal of Corporation Law*, 31 (2006), 489–502.

Srinivasan, T. N., "Nondiscrimination in GATT/WTO: Was there Anything to Begin With and is there Anything Left?," *World Trade Review*, 4 (2005), 69–95.

Stepkowska, U. M., "Process and Production Methods (PPMs) in the GATT Agreement," *Zeitschrift für europarechtliche Studien*, (2007), 273–329.

Steuer, R. M., "Standards of Proof and Judicial Review: A US Perspective," in B. E. Hawk (ed.), *Annual Proceedings of the Fordham Corporate Law Institute, International Antitrust Law & Policy,* New York: Juris Publishing, 2006, pp. 143–156.

Stevens, W. H. S., "The Federal Trade Commission's Contribution to Industrial and Economic Analysis: The Work of the Economic Division," *George Washington Law Review*, 8 (1940), 545–580.

Stigler, G. J., "The Economist and the Problem of Monopoly," 72 *American Economic Review*, 72 (1982), 1–11.

The Theory of Price, 3rd edn., New York: Macmillan, 1966.

Stigler, G. J. and Sherwin, R. A., "The Extent of the Market," *Journal of Law & Economics*, 28 (1985), 555–585.

Sullivan, L. A., *Handbook of the Law of Antitrust*, St. Paul, MN: West Publishing, 1977.

Sykes, A. O., *An Introduction to Regression Analysis* (1992), available at: www.law.uchicago.edu/files/files/20.Sykes_.Regression_0.pdf.

"Comparative Advantage and the Normative Economics of International Trade Policy," *Journal of International Economic Law*, 1 (1998), 49–82.

Tanigichi, Y., "Understanding the Concept of Prima Facie Proof in WTO Dispute Settlement," in M. E. Janow, V. Donaldson, and A. Yanovich (eds.), *The WTO: Governance, Dispute Settlement, and Developing Countries,* New York: Juris Publishing, 2008, pp. 553–572.

Tarullo, D., "Norms and Institutions in Global Competition Policy," *American Journal of International Law*, 94 (2000), 478–504.

ten Kate, A. and Niels, G., "The Relevant Market: A Concept Still in Search of a Definition," *Journal of Competition Law & Economics*, 5 (2008), 297–333.

Thaggert, H. L., "A Closer Look at the Tuna-Dolphin Case: 'Like Products' and 'Extrajurisdictionality' in the Trade and Environment Context," in J. Cameron, P. Demaret, and D. Geradin (eds.), *Trade & the Environment: The Search for Balance*, vol. I, London: Cameron May, 1994, pp. 69–95.

The Supreme Court, 1963 Term, *Harvard Law Review*, 78 (1964), 143–312.

Tietje, C., *Normative Grundstrukturen der Behandlung nichttarifärer Handelshemmnisse in der WTO-GATT-Rechtsordnung: eine Untersuchung unter besonderer Berücksichtung des Countertrade*, Berlin: Duncker & Humblot, 1998.

Timmerbeil, S., "The Role of Expert Witnesses in German and U.S. Civil Litigation," *Annual Survey of International and Comparative Law*, 9 (2003), 163–187.

Traugott, R., "Zur Abgrenzung von Märkten," *Wettbewerb und Wirtschaft*, 9 (1998), 929–939.

Trebilcock, M. J. and Giri, S. K., "The National Treatment Principle in International Trade Law," in E. K. Choi and J. C. Hartigan (eds.), *Handbook of International Trade, vol. II: Economic and Legal Analyses of Trade Policy and Institutions*, Malden, MA: Blackwell, 2004, pp. 185–238.

Trebilcock, M. and Howse, R. L., *The Regulation of International Trade*, 3rd edn., London: Routledge, 2005.

Tribe, L. H., "Trial by Mathematics: Precision and Ritual in the Legal Process," *Harvard Law Review*, 84 (1971), 1329–1393.

Tsai, E. S., "'Like' is a Four-Letter Word: GATT Article III's 'Like Product' Conundrum," *Berkeley Journal of International Law*, 17 (1999), 26–60.

Turner, D. F., "The Role of the 'Market Concept' in Antitrust Law," *Antitrust Law Journal*, 49 (1980), 1145–1154.

Taylor, M. D., *International Competition Law: A New Dimension for the WTO?* Cambridge University Press, 2006.

Tyson, J. M., "Presumed Guilty Until Proven Innocent: Using Results of Statistical or Econometric Studies as Evidence," *St. Thomas Law Review*, 10 (1997), 387–406.

Unterhalter, D., "The Burden of Proof in WTO Dispute Settlement," in M. E. Janow, V. Donaldson, and A. Yanovich (eds.), *The WTO: Governance, Dispute Settlement & Developing Countries*, New York: Juris Publishing, 2008, pp. 543–552.

Utton, M. A., *International Competition Policy: Maintaining Open Markets in the Global Economy*, Cheltenham: Edward Elgar, 2006.

Verhoosel, G., *National Treatment and WTO Dispute Settlement: Adjudicating the Boundaries of Regulatory Autonomy*, Oxford: Hart, 2002.

Vesterdorf, B., "Standard of Proof in Merger Cases: Reflections in the Light of Recent Case Law of the Community Courts," *European Competition Journal*, 1 (2005), 3–33.

Vogel, L., "Le juriste face à l'analyse économique," *Revue de la Concurrence et de la Consommation*, 134 (2003), 812–817.

Vogel, L. and Vogel, J., "Demand and Elasticities: How to Assess the Relevant Market," *Concurrences*, 4 (2009).

Vranes, E., *Trade and the Environment: Fundamental Issues in International Law, WTO Law, and Legal Theory*, Oxford University Press, 2009.

Waelbroeck, M., "Comments on Damien Neven's Paper," in T. Cottier and P. C. Mavroidis (eds.), *Regulatory Barriers and the Principle of Non-discrimination in World Trade Law*, Ann Arbor, MI: University of Michigan Press, 2000, pp. 343–344.

Waincymer, J., *WTO Litigation: Procedural Aspects of Formal Dispute Settlement*, London: Cameron May, 2002.

Walker, V. R., "Preponderance, Probability and Warranted Factfinding," *Brooklyn Law Review*, 62 (1996), 1075–1136.

Weiler, J. H. H., "The Rule of Lawyers and the Ethos of Diplomats," *Journal of World Trade*, 35 (2001), 191–207.

Werden, G. J., "A Perspective on the Use of Econometrics in Merger Investigations and Litigation," *Antitrust*, 16 (2002), 55–58.

"Demand Elasticities in Antitrust Analysis," *Antitrust Law Journal*, 66 (1998), 363–414.

"Making Economics More Useful in Competition Cases: Procedural Rules Governing Expert Opinions," in B. E. Hawk (ed.), *Annual Proceedings of the Fordham Corporate Law Institute, International Antitrust Law & Policy*, New York: Juris Publishing, 2006, pp. 601–613.

"Market Delineation and the Justice Department's Merger Guidelines," *Duke Law Journal*, (1983), 514–579.

"The 1992 Merger Guidelines and the Ascent of the Hypothetical Monopolist Paradigm," *Antitrust Law Journal*, 71 (2003), 253–275.

"The Admissibility of Expert Economic Testimony in Antitrust Cases," in ABA Section of Antitrust Law, *Issues in Competition Law and Policy*, vol. I, Chicago, IL: ABA Publishing, 2008, pp. 801–817.

"The History of Antitrust Market Delineation," *Marquette Law Review*, 76 (1992), 123–215.

Wish, R., *Competition Law*, 6th edn., Oxford University Press, 2009.

White, L. J., "Economics, Economists, and Antitrust: A Tale of Growing Influence," in J. J. Siegfried (ed.), *Better Living Through Economics*, Cambridge, MA: Harvard University Press, 2010, pp. 226–248.

Wille, S. B., "Recapturing a Lost Opportunity: Article III:2 GATT 1994 *Japan – Alcoholic Beverages* 1996," *European Journal of International Law*, 9 (1998), available at: http://207.57.19.226/journal/Vol9/No1/sr1b.html.

WilmerHale, *Memorandum: Consultation concerning DG Competition: Best Practices on Article 101 and 102 TFEU proceedings; Submission of Economic Evidence and Data Collection in Article 101 and 102 TFEU and merger cases; Guidance on Procedures of the Hearing Officers in relation to Article 101 and 102 TFEU*, March 3, 2010, available at: http://ec.europa.eu/competition/consultations/2010_best_practices/wilmerhale_en.pdf.

Wils, W., "The Combination of the Investigative and Prosecutorial Function and the Adjudicative Function in EC Antitrust Enforcement: A Legal and Economic Analysis," *World Competition*, 27 (2004), 201–224.

Wooldridge, J. M., *Introductory Econometrics: A Modern Approach*, 2nd edn., Mason, OH: Thompson South Western, 2003.

Young, M. K., "Dispute Resolution in the Uruguay Round: Lawyers Triumph over Diplomats," *The International Lawyer*, 29 (1995), 389–410.

Zedalis, R. J., "A Theory of the GATT 'Like' Product Common Language Cases," *Vanderbilt Journal of Transnational Law*, 27 (1994), 33–134.

Zhou, W., *Non-discrimination and the Accordion of "Like Product"* (2007), available at: http://ssrn.com/abstract=1000173.

Documents

GATT/WTO-related documents

Appellate Submission by the European Community to the Appellate Body, *Japan – Taxes on Alcoholic Beverages* (u.d.) (on file with the author).

Appellate Submission by the United States to the Appellate Body, *Japan – Taxes on Alcoholic Beverages*, August 23, 1996 (on file with the author).

First written submission of the European Communities to the Panel on *Japan – Taxes on Alcoholic Beverages*, December 4, 1995 (on file with the author).

Group of Negotiations on Services, Note on the Meeting of September 15–17, 1987, MTN.GNS/10, October 15, 1987.

Working Party Report on Border Tax Adjustments, BISD 18S/97, December 2, 1970.

WTO, Working Group on the Interaction between Trade and Competition Policy, Report on the Meeting of September 16/17, 1997, WT/WGTCP/M/2, November 12, 1997.

Working Group on the Interaction between Trade and Competition Policy, Report on the Meeting of November 27/28, 1997, WT/WGTCP/M/3, February 26, 1998.

Working Group on the Interaction between Trade and Competition Policy, Synthesis Paper on the Relationship of Trade and Competition Policy to Development and Economic Growth, WT/WGTCP/W/80, September 18, 1998.

World Trade Report, *Quantitative Economics in WTO Dispute Settlement*, 2005, pp. 171–211, available at: www.wto.org/english/res_e/booksp_e/anrep_e/world_trade_report05 _e.pdf.

European Union documents

Commission Guidance on the Commission's enforcement priorities in applying Article 82 of the EC Treaty to abusive exclusionary conduct by dominant undertakings [2009] OJ C45 7.

Commission Guidelines on the assessment of horizontal mergers under the Council Regulation on the control of concentrations between undertakings [2004] OJ C31 5.

Commission Notice on the definition of relevant market for the purpose of Community competition law [1997] OJ C372 5.

Commission Notice on agreements of minor importance which do not appreciably restrict competition under Article 81(1) of the Treaty establishing the European Community (de minimis) [2001] OJ C368 12.

Commission Regulation No. 330/2010 on the application of Article 101(3) of the Treaty on the Functioning of the European Union to categories of vertical agreements and concerted practices [2010] OJ L102 1.

Commission Regulation No. 773/2004 relating to the conduct of proceedings by the Commission pursuant to Articles 81 and 82 of the EC Treaty [2004] OJ L123 18.

Commission Regulation No. 802/2004 implementing Council Regulation No. 139/2004 on the control of concentrations between undertakings [2004] OJ L133 1.

European Commission, *XXIVth Report on Competition Policy 1994*, 1995.

XXVIIth Report on Competition Policy (1997), available at: http://ec.europa.eu/competition/publications/annual_report/1997/broch97_en.pdf.

Best Practices for the Submission of Economic Evidence and Data Collection in Cases Concerning the Application of Article 101 and 102 TFEU and in Merger Cases (2010), available at: http://ec.europa.eu/competition/consultations/2010_best_practices/best_practice_submissions.pdf.

Staff Discussion Paper on the Application of Article 82 of the Treaty to exclusionary abuses (December 2005), available at: http://ec.europa.eu/competition/antitrust/art82/discpaper2005.pdf.

Documents of European national competition authorities

Autorité de la concurrence, *Lignes directrices relatives au contrôle des concentrations*, (2009), available at: www.autoritedelaconcurrence.fr/doc/ld_concentrations_dec09.pdf.

Bundeskartellamt, *Best Practices for Expert Economic Opinions*, 20 October 2010, available at: www.bundeskartellamt.de/wEnglisch/download/pdf/Merkblaetter/Bekanntmachung_Standards_Englisch_final.pdf.

Diskussionspapier: Wettbewerbsschutz und Verbraucherinteressen im Lichte neuerer ökonomischer Methoden (2004), available at: www.bundeskartellamt.de/wDeutsch/download/pdf/Diskussionsbeitraege/04_AKK.pdf.

Competition Commission, *Suggested Best Practice for Submissions of Technical Economic Analysis from Parties to the Competition Commission* (2009), available at: www.competition-commission.org.uk/rep_pub/corporate_documents/corporate_policies/best_practice.pdf.

Conseil de la concurrence, *Rapport annuel 2001*, Deuxième partie, Titre I, Le marché pertinent, available at: www.autoritedelaconcurrence.fr/user/standard.php?id_rub=31&id_article=58#p2t1.

Office of Fair Trading (Armstrong, M. and Huck, S.), *Behavioural Economics as Applied to Firms: A Primer* (2010), available at: www.oft.gov.uk/shared_oft/economic_research/oft1213.pdf.

Quantitative Techniques in Competition Analysis (1999), available at: www.oft.gov.uk/shared_oft/reports/comp_policy/oft266.pdf.

The Role of Market Definition in Monopoly and Dominance Inquiries: A Report Prepared by National Economic Research Associates (2001), available at: www.oft.gov.uk/shared_oft/reports/comp_policy/oft342.pdf.

What Does Behavioural Economics Mean for Competition Policy? (2010), available at: www.oft.gov.uk/shared_oft/economic_research/oft1224.pdf.

Office of Fair Trading and Competition Commission, *Good Practice in the Design and Presentation of Consumer Survey Evidence in Merger Inquiries* (2010), available at: www.oft.gov.uk/shared_oft/consultations/OFT1230con.pdf.

United States documents

US Department of Justice, *Merger Guidelines* (1968), 4 Trade Reg. Rep. (CCH) § 13,101.

Merger Guidelines (1982), 4 Trade Reg. Rep. (CCH) § 13,102.

US Department of Justice and Federal Trade Commission, *Commentary on the 1992 Horizontal Merger Guidelines* (2006), available at: www.ftc.gov/os/2006/03/CommentaryontheHorizontalMergerGuidelinesMarch2006.pdf.

Horizontal Merger Guidelines (1992), 4 Trade Reg. Rep. (CCH) § 13,104.

Horizontal Merger Guidelines (2010), available at: www.justice.gov/atr/public/guidelines/hmg-2010.html.

US Federal Trade Commission, *Best Practices for Data, and Economics and Financial Analyses in Antitrust Investigations* (u.d.), available at: www.ftc.gov/be/bestpractices.shtm#_ftn2.

INDEX

For EU product safety concerns, contact us at Calle de José Abascal, 56–1°,
28003 Madrid, Spain or eugpsr@cambridge.org.

www.ingramcontent.com/pod-product-compliance
Lightning Source LLC
LaVergne TN
LVHW011530200926
848484LV00001B/216